THE ROMANTIC MOVEMENT

GARLAND REFERENCE LIBRARY
OF THE HUMANITIES
(VOL. 216)

THE ROMANTIC MOVEMENT
A Selective and Critical Bibliography for 1981

Edited by
David V. Erdman

with the assistance of
Brian J. Dendle
Robert R. Mollenauer
Augustus Pallotta
James S. Patty

GARLAND PUBLISHING, INC. · NEW YORK & LONDON
1982

Library of Congress Cataloging in Publication Data
Main entry under title:

The Romantic movement.

   (Garland reference library of the humanities ; v. 216)
   1. Romanticism—Bibliography.   I. Erdman, David V.
II. Title. III. Series.
Z6514.R6R644 1982 [PN603] 016.809′9145   82-48435
ISBN 0-8240-9508-1

Printed on acid-free, 250-year-life paper
Manufactured in the United States of America

This bibliography is compiled by a joint bibliography committee of the Modern Language Association representing groups General Topics II (now Comparative Studies in Romanticism and the Nineteenth Century), English 9 (English Romantic Period), French 6 (Nineteenth-Century French Literature), German 4 (Nineteenth- and Early Twentieth-Century German Literature), Italian 2 (Italian Literature, Seventeenth Century to the Present), and Spanish 4 (Eighteenth- and Nineteenth-Century Spanish Literature). It is designed to cover a "movement" rather than a period; though the English section, for example, is largely limited to the years 1789–1837, other sections extend over different spans of years.

It is our intent to include, with descriptive and, at times, critical annotation, all books and articles and reviews of substantial interest to scholars of English and Continental Romanticism. Studies of American Romanticism that relate to this interest are selectively included. We also make note of items of minor but scholarly interest, except those which may be expected to appear in the annual *MLA International Bibliography*. Major and controversial works are given what is intended to be judicious if necessarily brief review.

The approximate size of a book is indicated by report of the number of pages. Book prices are noted when available.

We continue the practice of including available current (1982) reviews of listed books.

The editorial committee gratefully acknowledges the help of its collaborators, whose names are given at the heads of the respective sections.

To ensure notice in the next issue of the bibliography, authors and publishers are invited to send review copies of relevant books or monographs and offprints of articles to: David V. Erdman, 58 Crane Neck Road, Setauket, N.Y. 11733.

CONTENTS

JOURNALS SEARCHED

All journals regularly searched are listed here. The editor welcomes notice of omissions, to be made good in the next annual.

ABC	American Book Collector (new series)
ABI	Accademie e Bibliotheche d'Italia
	Académie d'Angers. Mémoires
AConf	Les Annales, Conferencia
ActaG	Acta Germanica (Capetown)
	Acta Musicologicae
ActaN	Acta Neophilologica
	Adam: International Review
ADPh	Arbeiten zur deutschen Philologie
	Aevum: Rassegna di Scienze Storiche, Linguistiche, Filologiche
AFLSHA	Annales de la Faculté des Lettres et Sciences Humaines d'Aix
AG	Anglica Germanica
AHR	American Historical Review
AHRF	Annales Historiques de la Revolution Française
AI	American Imago
AION-SG	Annali Instituto Universitario Orientale, Napoli, Sezione Germanica
AJ	Art Journal
AJES	Aligarh Journal of English Studies
AJFS	Australian Journal of French Studies
AKG	Archiv für Kulturgeschichte
	Akzente: Zeitschrift für Literatur
AL	American Literature
	Albion
ALett	L'Approdo Letterario
ALittASH	Acta Litterarica Academiae Scientiarum Hungaricae. Magyar Tudomanyos Akademia. Budapest
	Allegorica
ALM	Archives des Lettres Modernes
	American Art Journal
	American Art Review
	American Journal of Sociology
	American Political Science Review
AmG	L'Amitié Guérinienne

Journals Searched

AN&Q	American Notes & Queries
AnBret	Annales de Bretagne
	Anglia
	Annales de Bourgogne
	Annales de l'Academie de Mâcon
	Annales de l'Est
	Annales de l'Université de Dakar
	Annales de l'Université de Toulouse-le Mirail
	Annales du Centre Universitaires Méditerranéen
	Annales du Midi
	Annales Universitaires (Avignon)
	Annales: Economies, Sociétés, Civilisations
	Annali della Facoltà di Lingne e Letterature Straniere (Bari)
	L'Année Balzacienne
AnS	Annals of Science
	Antaeus
Anzeiger	Anzeiger, Oesterreichische Akademie der Wissenschaften, philosophisch-historische Klasse
APh	Archives Philosophiques
APhilos	Archives de Philosophie
	Apollo
AQ	American Quarterly
AR	Antioch Review
	Arbor: Revista General de Investigación y Cultura
	L'Arc: Cahiers Méditerranéens (Aix-en-Provence)
	Arcadia: Zeitschrift für vergleichenden Literaturwissenschaft
Arch	Archivum
Archiv	Archiv für das Studium der Neueren Sprachen und Literaturen
ArH	Archivo Hispalense
ArielE	Ariel: A Review of International English Literature
ArM	Archiv für Musikwissenschaft
ArQ	Arizona Quarterly
ArtB	Art Bulletin
	Art History
ArtQ	Art Quarterly
	Arts Magazine
ASch	American Scholar
ASLHM	American Society Legion of Honor Magazine
	Association des Amis d'Alfred de Vigny. Bulletin
ASSR	Archives de Sciences Sociales des Réligions
AUB	Analele Universitatü, Bucuresti
AUMLA	Journal of the Australasian Universities Language and Literature Association
Aurora	Aurora: Eichendorff-Almanach
AWR	Anglo-Welsh Review

BAAD *Bulletin de l'Association des Amis d'Alexandre Dumas*
BAGB *Bulletin de l'Association Guillaume Budé*
BAWS *Bayerische Akademie der Wissenschaften. Philosophischhistorisch Klasse, Sitzungsberichte*
B&BM *Books & Bookmen*
BB *Bulletin of Bibliography*
BBaud *Bulletin Baudelairien*
BBMP *Boletin de la Biblioteca Menéndez Pelayo*
BC *Book Collector*
BCLF *Bulletin Critique du Livre Français*
BduB *Bulletin du Bibliophile*
    Belfagor: Rassegna di varia Umanità
    Bennington Review
    Berkshire Review (Williams College)
BF *Book Forum*
BFE *Boletín de Filología Española*
BGDSL *Beiträge zur Geschichte der deutschen Sprache und Literatur*
BH *Bulletin Hispanique*
BHR *Bibliothèque d'Humanisme et Renaissance*
BHS *Bulletin of Hispanic Studies*
    Bibliothèque de l'Ecole des Chartres
BIHR *Bulletin of the Institute of Historical Research (London)*
BioC *Biologia Culturale*
BIQ *Blake: An Illustrated Quarterly*
BJA *British Journal of Aesthetics*
BJHS *British Journal for the History of Science*
BJRL *Bulletin of the John Ryland Library*
BL *Beiträge zur Literaturkunde*
    Blackwood's Magazine
BLAM *Bulletin de la Librairie Ancienne et Moderne*
BLR *The Bodleian Library Record*
BM *The Burlington Magazine*
BMMLA *Bulletin of the Midwest MLA*
    Boletin de la Academía argentina de Letras
    Les Bonnes Feuilles
    Boundary
BPhilos *Bibliography of Philosophy*
BRAE *Boletín de la Real Academia Española*
BRAH *Boletín de la Real Academia de la Historia*
BRH *Bulletin of Research in the Humanities*
    The British Library Journal
BRP *Beiträge zur romanischen Philologie (Berlin)*
BS *Blake Studies*
BSAP *Bulletin de la Société des Amis de Marcel Proust et des Amis de Combray*
BSUF *Ball State University Forum*
BUJ *Boston University Journal*

Bulletin de l'Académie royale de Langue et de
   Littérature Françaises (Brussels)
Bulletin de l'Association des Amis d'Alain
Bulletin de l'Association des Amis de J.-J.
   Rousseau
Bulletin de l'Association des Amis de Rabelais
   et de La Devinière
Bulletin de l'Association J.-K. Huysmans
Bulletin de la Bibliothèque Nationale
Bulletin de la Société Belge des Professeurs de
   Français
Bulletin de la Société d'Histoire du Protestantisme
   Français
Bulletin de la Société Jules Vernes
Bulletin des Amis d'André Gide
Bulletin des Amis de Flaubert
Bulletin des Amis de Jules Romains
Bulletin of the Faculty of Literature (Kyushu
   University)
Byron Journal

BYUS	Brigham Young University Studies
CA	Cuadernos americanos
CACP	Cahiers de l'Amitié Charles Peguy
	Cahiers Canadien Claudel
CahiersC	Cahiers Césairiens
	Cahiers d'Analyse Textuelle
	Cahiers d'Histoire
	Cahiers de l'Ecole Supérieure des Lettres de Beyrouth
	Cahiers des Amis de Valery Larbaud
	Cahiers Diderotiens
	Cahiers François Mauriac
	Cahiers Internationaux du Symbolisme
	Les Cahiers Naturalistes
CahiersS	Cahiers Staëliens
CAIEF	Cahiers de l'Association Internationale des Etudes Françaises
CalSS	California Slavic Studies
CamR	Cambridge Review
	Canadian Journal of Research in Semiotics
CB	Cuadernos bibliográficos
CE	College English
CentR	Centennial Review
CeS	Cultura e Scuola
CG	Colloquia Germanica
CH	Church History
CHA	Cuadernos Hispanoamericanos (Madrid)
ChLB	Charles Lamb Bulletin
CHR	Catholic Historical Review

ELWIU	*Essays in Literature (Western Illinois University*
EM	*English Miscellany*
	Encounter
	English
EnlE	*Enlightenment Essays*
EP	*Etudes philosophiques*
ES	*English Studies*
ESA	*English Studies in Africa (Johannesburg)*
ESC	*English Studies in Canada*
	Esprit
ESQ	*Emerson Society Quarterly*
ESR	*European Studies Review*
	Essays in French Literature
EstF	*Estudios Filosóficos*
ETJ	*Educational Theater Journal*
ETR	*Etudes Théologiques et Réligieuses*
	Etudes Bernanosiennes
	Etudes Françaises
	Etudes Gobiniennes
	Euphorion: Zeitschrift für Literaturgeschichte
	Europe
	Explicator
Fabula	*Fabula: Zeitschrift für Ersählforschung*
FemS	*Feminist Studies*
FHS	*French Historical Studies*
FilM	*Filologia Moderna*
FL	*Le Figaro Littéraire*
	Le Flambeau (Haiti)
FLe	*Fiera Letteraria*
FM	*Le Français Moderne*
FMLS	*Forum for Modern Language Studies*
	Foi et Vie
	Folklore
	Fontes Artis Musicae
	Forum Italicum
FR	*The French Review*
	Francia
	French Forum
	French Monographs (Macquarie University)
	French News
	The French-American Review
FS	*French Studies*
FSSA	*French Studies in Southern Africa*
FurmS	*Furman Studies*
GaR	*Georgia Review*
GBA	*Gazette des Beaux-Arts*
	Genre
	Germanistik

GGA   Göttingsche Gelehrte Anzeigen
GIF   Giornale Italiano di Filologia
GL&L   German Life and Letters
         Glyph
GN   Germanic Notes
GoetheJ Goethe-Jahrbuch
GoetheJT Goethe Jahrbuch Tokyo
GQ   German Quarterly
GR   Germanic Review
         Gradiva
GRM   Germanisch-romanische Monatsschrift, Neue Folge
GSlav   Germano-Slavica
GSLI   Giornale Storico della Letteratura Italiana
GSR   German Studies Review
         Gulliver
GW   Germanica Wratislaviensia
H   History
HAHR   Hispanic American Historical Review
         Harvard English Studies
         The Hebrew University Studies in Literature
HeineJ   Heine Jahrbuch
Hisp   Hispania
Hispano Hispanófila
         Historia
         The Historian
         History and Theory
         History of Religions
HJ   Historical Journal
HLB   Harvard Library Bulletin
HLQ   Huntington Library Quarterly
HÖJB   Hölderlin Jahrbuch
         Horizon
HPE   The History of Political Economy
HR   Hispanic Review
HSL   Hartford Studies in Literature
HT   History Today
HudR   Hudson Review
Hum   Humanities
         Humanities Association Review
IASL   Internationales Archiv für Sozialgeschichte der
             deutschen Literatur
I&L   Ideologies and Literature
IdS   Idealistic Studies
IHA   L'Information d'Histoire de l'Art
IL   L'Information Littéraire
         L'Information Historique
         Inti: Revista de Literature Hispánica
         International Fiction Review

	Interpretations (Memphis State University)
IPQ	*International Philosophical Quarterly*
IQ	*Italian Quarterly*
IS	*Italian Studies*
	Italica
	Italianistica
IUB	*Indiana University Bookman*
JAAC	*Journal of Aesthetics and Art Criticism*
JAF	*Journal of American Folklore*
JBS	*Journal of British Studies*
JDH	*Jahresverzeichnis der deutschen Hochschulschriften*
JDSG	*Jahrbuch der deutschen Schiller-Gesellschaft*
JEGP	*Journal of English and Germanic Philology*
JEH	*Journal of Ecclesiastical History*
JES	*The Journal of European Studies*
JFDH	*Jahrbuch des Freien deutschen Hochstifts (Tübingen)*
JFI	*Journal of the Folklore Institute*
JfV	*Jahrbuch für Volksliedforschung*
JHA	*Journal of the History of Astronomy*
JHI	*Journal of the History of Ideas*
JHK	*Jahrbuch der Hamburger Kunstammlungen*
JHP	*Journal of the History of Philosophy*
JIG	*Jahrbuch für internationale Germanistik*
JIH	*Journal of Interdisciplinary History*
JJPG	*Jahrbuch der Jean-Paul-Gesellschaft*
JLS	*Journal of Literary Semantics*
JMH	*Journal of Modern History*
JML	*Journal of Modern Literature*
JMRS	*Journal of Medieval and Renaissance Studies*
JNH	*Journal of Negro History*
JNL	*Johnsonian News Letter*
JNT	*Journal of Narrative Technique*
	Journal of Library History
	Journal of Religious History
	Journal of Women's Studies in Literature
JPC	*Journal of Popular Culture*
JR	*Journal of Religion*
JRG	*Jahrbuch der Raabe-Gesellschaft*
JS	*Journal des Savants*
JSH	*Journal of Social History*
JSUB	*Jahrbuch der schlesischen Friedrich-Wilhelms-Universität zu Breslau*
JWCI	*Journal of the Warburg and Courtauld Institutes*
JWGV	*Jahrbuch des Wiener Goethe-Vereins*
KantS	*Kant-Studien*
	Kenyon Review
KFLQ	*Kentucky Foreign Language Quarterly*
	Konsthistorisk Tidskrift
KRQ	*Kentucky Romance Quarterly*

KSJ	Keats-Shelley Journal
KSMB	Keats-Shelley Memorial Bulletin
KuL	Kunst und Literatur
	Das Kunstwerk
Kurbiskern	Kurbiskern: Literatur und Kritik
L&H	Literature and History
	Langages
Lang&L	Language & Literature
	Language and Style
LanM	Les Langues modernes
L&P	Literature and Psychology
	Lavoro critico
LC	Library Chronicle (University of Pennsylvania)
LCUT	Library Chronicle of the University of Texas
LE&W	Literature East and West
LenauA	Lenau-Almanach (Wien)
LenauF	Lenau-Forum. Vierteljahresschrift für vergleich- ende Literaturforschung (Wien)
LetN	Lettres Nouvelles
	Letras
LHR	Lock Haven Review (Lock Haven State College, Pa.)
LI	Lettere Italiane
	Library
	The Library Quarterly
	La Licorne (Faculté des Lettres et des Langues de l'Université de Poitiers)
LiLi	Zeitschrift für Literaturwissenschaft und Linguistik
	Lingua et Stile
	Literature and Ideology
LitR	Literary Review
	Littérature
	Littératures
LJ	Library Journal
LJGG	Literaturwissenschaftliches Jahrbuch. Im Auftrage der Littérature Gorres-Gesellschaft. N.F.
LMFA	Literature, Music and Fine Arts
LNL	Linguistics in Literature
LR	Les Lettres Romanes
LSoc	Language in Society
LuK	Literatur und Kritik
	Lumière et Vie
LWU	Literatur in Wissenschaft und Unterricht
LY	Lessing Yearbook
MA	Le Moyen Age
M&L	Music and Letters (London)
	Marche Romane

REE   *Revista de Estudios Extremenos*
REG   *Revue des Etudes Grecques*
REH   *Revista de Estudios Hispanicos*
REI   *Revue des Etudes Italiennes*
REL   *Review of English Literature (Leeds)*
RES   *Review of English Studies*
RevEH   *Revue d'Histoire Ecclésiastique Review*
         Reviews in European History
RevR   *Revue Romane*
         Revue Belge de Musicologie
         Revue d'Esthétique
         Revue d'Histoire et de Philosophie Religieuses
         Revue de l'Histoire des Religions
         Revue de l'Art
         Revue de l'Université de Bruxelles
         Revue de Metaphysique et de Morale
         Revue des Etudes Juives
         Revue des Etudes Slaves
         Revue des Sciences Religieuses
         Revue du Louvre et des Musées de France
         Revue du Monde Russe et Soviétique
         Revue du Pacifique
         Revue Française d'Histoire du Livre
RF   *Romanische Forschungen*
RFE   *Revista de Filologia Española*
RFNS   *Revista di Filosophia Neo-Scolastica*
RG   *Revue Générale*
RGer   *Recherches Germaniques*
RH   *Revue Historique*
RHEF   *Revue d'Histoire de l'Eglise de France*
RHL   *Revue d'Histoire Littéraire de la France*
RHM   *Revista Hispánica Moderna*
RHT   *Revue d'Histoire du Théâtre*
RHV   *Revue Historique Vaudoise*
RI   *Revista Iberoamericana*
RIE   *Revista de Ideas Estéticas*
         Rimbaud Vivant
RJ   *Romantisches Jahrbuch*
RL   *Revista de Literatura*
RLC   *Revue de Littérature Comparée*
RLI   *Rassegna della Letteratura Italiana*
RLM   *Revue des Lettres Modernes*
RLMC   *Rivista di Letterature Moderne e Comparate (Firenze)*
RLR   *Revue des Langues Romanes*
RLSt   *Rackham Literary Studies*
RLV   *Revue des Langues Vivantes*
RMM   *Revue de Métaphysique et de Morale*

RMus *Revue de Musicologie*
RNL *Review of National Literatures*
RO *Revista de Occidente*
  Romania
  Romanica Wratislaviensia
  Romanistische Zeitschrift für Literaturgeschichte/
    Cahiers d'Histoire des Littératures Romanes
  Romantisme
RomN *Romance Notes (University of North Carolina)*
RP&P *Romanticism Past and Present*
RPFE *Revue Philosophique de la France et de l'Etranger*
RPh *Romance Philology*
RPL *Revue Philosophique de Louvain*
RPP *Revue Politique et Parlementaire*
RR *Romanic Review*
RS *Research Studies (Washington State University)*
RSC *Royal Society of Canada*
RSH *Revue des Sciences Humaines*
RSPT *Revue des Sciences Philosophiques et Théologiques*
RUO *Revue de l'Université d'Ottawa*
RUS *Rice University Studies*
RusL *Russian Literature*
S *Spectator*
Saeculum *Saeculum: Jahrbuch für Universalgeschichte*
Saggi *Saggi e Ricerche di Letteratura Francese*
  Salmagundi
  San Jose Studies
SAQ *South Atlantic Quarterly*
S&S *Science and Society*
SAR *South Atlantic Review*
SatR *Saturday Review*
SB *Studies in Bibliography*
SC *Stendhal Club*
SCB *South Central Bulletin*
Scheidewege *Scheidewege: Vierteljahresschrift für skeptisches*
    Denken
SchM *Schweitzer Monatshefte für Politik, Wirtschaft,*
    Kultur
ScHR *Scottish Historical Review*
SCR *South Carolina Review*
SCr *Strumenti Critici*
SECC *Studies in Eighteenth-Century Culture* (Univ. of Wisconsin)
SEEJ *Slavic and East European Journal*
SEL *Studies in English Literature, 1500-1900 (Rice*
    University)
  Seminar: A Journal of Germanic Studies
  Semiolus
  Semiotext
  Semiotica: Revue Publiée par l'Association Inter-
    nationale de Sémiotique

SFI   *Studi di Filologia Italiana*
SFR   *Stanford French Review*
SFr   *Studi Francesi*
SGr   *Studi Germanici*
ShawR   *The Shaw Review*
        Shenandoah
SHPS   *Studies in the History and Philosophy of Science*
SHR   *Southern Humanities Review*
ShS   *Shakespeare Survey*
        Signs
SiR   *Studies in Romanticism (Boston University)*
SJP   *Southern Journal of Philosophy*
SJW   *Shakespeare Jahrbuch (Weimar)*
SlavR   *Slavic Review*
SLIm   *Studies in the Literary Imagination*
SLJ   *Scottish Literary Journal*
SN   *Studia Neophilologica*
SNNTS   *Studies in the Novel (North Texas University)*
SÖAW   *Sitzungsberichte der Österreichischen Akademie*
        der Wissenschaften im Wien, Philosophisch-
        historisch Klasse
        Société Chateaubriand, Bulletin
        Société de Linguistique de Paris. Bulletin
        Société des Amis de Montaigne. Bulletin
        Société Paul Claudel. Bulletin
SoR   *Southern Review (Louisiana State University)*
SoRA   *Southern Review (Adelaide, Australia)*
        Soundings: A Journal of Interdisciplinary Studies
        Soviet Studies in Literature
SovL   *Soviet Literature*
SP   *Studies in Philology*
SPCT   *Studi e Problemi de Critica Testuale*
        Sprachkunst
SQ   *Southern Quarterly*
SR   *Sewanee Review*
SSEL   *Salzburg Studies in English Literature*
SSF   *Studies in Short Fiction*
SSL   *Studies in Scottish Literature (University of*
        South Carolina)
StF   *Studia Filozoficzne*
        Storia dell'Arte
        Structuralist Review
        Studi de Letteratura Francese
        Studi Piemontesi
        Studies in Browning
        Studies in the Humanities
        Style

THE ROMANTIC MOVEMENT

GENERAL

(Compiled by David V. Erdman with the assistance of
Thomas L. Ashton, Robert A. Brinkley, Irene H. Chayes,
Jerome C. Christensen, Julia M. DiStefano, Bishop C.
Hunt, Robert Mollenauer, Augustus Pallotta, James S.
Patty, Jeffrey C. Robinson, and Robert Michael Ryan)

1. BIBLIOGRAPHY

See the respective "Bibliography" and "General" sections for
each language, below. *The Romantic Movement Bibliography* has
been published in its present form beginning with the *Bibliography for 1979*, in 1980. For previous years, see the "Bibliography of the Romantic Movement" in *English Language Notes* (*ELN*),
September supplements, 1965-79. In 1973 a cumulative reprint
since 1936 was published in seven volumes by the Pierian Press
and R.R. Bowker, New York. For the most extensive general listing, in all languages, without commentary, see the annual *MLA International Bibliography*, Vols. I and II.

Allen, Robert R., ed. *The Eighteenth Century: A Current
Bibliography*. New York: AMS Press. (Abbrev. ECCB)

New series, continuing, of the famous annual bibliography
that began in *PQ* in 1926 (ten years before *RMB*, but not
managing to be quite as current; the volume "for 1978"
appeared in 1981).

Arntzen, E., and R. Rainwater. *Guide to the Literature of Art
History*. London: The Art Book Company, 1981. Pp. 635.
£45.00.

Developed from *Chamberlin's Guide to Art Reference Books*;
double its length.

Pingree, Elizabeth E., ed. *Humanities Index*, Vols. 7, 8. April
1980 to March 1982. New York: H.W. Wilson Co., 1980-82.

Continuing and cumulative.

Tanselle, G. Thomas. "From Bibliography to *histoire totale*:
The History of Books as a Field of Study." *TLS*, June 5,
1981, pp. 647-48.

Second Hanes Lecture on the History of the Book, April 15,
1981.

Wearing, J.P. *American and British Theatrical Biography: A
Directory*. Metuchen, N.J., and London: The Scarecrow Press,
1979. Pp. v+1007. $37.50.

Rev. by Cecil Price in *N&Q* 28 (1981): 569-70.

2. ENVIRONMENT: ART, PHILOSOPHY,
POLITICS, RELIGION, SOCIETY

Allen, Margaret Vanderhaar. *The Achievement of Margaret Fuller*.
Pennsylvania State University Press, 1979. Pp. xi+212.
$13.50.

Rev. by Marie Olessen Urbanski in *NEQ* 54 (1981): 286-87.

Anderson, Wilda. "Translating the Language of Chemistry:
Priestley and Lavoisier." *ECent* 22 (Winter 1981): 21-31.

Baker, Keith Michael. "Enlightenment and Revolution in France:
Old Problems, Renewed Approaches." *JMH* 53 (1981): 281-303.

An excellent status report on the search for the ideological origins of the French Revolution. (T.L.A.)

Baker, Keith Michael. "A Script for a French Revolution: The
Political Consciousness of the Abbé Mably." *ECS* 14 (1981):
235-63.

Beck, Thomas. "The French Revolution and the Nobility: A Reconsideration." *JSH* 2 (1981): 219-33.

Bergeron, Louis, and Guy Chaussinard-Nagaret. *Les "Masses de
granit": cent mille notables du Premier Empire*. (Editions
de l'Ecole des Hautes Etudes en Sciences Sociales.) Paris:
Touzot, 1979. Pp. 122.

Rev. by Isser Walach in *AHR* 86 (1981): 145-46.

Bertaud, Jean-Paul. *La Révolution armée: Les Soldats-citoyens
et la Révolution française*. Paris: Robert Laffont, 1979.
Pp. 382.

Rev. by Peter Paret in *JMH* 53 (1981): 121-23 as weak.

Billington, James H. *Fire in the Minds of Men: Origins of the Revolutionary Faith*. New York: Basic Books, 1980. Pp. viii+ 677.

Rev. by Naomi Bliner in *NY* 47 (Jan. 12, 1981): 97–101; by Charles Tilley in *AHR* 86 (1981): 1060–61.

Bosher, J.F. "Current Writing on Administration and Finance in Eighteenth-Century France." *JMH* 53 (1981): 73–83.

Includes among its judicious commentary remarks on Robert D. Harris, *Necker: Reform Statesman* (see *RMB* for 1980, p. 9). (T.L.A.)

Braham, Allan. "A Hidden Portrait by Goya." *BM* 123 (Sept. 1981): 541–42; 5 illus.

Brown, Marshall. "Mozart and After: The Revolution in Musical Consciousness." *CritI* 7 (1981): 689–706.

"What emerges in both the literature and the music of the 1780s is not only a new type of experience but also a new conception of form. No longer does consciousness begin with external perception or artistic form with inherited convention; now the basic structural orientation is generated from within, from the flow of time." A subtle and illuminating study of the musical reverie, centered on the introduction to Mozart's so-called Dissonance Quartet in C Major. (I.H.C.)

Brush, Stephen G. *The Temperature of History: Phases of Science and Culture in the Nineteenth Century*. New York: Burt Franklin, 1978. Pp. xii+210. $18.95.

Rev. by Crosbie Smith in *BJHS* 13 (1980): 272–73.
An examination of "some of the relations between nineteenth-century theoretical physics and wider cultural movements of the period."

Cash, Philip, Eric H. Christianson, and J. Worth Estes, eds. *Medicine in Colonial Massachusetts, 1620-1820*. The Colonial Society of Massachusetts, Distributed by the University Press of Virginia, 1980. Pp. xxiii+425. $25.00.

Rev. by John H. Ellis in *NEQ* 54 (1981): 583–85; by Charles E. Rosenberg in *PMHB* 105 (1981): 344–45, who finds that "this handsomely produced book marks a new level of interest and sophistication in the study of medicine in colonial and early national America."
Of particular interest will be essays by C. Helen Brock on European influences. (R.A.B.)

Clay, Jean. *Le Romantisme.* (Réalités.) Paris: Hachette, 1980.
Pp. 320. Trans. Dan Wheeler: *Romanticism.* Vendome, 1981.
$60.00.

Rev. by Georges Raillard in *QL* 340 (Jan. 16-31, 1981): 20.
A fresh, even dazzling look at Romantic painting in western
Europe. Over 120 different artists are represented by hundreds
of reproductions, nearly all in color. The originality of
Clay's approach is in the organization of material by pictorial or painterly motifs, rather than by country, by genre,
or by artist. The five general headings, "L'aplat," "La
ligne," "Le flou," "La couleur," and "L'assemblage," are
each broken down into dozens of subheadings. For instance,
animal scenes by Stubbs and Delacroix are given the following titles: "Le cheval, idéogramme de l'énergie," "Zigzags
de la main, fureur de peindre," "Une frénédie circulaire
brasse en une seule masse hommes et bêtes, formes et couleurs,"
"Un geste automatique tresse la crinière des fauves." Thus,
while the themes and motifs are often grouped in a familiar
way (animals, Ossian, ruins, odalisques, etc.), Clay's headings, the accompanying texts, and especially the close-ups
of details bring out the visual effects and the painterly
techniques involved. It should be pointed out that, although,
as usual, French art dominates, Clay is generous to English
and German painting, and not only to the inevitable Blake,
Fuseli, Constable, Turner, and Friedrich (Spain, however,
has only Goya to represent her, in this account).
The main body of the text is overshadowed by the quantity
and quality of the illustrations and by Clay's approach,
which might be called atomistic. (One troublesome detail:
O.A. Lovejoy is apparently regarded as having unearthed
"deux érudits de la Ferté-sous-Jouarre, MM. Dupuis et Cotonet";
Alfred de Musset would be surprised by this "discovery.")
All in all, the most spectacular survey of Romantic painting this reviewer has seen. (J.S.P.)

Cobb, Richard. "Thermidor or the Retreat from Fantasy." *Encounter* 57 (1981): 30-42.

On the changes in language which accompanied the political
changes in France after the death of Robespierre.

Cohen, Lester H. "Narrating the Revolution: Ideology, Language,
and Form." *SECC* 9 (1980): 455-76.

"To make history the vehicle for an American vision,"
the historian of the American Revolution "had to be a revolutionary historian--one who perceived himself as standing
at the nexus of history-as-lived and history-as-written,

a location at which the very writing of history was a
revolutionary act." Elaborately annotated.

Conkin, Paul K. *Prophets of Prosperity: America's First Political
Economists.* Indiana University Press, 1980. Pp. xii+333.
$25.00.

   Rev. by Herbert Ershkowitz in *PMHB* 105 (1981): 232-34.

Dann, John C., ed. *The Revolution Remembered: Eyewitness
Accounts of the War for Independence.* University of Chicago
Press, 1980. Pp. xxvi+446. $20.00.

   Rev. by George B. Kirsch in *NEQ* 54 (1981): 435-37; by
Russell F. Weigley in *PMHB* 105 (1981): 220-22.

Doyle, William. *Origins of the French Revolution.* Oxford University Press, 1981. Pp. 272. $37.50.

   Rev. by Douglas Johnson in *S*, March 7, 1981, pp. 23f.

Dumoulin, Heinrich. "Buddhism and Nineteenth-Century German
Philosophy." *JHI* 42 (1981): 457-70.

   Kant, Hegel, Schopenhauer, and Nietzsche were all intrigued
by what they regarded as "the dark and pessimistic world
view of the Buddhists." Fascination with Buddhism involves
a shift of interest away from China "to India as the Wonder-
land" at the end of the eighteenth century. (R.A.B.)

Duncan, Carol. "Fallen Fathers: Images of Authority in Pre-
Revolutionary French Art." *Art History* 4 (1981): 186-202.

   Years before the Revolution, French artists communicated
"a growing ambivalence toward established authority" through
images of "overthrown kings and fallen fathers."

Ferguson, E. James, and John Catanzariti, eds. *The Papers of
Robert Morris, 1781-1784.* Vol. V: April 16-July 20, 1782.
University of Pittsburg Press, 1980. Pp. xxxix+649. $27.50.

   Rev. by Carl E. Prince in *PMHB* 105 (1981): 496.
See *RMB* for 1979, p. 6, for earlier volumes.

Ferling, John E. *A Wilderness of Miseries: War and Warriors
in Early America.* Westport, Ct.: Greenwood Press, 1980.
Pp. xiv+227. $25.00.

   Rev. by Peter Karsten in *PMHB* 105 (1981): 219-20.

Fink, Karl J., and James W. Marchand, eds. *The Quest for the
New Science: Language and Thought in Eighteenth-Century
Science*. Southern Illinois University Press, 1979. Pp. ix+
101.

> Summarized by Karl J. Fink in *History and Theory* 19 (1980):
> 242.
> Vico and late eighteenth-century German writers.

Fleming-Williams, Ian. "The Early Constable: New Watercolours
& Drawings." *Connoisseur* 206 (Jan. 1981): 58-61.

> They date from 1805-06 and include views of the Lake
> District.

Forrest, Alan. *The French Revolution and the Poor*. Oxford:
Blackwell, 1981. Pp. 175. £12.50.

> Rev. by Olwen Huften in *HT* (Sept. 1981): 33-34, approving
> of its scholarship and its telling "simply and cogently"
> how revolutionary governments sought to cope with poverty.

Furet, François. *Interpreting the French Revolution*. Trans.
Elborg Forster. Cambridge University Press and Maison des
Sciences de l'Homme, 1981. Pp. x+204. Cloth or paper.

> Rev. by William Doyle in *HT* (Dec. 1981): 54.
> Published in French as *Penser la Revolution Française*,
> 1978.
> The proposition is not to "re-think" the Revolution but
> (for the first time) to "think" it rigorously. Unlike earlier
> revisionist historians, Furet urges us "to concentrate on
> the conceptual core of the Revolution, without diluting it
> with vague notions of linear development designed to add a
> layer of dignity to the virtues of its protagonists."
> Furet drops what have been distorting formulas of explana-
> tion, requiring the Revolutionary power shifts to open-and-
> shut class definitions, which become less and less clear
> the more we learn about the particulars of "feudalism" and
> "capitalism." What was special about France, he argues, was
> not that "it had gone from an absolute monarchy to a repre-
> sentative regime or from a world of noble privilege to a
> bourgeois society. After all, the rest of Europe went
> through the same process without a revolution and without
> Jacobins.... What sets the French Revolution apart is that
> it was not a transition but a beginning and a haunting
> vision of that beginning.... it was the first experiment
> with democracy" (79). Furet's way of opening up the debate
> is to examine side by side Tocqueville's thesis that the

Revolution was a culmination and the Jacobin view (investigated by Augustin Cochin, who "wanted to re-write Michelet in conceptual terms" [28]) that it constituted a political and cultural discontinuity.

A book that is intellectually absorbing and at the same time practically helpful to anyone trying to make sense out of the "events" or "journées" or out of the debates and declamations in the Jacobin Club—or the Paris press. But for balance one might read Soboul's latest volume, listed below. But then see also Wallerstein, below. (D.V.E.)

Fuss, Peter, and John Dobbins. "Spirit as Recollection: Hegel's Theory of the Internalizing of Experience." *IdS* 11 (1981): 142-50.

Gay, Peter. "Peter Gay on 'Voltaire's Politics.'" *TLS*, June 12, 1981, pp. 673-74.

Gendron, François. *La Jeunesse Dorée: Episodes de la Révolution française*. Presse de l'Université du Québec, 1979. Pp. xiv+448.

Rev. by Martyn Lyons in *JMH* 53 (1981): 119-20.

Grafton, Anthony. "Wilhelm von Humboldt." *ASch* 50 (1981): 371-81.

Handlin, Oscar. *Truth in History*. Belknap Press of Harvard University, 1979. Pp. xii+437. $17.50.

Rev. by Gordon S. Woof in *JMH* 53 (1981): 84-90.

Haraven, Tamara K., and Robert Wheaton, eds. *Family and Sexuality in French History*. University of Pennsylvania Press, 1980. Pp. xii+274. $22.50.

Rev. by Olwen Hufton in *JMH* 53 (1981): 552-54.

Harbison, Robert. *Deliberate Regression: The Disastrous History of Romantic Individualism in Thought and Art, from Jean-Jacques Rousseau to Twentieth-Century Fascism*. New York: Knopf, 1980. $15.00.

Rev. by Alfred Corn in *YR* 70 (1981): 304-11: "Romanticism as Lucifer?"

Hartmann, Jørgen Birkedal. *Antike Motive bei Thorvaldsen: Studien zur Antikenrezeption des Klassizismus*. Bearbeitet und Herausgegeben von Klaus Parlasca. Ernst Wasmuth, 1980. Pp. 224; 338 illus. DM 110.00.

Rev. by Nicholas Penny in *BM* 123 (Jan. 1981): 41; 5 illus.

Haskell, Francis, and Nicholas Penny. *Taste and the Antique:
The Lure of Classical Sculpture, 1500-1900.* Yale University
Press, 1981. Pp. 376; 180 illus. $45.00.

Rev. by Joseph Alsop ("A Revolution in Taste") in *NR*,
Nov. 4, 1981, pp. 34-37; by J. Mordaunt Crook in *TLS*, April
3, 1981, p. 373; by Alex Potts in *BM* 123 (Oct. 1981): 618-
19.

"Antique" and "classical" here refer to the surviving
sculpture, mostly Roman copies of lost Hellenistic originals,
which began to come to light in sixteenth-century Rome and
eventually became known all over the Western world through
further copies "in every medium." The height of its prestige
was reached at the time of Napoleon's plunders near the end
of the eighteenth century, although through the influence of
Winckelmann and others, "taste" was already changing.

The authors' historical text, based on contemporary writings in the periods covered, is followed by an illustrated
and fully annotated catalogue of ninety-five individual
statues, among them such famous pieces as the Apollo Bel-
vedere, Laocoön, and Medici Venus, which now can be seen
in the company of which they often were judged the most
excellent.

As a reference source, the catalogue should be especially
useful to readers who are *not* art historians. The bibliography is a scholarly achievement in itself. (I.H.C.)

Heyd, Michael. "The Reaction to Enthusiasm in the Seventeenth
Century." *JMH* 53 (1981): 258-80.

Consulting some two dozen books, essays, and unpublished
dissertations, Heyd makes an important contribution to an
integrative approach. (T.L.A.)

Heywood, Colin. "The Market for Child Labour in Nineteenth-
Century France." *H* 66 (1981): 34-49.

"... the offspring of the *classes populaires* abandoned
their labours in the fields and workshops in order to move,
definitively, to the school benches" in the 1820s and 1830s.

Hibbert, Christopher. *Days of the French Revolution.* New
York: Morrow, 1980. Pp. 351; 28 plates.

Rev. by Gwynne Lewis in *TLS*, Jan. 9, 1981, p. 37.
Nothing new for scholars.

Hobson, Charles F., and Robert A. Rutland, eds. *The Papers
of James Madison.* Vol. V: Jan. 20, 1790--Mar. 31, 1791.
University Press of Virginia, 1981. Pp. xxviii+423. $20.00.

Rev. by Charles M. Harris in *PMHB* 105 (1981): 497-98.

Hunt, John Dixon. "Picturesque Mirrors and the Ruins of the Past." *Art History* 4 (1981): 254-70.

Another of Hunt's searching studies of nature, the arts, and consciousness in the later eighteenth century. Changes in the ways ruins were viewed and the image of the mirror was used were part of a "fresh alliance" of poetry and painting, word and image, which was not lost in the Romantic period. (I.H.C.)

Hutson, James H. *John Adams and the Diplomacy of the American Revolution*. University Press of Kentucky, 1980. Pp. vii+199. $13.00.

Rev. by Ralph Adams Brown in *PMHB* 105 (1981): 111-14, who finds that while a "tendency to psychoanalyze John Adams leads Hutson into contradictions," when "the author writes history, ... his study has major significance."

Ingraham, Barton L. *Political Crime in Europe: A Comparative Study of France, Germany, and England*. University of California Press, 1979. Pp. xvi+380. $22.50.

Rev. by Dirk Blasius in *JMH* 53 (1981): 98-99.

Irwin, David. *John Flaxman 1755-1826, Sculptor, Illustrator, Designer*. New York: Rizzoli International Publications, 1980. Pp. xviii+249; 282 illus. $55.00.

Rev. by Janice Lyle in *BIQ* 15 (1982): 176-78 as a valuable presentation of factual information in an organized format.

Isherwood, Robert M. "Entertainment in the Parisian Fairs in the Eighteenth Century." *JMH* 53 (1981): 24-48.

First a survey by type: animals, freaks, puppets, pseudo-science, and satire—including Le Marchand de merde—and then an argument showing increased popularity as the Revolution nears and among upper classes as well—the whole of use and very reminiscent of the *Prelude*: VII. (T.L.A.)

Kaiser, Colin. "The Deflation in the Volume of Litigation at Paris in the Eighteenth Century and the Waning of the Old Judicial Order." *ESR* 10 (1980): 309-36.

A look at "one of the routes which led France to revolution."

Kaiser, Thomas E. "Enlightenment and Public Education during
the French Revolution: The View of the Ideologues." *SECC*
10 (1981): 95-112.

It remains "an open question" which was greater: "the
influence of the Enlightenment on the Revolution" or "the
influence of the Revolution on the Enlightenment."

Kelly, G.A. "From *Lèse-Majesté* to *Lèse-Nation*: Treason in
Eighteenth-Century France." *JHI* 42 (1981): 269-86.

The concept of majesty is not abandoned but revolutionized
and nationalized. (R.A.B.)

Keohane, Nannerl O. *Philosophy and the State in France: The
Renaissance to the Enlightenment*. Princeton University Press,
1980. Pp. xii+450. $30.00.

Rev. by J.H.M. Salmon in *JMH* 53 (1981): 547-49.
"This approach proves particularly rewarding with Rousseau,
whose distinction between the artificial self-interest of
amour-propre and the natural and beneficent *amour de soi-
même* assumes added meaning when it is related to the earlier
ideas of the *moralistes*," finds Salmon.

Kerber, Linda K. *Women of the Republic: Intellect and Ideology
in Revolutionary America*. University of North Carolina Press,
1980. Pp. xv+304. $16.50.

Rev. by Carol Berkin in *NEQ* 54 (1981): 437-39, who finds
the book "an important contribution" which shows that "the
Revolution is different when viewed through women's eyes."
(R.A.B.)

Knight, David M. *The Transcendental Part of Chemistry*.
Folkestone: Dawson, 1978. Pp. viii+289. £12.00.

Favorably rev. by Trevor H. Levere in *BJHS* 13 (1980):
171-71.
Knight's "theme is the fundamental simplicity of matter
from Boyle to J.J. Thomson, approached as part of intellectual history," and he touches on the Romantics.

Knox, T.M., trans. *Hegel's Introduction to Aesthetics*. Oxford
University Press, 1979. Pp. lxxvi+94. $16.95.

Rev. by Gary Shapiro in *JAAC* 40 (1981/82): 231-33.

Laslett, Peter, K. Oosterveen, and R.M. Smith, eds. *Bastardy
and Its Comparative History*. Harvard University Press,
1980. Pp. xvi+431. $35.00.

Rev. by Edward Shorter in *JMH* 53 (1981): 713-14.
"The chief issue in this field of research continues to
be why illegitimacy and 'pre-bridal pregnancy' increased
so dramatically in the years 1750 to 1850," writes Shorter
of an important work. (T.L.A.)

Le Bris, Michel. *Romantics and Romanticism*. New York: Rizzoli
International Publications, 1981. Pp. 215; 124+90 illus.
$85.00.

A book that brings the coffee table into the classroom;
or, rather, an exhibition that is itself a performance, with
brilliant color-printing that renders the three-dimensionality
of Turner and Runge and Martin; with a showman's running
commentary excited about poetry (often quoted), mental war,
effects of technique and idea. There had to be *nine* chapters,
beginning with "The Masks of Reason" and ending in "The
East of the Imagination," i.e., from "Paradise Lost" to "Turner
and the end of art." An exciting book to read in, confront-
ing concepts with pictures, stressing multeity and diversity,
demonstrating that the third word in the title should be
"Romanticisms."
Ninety painters are exhibited, the greatest space being
given to Delacroix, Friedrich, Fuseli, Goya, Runge, and
Turner. The authors most heavily quoted are Baudelaire,
Blake, Byron, Delacroix, Diderot, Gautier, Gericault, Goethe,
Gothic novelists and Austen, Hugo, Novalis, Ossian, Rousseau,
Schiller, Tieck, de Vigny, Wackenroder, and Winckelmann.
(D.V.E.)

Lenoir, Timothy. "Theology Without Regrets. The Transformation of Physiology in Germany: 1790-1847." *SHPS* 12 (1981):
293-354.

Lowance, Mason I. *The Language of Canaan: Metaphor and Symbol
from the Puritans to the Transcendentalists*. Harvard University Press, 1980. Pp. x+335. $20.00.

Rev. by Michael J. Crawford in *NEQ* 54 (1981): 432-35, who
notes that "Lowance asks in what ways the sources of the
American Renaissance are to be found in American Puritanism
rather than in European Romanticism."

Maier, Pauline. *The Old Revolutionaries: Political Lives in
the Age of Samuel Adams*. New York: Alfred A. Knopf, 1980.
Pp. xxii+309. $15.00.

Rev. by Richard R. Beeman in *PMHB* 105 (1981): 348-50,
who writes that "the great merit of this book ... is not

its success in capturing a common pre-revolutionary mentality, but rather its sensitive portrayal of five men": Sam Adams, Isaac Sears, Dr. Thomas Young, Richard Henry Lee, and Charles Carroll.

Mansel, Philip. *Louis XVIII*. New York: State Mutual Book Service, 1980. Pp. 460. $70.00.

    Rev. by Douglas Johnson in *S*, Jan. 31, 1981, pp. 18f.

McClelland, Charles E. *State, Society, and University in Germany: 1700-1914*. Cambridge University Press, 1980. Pp. x+381. $29.95.

    Rev. by Steven Turner in *JMH* 53 (1981): 573-74 as an "impressive contribution to university history."

Mehra, Marlis. "The Art of Landscape Gardening in Goethe's Novel *Die Wahlverwandtschaften*." *SECC* 10 (1981): 239-78.

Moran, Michael. "On the Continuing Significance of Hegel's *Aesthetics*." *BJA* 21 (1981): 214-39.

Morris, Richard B., and Ene Sirvet, eds. *John Jay, the Winning of the Peace: Unpublished Papers, 1780-1784*. New York: Harper & Row, 1980. Pp. xi+765. $30.00.

    Rev. by Louis M. Waddell in *PMHB* 105 (1981): 352-53.

Moser, Walter. "Translating Discourses: Inter-Discursive Mobility in the Early Romantic Encyclopedia." *The Eighteenth Century: Theory and Interpretation* 22 (Winter 1981): 3-20.

Nybakken, Elizabeth I. *The "Centinel": Warnings of a Revolution*. University of Delaware Press, 1980. Pp. 234. $19.50.

    Rev. by Frederic Trautmann in *PMHB* 105 (1981): 217-18, who finds that by supplying the texts of the Centinel Series which appeared in 1768 in William Bradford's *Pennsylvania Journal and Weekly Advertiser*, "Nybakken has shown with reasonable probability the significant revolutionary influence" of the series as it "fixed in the minds of Pennsylvanians a definition of colonial rights that helped unite inhabitants of the middle colonies."

Ousterhout, Anne M. "Controlling the Opposition in Pennsylvania During the American Revolution." *PMHB* 105 (1981): 3-34.

Perkins, Edwin J. *The Economy of Colonial America*. Columbia
University Press, 1980. Pp. xii+177. $17.50; paper $6.00.

Rev. by Joanne Fraser in *PMHB* 105 (1981): 216-17, who
finds the book "more of an annotated bibliography" than
the "historical synthesis" it purports to be.

Petersen, Susanne. *Lebensmittelfrage und Revolutionäre Politik
in Paris, 1792-1793: Studien zum Verhältnis von revolutionärer
Bourgeoise und Volksbewegung bei Herausbildung der Jakobin-
erdictatur*. Munich: R. Oldenbourg, 1979. Pp. 304.

Rev. by Lynn Hunt in *AHR* 86 (1981): 144-45.

Pocock, J.G.A. "*The Machiavellian Moment* Revisited: A Study
in History and Ideology." *JMH* 53 (1981): 49-72.

Pocock reviews scholarship since the publication of his
magnum opus on Florentine political thought and the Atlantic
Republican tradition. (T.L.A.)

Popkin, Jeremy D. *The Right-Wing Press in France, 1792-1800*.
University of North Carolina Press, 1980. Pp. xx+234. $22.00.

Rev. by Jack R. Censer in *JMH* 53 (1981): 339-40; by Emmet
Kennedy in *AHR* 86 (1981): 143-44.

Potts, A.D. "Greek Sculpture and Roman Copies: I. Anton
Raphael Mengs and the Eighteenth Century." *JWCI* 43 (1980):
150-73; 19 illus.

Anticipations of the changes in taste and valuation which
occurred after the arrival of the Elgin Marbles in England.
Blake is cited briefly in reference to his and Mengs's
theories of "copies."

Ragsdale, Hugh. *Détente in the Napoleonic Era: Bonaparte and
the Russians*. Lawrence: Regents Press of Kansas, 1980. Pp.
xii+183.

Rev. by Owen Connelly in *AHR* 86 (1981): 570.

Rather, L.J. *The Dream of Self-Destruction: Wagner's "Ring"
and the Modern World*. Louisiana State University Press,
1979. Pp. xx+215.

Rev. by William Weber in *AHR* 86 (1981): 112.

Rex, Walter E. "On the Background of Rousseau's First Discourse." *SECC* 9 (1980): 131-50.

"It is the diversity and intensity of the human experience reflected in the Discourse that make it even today such a compelling work...."

Rollins, Richard M. *The Long Journey of Noah Webster*. University of Pennsylvania Press, 1980. Pp. xi+195. $16.00.

Rev. by Earl N. Narbert in *NEQ* 54 (1981): 600-601; by Willard Thorp in *PMHB* 105 (1981): 116-18.

Rorty, Richard. *Philosophy and the Mirror of Nature*. Princeton University Press, 1979. Pp. xvi+401. $20.00.

Rev. by C.C. Prado in *QQ* 88 (1981): 591-93 as "probably the best available summary of and running commentary on some of the major philosophical developments of the seventeenth and eighteenth centuries" and as "the most exciting book I have read in the past dozen years." The temptation to comment on this last should be resisted. (B.C.H.)

Rothenberg, Albert. *The Emerging Goddess: The Creative Process in Art, Science, and Other Fields*. University of Chicago Press, 1979. Pp. 440. $22.50.

Rykwert, Joseph. *The First Moderns: The Architects of the Eighteenth Century*. Cambridge, Mass., and London: MIT Press, 1981. Pp. 585; 275 illus. $45.00; £27.50.

Rev. by John Lubbock in *Art History* 4 (1981): 233-34; by J.M. Richards ("Ways of Looking Back: Architectural Books") in *Encounter* 56 (1981): 66-67.
According to reviewer Richards, the author is concerned "to show how architecture, and especially neo-classical architecture, reflected the revolution in intellectual thought which characterised that century."

Saisselin, R.G. "Neo-Classicism: Images of Public Virtue and Realities of Private Luxury." *Art History* 4 (1981): 14-36.

Salmon, J.H.M. "Storm over the Noblesse." *JMH* 53 (1981): 242-57.

A lucid treatment of recent books and articles dealing with conflict and interchange between the nobility of the sword and the nobility of the gown in France during the 300 years before the Revolution. (T.L.A.)

Schwarzfuchs, S. *Napoleon, the Jews and the Sanhedrin*. London: Routledge & Kegan Paul, 1979. Pp. xii+218. £5.50.

Rev. by John Dunne in *ESR* 10 (1980): 383-92.

Sewell, William H., Jr. *Work and Revolution in France: The Language of Labor from the Old Regime to 1848.* Cambridge University Press, 1980. Pp. x+340. $39.50.

Rev. by François Furet in *JMH* 53 (1981): 557-59.

Shaw, Peter. *American Patriots and the Rituals of Revolution.* Harvard University Press, 1981. Pp. 279. $17.50.

Rev. by Edmund S. Morgan in *NYRB* 6 (April 16, 1981): 29-38; and by Douglas Greenberg in *PMHB* 105 (1981): 345-48, who finds that Shaw's book, while occasionally wrong, is "one of the most thought-provoking works on American history that I have read in a long time." Using "methods derived from anthropology, psychology, and literary criticism," Shaw "draws on traditional historical sources" in order "to interpret the relationship between ... crowd disturbances in the pre-Revolutionary decade" and "the private histories of four 'conscience patriots'--James Otis, Jr., John Adams, Joseph Hawley, and Josiah Quincey, Jr."--as they "interacted with the public events of the 1760s and 1770s."

Slavin, Morris, and Agnes M. Smith, eds. *Bourgeois, Sans-culottes, and Other Frenchmen: Essays on the French Revolution in Honor of John Hall Stewart.* Wilfrid Laurier University Press, 1981. Pp. x+139. $9.50.

Seven essays, including Stanley J. Idzerda, "When and Why Lafayette Became a Revolutionary" (7-24); Themistocles Rodis, "Marriage, Divorce, and the Status of Women During the Terror" (41-58); James R. Harkins, "The Intellectual Origins of Babouvism"; and discussions of the historians Toulongeon (by Agnes M. Smith: 97-112) and Mathiez (by James Friguglietti: 113-30).

Smith, Laura E. "Prisons, Prisoners, and Punishment: French Caricature and Illustration on Penal Reform in the Early Nineteenth Century." *Arts Magazine* 55,vi (1981): 134-45.

Smith, Paul H., et al., eds. *Letters of Delegates to Congress, 1774-1789.* Vol. III, Jan. 1-May 15, 1776; Vol. IV, May 16-Aug. 15, 1776. Washington, D.C.: U.S. Government Printing Office, 1978. Pp. 735; 739. $10.25; $11.25.

Rev. by Roland M. Baumann in *PMHB* 105 (1981): 105-106 (see *RMB* for 1979, p. 13, for earlier volumes).

Soboul, Albert. *Comprendre la Révolution: Problèmes politiques de la Révolution Française, 1789-1797.* Paris: Maspero, 1981. Pp. 379.

Rev. by George Rudé in *TLS*, Oct. 16, 1981, p. 1211, along with Alan Forrest, *The French Revolution and the Poor*.

The title, at least, is a response to Furet's book (listed above), called in French *Penser la Revolution*, though cited, with intent to wither, is only the Furet and Richet history of 1966, 1972. Soboul's epigraph is "Il ne suffit pas de penser la Revolution. Encore faut-il la comprendre." There is some rethinking in these chapters, but mostly in confirmation of the Lefebvre-Soboul paradigm. (D.V.E.)

Solomon, Maynard. "On Beethoven's Creative Process: A Two-Part Invention." *M&L* 61 (1980): 272-83.

The Romantic notion of Beethoven's inspired, effortless mode of composition was derived from two spurious reports.

Stanley, Linda. "James Carter's Account of His Sufferings in Slavery." *PMHB* 105 (1981): 335-39.

The 1807 account of an escaped slave, written for Pennsylvania Quakers in the antislavery movement. (R.A.B.)

Stapleton, Darwin H., ed. *The Engineering Drawings of Benjamin Henry Latrobe*. Yale University Press, 1980. Pp. xx+256. $60.00.

Rev. by George E. Thomas in *PMHB* 105 (1981): 353-54.

Starobinski, Jean. *1789: The Emblems of Reason*. Trans. by Barbara Bray. University Press of Virginia, 1981. ca. 60 illus. $24.95.

A reading of European art--Goya, David, Fuseli ... Blake, Mozart--which "attempts to illuminate the images, the myths, and the emblems with which men [in 1789] tried to understand ... history as they lived it." We are often shown how much more is meant than meets the eye. (D.V.E.)

Traer, James F. *Marriage and the Family in Eighteenth-Century France*. Cornell University Press, 1980. Pp. 208. $15.00.

Rev. by Olwen Hufton in *JMH* 53 (1981): 552-54.

Trautmann, Frederic. "Pennsylvania Through a German's Eyes: The Travels of Ludwig Gall, 1819-1820." *PMHB* 105 (1981): 35-65.

Material on Pennsylvania from *My Travels in the United States*, the diary of a German socialist who grew up during the Napoleonic Wars, sought "an answer to the social ques-

tion" in "the promised land," changed from an admirer to a
critic of America, returned to Germany, wrote widely, "influenced Karl Marx, and came to be called Germany's first
utopian socialist." Goethe reviewed the diary when it was
published in 1822, and Gall's book influenced *Wilhelm Meisters
Wanderjahre*. (R.A.B.)

Urbanski, Marie Mitchell Olesen. *Margaret Fuller's "Woman in
the Nineteenth Century": A Literary Study of Form and Content, of Source and Influence*. Westport, Ct.: Greenwood
Press, 1980. Pp. x+189. $17.95.

Rev. by Florence Turner in *NEQ* 54 (1981): 144-46.

Wall, Charles Cecil. *George Washington: Citizen-Soldier*.
University Press of Virginia, 1980. Pp. xiv+217. $12.50;
paper $6.95.

Rev. by Nicholas B. Wainwright in *PMHB* 105 (1981): 110-11.

Wallerstein, Immanuel. *The Modern World System II: Mercantilism
and the Consolidation of the European World-Economy, 1600-
1750*. New York: Academic Press, 1980. $22.00.

Rev. by Samir Amin in *Monthly Review*, 34,i (1982): 47-53.
Apropos of the dispute whether the French Revolution was
a bourgeois revolution (see Furet and Soboul, above), here
is a reading that the new states which crystallized around
1650--England, the United Provinces, and France--were already capitalist, the aristocracy having already become an
agrarian-capitalist class and having fused with the bourgeoisie. The "revolutions" that occurred in the seventeenth
and eighteenth centuries, including that of 1789, marked
a transformation of the new absolutist state into a liberal
state, necessary for economic expansion. In this view the
notion that in 1789 feudalism was defeated by capitalism is
an invention of bourgeois ideology. And between nations
what really mattered was hegemony. Wallerstein's next
volume will evidently develop his thesis that it was England's
hegemonic position, secured during the mercantile period,
that gave the Empire its decisive advantage in the world
in the nineteenth century, the "industrial revolution" being
an ideological myth. (D.V.E.)

Wegert, Karl H. "Patrimonial Rule, Popular Self-Interest,
and Jacobinism in Germany, 1763-1800." *JMH* 53 (1981): 440-
67.

"The French Revolution, through its disparate ramifications on German sociopolitical life, contributed massively toward facilitating a patrimonial excursion along a road that would lead to administrative efficiency and bad government. The result was a stifling of the opportunities for the emergence of a German middle way between enlightened absolutism and Jacobin democracy."

See also Arntzen, Stern ("General 1. Bibliography"); Cooper ("English 4. Darley").

Reviews of books previously listed:

DONAKOWSKI, Conrad L., *A Muse for the Masses: Ritual and Music in an Age of Democratic Revolution* (see *ELN* 17, Supp., 18), rev. by Sandra S. Sizer in *History of Religions* 19 (1980): 275-77; by Calvin R. Stapert in *CSR* 9 (1980): 367-69; DOYLE, William, *Origins of the French Revolution* (see *RMB* for 1980, p. 7), rev. by Colin Lucas in *TLS*, May 8, 1981, p. 525; HAMPSON, Norman, *Danton* (see *RMB* for 1979, p. 7), rev. by James F. Fraer in *ECS* (Summer 1981): 490-92; HONOUR, Hugh, *Romanticism* (see *RMB* for 1979, p. 8), rev. by Karl Kroeber in *SiR* 20 (1981): 268-70; MANUEL, Frank E., and Fritzie P. Manuel, *Utopian Thought in the Western World* (see *RMB* for 1980, p. 11), rev. at length by Bronislaw Baczko in *JMH* 53 (1981): 468-76; ROYSTER, Charles, *A Revolutionary People at War: The Continental Army and American Character, 1775-1783* (see *RMB* for 1980, p. 13), rev. by George Athan Billias in *NEQ* 54 (1981): 127-29; by Samuel F. Scott in *ECS* 13 (1980): 218-21; WOLOCH, Isser, *The French Veteran from the Revolution to the Restoration* (see *RMB* for 1980, p. 14), rev. by Peter Paret in *JMH* 53 (1981): 121-23 with praise.

Review articles:

Clayton, John Powell. "Perspectives on Protestant and Catholic Thought in the Nineteenth Century." *ESR* 10 (1980): 247-62.

Review of a series of monographs on nineteenth-century theology published by a German company, Vandenshoeck-Ruprecht.

Holtman, Robert B. *JMH* 53 (1981): 554-57.

An essay reviewing new directions in Napoleonic studies: Irene Collins, *Napoleon and His Parliaments, 1800-1815* (see *RMB* for 1980, p. 7); Armgard von Reden-Dohna, *Deutschland und Italien im Zeitalter Napoleons* (Wiesbaden: Franz Steiner Verlag, 1979; pp. viii+189; DM 28.00); Domokos Kosáry, *Napoleon et la Hongrie* (Budapest: Akadémia Kiadó, 1979; pp. 122; $10.00); Angelo Varni, *Bologna napoleonica: Poteree società dalla Republica Cisalpina al regno d'Italia: 1800-1806* (Bologna: Massimiliano Boni Editore, 1973; pp. xviii+ 288; L4,500)--excellent background. (T.L.A.)

Warner, Marina. "Tears in the Mind's Eye: From David to Pissarro." *Encounter* 56 (1981): 67-74.

Relevant titles discussed are Anita Brookner, *Jacques-Louis David*; Hubert Wellington, ed., *The Journals of Eugène Delacroix*; and William Vaughan, *German Romantic Painting.* See *RMB* for 1980, pp. 149, 189, and 272, respectively.

3. CRITICISM

Agulhon, Maurice. *Marianne into Battle: Republican Imagery and Symbolism in France, 1789-1880.* Trans. by Janet Lloyd. Cambridge University Press, 1981. $32.50.

Not seen.

Altizer, Thomas J.J. "The Apocalyptic Identity of the Modern Imagination." *JAAR Thematic Studies* 48,ii (1981): 19-29.

"In entering the world of the modern imagination we discover a strange counterpart to the apocalyptic faith of primitive Christianity."

Andrews, William L., ed. *Literary Romanticism in America.* Louisiana State University Press, 1981. Pp. 168. $14.95.

Rev. by Lachlan Mackinnon in *TLS*, Oct. 23, 1981, p. 1242.

Arac, Jonathan. *Commissioned Spirits: The Shaping of Social Motion in Dickens, Carlyle, Melville, and Hawthorne.* Rutgers University Press, 1979. Pp. xiii+200.

Favorably rev. by Michael Sprinkler in *MLN* 95 (1980): 1437-42.

Avens, Robert. "Recovering Imagination--Discovering the East." *Thought: A Review of Culture and Idea* 55 (1980): 153-68.

Includes section on Romantic authors.

Bahti, Timothy. "The Indifferent Reader: The Performance of
Hegel's Introduction to the *Phenomenology*." *Diacritics* 11
(Spring 1981): 68-82.

Bell, Michael Davitt. *The Development of American Romance: The
Sacrifice of Relation*. University of Chicago Press, 1981.
Pp. 219.

  Rev. by Larzer Ziff in *TLS*, June 12, 1981, pp. 663-64 as
deserving "every centimetre of the space it will occupy on
the shelf of standard works on the evolution of an American
literature." (Main figures: Irving, Hawthorne, Melville.)

Bloom, Harold. "Agon: Revisionism and Critical Personality."
Raritan (Summer 1981): 18-47.

  His workouts with Richard Rorty's versions of Jamesian
pragmatism have resulted in a more muscular and cheerful
Bloom. Fueling the polemic here are several splendidly
provocative quotations from Emerson and some agonizingly
opaque comments on Whitman--personalities who, according
to Bloom, have something to say "about agon, about the
struggle between adverting subject or subjectivity and the
mediation that consciousness hopelessly wills language to
constitute." (J.C.C.)
  (A fuller version of this essay appears as the first chapter of Bloom's *Agon: Towards a Theory of Revisionism* (Oxford
University Press, 1982.)

Booth, Wayne C. "Do Reasons Matter in Criticism? or: Many
Meanings, Many Modes." *BMMLA* 14 (1981): 3-23.

  This amounts to a reading of Keats's *La Belle Dame*, with
responses (pp. 24-34) by David Bleich, Patricia H. Sosnoski,
and Lawrence Lipking. (T.L.A.)

Chase, Cynthia. "Paragon, Parergon: Baudelaire Translates
Rousseau." *Diacritics* 11 (Summer 1981): 42-51.

  Readings of Baudelaire, Rousseau, Kant, and Derrida.

Coogan, Robert M. "The Triumph of Reason: Sidney's *Defense*
and Aristotle's *Rhetoric*." *PLL* 17 (1981): 255-70.

  A clarification of a legacy which Sidney bequeathed the
Romantics: the distinction between prophetic and fictive
poetry. (R.A.B.)

Crow, Brian. "Romantic Ambivalence in *The Master Builder*." *SiR*
20 (1981): 203-23.

"In *The Master Builder*, ... as in *Alastor* and other Romantic quest poems, the quest for spiritual insight and creative
fulfillment is presented as fraught with danger and involving the risk of self-destruction."

Culler, Jonathan. *The Pursuit of Signs: Semiotics, Literature,
Deconstruction*. Cornell University Press, 1981. Pp. xiii+
242. $15.00.

Includes three essays of particular interest to students
of Romanticism: "Semiotics as a Theory of Reading," which
deploys the gamut of readings of Blake's "London" to illustrate its thesis; "Apostrophe," which engages Keats, Shelley,
and Wordsworth; and "The Mirror Stage," a consideration of
M.H. Abrams's *The Mirror and the Lamp* that was also published
in the festschrift *High Romantic Argument*.

Derrida, Jacques. "Economimesis." *Diacritics* 11 (Summer 1981):
3-25.

A reading of Kant's *Critique of Judgment*.

Donato, Eugenio. "Divine Agonies: Of Representation and Narrative in Romantic Poetics." *Glyph* 6 (1979): 90-122.

Engages the problem of representation as it is formulated
in Nietzsche and Hegel and as it emerges in both European
and English Romantic poets. Comments on the epistemological
debate between Paul De Man and Earl Wasserman.

Engell, James. *The Creative Imagination: Enlightenment to
Romanticism*. Harvard University Press, 1981. Pp. xix+416.
$16.00.

Rev. by Stuart Peterfreund in *RP&P* 5,ii (1981): 57-62.
As the book jacket says: "James Engell traces the evolution of the creative imagination, from its emergence in
British empirical thought through its flowering in Romantic
art and literature." The word "trace" is particularly apt
for a work that, exhibiting an enormous range of knowledge,
records precisely the presence of the word "imagination"
without providing much insight into how to evaluate it. More
specifically, the evaluation of "imagination," which is
utterly positive and unquestioned, reminds one immediately
of one of Engell's mentors, W.J. Bate, in his *From Classic
to Romantic* (1946). Nothing, it seems, has significantly
changed since then; as a result, while the book is clearly
and energetically written, it provides the reader with no
new insights on what we are to make of (often) familiar
material.

Engell distorts, or evades, context in a manner which leads
to the "triumph" of imagination in the work of Coleridge.
Subordinated to Coleridge in importance are (to pick two
glaring examples) Blake (about whom Engell says: "Compared
with Keats or Schiller, Blake approached a kind of fanaticism")
and Hazlitt, the discussion of whom anachronistically pre-
cedes that of Coleridge even though some of Hazlitt's most
important thinking about imagination is a critique of Coleridge. But the main contextual distortions concern the treatment of the idea--particularly with regard to political,
sexual, and psychological implications. Of Blake we hear that
his notion of imagination is "frankly Christian," but we
never hear about how *radical* that Christianity is; imagination as a way of opposing a "true" to a false religion is
never discussed. Nor does Engell, amazingly, connect Blake's
"imagination" with sexuality. The effect of this treatment
is to blend Blake's radicalism into the liberal-conservative
continuum of the other Romantics. The same is true of Engell's
section on Hazlitt, which has nothing about politics and the
imagination (although he mentions John Kinnaird's study of
Hazlitt, Engell shows no assimilation of Kinnaird's brilliant
account of Hazlitt's growing skepticism about imagination
and disinterestedness as in the *Coriolanus* essay).

Finally, the book, which is primarily about theoretical
statements of imagination, imports poetry for evidence in
arbitrary ways, most notably in the discussion of Keats.
There is, of course, a tradition for discussing Keats's
ideas by discussing his poetry, but doing that here simply
adds to the uncritical nature of the book. (J.C.R.)

Feder, Lillian. *Madness in Literature*. Princeton University
Press, 1980. Pp. xvi+331. $17.50.

Rev. by Jeffrey Berman in *ELN* 19 (1981): 169-71; by Edward
Butscher in *GaR* 35 (1981): 675-78.

Frye, Northrop. *The Great Code: The Bible and Literature*.
New York: Harcourt Brace Jovanovich, 1981. Pp. xxiii+261.
$14.95.

Work derived from Frye's teaching of the Bible. He describes
it as a book "concerned with the impact of the Bible on the
creative imagination."

Garber, Frederick. "Beckford, Delacroix and Byronic Orientalism." *CLS* 18 (1981): 321-32.

If the Orient "has helped to define Europe (or the West)
as its contrasting image, idea, personality, experience"

(Said), as "a sort of antiworld against which we pit ourselves for definition" (Crapanzano), then Orientalism is part
of the essential process of self-making--"and it is in that
light that Orientalism gains a large part of its meaning for
Beckford and his Romantic successors" (Garber). A valuable
essay, perhaps especially for its precision in distinguishing the Orientalisms of Beckford, Byron, and Delacroix.
(*Vathek*, for instance, "has been called a counterpart of the
Gothic" but shows none of the Gothic's "calculated fuzziness.")
(D.V.E.)

Grady, Hugh H. "Notes on Marxism and the Lyric." *Contemporary
Literature* 22 (1981): 544-55.

"The lyric has become the specialized literary genre for
Utopian vision, for the construction of realms of imaginative freedom that would escape the very conditions which
have given rise to their expression (only) as poetry." The
theoretical section (drawing valuably on Christopher Caud-
well) is very suggestive and superior to the author's application of it to Coleridge's "Kubla Khan." (J.C.R.)

Gram, Moltke S. "Intellectual Intuition: The Continuity Thesis."
JHI 42 (1981): 287-304.

Against Hearing, Kroner, and Lovejoy who argue that "intellectual intuition" in Fichte and Schelling means what it
meant in Kant, Gram argues that "there is no continuity
within Kant's thought in the use of the term, and there is
none between Kant and Fichte or between Fichte and Schelling."
(R.A.B.)

Grossman, Marshall. "Hayden White and Literary Criticism:
The Tropology of Discourse." *PLL* 17 (1981): 424-45.

White seeks to demystify post-structuralism and its
"mythology of the negative." His tropology provides "a useful classificatory system with which to characterize literary
and factual texts and the relations between texts within
and across given historical periods." (R.A.B.)

Hamacher, Werner. "The Reader's Supper: A Piece of Hegel."
Diacritics 11 (Summer 1981): 52-67.

Hammond, J.R. *An Edgar Allan Poe Companion.* London: Macmillan,
1981. Pp. 205. £15.00.

Rev. by Stoddard Martin (along with Raymond Foye, ed.,
The Unknown Poet: An Anthology of Fugitive Writings [San

Francisco: City Lights Books, $5.95]) in *TLS*, Sept. 18, 1981, p. 1077, emphasizing Poe's role as "the conduit through which many early Romantic motifs [deriving from Coleridge, Godwin, Shelley] were passed on to French writers of the late nineteenth century, who in turn passed them on to Wilde, Symons, Yeats, et al. The fugitive writings of Poe include a fragment on "Shelley and the Poetic Abandon" and a piece called "The Flame of Love" citing Byron's "boyish poet-love."

Hartman, Geoffrey. *Saving the Text: Literature/Derrida/Philosophy*. The Johns Hopkins University Press, 1981. Pp. xxvii+ 184. $12.95.

 Rev. by James Mall in *JAAC* 40 (1981/82): 227-29 as flawed. Not seen.

Johnson, Barbara. *The Critical Difference: Essays in the Contemporary Rhetoric of Reading*. The Johns Hopkins University Press, 1981. Pp. 176. $12.00.

 Studies of Balzac, Mallarmé, Baudelaire, Apollinaire, Melville, Poe, Barthes, Lacan, Austin, and Derrida. (Not seen.)

Kenshur, Oscar S. "Fragments and Order: Two Modern Theories of Discontinuous Form." *PLL* 17 (1981): 227-44.

 In connection with Joseph Frank and Umberto Eco, Thomson's *Seasons* call into question the premises of modern critical theory. (R.A.B.)

Kermode, Frank. *The Genesis of Secrecy: On the Interpretation of Narrative*. Harvard University Press, 1979. Pp. xii+163. $3.95 (paper).

 Rev. by Ruth F. Smith in *JAAC* 40 (1981/82): 94-96.

Kier, Kathlene E. "Only Another Suspension of Disbelief: Emily Dickinson's 'I heard an organ talk, sometimes.'" *MSE* 8 (1981): 40-48.

Klein, Richard. "Kant's Sunshine." *Diacritics* 11 (Summer 1981): 26-41.

 A reading of Derrida's reading of Kant. See Derrida, Jacques, above. (J.C.C.)

Lobb, Edward. *T.S. Eliot and the Romantic Critical Tradition*. London and Boston: Routledge & Kegan Paul, 1981. Pp. xiii+ 194. $20.00.

Although this book does not contain a full-scale analysis
of Romantic aesthetic, it does demonstrate, by analysis of
Eliot's published works and "Clark Lectures," common denomi-
nators between Eliot's and the English Romantics' critical
theories. Most of the Romantics are given but brief mention
(Hazlitt on two pages; Byron on three; Shelley on five;
Wordsworth on ten), although Coleridge and Keats are treated
in greater breadth if not depth. "Nostalgia," Lobb claims,
is central to the aesthetic of some of the Romantics and of
Eliot. Lobb's remarks on Keats best represent the offerings
of this book: "Eliot's direct references to Keats are admittedly few in number. The affinities are nevertheless clear,
though they are obscured somewhat by the different forms of
expression ..., and Eliot's praise of Keats as a critic ...
is unqualified.... Keats's influence can perhaps be reduced
to this: Eliot, believing that feeling was the basis of all
poetry but distrustful of subjective and uncontrolled emotion, found in Keats a theory analogous to his own, embodied
in a historical myth, accompanied and supported by a finally
successful, 'impersonal' practice of poetry. He was therefore encouraged in his own habit of thinking of poetry not
as issuing from heart or head (for from either source it
was feeling), but as focused on subject or object. Eliot's
own poetry, always the best index to his preferences, contains several Keatsian echoes" (68). (C.E.R.)

Martinet, Marie-Madeleine, ed. *Art et nature en Grande-
Bretagne au XVIIIe siècle: de l'harmonie classique au pittoresque du premier romantisme.* Paris: Aubier-Montaigne,
1980.

Mellow, James R. *Nathaniel Hawthorne in His Times.* Boston:
Houghton Mifflin Company, 1980. Pp. 600. $19.95.

Rev. by Richard Conway in *NEQ* 54 (1981): 442-44.

Miller, J. Hillis. "A 'Buchstabliches' Reading of *The Elective
Affinities.*" *Glyph* 6 (1979): 1-23.

Unravels the "figures of lines" that stitch together
Goethe's text. (J.C.C.)

Müllenbrock, Heinz-Joachim. *Der historische Roman des 19.
Jahrhunderts.* (Forum Anglistik.) Heidelberg: Carl Winter,
1980. Pp. 139. DM 20.00 (paper).

Neufeldt, Leonard N. "Emerson, Thoreau and Daniel Webster."
ESQ 26 (1980): 26-37.

Olechowski, Christopher H. "The Napoleonic Legend and Its
   Aftermath: Polish Romanticism and Stendhal." *CLS* 17 (1980):
   368-75.

Orsini, Daniel J. "Emily Dickinson and the Romantic Use of
   Science." *MSE* 8 (1981): 57-69.

Pajak, Edward F. "Washington Irving's *Ichabod Crane*: American
   Narcissus." *AI* 38 (1981): 127-35.

   "The very name, 'Sleepy Hollow,' the setting of the story,
   suggests reference to the womb," argues Pajak, and Ichabod
   pays the price for "having withdrawn his libidinal cathexis
   from her and returned it to his own ego"--a matter of heads
   up or heads off you might say. (T.L.A.)

Papers in Language and Literature. "A *Symposium*: Hermeneutics,
   Post-Structuralism, and 'Objective' Interpretation." *PLL*
   17 (1981): 48-87.

   A series of papers which take Heidegger as their point of
   departure and which were originally presented at a 1979
   MLA session on "Literary Worlds and Actual Worlds: The Problem of Reference." Contents: Vernon Gras, "Understanding,
   Historicity, and Truth" (48-53); Michael Murray, "Poetic
   Sense and Poetic Reference" (53-61); James E. Swearingen,
   "The Poet and the Phenomenon of World" (62-71); David Halliburton, "From Poetic Thinking to Concrete Interpretation"
   (71-79); Robert Magliola, "Grounds and Common(s), and a
   Heideggerian Recension" (80-87). Gras focuses contemporary
   critical debate in terms appropriate for a theory of Romanticism. "The question becomes, 'Is self-reference and emancipatory truth sufficient basis for a literary theory?...
   Ultimately, language as a metaphysically pointless human
   game undercuts the emancipatory reach of this criticism.
   Why emancipate man from his mythologies if no genuine dialogue
   with Being can ever take place?" Only "when our conversation with Being is cognitive and revelatory even though
   partial and temporal" does it "seem to be worthwhile to
   write about writing." Halliburton's essay, which uses
   Heidegger and Benjamin to read "Michael" and Wordsworth
   to read Heidegger and Benjamin, demonstrates the worth.
   (R.A.B.)

Pavel, Thomas G. "Ontological Issues in Poetics: Speech Acts
   and Fictional Worlds." *JAAC* 40 (1981/82): 167-78.

   Contra speech act theory.

Price, Kenneth M. "Whitman on Other Writers: Controlled 'Graciousness' in *Specimen Days*." *ESQ* 26 (1980): 79–87.

Carlyle and Poe figure.

Reed, Arden. "Abysmal Influence: Baudelaire, Coleridge, De Quincey, Piranesi, Wordsworth." *Glyph* 4 (1978): 189–206.

Uses the relationships among various texts to demonstrate that "just where one is confidently following the line of influence, the text itself inscribes a labyrinth, doubling and redoubling the line, folding it over and in on itself."

Rees, John O. "Aminadab in 'The Birth-Mark': The Name Again." *Names* 28 (1980): 171–82.

Connects Hawthorne's tale with Goldsmith and late eighteenth-century farce.

Reiss, Edmund. "Medieval Irony." *JHI* 42 (1981): 209–26.

A consideration of texts which led to a consciousness of irony in the nineteenth century. (R.A.B.)

Rykwert, Joseph. *The First Moderns: The Architects of the Eighteenth Century*. Cambridge, Mass., and London: MIT Press, 1980. Pp. 585; 275 illus. £27.50.

Favorably rev. by Jules Lubbock in *Art History* 4 (1981): 233–34.

Sandler, Florence, and Darrell Reeck. "The Masks of Joseph Campbell." *Religion* 11 (1981): 1–20.

An examination of the salient features of Campbell's allegiances and thought "over the 20 years from *The Hero with a Thousand Faces* through the volumes of *The Masks of God*." Despite "considerable blemishes" in presentation, "his work has power and attractiveness" which the authors consider to be "not necessarily for the wrong reasons." To the frustration of "those who take their labels seriously," he appears to be a "dilettante among symbols" (as he has been called); more accurately, he is "a comparative esotericist." But to get beyond labels, this sympathetic, judicious pursuit of Campbell, through changing influences and shifting emphases, must be read in full. Campbell is seen as not merely elucidating the myths but converting them from one cultural viewpoint to another—to those whose myths are appropriated, "the process is a form of cultural imperialism." In his biographical note in the Viking/Penguin *Masks* he re-

calls his childhood fascination with American totem poles,
but in his peroration it is beyond American Primitivism and
to Romanticism, to "a romantic or gnostic version of Christianity" that he appeals, invoking Shelley's *Prometheus
Unbound* as to the improbability that "within the time of
our lives ... any solid rock will be found to which Prometheus
can again be durably shackled...." (D.V.E.)

Schneider, Richard J. "*Cape Cod*: Thoreau's Wilderness of
Illusion." *ESQ* 26 (1980): 184-96.

   Evolving relations with nature from Ktaadn to Provincetown.
(T.L.A.)

Schoenholtz, Andrew I. "The Temptations of Truth: Imagination,
Doubt and the 'Imposing Completeness of a Delusion' in Keats
and Flaubert." *MLN* 96 (1981): 1051-65.

   Finds in Flaubert an attitude resembling Negative Capability.

Shackleton, Deborah. "Canadian Energy: Dialogues on Creativity:
Northrop Frye." *Descant* 31-32 (1981): 216-26, with port.

   There is "a psychological difference ... between the ego-
centric interpretation and the interpretation which tries,
at any rate, to follow what is suggested by the data."

Sinfield, Alan. "Against Appropriation." *EiC* 31 (July 1981):
181-96.

   "Appropriation--the attempt to juggle the text into ac-
ceptability--produces imprecise thought and emotion and en-
courages a complacent 'discovery' of what we wanted to find."
Cites various examples of strategies of appropriation in
criticism from the Romantics to contemporary Marxists. Proposes that we "resist and reduce appropriative tendencies
in our reading" by attending "to the gap between the text
and ourselves."

Singh, Pratap. *Poets' Vision of History*. (SSEL, Romantic Reassessment, 103.) University of Salzburg, Austria, 1981.
Pp. iv+106. $13.50.

   A superficial, conventional treatment of the historical
views of Coleridge, Wordsworth, Shelley, Meredith, Hardy,
and T.S. Eliot. Prof. Singh's "Concise Bibliography" is
dated. (J.M.D.)

Solomon, Maynard. "Franz Schubert's 'My Dream.'" *AI* 38 (1981): 137-54.

The *dream* is a brief tale written in 1822, here teased into a skillful comment on homosexuality and the artist. (T.L.A.)

Stafford, Barbara Maria. *Symbol and Myth: Humbert de Superville's Essay on Absolute Signs in Art.* University of Delaware Press, 1979. Pp. 206; illus. $35.00.

Rev. by F. David Martin in *JAAC* 40 (1981/82): 233-34.

The essay by a literal Dutch painter was first published in 1827-32: "Through Humbert seemed to flow every stream that was relevant to the central problem of early Romanticism: the relationship between the subjective world and the objective world." (T.L.A.)

Ullman, Pierre L. "Romanticism and Irony in *Don Quixote*: A Continuing Controversy." *PLL* 17 (1981): 320-33.

Much more is here than a good survey dealing with Romanticism and impossible dreams. (T.L.A.)

Vendler, Helen. "I.A. Richards at Harvard." *New Boston Review* 6,ii (1981): 3-5.

(Appeared first in *The American Scholar*; to be part of a book, *Masters*.)

Vendler, Helen. "Understanding Ashbery." *NY* 4 (March 12, 1981): 108-36.

Warminski, Andrezej. "Reading for Example: 'Sense-Certainty' in Hegel's *Phenomenology of Spirit*." *Diacritics* 11 (Spring 1981): 83-94.

Weber, Eugen. "Fairies and Hard Facts: The Reality of Folktales." *JHI* 42 (1981): 93-113.

The folktales which the Grimm brothers collected were not based on fantasy but on "grim everyday experience." They are "popular stories that we describe as fairytales" and--despite our description--they "can tell us a great deal about real conditions in the world of those who told and those who heard the tales." The genre began to die out when "the realistic substance of *märchen* no longer matched experience," when "their wisdom became nonsense and superstition." (R.A.B.)

Wohlfarth, Irving. "The Politics of Prose and the Art of
Awakening: Walter Benjamin's Version of a German Romantic
Motif." *Glyph* 7 (1980): 131-48.

See also Garber ("English 4. Byron"); Hennelly, Paulson
("English 4. The Gothic Novel"); Homans ("English 4. D.
Wordsworth").

Reviews of books previously listed:

BLOOM, Harold, et al., *Deconstruction and Criticism* (see
RMB for 1980, p. 16), rev. by A.C. Goodson in *TWC* 12 (1981):
200-02; by Donald G. Marshall ("The Inflation of Theory")
in *PR* 48 (1981): 294-96; by Carl Woodring in *KSJ* 30 (1981):
191-94; BOOTH, Wayne C., *Critical Understanding: The Powers
and Limits of Pluralism* (see *RMB* for 1980, p. 17), rev. by
Terry Heller in *ArQ* 37 (1981): 85-90; by Stephen Trombley
in *RES* 32 (1981): 365-67; CONRAD, Peter, *Romantic Opera and
Literary Form* (see *ELN* 17, Supp., 28), rev. by John Warrack
in *M&L* 61 (1980): 186-88; DE MAN, Paul, *Allegories of Reading: Figural Language in Rousseau, Nietzsche, Rilke, and
Proust* (see *RMB* for 1979, p. 19), rev. by George McFadden
in *JAAC* 39 (1980/81): 337-41; by Hayden White ("Critic,
Critic") in *PR* 48 (1981): 311-15; FURST, Lilian R., *The
Contours of European Romanticism* (see *RMB* for 1980, p. 19),
rev. by Elizabeth Boa in *BJA* 21 (1981): 85-88; FURST,
Lilian R., ed., *European Romanticism: Self-Definition* (see
RMB for 1980, p. 19), rev. by Robert T. Denommé in *FR* 55
(1981): 411; by Edith Kern, briefly, in *MLR* 76 (1981): 919-
20; HAGSTRUM, Jean H., *Sex and Sensibility: Ideal and Erotic
Love from Milton to Mozart* (see *RMB* for 1980, pp. 19-20),
rev. by Robert A. Logan III in *HSL* 13 (1981): 187-90; HART-
MAN, Geoffrey, *Criticism in the Wilderness: The Study of
Literature Today* (see *RMB* for 1980, p. 20), rev. by James
Mall, negatively, in *JAAC* 40 (1981/82): 227-29; by Robert
Moynihan in *ArQ* 37 (1981): 187-90; by Paul C. Ray in *WHR*
35 (1981): 367-69; by Hayden White in *PR* 48 (1981): 646-49;
LENTRICCHIA, Frank, *After the New Criticism* (see *RMB* for
1980, p. 22), rev. by William F. Cain in *WHR* 35 (1981):
192-95; by Thomas McLaughlin in *JAAC* 39 (1981): 466-68;
RAJAN, Tilottama, *Dark Interpreter: The Discourse of Roman-
ticism* (see *RMB* for 1980, p. 24), rev. by Helen Regueiro
Elam in *TWC* 12 (1981): 197-99; by Scott P. Sanders in *ELN*
19 (1981): 149-52; by David Wagenknecht in *SiR* 20 (1981):
525-32; SCHLEIFER, James T., *The Making of Tocqueville's
Democracy in America* (see *RMB* for 1980, p. 162), rev. by
Richard Herr in *JMH* 53 (1981): 731-33 with great apprecia-

tion; SCHMIDGALL, Gary, *Literature as Opera* (see *ELN* 16,
Supp., 24), rev. by John Warrack in *M&L* 61 (1980): 186–88;
SPENGEMANN, William C., *The Forms of Autobiography: Episodes
in the History of a Literary Genre* (see *RMB* for 1980, p. 27),
rev. by Gay Wilson Allen in *GaR* 35 (1981): 411–15; by John N.
Morris in *ELN* 18 (1981): 229–33; TURNER, Arlin, *Nathaniel
Hawthorne: A Biography* (see *RMB* for 1980, p. 28), rev. by
Kent Bales in *WHR* 35 (1981): 183–88; VAUGHAN, William,
German Romanticism and English Art (see *RMB* for 1979, p. 46),
rev. by Andrew Sanders in *VS* 24 (1981): 247–48.

Review article:

Adamowski, T.H. "The Disenchantment of the Word." *QQ* 88 (1981):
442–56.

An excellent review essay of: Geoffrey Hartman, *Criticism
in the Wilderness: The Study of Literature Today* (see *RMB*
for 1980, p. 20); Frank Lentricchia, *After the New Criticism*
(see *RMB* for 1980, p. 22); John Fekete, *The Critical Twi-
light* (Boston: Routledge and Kegan Paul, 1978; pp. xxviii+
300; $27.95); and Grant Webster, *The Republic of Letters:
A History of Postwar American Literary Opinion* (Johns Hopkins University Press, 1979; pp. xviii+381; $22.50). Those
of us who joined Bishop Hunt in cheering for the Canadian
league of the British empirical tradition last year will
enjoy Adamowski's summary comment on the voice of critical
addiction––"the solitude of epistemological narcissism"
echoes. (T.L.A.)

ENGLISH

(Compiled by Thomas L. Ashton, University of Massachusetts; Robert A. Brinkley, University of Southern Mississippi; Irene H. Chayes, Kensington, Md.; Jerome C. Christensen, The Johns Hopkins University; Julia M. DiStefano, New Hampshire College; David V. Erdman, State University of New York, Stony Brook; Philip A. Everson, University of Delaware; Moira Ferguson, University of Nebraska, Lincoln; Bishop C. Hunt, College of Charleston; John E. Jordan, University of California, Berkeley; Charles E. Robinson, University of Delaware; Jeffrey C. Robinson, University of Colorado; Robert Michael Ryan, Rutgers University, Camden)

1. BIBLIOGRAPHY

Bell, Alan. "Accessions of Scottish Literary Manuscripts, National Library of Scotland, 1979-80." *SLJ* 8 (1981): supp. 15, pp. 55-56.

Letters of Scott and Carlyle and an annotated set of *The Mirror* (1779-80) with tipped manuscript drafts from the Arthur A. Houghton sale.

Brogan, T.V.F. *English Versification, 1570-1980: A Reference Guide with a Global Appendix.* The Johns Hopkins University Press, 1981. Pp. 832. $47.50.

Nearly 6000 entries listing known source materials on English versification, carefully annotated.

Davis, Adina. "John Morice, F.S.A. 1768-1844: Portrait of a Bibliophile XXII." *BC* 29 (1980): 37-49.

A look at Morice's life and the contents of his library of over 4000 volumes.

Essick, Robert N., and Michael C. Young. "Blake's 'Canterbury' Print: The Posthumous Pilgrimage of the Copperplate." *BIQ* 15 (1981): 78-82; illus.

Halsband, Robert. "A Collector's Connections." *TLS*, June 12, 1981, pp. 681-82.

   A summarizing review of the 42-volume *Correspondence of Horace Walpole* (Yale University Press), upon publication of the 42nd volume (1981). (Still to come, a volume of Additions and Corrections and a 5-volume Index.)

Loudon, J.H. *James Scott and William Scott, Bookbinders*. London: Scolar Press, 1980. Pp. 414. £30.00.

   Rev. by Dorothy A. Harrop in *Library* 3 (1981): 74-77. On Scots binding in the 1770s and 1780s.

Orr, Leonard. *A Catalogue Checklist of English Prose Fiction 1750-1800*. Troy, N.Y.: Whitston, 1981. Pp. xi+204. $13.50.

   A chronological list compiled from published library catalogues; almost 1200 novels.

Owings, Frank N., Jr. "Keats, Lamb, and a Black-Letter Chaucer." *PBSA* 75 (1981): 147-55.

   Speculation that Lamb acquired Keats's copy of the 1598 edition.

Pitcher, E.W. "Anthologized Fiction for the Juvenile Reader, 1750-1800: A Preliminary View." *Library* 3 (1981): 132-41.

   Pitcher is on to something of interest in his new campaign (here he gives the contents of three anthologies)--consider the collection for children entitled *Allegories and Visions* published in 1769. (T.L.A.)

Sait, J.E. "The Year's Work in Scottish Literary and Linguistic Studies 1978: 1800-1900." *SLJ* 7 (1980): supp. 13, pp. 39-42.

Sait, J.E. "The Year's Work in Scottish Literary and Linguistic Studies 1979: 1800-1900." *SLJ* 8 (1981): supp. 15, pp. 35-42.

Wellens, Oskar. "Henry Crabb Robinson, Reviewer of Wordsworth, Coleridge, and Byron in the *Critical Review*: Some New Attributions." *BRH* 84 (1981): 98-120.

   Seventeen reviews from May 1816 through June 1817 are attributed to Robinson, only two conjecturally. They include *Christabel*, Constant's *Adolphe*, Byron's *Childe Harold* III and *Manfred*, Wordsworth's *Letter to a Friend of Robert Burns &c.*, Coleridge's *Statesman's Manual* and *Lay Sermon*, and several of Southey's works including the 1817 *Wat Tyler*. Material here for the revision of several chapters on the reception of the Romantics.

See also Wearing ("General 1. Bibliography"); Temperley
("English 2. Environment"); and in "English 4": Minnick
("Blake"); Milton ("Coleridge"); Bareham, Gatrell ("Crabbe");
Dendurent ("De Quincey"); Frank ("The Gothic Novel"); Keynes
("Hazlitt"); Becker, Hearn ("Keats"); Murray ("Shelley,
Mary").

Reviews of books previously listed:

BAUER, N.S., *William Wordsworth: A Reference Guide to British
Criticism, 1793-1899* (see *ELN* 17, Supp., 34), rev. by Patricia
M. Ball in *YES* 11 (1981): 298-300; HARTLEY, Robert A., ed.,
*Keats, Shelley, Byron, Hunt, and Their Circles: A Bibliog-
raphy, 1962-1974* (see *RMB* for 1979, p. 30), rev. by J.
Drummond Bone in *YES* 11 (1981): 304-05; HOUGHTON, Walter E.,
and Esther Rhoads Houghton, eds., *The Wellesley Index to
Victorian Periodicals, 1824-1900*, Vol. III (see *RMB* for
1980, p. 32), rev. by Ian Jack in *RES* 32 (1981): 346-48;
REIMAN, Donald H., *English Romantic Poetry, 1800-1838: A
Guide to Information Sources* (see *RMB* for 1979, p. 31),
rev. by Charles W. Hagelman, Jr., in *KSJ* 30 (1981): 216-18.

2. ENVIRONMENT: ART, PHILOSOPHY, POLITICS, RELIGION, SOCIETY

Agrawal, R.R. *Tradition and Experiment in the Poetry of James
Thomson.* (SSEL.) University of Salzburg, Austria, 1981.
Pp. viii+273.

A fairly routine survey of Thomson's life and work, written
in a language that is not quite English, e.g., "*The Seasons*
is Thomson's principal and, perhaps, his best work, so far
as its popularity and literary influence are concerned"
(59); "Thomson's imitation of the archaic words and expressions of Spenser was not a laboured copy of his master"
(159); "He paid him a glowing homage" (222). One hates to
be cruel, especially to a scholar toiling at a far-off college in India. Nevertheless, like many of the books in the
"Salzburg Studies," this one should never have been published. (B.C.H.)

Ashton, Geoffrey. "Paintings in the Mander and Mitchenson
Theatre Collection." *Apollo* 114 (1981): 88-92.

Includes paintings of actors, actresses, and scenes, 1750-
1850.

Baeyer, Hans C. von. "The Universe According to St. George
Tucker." *ECL* 6 (1980): 67-79.

In his notebooks and letters from 1782 to 1819, Tucker
left a record of his model of the universe.

Baker, William J. *Beyond Port and Prejudice: Charles Lloyd
of Oxford, 1784-1829.* University of Maine at Orono Press,
1981. Pp. xvi+245; illus.

Rev. by G. Hewett Joiner in *Albion* 13 (1981): 314 as "a
valuable counterweight to the widely held view of Oxford's
academic climate in this period but ... counterweight,
rather than 'corrective,' as Baker calls it."
A precisely documented and lively "study of the inter-
section of the academic, ecclesiastical, and political worlds
in Pre-Victorian England," Lloyd being eloquent and influential in all three. "The center of the scene is Christ
Church, largest and most prestigious of the Oxford colleges."
I quote the jacket copy, but have read the book, edified
and amused. (D.V.E.)

Bayliss, Robert A., and C. William Ellis. "Neil Arnott, F.R.S.,
Reformer, Innovator and Popularizer of Science, 1788-1874."
NRRS 36 (1981): 103-23.

Bennett, Shelley M. "Changing Images of Women in Late-Eigh-
teenth-Century England: The *Lady's Magazine*, 1770-1810."
Arts Magazine 55,ix (1981): 138-41.

The *Lady's Magazine*, "a reflective and accurate index of
widespread popular taste," shows that from 1770 to 1810
there is a decline in the depiction of women as actively
sexual persons. Sexuality is replaced by domesticity as a
goal for the modern woman.

Bentley, G.E., Jr. "Flaxman in Italy: A Letter Reflecting the
Anni Mirabiles, 1792-93." *ArtB* 63 (1981): 658-64.

Berkowitz, Roger M. "The Patriotic Fund Vases: Regency Awards
to the Navy." *Apollo* 113 (1981): 104-05.

Bindman, David. *Hogarth.* London: Thames and Hudson, 1981. Pp.
213; 166 illus.; 17 col. pls. £5.95.

Rev. by Graham Reynolds in *TLS*, April 3, 1981, p. 380, as
a "concise study ... to be warmly welcomed."

Blum, Jerome. "English Parliamentary Enclosure." *JMH* 53 (1981):
477-504.

In this magnificent essay (based on forty or more sources)
historical revisionism falls to the data of earlier scholar-
ship--a not to be missed summary discussion for all interested
scholars. (T.L.A.)

Brigstocke, Hugh. "William Buchanan: His Friends and Rivals."
Apollo 114 (1981): 76-84.

"The importation of Old Master Paintings into Great Britain
during the first half of the Nineteenth Century" is the focus
of this study of a Scottish art dealer and speculator (1777-
1864).

Campbell, Anne. "A Scrapbook of Drawings by William Hamilton."
HLQ 43 (1979/80): 327-34.

Description of a scrapbook (at the Huntington Library)
which contains seventy-eight drawings--mostly preliminary
sketches--from the last fifteen years (1786-1801) of Hamilton's life. Four illustrations. "This new-found scrapbook
helps to explain and substantiate the high reputation Hamilton enjoyed with his contemporaries and to rehabilitate him
as a gifted and versatile narrative artist." (R.A.B.)

Campbell, T.D., and I.S. Ross. "The Utilitarianism of Adam
Smith's Policy Advice." *JHI* 42 (1981): 73-92.

While Smith "is consistently hostile to utility both as
an explanation for the origin of moral rules and as a principle to be applied routinely in everyday circumstances, it
is to the criterion of utility--the maximization of human
happiness--that he has recourse in his evaluations of practices, institutions, and systems (social, political, or
economic) as a whole." A study of the biographical record
suggests that "in his own case" Smith "was prepared to support
practical as well as contemplative judgments by a direct
appeal to utility as the sole moral criterion." Furthermore
his distrust of some utilitarian reasoning was itself utilitarian. He objected to it when its practical effect was "to
diminish rather than augment the sum of human happiness."
A crucial article. (R.A.B.)

Carr, Leo, and Peggy A. Knapp. "Seeing through *Macbeth*." *PMLA*
96 (1981): 837-47.

Critical illumination of the tragedy is found through the
different illustrations of the same scene (II.ii) by Zoffany
and Fuseli.

Chamberlin, J.E. "An Anatomy of Cultural Melancholy." *JHI* 42
(1981): 691-705.

  Nineteenth-century England became increasingly obsessed
by "arguments not as to what constituted but rather as to
what afflicted culture." Evidence in such arguments "was
marshalled along lines supplied by the sciences, for science
in general was beginning to take a particular interest in
abnormal or pathological states, from perturbations of the
planets to the palpitations of the heart." Analogies from
the sciences seemed authoritative. "For our nineteenth-century chroniclers any culture that allowed itself to become
like the sea-urchin might move quickly but certainly was
headed in the wrong (evolutionary) direction." (R.A.B.)

Cherry, Conrad. *Nature and Religious Imagination from Edwards
to Bushnell*. Philadelphia: Fortress Press, 1980. Pp. xii+
242. $12.95.

  Rev. by William Breifenbach in *WMQ* 38 (1981): 525-26 as
"an excellent study."

Chinnici, Joseph P. *The English Catholic Enlightenment: John
Lingard and the Cisalpine Movement, 1780-1850*. Shepherds-
town, W. Va.: Patmos Press, 1980. Pp. xii+261.

  Rev. by Donald F. Shea in *AHR* 86 (1981): 132.

Clement, Priscilla Ferguson. "The Philadelphia Welfare Crisis
of the 1820s." *PMHB* 105 (1981): 150-65.

  Useful for those interested in how "repressive relief
programs in England" in the 1820s were mirrored by "a singularly harsh response to need" in the United States. (R.A.B.)

Cooper, Robert Alan. "Jeremy Bentham, Elizabeth Fry, and
English Prison Reform." *JHI* 42 (1981): 675-90.

  "It is more valid to see Bentham and Mrs. Fry as representatives of a single prison reform tradition than as the
progenitors of opposing approaches to the question of prison
discipline."
  On Mrs. Fry, see also Rose (below).

Cressy, David. *Literature and the Social Order: Reading and
Writing in Tudor and Stuart England*. Cambridge University
Press, 1980. Pp. x+246. $29.50.

  Rev. by Peter A. Clark in *JMH* 53 (1981): 535-36 as "a
mountain of data not well interpreted."

English / 2. Environment   41

Cross, Donald. "Country and City." *CQ* 10 (1981): 76-77.

Interesting discussion, by someone with the same social
and intellectual background as Raymond Williams, of the
historical inaccuracies of the latter's analysis of the
tension between rural and city life. (B.C.H.)

Crown, Patricia. "An Album of Sketches from the Royal Academy
Exhibitions of 1780-1784." *HLQ* 44 (1980/81): 61-66.

In an album now at the Huntington, Edward Francis Burney
sketched some of the English works exhibited at the Royal
Academy from 1780 to 1784. (R.A.B.)

Daniels, Jeffrey. "Gainsborough the European." *The Connoisseur*
206 (1981): 110-15.

Downey, James. "Barnabas and Boanerges: Archetypes of Eighteenth-Century Preaching." *UTQ* 51 (1981): 36-46.

Duncan, Erika. "Portrait of Kathleen Raine." *BF* 5 (1981):
511-24.

This warm and informative study reminds Romanticists that
Raine was drawn to far more than the study of Blake, including the writing of her own poetry. (J.C.R.)

Dyson, Ketaki Kushari. *A Various Universe: A Study of the
Journals and Memoirs of British Men and Women in the Indian
Subcontinent, 1765-1856.* Delhi: Oxford University Press,
1979. Pp. xii+406. £8.25.

Rev. by Prabhu S. Guptara in *RES* 32 (1981): 335-37.

Erdman, David V. "Grub Street Behind the Skirts of Margaret
Nicholson." *Factotum: Newsletter of the XVIIIth Century
STC*, no. 12 (July 1981): 25-27; illus.

Two satiric items of 1786 by John Oswald but signed "H.K."
and making satiric use of Payne Knight's *Worship of Priapus*.
Did Wordsworth know his Napoleon was up to such tricks?

Fetter, Frank Whitson. *The Economist in Parliament: 1780-1868.*
Duke University Press, 1980. Pp. xii+306.

Rev. by Anthony Brundage in *AHR* 6 (1981): 132-33.

Filteau, Claude. *Le Statut narratif de la transgression:
essais sur Hamilton et Beckford.* (Etudes, 26.) Sherbrooke
(Quebec): Naaman, 1981. Pp. 200. Fr. 108.00.

Finlay, Nancy. "Thomas Stothard's Illustrations of Thomson's
    Seasons for the Royal Engagement Pocket Atlas." *PULC*, Spring
    1981.

Finley, Gerald. *Landscapes of Memory*. London: Scolar Press,
    1980. Pp. 272; 108 illus. £30.00.

    Rev. by Lindsay Errington in *Art History* 4 (1981): 232-33;
    by John Gage in *TLS*, Jan. 30, 1981, pp. 119-20.
    Looks at relations between J.M.S. Turner and Sir Walter
    Scott.

Fleming-Williams, Ian. "The Early Constable: New Watercolours
    & Drawings." *The Connoisseur* 206 (1981): 58-61.

Flinn, Derek. "John MacCulloch, M.D., F.R.S., and His Geological
    Map of Scotland: His Years in the Ordnance, 1795-1826." *NRRS*
    36 (1981): 83-101.

Ford, Brinsley. "The Grand Tour." *Apollo* 114 (1981): 390-400.

    Deals mainly with the period 1750-1800.

Fores, Michael. "The Myth of a British Industrial Revolution."
    H 66 (1981): 19-38.

    "Instead of having experienced an 'industrial revolution,'
    England experienced an urban evolution, as part of an age-
    old process of a shift of population to the towns."

Fradan, Cyril. "Gainsborough." *ContR* 238 (1981): 32-37.

    A look at Gainsborough's style and its weaknesses.

Frew, John. "An Aspect of the Early Gothic Revival: The Trans-
    formation of Mediaevalist Research, 1770-1800." *JWCI* 43
    (1980): 174-85; 9 illus.

    Richard Gough and the London Society of Antiquaries were
    among those responsible for the growth of interest in medieval
    architecture.

Garland, Martha McMackin. *Cambridge Before Darwin: The Ideal
    of a Liberal Education 1800-1860*. Cambridge University Press,
    1980. Pp. ix+196. £14.00; $34.00.

    Rev. by Arthur Engel in *VS* 25 (1981): 104-05.

Gold, Joel J. "Mr. Serjeant Glynn: Radical Politics in the
    Courtroom." *HLB* 29 (1981): 197-209.

The legal career and courtroom performances of John Glynn, radical member of Parliament (1768-79) and John Wilkes's attorney. (R.A.B.)

Hayes, John. *Thomas Gainsborough*. London: Tate Gallery, 1980. Pp. 58; 194 illus., 20 col. pls. £2.50.

Rev. by John Gage ("'A Little Business for the Eye'") in *Art History* 4 (1981): 118-21.

Heleniak, Kathryn. *William Mulready*. Paul Mellon Centre for Studies in British Art. Yale University Press, 1980. Pp. 287; 200 illus., 8 in color. $60.00.

Rev. by John Murdoch in *BM* 123 (April 1981): 244-45.

Henderson, John P. "David Ricardo on Religious Liberty." *CentR* 25 (1981): 294-313.

A moving and interesting biographical account of Ricardo's rejection of his family's Judaism and his growing isolation resulting from his outspoken remarks on religious freedom. (J.C.R.)

Henkle, Roger B. *Comedy and Culture: England, 1820-1900*. Princeton University Press, 1980. Pp. x+373. $22.50; $8.95 paper.

Rev. by Harry Levin in *NCF* 35 (1981): 551-55; by Sam Pickering in *SR* 89 (1981): lii-liv. Not seen.

Hindle, Wendy. *Castlereagh*. London: Collins, 1981. Pp. 320. £16.00.

Rev. by Norman Gash in *HT*, Nov. 1981, p. 57: "Castlereagh baffled men in his lifetime; he baffles still."

Holme, Thea. *Caroline of Brunswick: A Biography*. London: Hamish Hamilton, 1980. £8.95.

Favorably rev. by Cecil Northcott in *ContR* 236 (1980): 109.

Horsman, Reginald. "Nantucket's Peace Treaty with England in 1814." *NEQ* 54 (1981): 180-98.

Hughes, Clair. "Zoffany's Trial Scene from *The Merchant of Venice*." *BM* 123 (May 1981): 290-94; 12 illus.

The painting is related to a court trial involving the actor Charles Macklin in 1775.

Ippel, Henry P. "Blow the Trumpet, Sanctify the Fast." *HLQ* 44
(1980/81): 42-60.

   The call for a sanctifying fast day to mark the commence-
ment of the American Revolution again demonstrates internal
division in Britain. (T.L.A.)

Irwin, Helen. "Samuel Palmer, Poet of Light and Shade: His
Last Years at Reigate, Surrey." *Apollo* 114 (1981): 109-13.

Issawi, Charles. "The Struggle for Linguistic Hegemony, 1780-
1980." *ASch* 50 (1981): 382-87.

   English *vs*. French as international languages.

James, Patricia. *Population Malthus: His Life and Times*.
London: Routledge & Kegan Paul, 1979. Pp. xviii+524. $43.50.

   Rev. by Donald Winch in *JMH* 53 (1981): 110-12.

Jordanova, L.J., and Roy Porter, eds. *Images of the Earth:
Essays in the History of the Environmental Sciences*. (BSHS
Monographs, 1.) Chalfont St. Giles: British Society for the
History of Science, 1979. Pp. xx+282. £5.95.

   Rev. by Joe D. Burchfeld in *BJHS* 13 (1980): 162-63.
"Ten of the eleven essays deal primarily or entirely with
British geology, and nine concentrate on the familiar period
from 1750 to 1830--geology's so called 'golden age.'"

Leavis, Q.D. "The Englishness of the English Novel." (*New*)
UQ 35 (1981): 149-71.

   Includes some mention of Austen and the Brontës.

Lenoski, D.S. "The Symbolism of the Early Yeats: Occult and
Religious Backgrounds." *SLI* 14 (1981): 85-100.

   The influence of Blake, and Yeats's shifting views of
Blake and, to a lesser extent, Shelley, take up much of the
discussion.
   Other articles in this issue (Spring 1981) of *SLI*, devoted
to "W.B. Yeats: The Occult and Philosophical Backgrounds,"
touch on these matters occasionally.

Liscombe, R.W. *William Wilkins, 1778-1839*. Cambridge University
Press, 1981. Pp. 297; 107 illus. £22.50.

   Rev. by David Watkin in *BM* 123 (May 1981): 316-17.

Lyte, Charles. *Sir Joseph Banks: 18th Century Explorer, Botanist and Entrepreneur.* London: David and Charles, 1981. Pp. 248. £10.50.

Martinet, Marie-Madeleine. *Art et nature en Grande-Bretagne au XVIIIe siècle: de l'harmonie classique au pittoresque du premier romantisme.* Paris: Aubier-Montagne, 1980. Pp. 286.

Rev. by Harold Osborne in *BJA* 21 (1981): 89-90; by Pat Rogers in *N&Q* 28 (1981): 558-59.

Not seen; from the reviews it appears to be a very well-executed anthology, not a critical study.

Mathias, Peter. *The Transformation of England: Essays in the Economic and Social History of England in the Eighteenth Century.* Columbia University Press, 1979. Pp. x+324. $18.50.

Rev. by W.W. Rostow in *JMH* 53 (1981): 108-10.

Mayes, Jan. "John Bell, *The British Theatre*, and Samuel de Wilde." *Apollo* 113 (1981): 100-03.

McCahill, Michael W. "Peerage Creations and the Changing Character of the British Nobility, 1750-1830." *EHR* 96 (1981): 259-84.

Not only the number of peers increased significantly during this period but also the number of Scottish and Irish noblemen entering the ranks. After 1800 many individuals became peers as a reward for outstanding accomplishment. (J.C.R.)

McClary, Ben Harris. "Samuel Rogers' Historic War Story: A Letter for Lady Bessborough." *HLQ* 44 (1980/81): 223-25.

Sir Frederic Cavendish Ponsonby's account of "battlefield experiences at Waterloo ... is actually the compilation of Samuel Rogers, poet-banker, who, having heard the story from Ponsonby, put it together for the officer's mother, Lady Bessborough." The compilation is further testimony that Rogers was a "consummate artist in words." (R.A.B.)

McConville, Sean. *A History of English Prison Administration.* Vol. *I*: 1750-1877. London: Routledge and Kegan Paul, 1981. Pp. 535. £25.00.

Rev. by Michael Agnatieff in *TLS*, Oct. 23, 1981, p. 1230.

McDowell, R.B. *Ireland in the Age of Imperialism and Revolution, 1760-1801.* Oxford: Clarendon Press, 1979. Pp. viii+ 740. $73.00.

Rev. by Samuel Clark in *JMH* 53 (1981): 717-18; by Francis
G. James in *AHR* 86 (1981): 139-40.

McKerrow, Ray E. "Richard Whately on the Nature of Human
Knowledge in Relation to Ideas of His Contemporaries."
JHI 42 (1981): 439-55.

Archbishop of Dublin from 1831 to 1863, Whately was an
important popularizer of the philosophical ideas of his day.
"Largely ignored by his more famous contemporaries" and by
later historians, his "common-sense views were nonetheless
the staple fare of such journals as *Leisure Hour*, *Good Words*,
Catholic Layman, *Saturday Magazine*, and others." (R.A.B.)

Middleton, R.D. "Viollet-le-Duc's Influence in Nineteenth-
Century England." *Art History* 4 (1981): 203-19.

A questioning of the real extent of the influence of
Viollet-le-Duc on English architects.

Munsche, P.B. "The Gamekeeper and English Rural Society 1660-
1830." *JBS* 20 (1981): 82-105.

Neale, R.S. *Class in English History, 1680-1850*. Totowa, N.J.:
Barnes and Noble, 1981. Pp. 250. $28.50.

Rev. by Anthony Brundage in *Albion* 13 (1981): 154-55.
Not seen, but it sounds valuable, dwelling on the "middling
class" as most dynamic and deriving evidence from Adam Smith,
Jane Austen, William Hogarth, Thomas Paine, and William
Blake, as well as such writers as Hone and Mill.

Noon, Patrick J. "Bonington and Boys: Some Unpublished Documents at Yale." *BM* 123 (May 1981): 294-300; 7 illus.

Pace, Claire. "Gavin Hamilton's *Wood and Dawkins Discovering
Palmyra*: The Dilettante as Hero." *Art History* 4 (1981):
271-90; 13 illus.

Parry, Graham. "The Grand Delusions of Benjamin Haydon." *KSMB*
31 (1980): 10-21.

Though he convinced himself and others of his genius, even
his best work wasn't very good.

Pazos, Fernando Berckemeyer. "British Artists and the Bull-
fight." *Apollo* 113 (1981): 296-301.

Pocock, J.G.A., ed. *Three British Revolutions: 1641, 1688,
1776*. Princeton University Press, 1980. Pp. xiv+468. $32.50;
$12.50 paper.

Rev. by J. Jean Hecht in *NEQ* 54 (1981): 597-600; by Isaac Kramnick in *JMH* 53 (1981): 716-17.

Contents: Lawrence Stone, "The Results of the English Revolutions of the Seventeenth Century"; Christopher Hill, "A Bourgeois Revolution?"; G.E. Aylmer, "Crisis and Regrouping in the Political Elites: England from the 1630s to the 1660s"; Charles Carlton, "Three British Revolutions and the Personality of Kingship"; Lois G. Schworer, "The Bill of Rights of the Revolution of 1688-89"; David S. Lovejoy, "Two American Revolutions, 1689 and 1776"; John Brewer, "English Radicalism in the Age of George III"; John M. Murrin, "The Great Inversion, or Court Versus Country: A Comparison of the Revolutionary Settlements in England (1688-1721) and America (1776-1816)." See especially the Brewer essay.

Pressly, William L. *The Life and Art of James Barry*. The Paul Mellon Centre for Studies in British Art. Yale University Press, 1981. Pp. xiii+320; 149 illus., 8 col. pls. $65.00.

Rev. by David Bindman in *New Statesman*, Sept. 11, 1981, pp. 19-20; by Graham Reynolds ("The End of the Grand Manner") in *TLS*, Oct. 30, 1981, pp. 1251-52, in a review essay.

Full-scale study of an artist who is relatively neglected today. Pressly combines the biography of a difficult and turbulent personality with art history, giving a full account of Barry's individual works, his aims and values in art, relations with his contemporaries, and influence on his successors (who included Girodet and Ingres). A complete catalogue raisonné is appended. (I.H.C.)

Preyer, Robert O. "Bunsen and the Anglo-American Literary Community in Rome." Pp. 35-44 in Erich Geldbach, ed., *Der Gelehrte Diplomat: Zum Wirken Christian Carl Josias Bunsens*. Leiden: E.J. Brill, 1980.

The significant ramifications of the career of Christian Bunsen which buttressed the hyphen in the grouping of Cambridge and Oxford Englishmen known as "the Germano-Coleridgians." Bunsen's appointment in 1842 as Prussian ambassador to the Court of St. James appeared to seal and signify the victory in intellectual life "of German learning and Broad Church principles."

Preyer, Robert O. "The Romantic Tide Reaches Trinity: Notes on the Transmission and Diffusion of New Approaches to Traditional Studies at Cambridge, 1820-1840." *Annals of the N.Y. Academy of Sciences* 360 (1981): 39-68.

A charting, too complex to summarize here, of what the
running title calls "Science and Romanticism at Cambridge"
in the second quarter of the nineteenth century. "We need
to learn from what is strange, other, and mysterious—but
which was taken for granted by our Victorian forebears. If
their problem was 'superstition,' then ... our problem is
'desiccation.'" (D.V.E.)

Prothero, I.J. *Artisans and Politics in Early Nineteenth-
Century London: John Gast and His Times.* Louisiana State
University Press, 1979. Pp. xi+418.

Rev. by Geoffrey Crossick in *AHR* 86 (1981): 134; by R.S.
Neale in *JMH* (1981): 538-39 as "a richer study than we may
think." (Listed in *RMB* for 1980, p. 44, but not reviewed.)
Prothero's Introduction explains why John Gast is the
central figure in the book: he was leader of the shipwrights
from about 1800 to 1837, played a leading role in strikes
of 1802 and 1825, and helped set up "the world's first trade
union journal, the *Trades' Newspaper*," drawn upon heavily
for this book—which is, however, "primarily a study of
London artisans, not of Gast."
"The first five chapters deal with different aspects of
artisan activity up to 1818" and "establish the basic artisan features from which the events of the rest of the book
can be 'deduced.' The remainder of the book is broadly
chronological, dealing with the radical politics of the
post-war period, the multiform artisan activities of the
1820s ending with co-operation, and the developments of the
1830s which led up to Chartism."
In a sense this is a sequel—and a worthy, very readable
one—to E.P. Thompson's *Making of the Working Class*, dealing
this time with its resilience to attempts at its breaking.
(D.V.E.)

Pullen, J.M. "Malthus' Theological Ideas and Their Influence
on His Principle of Population." *HPE* 13 (1981): 39-54.

"... Malthus intended the *Essay* [on the Principle of
Population] to be as much a theological treatise as a
treatise in economics, demography, or sociology."

Purkis, John. *The World of the English Romantic Poets: A
Visual Approach.* London: Heinemann Educational Books, 1981.
£12.50 boxed.

Radner, John B. "The Art of Sympathy in Eighteenth-Century
British Moral Thought." *SECC* 9 (1980): 189-210.

"In 1800, in part because of continuing and changing
speculation about human sympathy, a number of standard
questions were posed and answered in ways generally unknown
a century earlier."

Rapaczynski, Andrzej. "Locke's Conception of Property and the
Principle of Sufficient Reason." *JHI* 42 (1981): 305-15.

Rashid, Salim. "Malthus' *Principles* and British Economic
Thought, 1820-1835." *HPE* 13 (1981): 55-79.

Set in the context of economic debates of the 1820s and
1830s.

Reardon, Bernard M.G. *Religious Thought in the Victorian Age:
A Survey from Coleridge to Gore*. New York: Longman, 1980.
Pp. 502. $15.95.

Rev. by Walter L. Arnstein in *Albion* 13 (1981): 161-62
as concentrating on "the highways and byways of Anglican
thought" with "scrupulous thoughtfulness." First published
in 1971 as *From Coleridge to Gore*.

Redgrave, Richard, and Samuel Redgrave. *A Century of British
Painting*. (Landmarks in Art History.) Cornell University
Press, 1981. Pp. viii+612; 100 illus. $9.95 paper.

First published in 1866; reprinted from the Phaidon Press
edition of 1947, ed. Ruthven Todd. Ranging from Hogarth
to the early Victorians, this first popular account of
British painting evidently was inspired by Johnson's *Lives
of the English Poets*, or perhaps even by Vasari. In the
biographical chapters, the emphasis is on anecdote and the
oddities of character; Turner's eccentricities, for example,
are recalled from the student days of one of the authors.
Other chapters concern such topics as genre, landscape
and animal painting, book illustration and design, "institutions affecting the spread of art," and the question of
state patronage. (I.H.C.)

Richards, Judith, Lotte Mulligan, and John K. Graham. "'Property' and 'People': Political Usages of Locke and Some Contemporaries." *JHI* 42 (1981): 29-51.

Although concerned with the seventeenth century and the
linguistic context within which Locke wrote, this article
will also be of interest for those who deal with the effects
of Locke's political definitions in the Romantic period.
"Locke, by his self-conscious and particular use of *property*,

arrived at a political definition of *the people* radically different from that of most of his political associates. Where they were rigorously and explicitly exclusive in their qualifications for full membership of the political nation, Locke was consistently inclusive." (R.A.B.)

Rose, James. *Elizabeth Fry: A Biography*. New York: St. Martin's Press, 1981. Pp. 218. $22.50.

Rev. by Thomas R. Knox in *Albion* 13 (1981): 404-05 as aiming "to desanctify" the "angel of the prisons" but not depreciate the human being; a chronological and reportorial narrative drawing upon the forty-six volumes of Fry's journals, largely ignoring context.
Not seen. (See also Cooper, above.)

Rubinstein, Jill. "Giving the Devil His Due: Lady Louisa Stuart and Henry Lord Brougham." *TWC* 12 (1981): 232-42.

Rule, John. *The Experience of Labour in Eighteenth-Century English Industry*. New York: St. Martin's Press, 1981. Pp. 227. $25.00.

Rev. by Eugene F. Stafford in *Albion* 13 (1981): 401-02 as a delightful book, "worth reading as much for its content as for its style" (sic); it includes a survey of both contemporary and modern scholarship.
Not seen.

Schaffer, Simon. "Herschel in Bedlam: Natural History and Stellar Astronomy." *BJHS* 13 (1980): 211-39.

Herschel saw himself as a natural historian, not as the founder of modern astronomy.

Schofield, R.B. "The Promotion of the Cromford Canal Act of 1789: A Study in Canal Engineering." *BJRL* 64 (1981): 246-78.

Simon, Robin. "Richard Wilson's 'Meleager and Atalanta.'" *BM* 123 (July 1981): 414-17; 5 illus.

On J.H. Mortimer's additions to Wilson's painting.

Solkin, David H. "Richard Wilson's Variations on a Theme by Gaspard Dughet." *BM* 123 (July 1981): 410-14; 5 illus.

Soltow, Lee. "The Distribution of Property Values in England and Wales in 1798." *EcHR* 34 (1981): 60-70.

"Multiple-property ownership in England and Wales was very common since only one property in five was occupied by its owner. Ownership distribution was strongly concentrated, with the few owning very substantial shares of the total aggregate value."

Stange, Douglas C. "Teaching the Means of Freedom to West Indian Slaves, or, Failure as the Raw Material for Anti-slavery Propaganda." *HLB* 29 (1981): 403-19.

On Robert Hibbert (1770-1849), a Jamaican slaveholder, who used the proceeds from his profession to further the cause of liberalism and Unitarianism in England. Thomas Cooper, a Unitarian minister whom Hibbert sent to Jamaica "to provide religious instruction to ... 'uncultured minds,'" found that Hibbert's liberalism had well-defined limits. (R.A.B.)

Stewart-Robertson, J.C. "The Well-Principled Savage, or, the Child of the Scottish Enlightenment." *JHI* 42 (1981): 503-25.

Thomas Reid and his contemporaries desired an education for children that would enable them to escape savagery without becoming skeptics. However, "Reid drew the searing and fateful conclusion: 'There seems to be no Medium between these two, either we must have Education along with its prejudices, or we must have no Education & be Savages.'" (R.A.B.)

Tait, A.A. "Robert Adam's Picturesque Architecture." *BM* 123 (July 1981): 421-22; 8 illus.

Teichgraeber, Richard, III. "Rethinking *Das Adam Smith Problem.*" *JBS* 20 (1981): 106-23.

Temperley, Nicholas, ed. *The Romantic Age 1800-1914.* (The Athlone History of Music in Britain, vol. 5.) London: The Athlone Press; Atlantic Highlands, N.J.: Humanities Press, 1981. Pp. xii+548. $90.00.

An encyclopedic survey, in twenty-three essay-chapters by fifteen scholars. The first of four Parts discusses "Music in Society," including music in education and music publishing. No great Romantic music before Elgar, but lots of other kinds. Four chapters deal with "Popular and Functional Music," twelve with "art music" from cathedral to opera, from glees to organ. And a final part divides "Writings on Music" into criticism, theory, and musicology. Frequent musical illustrations. (D.V.E.)

Thomas, William. *The Philosophic Radicals: Nine Studies in Theory and Practice, 1817-1841*. Oxford: Clarendon Press, 1980. Pp. ix+491. $45.00.

Rev. by John Clive in *JMH* 53 (1981): 718-20; by Gertrude Himmelfarb in *AHR* 86 (1981): 132; by David Roberts in *VS* 25 (1981): 91-92; by John M. Robson in *Albion* 13 (1981): 63-64.

The studies of "Bentham and His Circle" and "Radical Westminster" are particularly valuable, the latter especially for its judicious definition of the components and shifts of ground of the radicalism of Burdett and Hobhouse. When Whigs and parliamentary radicals were drifting apart, what united them "at one stroke" was Peterloo—not the news itself but Sidmouth's conveying "the Regent's approval of the conduct of the magistrates." (D.V.E.)

Tyrrell, Alex. "'Woman's Mission' and Pressure Group Politics in Britain (1825-60)." *BJRL* 63 (1980): 194-230.

Reproduces and briefly comments on B.R. Haydon's painting of the Great Meeting of Delegates assembled in June 1840 for the abolition of slavery and the slave trade.

Walker, Robert G. "Johnson in the 'Age of Evidences.'" *HLQ* 44 (1980/81): 27-41.

"In the history of Christian apologetics the Eighteenth Century stands as the period in which traditional 'external' evidences gave way to 'internal' evidences." In a period of transition, Johnson looked backward, Coleridge, forward ("*Evidences* of Christianity! I am weary of the word"). Paley and Jenyns looked both ways. (R.A.B.)

Waterhouse, Ellis. *The Dictionary of British 18th Century Painters*. Antique Collectors Club, 1981. £29.50.

Rev. by John Harris in *Apollo* 114 (1981): 348-49.

Watson, Jennifer C. "William Artaud and 'The Triumph of Mercy.'" *BM* 123 (April 1981): 228-31; 6 illus.

Artaud is identified as the author of a painting (ca. 1788) formerly attributed to Reynolds and Romney.

Weaver, Bruce J. "Debate and the Destruction of Friendship: An Analysis of Fox and Burke on the French Revolution." *QJS* 67 (1981): 57-68.

Weeks, Jeffrey. *Sex, Politics and Society: The Regulation of Sexuality Since 1800*. New York: Longman, Inc., 1981. Pp. 352. $25.00; paper $12.95.

  Chapters include "Sexuality and the Historian"; "Sex in Victorian Ideology"; "Moral Regulation in the Victorian Period"; and so on.

Weindling, Paul. "Science and Sedition: How Effective Were the Acts Licensing Lectures and Meetings, 1795-1819?" *BJHS* 13 (1980): 139-53.

Wellens, Oskar. "The *Critical Review*: 1805-1808." *Neophil* 65 (1981): 148-59.

Wickwire, Franklin, and Mary Wickwire. *Cornwallis: The Imperial Years*. University of North Carolina Press, 1980. Pp. xi+340. $16.50.

  Rev. by Paul David Nelson in *PMHB* 105 (1981): 114-15.
  Sequel to *Cornwallis: The American Adventure* (Boston: Houghton Mifflin Company, 1970).

Winfrey, John C. "Charity versus Justice in Locke's Theory of Property." *JHI* 42 (1981): 423-38.

Wormell, Deborah. *Sir John Seeley and the Uses of History*. Cambridge University Press, 1980. Pp. x+233. $32.50.

  Rev. by Sheldon Rothblatt in *JMH* 53 (1981): 505-06.
  Born in 1834, Seeley was a minor historian and major personality. (T.L.A.)

Wright, C.J. "The 'Spectre' of Science: The Study of Optical Phenomena and the Romantic Imagination." *JWCI* 43 (1980): 186-200.

  Rainbows, mirages, solar and lunar haloes, "glories," the Brocken Spectre, the kaleidoscope, etc., and contemporary responses. The early Romantics were interested, still "conditioned" by rationalism; the second generation began to be hostile to science.

Wright, Catharine Morris. "The Keats-Shelley Association: A Personal History." *KSJ* 30 (1981): 52-77.

  An extremely delightful and informative reconstruction of the events and persons involved in the purchase of the Keats House in Rome and the establishment of the Keats-Shelley Memorial Association in England and the Keats-Shelley

Association of America. Wright focuses on Robert Underwood Johnson in detailing the activities of 1903-09. To be continued in the next *KSJ*. (C.E.R.)

See also Finley ("English 4. Scott"); several entries under "English 4. Turner."

Reviews of books previously listed:

BARRELL, John, *The Dark Side of the Landscape* (see *RMB* for 1980, p. 35), rev. by Jonathan Cook ("Looking at the Poor") in *Art History* 4 (1981): 114-18 (the works of Gainsborough and Constable, Thomson and Wordsworth, helped "to console the rich about the state of the poor"); by Dennis Farr in *Apollo* 113 (1981): 34; by Kenneth Garlick, as biased politically, in *N&Q* 28 (1981): 559-60; by Andrew Hemingway in *BM* 123 (May 1981): 316; by Stuart M. Tave in *YES* 11 (1981): 290-93; BERMAN, Morris, *Social Change and Scientific Organization* (see *RMB* for 1980, p. 34), rev. favorably by Gerrylynn K. Roberts in *BJHS* 13 (1980): 154-57; GOODWIN, Albert, *The Friends of Liberty* (see *RMB* for 1979, p. 38), rev. by Alan Booth in *ESR* 10 (1980): 118-20; GORDON, Barry, *Economic Doctrine and Tory Liberalism* (see *RMB* for 1980, p. 39), rev. by Bernard Semmel in *AHR* 86 (1981): 591; HALSBAND, Robert, *The Rape of the Lock and Its Illustrations* (see *RMB* for 1980, p. 39), rev. as delightful in *JNL* 41,i (1981): 1-2; HATTON, Ragnhild, *George I: Elector and King* (see *RMB* for 1979, p. 39), rev. by Daniel A. Baugh in *JMH* 53 (1981): 106-08; IRWIN, David, *John Flaxman 1755-1826: Sculptor, Illustrator, Designer* (see *RMB* for 1979, p. 40), rev. by Nigel Llewellyn in *BJA* 21 (1981): 376-78 as "essential reading for British art in the period for many years to come"; KELLY, Linda, *The Kemble Era* (see *RMB* for 1980, p. 41), rev. by Rosaline Wade in *ContR* 237 (1980): 56; KROEBER, Karl, and William Walling, eds., *Images of Romanticism: Verbal and Visual Affinities* (see *ELN* 17, Supp., 44), rev. by Wolfgang Drost in *SFr* 25 (1981): 171; MORRIS, R.J., *Cholera 1832* (see *ELN* 16, Supp., 34), rev. anonymously in *QQ* 88 (1981): 130-34; PELLING, Margaret, *Cholera and English Medicine* (see *RMB* for 1979, p. 43), rev. anonymously in *QQ* 88 (1981): 130-34; PETERSEN, William, *Malthus* (see *RMB* for 1980, p. 43), rev. by Donald Winch in *JMH* 53 (1981): 110-12; SCHENK, H.G., *The Mind of the European Romantics* (see *RMB* for 1980, p. 26), rev. by J.R. Armsgathe in *Revue de l'Histoire des Religions* 198 (1981): 346-47; VAUGHAN, William, *German Romanticism and English Art* (see *RMB* for 1979, p. 46), rev. by Deborah Cherry ("'History Repeats Itself as Farce'") in *Art History* 4 (1981): 335-39.

Review article:

Mingay, G.E. *Albion* 13 (1981): 310-13.

Reviewing three books on the "lost countryside of old
England": *The English Heartland* by Robert and Monica Beckin-
sale (London: Duckworth; Totowa, N.J.: Biblio Distribution
Centre, 1981); *The Rural World, 1780-1850: Social Change in
the English Countryside*, by Pamela Horn (New York: St. Martin's, 1981); and *Change and Tradition in Rural England: An
Anthology of Writings on Country Life*, ed. Denys Thompson
(Cambridge University Press, 1981). Recommends strongly
only Pamela Horn's book.

3. CRITICISM

Aers, David, with Jonathan Cook and David Punter. *Romanticism
and Ideology: Studies in English Writing 1765-1830*. London:
Routledge & Kegan Paul, 1981. Pp. 194. $16.50.

A collection of polemical essays on Blake, Wordsworth,
Coleridge, Gothic fiction, Austen, Hazlitt, and Shelley--
some solo efforts, some collaborations by the trio. All
practice "methods of reading [that] try to grasp the complex
ways in which ideology is at work within literary texts,
without reducing the specific linguistic and aesthetic forms
in question to some other discourse." Success is intermittent.
The ideological investment in ideology leads to a reduction
of the poetry and prose to Marxist allegory of variable
subtlety, pertinence, and persuasiveness. Blake, with whom
the authors are in sympathy, comes off the best; in essays
on the themes of labor, sexuality, and childhood in Blake
the authors develop his criticism of repressiveness and
passivity without ignoring qualifications of the poet's
visionary Marxism. There are interesting essays on the
ideological strategies of Austen, the social relations of
Gothic fiction, and the "obsessional nature" of Hazlitt's
"preoccupation with the struggle between liberty and tyranny
in his own time." The commentary on Wordsworth, however, is
deplorably simplistic and unwisely condescending. Coleridge
fares somewhat better, although he too is condemned with
his quondam collaborator for "living off the surplus ex-
tracted from other men's labour power." Occasionally these
ardently engaged essays are as provocative as they consistently intend to be; too often doctrinal certainty begets
critical predictability. (J.C.C.)

Allen, Gay Wilson. *Waldo Emerson*. New York: Viking, 1981.
Pp. xxiv+751; 16 pls.

Rev. by R.W.B. Lewis in *NR*, Oct. 21, 1981, pp. 21-27.

Ashton, Rosemary. *The German Idea: Four English Writers and
the Reception of German Thought 1800-1860*. Cambridge University Press, 1981. Pp. 245. £14.50.

Bauer, Helen Pike. "Ruskin's Changing Evaluation of Poetic
Vision." *VN* 57 (1980): 27-31.

Beckett, J.C. "The Irish Writer and His Public in the Nineteenth Century." *YES* 11 (1981): 102-16.

Brekilien, Yann, ed. *Ossian: Saga des hautes terres*. Recueillié
par James MacPherson. Trad. de P. Christian. Paris: Editions
libres Hallier, 1980. Pp. 298.

Rev. by André Bourin in *RDM*, Sept. 1980, pp. 685-88; by
Kenneth White in *QL* 345 (April 1-15, 1981): 14-15.

Buckler, William E. "*Literature and Dogma* and Literature: New
Textual Perspective on Matthew Arnold's Critical Organicism."
VN 59 (1981): 6-16.

"This suggests how far Arnold (and criticism) have traveled
from the subjectivity of the prefaces of Wordsworth and the
Biographia Literaria"--perhaps in the wrong direction, some
will think. (T.L.A.)

Buckler, William E. "'The Thing Signified' in *The Dynasts*:
A Speculation." *VN* 57 (1980): 9-14.

An interesting explanation of Hardy's choice of subtitle:
"An Epic-Drama of the War with Napoleon." (T.L.A.)

Bump, Jerome. "Hopkins, Christina Rossetti, and Pre-Raphaelit-
ism." *VN* 57 (1980): 1-6.

Carefully following Hartman's earlier suggestion the line
is *traced* back to Coleridge and Keats. (T.L.A.)

Butler, Marilyn. *Romantics, Rebels, and Reactionaries*. Oxford
University Press, 1981. Pp. 213. $17.95.

Rev. critically by Rosemary Ashton in *TLS*, Oct. 9, 1981,
p. 1177.
Operating from the premise that "literature, like all art,
like language, is a collective activity, powerfully condi-

tioned by social forces," Marilyn Butler diverges from what
she regards as the psychological and philosophical biases of
contemporary criticism of Romantic poetry in order to situate
the major British writers of the period from 1790 to 1820 in
their historical context. Perhaps her most provocative stra-
tegy is to repudiate the pertinence of the term "Romantic"
for such writers as Blake, Wordsworth, Shelley, Peacock,
Byron, and Hazlitt in favor of "Neoclassicism," a category
which she owes to art historians and a mode which she finds
"co-existing with Romanticism" in the period. Although "Neo-
classicism" and its twin "Enlightenment" are defined too
loosely ("a radical simplicity of manner," "a liking for
the elemental," a commitment to "individualism," as well as,
puzzlingly, a belief "that art functioned within and for
the community") to do the revisionist work Butler intends,
neither the vagueness about the historical framework nor
the fuzziness about the dynamics of the interaction between
social forces and artistic decisions seriously damages Butler's accounts of the careers of individual writers. She
shrewdly foregrounds the social implications--the political
conditions and the ideological expression--of each and is
especially stimulating in her remarks on Coleridge, Austen,
Peacock, and Hazlitt. Most readers will balk at a handful
or so of Butler's generalizations, such as her claims for
the pervasiveness and genuineness of counterrevolution as
a "popular sentiment" in the 90s and the prominence she
idiosyncratically ascribes to Peacock and the "Marlow circle";
but the dominant theme of the "Romantic" writer as an intellectual who perforce had to adopt a position in the
treacherous political currents of post-revolutionary England
is an important one, which Butler argues with élan. One
irritating liability must be mentioned: the absence of footnotes severely restricts the usefulness of this book; the
section "Suggestions for Further Reading," which includes
a lightly annotated bibliography, is a weak substitute for
full documentation. (J.C.C.)

Bystrom, Valerie Ann. "The Abyss of Sympathy: The Conventions
of Pathos in Eighteenth and Nineteenth-Century British
Novels." *Criticism* 23 (1981): 211-31.

Christensen, Jerome. *Coleridge's Blessed Machine of Language.*
Cornell University Press, 1981. Pp. 276. $17.50.

A close pursuit of Coleridge's "method," i.e., Coleridge's
"prosaics," which requires close reading in turn and is
itself a "good read" (if you keep the margins of your mind
fresh with rereading the *Biographia* and *The Friend*). Even

if put down it never lets you down, because along the way
you get more vivid and distinct conceptions of Coleridge's
teleological associations with Hartley and Shakespeare and
Plato, of the chiasmic nature of hypopoesis. Of how we can
read the modern readings of the *Biographia*; of how the "man
of letters" can be the Friend of man, having instantiated
Wordsworth--talk about symbiosis!--and thus substantiated
the poetic Genius. "One consequence of Coleridge's inability
to master Hartley fully is that instead of adventurous
dialectic or patient deduction we get volatile diversions,
displacements, and digressions," all to the purpose (20).

In Chapter XI of the *Biographia* Coleridge "poignantly
advises the aspiring author that he 'be not *merely* a man of
letters!'" That admonition Christensen suggests as "slogan"
for the whole work (161). And he finds the work epitomized
in "a digression that attempts to excuse digressions ...
most of all by encouraging [the reader] to conceive of the
man beneath the letters, if only by imagining his pain"
(164). As for *The Friend*, Christensen "boldly" reads Coleridge's reading of the Falstaff-Quickley dialogue as dis-
combobulation threatening Hal's sovereignty, "because the
Friend habituates his readers to the reading of all language
as rhetoric and of all rhetoric as spanning the gap between
the common and the singular, the lapse between the joke and
the guillotine. What theme Mrs. Quickley has is the Friend's"
(249). "To conceive of language or text as a blessed machine ... both moots the opposition between free will and
determinism that is the pretext of the Coleridgean text and
disarms the antithesis of originality and plagiarism which
is its murderous offspring." Chiasmus rescues us from this
chasm, when we accept the distinction "between the loose
statement that the Chiasmus is the Friend's figure and the
more precise formulation that the chiasmus is the figure
of the Friend." (Note the chiasmatic shift of capitalization.)
In short, a successful tightrope journey, this befriending
essay. (D.V.E.)

Christensen, Jerome. "'Thoughts That Do Often Lie Too Deep
    for Tears': Toward a Romantic Concept of Lyrical Drama."
    TWC 12 (1981): 52-64.

Clubbe, John. "The 'Folklore' of English Romanticism." *Mosaic*
    14,iii (1981): 95-112.

A polemic against modern criticism of Romanticism with
some valuable retracing of the ideas of classical commentators like Arnold and Eliot. Clubbe's irritation with the
recent criticism of Romanticism is a familiar cry against
the general tendency of fashionable criticism to separate

language and theory from the social reality that produced the literature itself. (J.C.R.)

Cottom, Daniel. "Taste and the Civilized Imagination." *JAAC* 39 (1980/81): 367-79.

A useful treatment centered on Addison and extending into the nineteenth century. (T.L.A.)

Davie, Donald. "Personification." *EiC* 31 (1981): 91-104.

This, the first F.W. Bateson Memorial Lecture, has an interesting discussion of Bateson's hostility to the Romantics, and of the historical reasons for the current and widening gulf between English and American views of Romanticism.

Diehl, Joanne Feit. "Dickinson and Bloom: An Antithetical Reading of Romanticism." *TSLL* 23 (1981): 418-41.

Eastwood, David R. "Romantic Elements and Aesthetic Distance in Trollope's Fiction." *SSF* 4 (Fall 1981): 395-405.

Ehrenpreis, Irvin. *Acts of Implication: Suggestion and Covert Meaning in the Works of Dryden, Swift, Pope, and Austen.* University of California Press, 1981. Pp. x+158. $14.95.

Rev. by Pat Rogers in *TLS*, Sept. 18, 1981, p. 1052.

The subtitle of this book indicates the broad area of the study, but perhaps not its motive. Ehrenpreis is concerned to rescue the Augustan period from too great a critical emphasis upon artistic clarity. It was an age which, he admits, generally agreed with Lord Kames's pronouncement that "perspicuity ought not to be sacrificed to any other beauty whatever" (8). But Ehrenpreis demonstrates that enrichment rather than sacrifice is often entailed. Pope's "one clear, unchanging, universal light" can be seen to have around and behind it a multiple, ambiguous, shifting, and particular flicker--as an author's sophistication, profundity, or even changing ideas or need for protective coloration against possible charges of treason or libel result in a level of implicit meaning sometimes counterpointing, sometimes extending the explicit statement.

This book consists of a brief introduction setting forth the thesis, a briefer epilogue, and four chapters: on Dryden as Playwright, on Swift's *The Examiner* essays compared to *The Drapier's Letters*, on Pope's "Bipolar Implication"-- the conventionally didactic and the boldly subversive--and on "Austen: The Heroism of the Quotidian," which interestingly demonstrates her use of implication by various tech-

nical devices, especially metonymy and synecdoche, and
employing details to indicate moral judgments.
    These essays are admirable examples of close reading. The
interpretations do not claim striking novelty; Ehrenpreis's
footnotes recognize predecessors. Much of what he says about
Pope was seen by Mack. His essay on Austen contains the
most ranging evaluation--but seems not to use the related
work of Barbara Hardy. The chief value of the work is the
cumulative effect of meticulous investigation of ways in
which a playwright, essayist, poet, and novelist of a period
celebrated for correctness and precision could still "by
indirection find direction out." (J.E.J.)

Ferguson, Frances. "The Sublime of Edmund Burke, or The
    Bathos of Experience." *Glyph* 8 (1981): 62-78.

    "The sublime ... represents a kind of opting out of the
pressures and dangers of the social, because the sublime
elevates one's individual relations with that mountain (or
whatever natural object one perceives as sublime) above
one's relationship to other human beings." This elegant
demystification of the sublime and the beautiful may be the
most important essay on Romanticism of the year. It appears,
by the way, in an issue of *Glyph* which contains several
other fine essays not on Romanticism but relevant to it.
(J.C.R.)

Fryckstedt, Monica Correa. "The Early Industrial Novel:
    Mary Barton and Its Predecessors." *BJRL* 63 (1980): 11-30.

Frye, Northrop. "Literary History." *NLH* 12 (1981): 219-25.

Gaston, James. *London Poets and the American Revolution.*
    Troy, N.Y.: Whitston, 1981. Pp. x+257. $15.00.

    125 poems in London periodicals 1763-83; introductory
discussions; bibliography; index.

Green, Martin. *Dreams of Adventure, Deeds of Empire.* London:
    Routledge & Kegan Paul, 1980. Pp. 429. £10.50.

    Rev. by Andrew A. Noble ("Literary Empires and Scotch
Imperials") in *SLJ* 8 (1981): supp. 15, pp. 91-100.
    "This desire to be a critical Caesar with a domain rival-
ling that of King and Queenie Leavis provides the imperious,
subconscious drive for everything he [Green] says and, inevitably, leads him into an unhappy series of silly evaluations and manifest illogicalities"--so says Noble with
Carlyle's help. (T.L.A.)

English / 3. Criticism 61

Hart, Frances Russell. "The Regency Novel of Fashion." Pp.
84-133 in Samuel I. Mintz, Alice Chandler, and Christopher
Mulvey, eds., *From Smollett to James: Studies in the Novel
and Other Essays Presented to Edgar Johnson*. University
Press of Virginia, 1981.

Harvey, A.D. *English Poetry in a Changing Society, 1780-1825*.
New York: St. Martin's Press, 1980. 195pp. $25.00.

The sociological implications of Harvey's title are slightly
misleading: in his introduction he dismisses the influence
on late eighteenth- and early nineteenth-century poetry of
the major political event of the era, the French Revolution;
he disavows any theory of the effects of social change on
poetic practice; and he argues for the autonomy of the
"cultural superstructure." This is a history of taste, which
Harvey charts in terms of generic change. Harvey devotes
his attention to those poets, such as the Wartons, Blair,
Campbell, Bloomfield, and Scott, who were most representative
of the taste of their age rather than to the canonical Romantics. When Harvey does reach for a historical generalization
or suggest social causes he is not compelling; and his criticism of individual poets--most glaringly of Byron--is frequently more opinionated than judicious. But the book is a
useful survey both of the vogues for graveyard poetry, rural
poetry, the sonnet, the couplet, and the metrical romance
and of the poets who sedulously practiced them. (J.C.C.)

Havens, Michael K. "Coleridge, Eliot, and the Romantic Consciousness." *CSR* 10 (1980): 150-54.

A response to Walhout's article (see *RMB* for 1979, p. 61).
Havens questions his view that the Romantic assumptions have
unduly influenced literary criticism.

Hogg, James, ed. *Romantic Reassessment* 87:3 (SSEL). Salzburg,
Austria, 1981. Pp. 102. $12.50.

"Studies in Nineteenth Century Literature" that begin
with a think-piece by William Oxley on "The Imminent Imagination" (3-16) which ends in confused grammar, having con-
ceded early on that no one has described "the imaginative
experience more simply or better than did Wordsworth." Eric
Glasgow, on "Anglo-Greek Relations: 1800-1832" (17-25), is
followed by Maria Emanuela Eisl on "Lord Byron and His Religious Pronouncements in *Cain, Don Juan*, and *A Vision of
Judgment*" (26-62), after which we go to Greece with Edward
Lear, Swinburne, and Jowett--stopping on the way for "Pippa
Passes Reconsidered" (70-84) by Ashok Sengupta, who finds

that "by and large" the critics agree that it is "a play of arresting novelty." (D.V.E.)

Hogg, James, ed. *Romantic Reassessment* 81:2 (SSEL). Salzburg, Austria, 1981. Pp. 103. $12.50.

Six brief papers and one longer study. Leonard Orr, in "The Accomplishments of Memory in Coleridge's 'This Lime-Tree Bower my Prison,'" discovers "a vision achieved through repetition and recollection." D.P. Sen Gupta, in "The Sonnets of Coleridge," quickly surveys all 49 of them, pointing out varying rhyme schemes and the reversals of traditional sonnet order. B.G. Tandom writes on Keats's "Autumn," arguing that the focal point of the poem is sorrow not joy. Ingrid R. Kitzberger surveys Shelley's rising, falling, and rising reputation as a political and social revolutionary. Eric Glasgow details Byron's relation to the Greek struggle and warns that it is "perilous" and often "spurious ... to transfer Byron's message of freedom ... out of its Greek context of 1824." B.G. Tandom (again) adds a study of the imagery of "Prisoner of Chaillon." (D.V.E.)

Homans, Margaret. "Eliot, Wordsworth, and the Scenes of the Sisters' Instruction." *CI* 8 (Winter 1981): 223-41.

Argues that George Eliot's "choice of the realistic novel as the form for her vision is in part an effect, not a cause, of her ambivalent divergences from Wordsworth."

Hopkins, Brooke. "Pear-Stealing and Other Faults: An Essay on Confessional Autobiography." *SAQ* 80 (1981): 305-21.

Commentary on the stolen-boat episode in *The Prelude*, compared with Augustine (pears) and Rousseau (a ribbon).

Janssen, Anke. "Fruhe Lyrikerinnen des 18. Jahrhunderts in ihrem Verhältnis zur Poetik und zur *Poetic Diction*." *Anglia* 99 (1981): 111-33.

Lady poets with pre-Romantic tendencies (Mary Barber, Mary Chudleigh, Mary Leapor, et al.) and their reception as late as Wordsworth, Hazlitt, and Hunt.

Leavis, Q.D. "The Englishness of the English Novel." *ES* 62 (1981): 128-45.

A lecture at the 1980 Cheltenham festival, published here for the first time. Interesting for its (posthumous) vitriol. (B.C.H.)

Lewis, Paul. "Fearful Lessons: The Didacticism of the Early Gothic Novel." *CLA Journal* 23 (1980): 470–84.

A look at the "open, ambiguous" treatment of ideas, particularly in the works of Radcliffe and Lewis.

Lipking, Lawrence, ed. *High Romantic Argument: Essays for M.H. Abrams.* Cornell University Press, 1981. Pp. 182. $14.95.

Rev. by Donald H. Reiman ("The Rites of Theocriticism: A Review Essay") in *ELN* 19 (1981): 133–40 with witty severity.

High Romantic Argument collects six essays delivered at a 1978 conference in honor of M.H. Abrams. Two of the participants, Geoffrey Hartman and Jonathan Wordsworth, engage Abrams's work only by implication in essays that interpret what each calls the "gravitation" of Wordsworth's poetic language, Hartman finding it in the "strange blast of harmony" that is the prophetic word, Wordsworth locating it in an impressive silence.

The four essays by Wayne Booth, Thomas McFarland, Lawrence Lipking, and Jonathan Culler consider Abrams's historical method in *The Mirror and the Lamp* and *Natural Supernaturalism* and assess the place of Abrams's work in the tradition. The best commentary on the group is supplied by Abrams, who, in his truly impressive extemporaneous reply, remarks on their general excellence but notes a pervasive "preoccupation with a single aspect of my writings, ... my use of radical constitutive metaphors as one key to important shifts in the intellectual and cultural history of the West." As if dramatizing another aspect of his procedure that might have attracted critical attention, Abrams generously attributes this unanimity to "the spirit of the age." But to whatever agency one wants to ascribe the consensus it has the effect of rarifying the argument, elevating it somewhat too high to reflect more than a pale illumination on the challenging substantive problems of both detail and design that Abrams's definitive histories raise.

The indubitable value of this collection is, as Abrams suggests, as a document of the self-conception of literary studies in our time. As Lawrence Lipking claims in his introduction, the collection does have a plot, which is to raise speculatively the questions that trouble humanistic literary culture at the present time and to have those questions answered or left authoritatively unanswered by an acknowledged representative and gifted exponent of the tradition, M.H. Abrams. In this plot, more precisely characterized as a symposium, Jonathan Culler, who deftly poses a deconstructionist reading of *The Mirror and the Lamp*, is

the *pharmakos*, who is admitted to the table and permitted
his speech but whose poisonous insinuations are not merely
neutralized but transfigured into an invigorating tonic by
the adept Master of the Feast. If there is no actual argument between Abrams and those who, despite their intelligent,
lucid, and occasionally elegant reservations about his
method, essentially affirm his values, it is because the
only real difference that Abrams, that the age, conceives
is between two stances, two ways of writing, whose differences are so fundamental and so elusive that there can be
no true debate. (J.C.C.)

Mackey, Louis. "Anatomical Curiosities: Northrop Frye's
Theory of Criticism." *TSLL* 23 (1981): 442-69.

McFarland, Thomas. *Romanticism and the Forms of Ruin: Wordsworth, Coleridge, and Modalities of Fragmentation.* Princeton University Press, 1981. Pp. xxxiv+432. $30.00; paper
$9.50.

Rev. by Robert Ginsberg (mixed) in *JAAC* 40 (1981): 218-
20; by J.H. Haeger in *RP&P* 5,ii (1981): 45-50; by Anne K.
Mellor (mixed) in *MLQ* 42 (1981): 194-96; by Christopher
Salvesen ("Finite, fleeting fragments") in *TLS*, July 17,
1981, p. 806.

A mixed book invites mixed reviews. This book is itself
trapped in "the situation actually obtaining" since it
chooses to occupy the pole of Ruin--though how a pole can
be a clutch of fragments baffles this reviewer. McFarland's
Coleridge and the Pantheist Tradition (1969), a work of
triumphant integrity despite its nineteen "Excursus Notes,"
has trained a world of scholars to recognize "the urge to
system," the "thrust to unity," and to recognize in Coleridge, and in ourselves, "the need for reticulation." Even
so, there lurked the dark side, Coleridge's or any Romantic's
resistance to becoming indistinguishable in the noonday
All. This is now proclaimed to be the "situation actually
obtaining," i.e., "the contrary of unity: that is, one of
fragmentation, of things not tied together," which he now
instructs us to call "diasparaction," adjective "diasparac-
tive" (torn to bits), fragmentary consequents "diasparacts."
Fragments witness that there has been, or could be, a whole
(which we toil all our lives to find).

Central to the discussion is the idea of "The Symbiosis
of Coleridge and Wordsworth" (Chapter 1), a journal article
amplified for this occasion and extended (after a diasparac-
tive Chapter 2) in two marvelous essays demonstrating how
the thoughts and acts of each poet had a tidal pull on

those of the other. Chapter 2, another revised article,
concentrates on "Coleridge's Anxiety" and is striven against
by a new chapter (3) on Wordsworth's. Chapter 4, also new,
gets down to literary particulars with a strong essay on
"Problems of Style" in their poetry.

Chapter 5 discloses the centering occasion for the book:
"The Psychic Economy and Cultural Meaning of Coleridge's
Magnum Opus"--a preview of McFarland's editorial introduction to his own Opus in progress, the Bollingen edition of
Coleridge's. Here McFarland is able to show "why Coleridge
is so very much more than just another Christian conservative,"
because he (McFarland/Coleridge) "understood ... what was
really happening in the culture of his time" (363). To
achieve this shoring up of his diasparacts, McFarland makes
vital use of his own symbiosis with the multivalent reticula-
tions of S.T.C. (D.V.E.)

P.S.: I see that my own initials serendipitously dropped
beside Esteesi's commingle the force of STC ("he hath stood"/
"withstood") and of "God willing." (D.V.E. again)

McGann, Jerome. "The Text, the Poem, and the Problem of Historical Method." *NLH* 12 (1981): 269-88.

Interesting essay. (B.C.H.)

McSweeney, Kerry. *Tennyson and Swinburne as Romantic Naturalists.*
University of Toronto Press, 1980. Pp. xvii+222.

Rev. by Maggie Berg in *DR* (Spring 1981): 162-63.

While the title suggests the continuity between Romantic
and Victorian poetry, McSweeney's book is of considerable
value because it can be used to chart a "complex shift in
sensibility," the "mutation of Romantic into Victorian
literature" and the misreadings of the Romantics which resulted. While the book's argument balances uneasily between
stressing the continuity and describing the mutation, it
can only define Tennyson and Swinburne as Romantic poets by
accepting a reductive Victorian reading of Wordsworth as
the poet "of man's life as a part of nature" (McSweeney begins and ends with this reference to Pater). But Tennyson
and Swinburne were not *Romantic* naturalists because the
Romantics were not *naturalists*--at least as McSweeney defines
the term. They did not share the faith "that the natural-
istic given must and will suffice." Such a faith involves
a reduction of the dialectic in Romanticism between nature
and imagination, its transformation into the opposition in
which McSweeney finds both Tennyson and Swinburne engaged:
on the one hand, the natural given; on the other, Christianity. (R.A.B.)

Morère, Pierre. *L'Oeuvre de James Beattie: Tradition et perspectives nouvelles*. 2 vols. Paris: Librairie Honore Champion, 1980. Pp. 1069. F. 120.00.

Rev. by Ian Ross in *SLJ* 8 (1981): supp. 15, pp. 108-09 as a "remarkable achievement."

Morgan, P., ed. *Jeffrey's Criticism*. Columbia University Press, 1981. Pp. 200. $18.50.

Not seen.

Novak, Maximillian E. "'Appearances of Truth': The Literature of Crime as a Narrative System (1660-1841)." *YES* 11 (1981): 29-48.

Includes remarks on Godwin's *Caleb Williams*.

Polhemus, Robert M. *Comic Faith: The Great Tradition from Austen to Joyce*. University of Chicago Press, 1981. Pp. x+ 398. $25.00.

Rev. by Peter Kemp in *TLS*, April 17, 1981, p. 442; by R.D. McMaster in *NCF* 36 (1981): 352-55; by Garrett Stewart in *VS* 25 (1981): 112-14.
From *Emma* through Peacock to *Finnegans Wake*.

Pricket, Stephen, ed. *The Romantics*. (Context of Literature Series.) London and New York: Methuen, 1981. Pp. 267. £9.50; paper £4.95.

Rev. by Glen Cavaliero in *TLS*, Dec. 11, 1981, p. 1449, as too compressed to be recommended to students but "a refresher course for their teachers." "The effect of the collection as a whole is to prompt the recollection that it is the romantic poets' difference from their age, and not their contemporaneity, which makes it still vital to attend to what they wrote."
Prickett contributes two essays, on "The Religious Context" and "Romantic Literature," Colin Brooks one on "The Historical Context." Marcia Pointon writes on "Romanticism in English Art," T.J. Diffey on "The Roots of the Imagination."
Not seen.

Rafroidi, Patrick. *Irish Literature in English: The Romantic Period (1789-1850)*, Vols. I and II, Atlantic Highlands, N.J.: Humanities Press, 1980. Vol. I: pp. xxviii+364; Vol. II: pp. 392. $67.50.

Rev. by Vivian Mercier in *TLS*, April 17, 1981, p. 444; very favorably by Robert Tracy in *NCF* 36 (1981): 355-58. The original, in French, appeared in 1972; see *ELN* 12, Supp., 25.

Randel, Fred V. "The Mountaintops of English Romanticism." *TSLL* 23 (1981): 294-323.

Reed, Walter L. "Introduction: Romanticism and Criticism—the Co-ordinating Conjunction." *TSLL* 23 (1981): 287-93.

Introduces an issue of *TSLL* devoted to these two "isms" (no. 3: Fall 1981), with articles by F. Randel, G. Spivak, K. Heinzelman, L. Brisman, J. Diehl, and L. Mackey, listed separately elsewhere.

Reiman, Donald H. "Wordsworth, Shelley, and the Romantic Inheritance." *RP&P* 5,ii (1981): 1-22.

Cautiously distinguishes two Romantic sensibilities: the "pastoral" of Wordsworth and his inheritors Auden and Stevens, who assert the protectiveness of the Other (whether Nature, family, society, or God); and the "Gothic" of Shelley and his inheritors Eliot and Yeats, who deny the protectiveness or meaningfulness of the Other and seek to protect or at least assert the self through the primacy of art.

Reiman, Donald H., ed. *Romantic Context: Poetry. Significant Minor Poetry 1789-1830.* Printed in photo-facsimile in 128 volumes. New York: Garland Publishing, 1976-1979. (See *RMB* for 1980, pp. 143-44, for a summary of the series.)

The five volumes of *The Poetry of James Montgomery* are reviewed by Judy Page in *BIQ* 15 (1981): 28-35; illus. The two volumes of Erasmus Darwin's *The Botanic Garden* are reviewed by Nelson Hilton in *BIQ* 15 (1981): 36-48; illus. The four volumes of the works of William Hayley are reviewed by Joseph Wittreich in *BIQ* 15 (1981): 48-50.

Rozenberg, Paul. "Romantisme ou barbarie: le romantisme anglais, une utopie du sujet." *Littérature* 40 (Dec. 1980): 95-114.

Sambrook, James, ed. *James Thomson: The Seasons.* Oxford University Press, 1981. Pp. 397. £45.00.

Rev. by Pat Rogers in *TLS*, Oct. 2, 1981, pp. 1121-22.

Stevenson, Catherine Barnes. "Druids, Bards, and Tennyson's
   Merlin." *VN* 57 (1980): 14-23.

Stone, Donald D. *The Romantic Impulse in Victorian Fiction*.
   Harvard University Press, 1980. Pp. ix+396. $17.50.

   Rev. by Robert Kiely in *TWC* 12 (1981): 190-92; by Jean
Wilson in *TLS*, March 27, 1981, p. 358; in *ELN* 19 (1981):
156-58 by Karl Kroeber as a "pleasantly surprising" work of
traditional criticism on the "primary responses to 'Romantic
impulses'" in the novels of Trollope, Disraeli, Charlotte
Brontë, Elizabeth Gaskell, George Eliot, Dickens, and Meredith.
   Not seen.

Twitchell, James B. *The Living Dead: A Study of the Vampire
   in Romantic Literature*. Duke University Press, 1981. Pp.
   x+219. $14.75.

   Rev. by Daniel P. Deneau in *SSF* 4 (1981): 457-68; by A.N.
Wilson in *TLS*, March 20, 1981, p. 308; in *SiR* 21 (1982):
107-10 by Judith Wilt as a book that "offers provocative,
often deliberately controversialist, readings of major romantic poems and novels."
   James Twitchell says that the vampire myth, as it has been
used in literature, can be both profound and silly, and one
is tempted to say something like that about his book. He
covers the subject with enthusiastic thoroughness, from the
sensational literary debut of the creature in John Polidori's
adaptation of Byron's fragment through its most recent re-
spectable incarnation in D.H. Lawrence's parasitic lovers.
Along the way he offers analyses of works by Wordsworth,
Coleridge, Byron, Shelley, Keats, Poe, the Brontës, Wilde,
Henry James, and some lesser figures as well. While passing
along a rich abundance of traditional vampire lore, Twitchell
is more interested in showing how the idea of vampirism has
been used metaphorically in literature to express "the process of energy exchange involved in human interactions,"
and more specifically in the interactions among the artist,
the work of art, and the audience.
   Twitchell is at his best when discussing works where the
vampires or their female counterparts appear *in propria
persona*, as in *The Vampyre* and *Dracula*, *Christabel*, and
Lamia (though one must suspend disbelief energetically when
he argues that Christabel is a masculine figure). He is also
quite compelling when dealing with characters who behave
certifiably like vampires, such as Count Cenci, Heathcliff,
and the pale protagonists of some of Poe's tales. But when

he argues that such poems as *The Rime of the Ancient Mariner*
and *Resolution and Independence* not only lend themselves to
this kind of analysis but were actually intended by their
authors as "vampire poems" (much significance being attached
to the mariner's sucking blood from his arm and to the life-
style of leeches), the hobbyhorse-drawn black coach may leave
some skeptical readers behind. One suspects that Twitchell
could, given the challenge, find a vampire lurking in just
about any poem or novel. It is easy to imagine him asking
in a sequel, "Why is Lucy called 'a thing that cannot feel
the touch of earthly years,' and why does her lover visit
her, in a trance-like state, when the moon is full?"

But even when one can't go the distance with Twitchell,
one never feels that the time has been wasted. He can
occasionally irritate the reader with his style, which in
the attempt to be light and racy sometimes lapses into sloppy
syntax and imprecise diction, but the book is wonderfully
entertaining and informative, and it permanently adjusts
one's understanding of a large number of literary works.
(R.M.R.)

Vicinus, Martha. "'Helpless and Unfriended': Nineteenth-Century Melodrama." *NLH* 13 (1981): 127-43.

Webb, Igor. *From Custom to Capital: The English Novel and the
Industrial Revolution.* Cornell University Press, 1981. Pp.
219. $17.50.

A deft and swift demonstration "that *any* novel written
between, say, 1780 and the 1850s"--the choices here include
Pride and Prejudice, Mansfield Park, Jane Eyre, Shirley, and
Hard Times--"bears the impress of and is at its core a
response to that transformation of society somewhat inac-
curately called the Industrial Revolution" (16). "If the
writings of Macaulay and Marx may be called a form of social
autobiography, this is obviously and explicitly true of the
novel," in which Webb observes "the effort in consciousness
to interpret, to define, and then to affect the developing
social transformation" (44). "Cobbett shows that a particular notion of value implies a particular system of human
relationships. Partly the novel confronts social transformation directly in terms of the system of relationships, in
terms of class. But most deeply the novel investigates the
sources of value in the self ..." (45).

The discussions of these novels are thoughtful and thought-
provoking, particularly in the contrasting evaluations of
Austen, Brontë, and Dickens and in the differences noted
between *Pride* and *Mansfield.* (D.V.E.)

Wesling, Donald. "Difficulties of the Bardic: Literature and
the Human Voice." *CritI* 8 (1981): 69-81.

  Chatterton, MacPherson, Blake, and Wordsworth are cited
in passing as poets who "saw their own ideal selves in the
figure of the bard." In contrast to theirs is present-day
"Derridian" poetry (e.g., by John Ashbery) "where utterance
is not bound to personal consciousness."

See also in "English 4": Troy ("Burke"); Christensen ("Coleridge"); Hennelly, MacAndrew, Paulson ("The Gothic Novel").

Reviews of books previously listed:

ASHTON, Rosemary, *The German Idea: Four English Writers and
the Reception of German Thought 1800-1860* (see *RMB* for 1980,
p. 49), rev. by R.J. Dingley in *N&Q* 28 (1981): 272-73; by
Lilian Furst in *JEGP* 80 (1981): 95-97; by Robert Maniquis
in *VS* 24 (1981): 367-68; BRISMAN, Leslie, *Romantic Origins*
(see *ELN* 17, Supp., 51), rev. by Carolyn Bond in *QQ* 88 (1981):
777-81 as deeply influenced by Bloom and a case of frequent
"wrenched emphasis"; by Stuart M. Tave in *YES* 11 (1981):
290-93; BUTT, John, and Geoffrey Carnall, *The Mid-Eighteenth
Century* (see *RMB* for 1980, p. 52), rev. by Pat Rogers in
RES 32 (1981): 83-86; CAMPBELL, Ian, ed., *Nineteenth-Century
Scottish Fiction* (see *RMB* for 1979, p. 51), rev. by Kathryn
Sutherland in *SLJ* 8 (1981): Supp. 15, pp. 119-21, as a
"mixed bag"; CONRAD, Peter, *Shandyism: The Character of
Romantic Irony* (see *RMB* for 1979, p. 52), rev. by Melvyn New
in *ECS*, Spring 1981, pp. 361-66, as "adding little to our
understanding"; COOKE, Michael G., *Acts of Inclusion: Studies
Bearing on an Elementary Theory of Romanticism* (see *RMB* for
1979, p. 52), rev. by Carl Woodring in *KSJ* 30 (1981): 191-
94; DAVIES, R.T., and B.G. Beatty, eds., *Literature of the
Romantic Period 1750-1850* (see *ELN* 15, Supp., 39), rev. by
J.R. Strugnell in *YES* 11 (1981): 285-86; FARRELL, John P.,
*Revolution as Tragedy: The Dilemma of the Moderate from
Scott to Arnold* (see *RMB* for 1980, p. 54), rev. by Roger B.
Hemble (favorably) in *VS* 25 (1981): 389-91; by Jane Millgate
in *JEGP* 80 (1981): 583-85; FRY, Paul H., *The Poet's Calling
in the English Ode* (see *RMB* for 1980, p. 55), rev. by Marshall
Brown in *SiR* 20 (1981): 249-54; by Douglas Bush in *JEGP* 80
(1981): 133-35, devastatingly; by A. Harris Fairbanks in
ELN 19 (1981): 145-47; by Alan Rodway in *BJA* 21 (1981):
178-80, negatively; by Helen Vendler in *MLQ* 42 (1981): 87-
90, as "embarrassing" and "dismaying"; by Carl Woodring in
KSJ 30 (1981): 191-94, genially; GOLDSTEIN, Laurence, *Ruins*

and *Empire: The Evolution of a Theme in Augustan and Romantic Literature* (see *ELN* 16, Supp., 39), rev. by Brean S. Hammond in *ES* 62 (1981): 178-82; HOWELLS, Coral Ann, *Love, Mystery, and Misery: Feeling in Gothic Fiction* (see *RMB* for 1979, p. 55), rev. by Rosemary Jackson in *YES* 11 (1981): 293-94; JACKSON, James Robert de Jaeger, *Poetry of the Romantic Period* (The Routledge History of English Poetry, vol. 4) (see *RMB* for 1980, pp. 57-58), rev. by George Dekker in *TWC* 12 (1981): 186-87; by John E. Jordan in *ELN* 18 (1981): 307-09; by Donald H. Reiman in *SiR* 20 (1981): 254-60; by Jack Stillinger, enthusiastically, in *JEGP* 80 (1981): 581-83; JACKSON, Wallace, *The Probable and the Marvelous: Blake, Wordsworth, and the Eighteenth-Century Critical Tradition* (see *ELN* 17, Supp., 53), rev. by Stuart M. Tave in *YES* 11 (1981): 290-93; KEITH, W.J., *The Poetry of Nature: Rural Perspectives in Poetry from Wordsworth to the Present* (see *RMB* for 1980, pp. 58-59), rev. by Lore Metzger in *ELN* 19 (1981): 148-49; by Keith Sutton in *TWC* 12 (1981): 187-90; KELLEY, Gary, *The English Jacobin Novel 1780-1805* (see *ELN* 15, Supp., 41), rev. by Günther Lottes in *Anglia* 99 (1981): 248-50; KING, Everard H., *James Beattie* (see *RMB* for 1979, p. 55), rev. by Thomas J. Rountree in *SiR* 20 (1981): 396-99; LANGBAUM, Robert, *The Mysteries of Identity* (see *ELN* 16, Supp., 40), rev. by Michael McKie in *EiC* 31 (1981): 263-70; LINDENBERGER, Herbert, *Historical Drama: The Relation of Literature and Reality* (see *ELN* 15, Supp., 21), rev. by Ursula Mahlendorf in *P&L* 1 (1976-77): 244-45; LOCK-WOOD, Thomas, *Post-Augustan Satire: Charles Churchill and Satirical Poetry, 1750-1800* (see *RMB* for 1979, p. 55), rev. by Joel J. Gold in *JEGP* 80 (1981): 255-56; MELLOR, Anne K., *English Romantic Irony* (see *RMB* for 1980, p. 60), rev. by Paul A. Cantor in *Criticism* 23 (1981): 187-90; by Carl Dawson in *ELN* 19 (1981): 69-71; by L.J. Swingle in *MLQ* 42 (1981): 99-104 as important, but inadequate on Wordsworth; PUNTER, David, *The Literature of Terror: A History of Gothic Fictions from 1765 to the Present Day* (see *RMB* for 1980, p. 61), rev. by Julia Briggs in *N&Q* 28 (1981): 471-73; by Coral Ann Howells in *English* 30 (1981): 185-90; RAGUSSIS, Michael, *The Subterfuge of Art: Language and the Romantic Tradition* (see *ELN* 17, Supp., 56), rev. by Stuart M. Tave in *YES* 11 (1981): 290-93; ROPER, Derek, *Reviewing before the "Edinburgh": 1788-1802* (see *RMB* for 1979, p. 58), rev. by J.H. Alexander in *YES* 11 (1981): 294-96; SIMPSON, David, *Irony and Authority in Romantic Poetry* (see *RMB* for 1980, p. 63), rev. by William Keach in *SiR* 20 (1981): 539-43; by Anne K. Mellor in *TWC* 12 (1981): 196-97; by E.B. Murray in *RES* 32 (1981): 459-61; TAYLOR, Anya, *Magic and English*

Romanticism (see *RMB* for 1979, p. 59), rev. by Geoffrey
Little in *RES* 32 (1981): 339-40; TYSON, Gerald P., *Joseph
Johnson: A Liberal Publisher* (see *RMB* for 1979, p. 60), rev.
by James H. Averill in *SiR* 20 (1981): 129-31; by R.J. Roberts
in *N&Q* 28 (1981): 84-85; WITTREICH, Joseph Anthony, Jr.,
Visionary Poetics: Milton's Tradition and His Legacy (see
RMB for 1979, pp. 61-62), rev. by Gordon Campbell in *YES* 11
(1981): 255-56; by Martin Evans in *RES* 32 (1981): 329-31.

Composite reviews:

Hanley, Keith. *CritQ* 23,1 (1981): 88-90.

Reviews Cooke, *Coleridge* (see *RMB* for 1979, p. 91), and
Proudfit, *Landor as Critic* (see *RMB* for 1979, pp. 107f.).

Sperry, Stuart M. "Recent Studies in the Nineteenth Century."
SEL 21 (1981): 713-39.

Books pertaining to the Romantics cover such topics as the
concept of imagination, Romantic irony, and Romantic genre,
style, and taste. Represented by critical studies or new
editions are the six major Romantic poets plus Hazlitt, De
Quincey, Mary Shelley, John Clare, James Hogg, Sydney Smith,
and Robert Bloomfield.

Review article:

Reiman, Donald H. "The Poems and Letters of William Cowper."
BIQ 15 (1981): 149-51.

A review of the recent Oxford editions of the poetry and
prose (see *RMB* for 1979, p. 11, and *RMB* for 1980, p. 50):
"Cowper's early letters and poems are of greatest interest
to the student of Romantic Poetry."

4. STUDIES OF AUTHORS

AUSTEN

Baruch, Elaine Hoffman. "The Feminine *Bildungsroman*: Education
Through Marriage." *MR* 22 (1981): 335-57.

A little on Emma who "is already beginning to hint at the
romantic importance of a woman's self. Having neither economic
need nor romantic inclination, she eventually does consent
to have her Knightley in shining armor.... Whereas a traditional sign of manhood lies in the hero's ability to give

up guides, the test of womanhood has resided in the heroine's ability to find a mentor." (R.A.B.)

Bodenheimer, Rosemarie. "Looking at the Landscape in Jane Austen." *SEL* 21 (1981): 605-23.

Cottom, Daniel. "The Novels of Jane Austen: Attachments and Supplantments." *Novel: A Forum on Fiction* 14 (1981): 152-67.

Culler, Jonathan. "Convention and Meaning: Derrida and Austen." *NLH* 13 (1981): 15-30.

Hardy, Barbara. *A Reading of Jane Austen*. London: Athlone Press, 1979. Pp. 192.

>   Rev. by J.F. Burrows in *AUMLA* 54 (1980): 251-54.
>   Not seen.

Leavis, L.R., and J.M. Blom. "A Return to Jane Austen's Novels." *ES* 62 (1981): 313-23.

>   Largely hostile view of recent Austen scholarship.

Lenta, Margaret. "Jane Austen's Feminism: An Original Response to Convention." *CritQ* 23, no. 3 (1981): 27-36.

>   "Rather than include in her fiction argument against the limits on the moral autonomy of women, she has presented us [in *Emma*] with a woman who determinedly and successfully maintains her freedom ..., directing her [own] behaviour responsibly and well."

Lenta, Margaret. "Jane Fairfax and Jane Eyre: Educating Women." *ArielE* 12 (Oct. 1981): 27-41.

Odmark, John. *An Understanding of Jane Austen's Novels: Character, Value and Ironic Perspective*. Oxford: Blackwell, 1981. Pp. xvi+224.

>   Rev. by Robert Folkenflik in *TLS*, Nov. 13, 1981, p. 1338.

Olshin, Toby A. "Jane Austen: A Romantic, Systematic, or Realistic Approach to Medicine?" *SECC* 10 (1981): 313-26.

>   Neither the "romantic" nor the "rationalist" view would do for Jane.

Person, Leland S. "Playing House: Jane Austen's Fabulous Space." *PQ* 59 (1980): 62-75.

Pigrome, Stella. "'Jane!'" *ChLB* 36 (Oct. 1981): 70-81.

The etiquette of Christian names—and Miss Austen's preferences and innuendoes.

Roberts, Warren. *Jane Austen and the French Revolution*. New York: St. Martin's Press, 1980. Pp. xii+224. $14.00.

Rev. by Frank W. Bradbrook in *N&Q* 28 (1981): 268-69.
Warren Roberts, a historian, sets out to correct the view promulgated by such historians as Watson, Halévy, and Trevelyan that Austen's novels reflect isolation from the events of the outside world during her lifetime. He faces frankly the fact that in her novels and extant correspondence she never refers directly to the French Revolution, and then goes on to make a plausible case that she was nevertheless aware of and influenced by the cataclysms flowing from France.
Roberts offers chapters on Politics, War, Religion, and Women and the Family—chapters which provide admirable analyses of the effects of Burke's ideas, the impact on southern England of the conflict with France, the political relations of Evangelicalism, and the submergence of feminism in Victorianism. In each chapter Roberts shows the development of these ideas in Austen's novels, demonstrating that he is knowledgeable about what literary critics have said. Most interesting are his suggestions that the famous "neighbourhood of voluntary spies" passage in *Northanger Abbey* may have been not (as Harding thought) essentially a satirical reference to a meddling and hostile society, but actually an indication of Austen's recognition of the ubiquity of Pitt's spies; that Henry Tilney's allusion to riots may not simply go back to the Gordon Riots but may reflect Austen's awareness—perhaps through Eliza de Feuillide—of London rioting in the 1790s. Most ingenious are the deductions drawn from a passage of Austen's Aug. 30, 1805 letter to her sister Cassandra about the "evil intentions of the Guards" and spiritless "gentlemen of the neighbourhood." Roberts reads this as a coded reference to responses to troop movements which demonstrates the novelist's knowledge of the tensions of living in Kent under threat of French invasion.
A convenient "Conclusion" summarizes Roberts's view of Austen's career in three phases, showing as a reaction to the French Revolution a movement from temperamental conservatism to a more informed political and religious conservatism. He sees this movement as producing in the work beginning with *Mansfield Park* a greater respect for authority and ordered society, and a preference—retreating from her earlier feminism—for more reserved, gentle heroines and

more masculine, decisive heroes.
Austen scholars will welcome this historian's reading.
(J.E.J.)

Schapera, I. *Kinship Terminology in Jane Austen's Novels.*
(Occasional Paper No. 33.) London: Royal Anthropological
Institute of Great Britain and Ireland, 1977. £4.00.

Southam, Brian, ed. *Jane Austen's "Sir Charles Grandison."*
Oxford University Press, 1981. Pp. 128; 5 halftones. $24.00;
$19.20.

Rev. by J.B. in *CritQ* 23 (1981): 90-91; by Pat Rogers in
TLS, April 3, 1981, p. 369; defended by D.C. Measham in *TLS*,
April 17, 1981, p. 437.

Spence, Jon. "The Abiding Possibilities of Nature in *Persuasion*." *SEL* 21 (1981): 625-36.

Swanson, Janice Bowman. "Toward a Rhetoric of Self: The Art
of *Persuasion*." *NCF* 36 (1981): 1-21.

Tatham, Michael. "A Need for Tenderness." *New Blackfriars* 62
(1981): 465-72.

Finds in *Emma* "a scale of values which owes nothing to
social class or economic arrangements"; it is the heroine's
awareness of the ultimate importance of tenderness that
gradually transforms her understanding of human relationships.

Wilt, Judith. *Ghosts of the Gothic: Austen, Eliot, and
Lawrence*. Princeton University Press, 1980. Pp. xii+307.
$18.50.

Rev. by Peter Kemp in *TLS*, Jan. 2, 1981, p. 18.
Not seen.

See also Leavis, Neale ("English 2. Environment"); Aers,
Butler, Ehrenpreis, Polhemus, Webb ("English 3. Criticism");
Conger ("Shelley, Mary").

Reviews of books previously listed:

BROWN, Julia Prewitt, *Jane Austen's Novels: Social Change
and Literary Form* (see *RMB* for 1979, p. 65), rev. by Juliet
McMaster in *ELN* 18 (1981): 304-07; CECIL, David, *A Portrait
of Jane Austen* (see *ELN* 17, Supp., 59), rev. anonymously
in *ContR* 238 (1981): 56; MONAGHAN, David, *Jane Austen:
Structure and Social Vision* (see *RMB* for 1980, p. 69), rev.

by Jean Wilson in *TLS*, April 17, 1981, p. 446; MORGAN,
Susan, *In the Meantime: Character and Perception in Jane
Austen's Fiction* (see *RMB* for 1980, p. 69), rev. by Juliet
McMaster in *ELN* 18 (1981): 304-07; by Gene W. Ruoff in *TWC*
12 (1981): 169-72; by Mona Scheuermann in *SAR* 46 (1981):
94-97; PARIS, Bernard J., *Character and Conflict in Jane
Austen's Novels: A Psychological Approach* (see *RMB* for 1979,
p. 67), rev. by Sheila Ortiz Tayler in *ECS* (1981): 491-97.

BECKFORD

See Garber ("General 3. Criticism"); Garber ("French 2. Delacroix"); *Caïn de Lord Byron* ("French 2. Fabre d'Olivet").

BLAKE

Ackland, Michael. "Blake's System and the Critics." *AUMLA* 54
(1980): 149-70.

   "In short, 'some simplification of genuine Blake scholarship' is now urgently required, lest the poet become increasingly the property of a specialist elite, and his work
become ironically the subject of thoroughly mystifying
readings, which, in the words of one of his nineteenth-century reviewers, 'no ingenuity can solve.'" This is not an
argument against deconstruction which hasn't or can't make
it down under; unexpectedly the mystifiers are represented
by Erdman. (T.L.A.)

Allentuck, Marcia. "Ruskin and Blake Again: Unpublished Sources
Not in Bentley." *PBSA* 75 (1981): 447-49.

   Correspondence that demonstrates that Ruskin's "enthusiasm"
for Blake was considerably tempered by considerations of
changing taste--and changing market values.

Baine, Rodney M. "Bromion's 'Jealous Dolphins.'" *BIQ* 14 (1981):
206-07; illus.

   An allusion to the Galatea legend; the illustration shown
is Raphael's "Triumph of Galatea" as engraved by Goltzius.

Bentley, G.E., Jr. "A Portrait of Milton Engraved by William
Blake 'When Three Years of Age'? A Speculation by Samuel
Palmer." *UTQ* 51 (1981): 28-35; 4 illus.

Palmer had no factual basis for his speculation; Bentley has no answer to the problem. (I.H.C.)

Bentley, G.E., Jr. "William Blake's Techniques of Engraving and Printing." *SB* 34 (1981): 241-53.

Emphasizes the tecnical expertise and inventiveness Blake brought to his art.

Bogan, James J. "Apocalypse Now: William Blake and the Conversion of the Jews." *ELN* 19 (1981): 116-19.

Bogan, James. "Blake's City of Golgonooza in *Jerusalem*: Metaphor and Mandala." *CLQ* 17 (1981): 85-98.

BRH 84,iii (1981): 273-381. A Blake Issue; illus.

"Blake and the Night Sky" is the subject of two extensive studies by David Worrall ("The 'Immortal Tent'": 273-95) and Paul Miner ("Visionary Astronomy": 305-36) and a brief note by David V. Erdman ("Art Against Armies": 296-304), constituting the first concentrated investigation of this area of Blake's symbolism. Worrall and Miner independently found the constellation Tigris swimming into their ken; all three investigators engage in some debates with each other in the footnotes. In a somewhat related article, "The Human Entrails and the Starry Heavens: Some Instances of Visual Art as Patterns for Yeats's Mingling of Heaven and Earth" (363-81), Patrick Keane finds Boehme's celestial human form, admired by Blake, in the weavings of Yeats. Returning to Blake's visual art, Christopher Heppner offers a sophisticated methodology for "Reading Blake's Designs: *Pity* and *Hecate*" (337-62).

An article announced for this issue, Andrew Lincoln's "Blake's Lower Paradise: The Pastoral Passage in *The Four Zoas*, Night the Ninth," was postponed to *BRH* 85,i (1982) because of the expansiveness of these astronomers. Lincoln's probing of the enigmatic role of Vala as "the sinless Soul" in Luvah's "bodily house" brings unexpected aid to those of us still puzzling over the earlier enigma of Thel. (D.V.E.)

Brown, Catherine, ed. "S. Foster Damon (1893-1971): Selections from His Personal Journal." *Books at Brown* 28 (1981): 1-57.

Foster Damon was a canny man, who watched himself in many roles (including self-watching) and filled a file cabinet with notes to himself, some headed "Autobiography," "Spiritual Diary," or "Spit Dig" (perhaps, as the editor suggests,

"Spiritual Digest" but with a pun: Spit on your hands and Dig--how to face death is the subject of one such note). "More more!" is the cry of one who knew him in one role, upon reading that the present selection represents "but a small fraction of the material" (2). A mistaken cry? "A man is much bigger than himself," Damon warns (48). Damon extruded books about Shakespeare, musical compositions, his own poems; was even bold enough to give us a "Blake Dictionary," some entries in which are much bigger than the particulars in Blake. (There is almost no mention of the *Dictionary* in these "Selections," but they open to us the mind that invented it.) (D.V.E.)

Butlin, Martin. *The Paintings and Drawings of William Blake*. The Paul Mellon Centre for Studies in British Art. 2 vols. Yale University Press, 1981. Vol. I (Text): pp. xxiii+668. Vol. II (Plates): 1193 illus., 169 col. pls. $300.00 the set.

   Rev. by Harold Bloom in *New York Times Book Review*, Jan. 3, 1982, p. 4; by Michael Mason in *TLS*, Sept. 11, 1981, p. 1044.

   Long in preparation and in reaching final published form, this is the catalogue of Blake's visual art which comes nearest to being complete. It comprises all his known paintings, watercolors, drawings (including those attributed to his brother Robert and to Catherine Blake), and separate color prints. Although the monochrome engravings and the illuminated books as such are omitted because of the availability of other catalogues covering them specifically, further volumes adding those works to Butlin's compilation would provide the single authoritative source of reference information which is still desirable and needed.

   Originally, publication was planned for the text only. The volume of plates was added with the change of publisher from Trianon Press to Yale, and it is this that makes Butlin's catalogue a truly indispensable research tool. The only works not reproduced are those on which fully illustrated editions or monographs have already been published: *Tiriel*, the Notebook, *Four Zoas* manuscript and Blake-Varley Sketchbook, and the major series of illustrations to Young, Gray, and Dante. Even so, there are token reproductions from the latter group, and others related to the excluded illuminated books. Notable illustrations which now can be seen together are the different, and differing, sets of watercolors to Milton (all in color) and the Book of Job (one set in color), along with the series for *Pilgrim's Progress*, which has not been reproduced as a whole since 1941.

Butlin's descriptive entries are full and informative.
The color plates are clear and, in the absence of a detailed
comparison with the originals, seem to be true to the differing effects of the media used. (I.H.C.)

Carr, Stephen Leo. "Visionary Syntax: Nontyrannical Coherence
in Blake's Visual Art." *ECent* 22 (1981): 222-48.

Cooper, Andrew M. "Blake's Escape from Mythology: Self-Mastery
in *Milton*." *SiR* 20 (1981): 85-110.

"*Milton*'s 'parallelism' is purely functional. It is the
rehearsal of a single prophetic pattern on several different
levels which serve, first to expose the animating truth
behind the pattern (the Logos of the conclusion), but then
also serve to signal the falseness of reducing this truth
to any of the vehicles that shadow it forth...."

Corti, Claudia. *Il primo Blake. Testo e sistema*. Ravenna:
Longo, 1980. Pp. 250.

Rev. by Serena Cenni in *RLMC* 33 (1980): 313-15.

Cox, Stephen. "Adventures of 'A Little Boy Lost': Blake and
the Process of Interpretation." *Criticism* 23 (1981): 301-16.

"The history of [readers'] reactions provides an interesting study of a significant but seldom examined phenomenon--
the process by which an author's admirers dispose of particular texts that they do not greatly admire."

Damrosch, Leopold, Jr. *Symbol and Truth in Blake's Myth*.
Princeton University Press, 1981. Pp. xiv+395; 35 illus.
$25.00; $9.50 paper.

Rev. by Stuart Curran, favorably, in *MLQ* 42 (1981): 303-
05; by Nelson Hilton in *BIQ* 15 (1982): 192-96, with praise--
and severe criticism; by Daniel Karlin in *TLS*, June 26,
1981, p. 738.
The key to both the strengths and the weaknesses of this
new study is the imposing number of references to and quotations from other books, many other books, in philosophy,
anthropology, the history of religion, Bible hermeneutics,
linguistics, and inevitably post-modern criticism. There
is much that is illuminating in the direct discussions of
ideas, which add new names to Blake's philosophical ancestry,
and Damrosch's intellectual rigor is welcome on such topics
as "vision and perception," "the problem of dualism," and
"God and man."

On the debit side are the effects of the radical separation
and subordination reflected in the title, influenced perhaps by the theoretical formulations of Damrosch's secondary
authors. He is not comfortable in dealing with the designs,
tends to read the verse in search of ideas at the expense
of other meanings, and depends largely (and inhibitingly)
on received interpretations of the poems. Most questionable
is his understanding of Blake's concept of art and its
"symbols" (the term Damrosch insistently uses): that it,
and they, are limited, equivocal, and ultimately corruptive
of religious and moral "truth."

In the concluding chapter, after denying to the poems the
normal appeal of form, language, and shared human experience,
Damrosch is led to justify reading them at all on the uncertain ground of Blake's "religious vision" and "passionate
demand for moral commitment," which he says are "exciting
to many a reader who has only the sketchiest idea of what
[Blake] is actually talking about." Thus we have been taken
on a long and labyrinthine journey through Damrosch's hetero-
geneous texts only to be left with a barely modified version
of the common outsiders' view of Blake: as cult figure to a
few, in this instance non-believers nostalgic toward someone else's belief (see p. 370); irrelevant and unreadable
to the rest.

Damrosch has previously published a book on Samuel Johnson. Occasionally in digressions here--rare observations on
the language of the poems, or perceptive remarks about
Blake's personal psychic tensions and ambivalences--there
are hints of the very different, empirical Blake study he
might have written had he not apparently sought to update
the work of Percival and Frye. (I.H.C.)

Davies, J.M.Q. "'Embraces are Cominglings': Passion and
    Apocalypse in Blake's *Paradise Regained* Designs." *DUJ* 74
    (n.s. 43), i (1981): 75-116; 39 illus.

This concentrated and particularizing account of Blake's
Paradise Regained designs makes some valuable contributions
to their interpretation, hitherto most fully presented in
Joseph A. Wittreich's essay in *Calm of Mind* (1971: see *ELN*
10, Supp., 38) and his *Angel of Apocalypse* (1975). While in
"substantial agreement" with Wittreich's discussion of the
sequence of twelve designs as psychodrama, and with many of
his readings, Davies disputes (with some support from
Christopher Hill) the underlying assumption which allows
Wittreich to regard Blake's designs as an unqualified celebration of Milton's religion, the assumption that Christ
meant "the same thing" to Blake as to Milton, that what is

radical in one revolutionary era is still radical in the
next (76). Davies demonstrates that "the case can be made
that Blake is more critical of *Paradise Regained* than is
suggested in Wittreich's account of the designs as theodicy."
    This is a sound position, theoretically, and many of
Davies's particulars support it. Perhaps most of them do,
but he tends to base some of his readings on very slight
evidence. Many readers will be skeptical--I am not--of his
identification of certain shapes as iconic hearts and
phalluses. (Design 11 makes clear what is a nuance in 10,
for instance.) But his general reading can stand without
these particulars. One broadly helpful insight is the suggestion that the youthful Mary in these designs, especially
the final design, in which her position and gesture resemble
those of Ololon in the final plate of *Milton*, "may function
not as Jesus' mother but as his emanation" (79). (D.V.E.)

Doskow, Minna. "The Shape of Limitation: A Visual Pattern in
    the Illuminated Works of William Blake." *CLQ* 17 (1981):
    121-60.

Erdman, David V. See *BRH* Blake Issue (above).

Essick, Robert N. "Blake's 'Enoch' Lithograph." *BIQ* 14 (1981):
    180-84; illus.

Essick, Robert N. "New Information on Blake's Illuminated
    Books." *BIQ* 15 (1981): 4-13; 15 illus.; postscript, pp.
    59-60.

    Illustrates and describes several prints that have re-
cently turned up or that have not received full attention.
Among these are two from *Songs* copy BB (see Keynes, below);
Europe, posthumous copy c, plates 4, 9, 15; three variants
of *Milton* 13 (one in 1st state, two in 2nd); and two impressions of the title page for *Ahania* which constitute "a rare
set of progress proofs." (D.V.E.)

Essick, Robert N. *William Blake, Printmaker*. Princeton Uni-
    versity Press, 1980. Pp. xxii+283; 236 illus. $50.00.

    Rev. by David Alexander in *BM* 123 (May 1981): 311-12;
by Leopold Damrosch, Jr., in *SiR* 20 (1981): 544-45; by
John Gage in *Art History* 4 (1981): 470-74; by David Irwin
in *DUJ* 43 (1981): 112-13; by Bo Ossian Lindberg in *BIQ* 15
(1981): 140-47; by Michael Mason in *TLS*, Feb. 13, 1981,
p. 169; by David E. McKenty in *CollL* 8 (1981): 196-97; by
Peter Quennell in *Apollo* 114 (1981): 136-37. (All reviews
positive, some very strong.)

All earlier publications on the subject are made obsolete
by this remarkably detailed yet comprehensive study, which
is concerned with everything pertaining to Blake's "craft
and trade," from the conventions of printmaking in which he
was trained as an apprentice to the "synthesis and mastery"
of his own style in the intaglio engravings for the Book
of Job during the last years of his life. The most notable
chapters are those based on research and on painstaking
personal experiments with materials and techniques, which
reconstruct Blake's processes of relief etching and color
printing and their development from book to book, even from
plate to plate. After Essick's meticulously detailed descriptions and analyses, no reader of the illuminated books can
again be content with purely typographic texts.

Essick also tries to relate Blake's printing techniques
and printed effects to the verse, but except in his identifications of certain obvious allusions and metaphors he is
less persuasive in that endeavor. In contrast to the spirit
of his technical investigations, his interpretations of the
poems are disappointingly orthodox. (I.H.C.)

Ferber, Michael. "'London' and Its Politics." *ELH* 48 (1981):
310-38.

An impressively thorough and sound reading of "London,"
which politely but firmly corrects small and large inaccuracies and misreadings in previous interpretations of the
poem--in the process supplying a severe critique of Harold
Bloom's careless dealings with the words in the poem. Ferber
should be encouraged to write the "amusing essay" which he
says, in footnote 17, "could be written on the impact of
the *American Heritage Dictionary* (1969) on the Yale English
Department," from misapplying the dictionary's etymological
information to questions of meaning. (D.V.E.)

Gleckner, Robert F. "Antithetical Structure in Blake's *Poetical
Sketches*." *SiR* 20 (1981): 143-62.

A valuable examination of Blake's early "Songs" which
brings to our attention instances and anticipations of the
"dialectical debate and symbolic mental warfare" which
become Blake's habitual poetic procedure. (D.V.E.)

Heppner, Christopher. See *BRH* Blake Issue (above).

Herrstrom, David Sten. "Blake's Transformations of Ezekiel's
Cherubim Vision in *Jerusalem*." *BIQ* 15 (1981): 64-77; illus.

"By a series of meditative transformations ... Blake
brings the exiled chariot-vision back inside its landscape
of the rider-visionary, thereby restoring man to psychic
and bodily wholeness."

Hilton, Nelson. "Blake and the Mountains of the Mind." *BIQ*
14 (1981): 196-204; illus.

This exploration of passages in which "Blake's mountains
reflect an interior vision of the mountains of mythology
and ... of the Bible" gives distinct outline to images ranging from the tent cross section dropping around plates 1
and 21 of *Job*, to the "visionary continuity joining the
Druid monuments, Calvary, and Tyburn." The scaffold at
Tyburn, for instance, was made of three posts held apart
by three cross-bars at the top, "a ruined version of a
Druidic temple made of trilithons"--information that eluci-
dates the drama of *Milton* 3. (D.V.E.)

Hilton, Nelson. "Spears, Spheres, and Spiritual Tears: Blake's
Poetry as 'The Tyger,' 11. 17-20." *PQ* 59 (1980): 515-29.

"The lines present--as does the poem--a scene of writing:
of framing: of creation which is the passage from imagination to text, from Blake's 'Eternity' into time, and so
practically done that through its thirteen 'words' we assume
that creation."

Keane, Patrick. See *BRH* Blake Issue (above).

Keynes, Geoffrey, Kt. *The Gates of Memory*. Clarendon Press;
Oxford University Press, 1981. Pp. xi+428; 55 illus. $22.50.

In this his nonagenarian autobiography, Sir Geoffrey has
yielded to the pleadings of the Spectre to "unbar the gates
of memory" (*Four Zoas* 7:347); yet while thus releasing the
story of his own life, he generally manages to keep from
falling "Into his own chaos, which is the memory between
man & man" (*Jerusalem* 54:8). For those who know him primarily
as a collector, bibliographer, and editor (in that order)
any disappointment we feel at his saying very little about
his Blake work is forgotten in our gratitude for his inviting us into the theater of his distinguished surgical
career (he was a pioneer in the use of blood transfusion
and the rational treatment of breast cancer) and the more
intimate domestic and social paths of his daily converse.
In an Epilogue he apologizes to his friends for having
given "too much" about himself and "too little about the
'interesting people'" in his life; but these are symbiotic

strands in a warmblooded, interesting life. From the modest,
matter-of-fact narrative, free of italics, we discover what
a mental prince has been living amongst us. (D.V.E.)

Keynes, Geoffrey, Kt. "'To the Nightingale': Perhaps an Unrecognized Poem by William Blake." *BC* 30 (1981): 335-45;
illus.

   To his own satisfaction Sir Geoffrey proves that the
poem of four sextains etched and counterproofed in 1784,
here reproduced, was "written by [George] Cumberland himself" on the plate. And he quotes part of "A Poem on the
Landscapes of Great Britain" by Cumberland; there is a
similar ring. But, as a non sequitur, Keynes concludes by
attributing the poem to Blake, with some courteous support-
ing remarks by others not quite to that effect. A concordance
test gives only negative evidence. (D.V.E.)

Keynes, Geoffrey. "An Undescribed Copy of Blake's *Songs of
Innocence and of Experience*." *BC* 30 (1981): 39-42; illus.

   Census copy BB turned up at a Sotheby sale, May 1, 1980.
It consists of 55 plates instead of the usual 54, having
"A Divine Image" in the *Experience* section between "Holy
Thursday" and "Nurses Song." It was "Bought of Blake May
1816" by (Keynes conjectures) Robert Balmanno, a frequent
customer with whose collection the volume was sold in 1830.

Keynes, Geoffrey, Kt., and Peter Davidson, eds. *A Watch of
Nightingales*. London: Stourton Press, 1981. Pp. 64. £35.00
(signed); £12.50 (numbered).

   An anthology of "nearly fifty poems from Chaucer to de
la Mare which celebrate the song of the nightingale";
promised to contain some surprises. A gesture of confidence
in Sir Geoffrey's adding a nightingale poem to the Blake
canon (see entry above).

Kirk, Eugene. "Blake's Menippean *Island*." *PQ* 59 (1980): 194-
215.

   An Island in the Moon as an example of Menippean satire:
the "island" is England and "she has attained that absurd
sphere through the ambitions, perversions, and greeds of
those who pass for her finest minds."

Leader, Zachary. *Reading Blake's Songs*. London: Routledge &
Kegan Paul, 1981. Pp. xxiii+259; 25 illus. $27.50.

Rev. by David Bindman in *TLS*, Sept. 4, 1981, p. 1017; by
Susan Matthews in *English* 30 (1981): 296-302.

Excellent readings, most of the time "right on"; yet an
untrustworthy book. It opens with a well-pointed discussion
of "Children's books, education, and vision," but it develops
a scenario that won't let Blake's Christ become Jehovah or
let Blake sustain his vision.

As Leader discusses individual Songs, relating the particulars of poem and design, he makes sensible if not always
persuasive readings, bringing into the discussion a range
of previous interpretations and, as discussion leader, sometimes playing the Devil's advocate to stimulate thoughts.
Some of his visual reactions seem strained. Leader offers
a phobic response to "vaguely disturbing" vegetation (as
on pp. 43, 66, 107), and I am as nonplussed as David Bindman,
in his review, at Leader's finding the tree in the *Innocence* title page "singularly unpleasant" and to be taken
as "threatening" the children. Yet many of his disturbed
reactions are intelligently incorporated. By p. 74, however,
Leader is moving too fast and a hypothesis ("perhaps Blake
wants us to realize") is at once restated as "the fact."
Even the first "Nurse's Song" becomes scary: "When we look
at the green and the empty hills ... we cannot help but
[sic] imagine the dangers they will hold ..." (107). And
gradually we discover that Leader, at whim, can suppress
interpretations that fail to fit his blend. A very un-
Blakean reading of "The Little Black Boy" sees the white
boy and Christ as an exclusive club, with the excluded
black boy "tentatively asking, or pathetically pretending,
to be included" (111)--and silently ignores the apt and
frequently cited emblem analogue of Cupid introducing Psyche
to Christ. (Citing "Erdman," he selects out the pertinent
interpretation.) Two pages later he is making Christ into
"Creeping Jesus" and seems ready to see Innocence destroyed
by the Savior figures in "The Little Vagabond" and "The
Little Boy Found." It is hard to trust the chapter labeled
"False Innocence," in which "we" develop "doubts" about the
trustworthiness of the Bard and then, as these diminish,
feel "confusion about the degree of control Blake exercises
over his meanings" (190). Perhaps a subtle way of saying
we have lost contact with Blake--as seems to happen as we
wind along through "The Bard Redeemed," mistaking the aged
wanderer pictured in "London" for the speaker, disappointed
at the design to "The Tyger"--dismissed earlier (47-48) as
a joke on us, or on the speaker or the tiger or the Creator
himself. Who's afraid of "fearful symmetry"!

Leader is a good moderator, but the kind "we" have to
contradict. His climactic/anticlimactic reading, only

seeming to be supported by the critics cited, exhibits a
"To Tirzah" in which "It is raised a spiritual body" is
taken to reveal Blake's reversion to a body/soul dichotomy
he should have outgrown. But does the design show a soul
departing from a body? In that case the man with the pitcher
should be using a spade, to bury the already vegetating
body. Blake, though, has him reviving that body's life with
an ample pitcher of nutbrown ale (I take that detail from
"The Little Vagabond") with the aim, surely, of raising
that body not "as soul" but as a spiritual *body*. This ob-
tuseness is apparently necessary for Leader's scenario;
yet the book is seldom that bad; indeed it is a major
contribution *to the discussion.* (D.V.E.)

Magno, Concettina Tramontano. "L'Imagery poetico-pittorica
di W. Blake nei romanzi di P. White." Estratto dagli Atti
del Convegno di Studi Australiani: *L'Australia Negli Anni
'80*, Universita di Messina 8-10 Gennaio 1981. Pp. 45.

Miner, Paul. See *BRH* Blake Issue (above).

Minnick, Thomas L., and Detlef W. Dörrbecker. "Blake and His
Circle: A Checklist of Recent Scholarship." *BIQ* 15 (1981):
83-93.

Murray, E.B. "Thel, *Thelyphthora*, and the Daughters of Albion."
SiR 20 (1981): 275-97.

The Court of King's Bench in 1781 ruled that the Marriage
Act of 1751 made void all marriages performed in chapels
erected since. (See *Blake: Prophet*, p. 62.) But God's
command from Mt. Sinai was that any man who "took" a virgin
had, in effect, married her for "all his days." Thus ruled
the Methodist preacher Martin Madan, holding not only that
all performed marriages were legitimate but also that all
copulations, polygamous or not, constituted permanent obli-
gations. Uproar! Blake commented on the King's Bench ruling
in *America* 15:19 (twelve years later); at the time he cannot
have been unaware of Madan's *Thelyphthora; or A Treatise on
Female Ruin*, sensationally reviewed. But Blake scholars
have been—not even aware that "thel" in Greek means woman
or female (if spelled with an eta), having noticed that
"thel" with an epsilon can mean will.
    Murray belatedly opens our minds to the "female ruin"
debate of the 1780s and skillfully reexamines, in its light,
the themes and ironies of *Thel* and *Visions.* (D.V.E.)

Pagliaro, Harold E. "Blake's 'Self-annihilation': Aspects of
Its Function in the *Songs*, with a Glance at Its History."
English 30 (1981): 117-46.

An extremely valuable discussion, both in redefining the
historical and psychological dimensions of the concept of
self-annihilation and in taking us minutely through the "con-
tinuous psychological process" represented in the *Songs of
Innocence* (part of the way) and *Songs of Experience* (more
completely). True, "it is not usual to think of the *Songs of
Experience* as primarily concerned with characters in the actual process of moving 'through' their vulnerability to death
and consequently of changing their way of seeing and the nature
of their being" (123-24). But Pagliaro's readings, particularly of "The Lilly," "A Poison Tree," and "The Tyger," are
meticulously developed and wholly convincing. How could
anyone have supposed that the speaker of "The Tyger" is
merely an average imaginative man? This critic's insight
derives from--or is evident in--his recognition that the
speaker's awe is real and deep, tellingly expressed, and
non-dismissable and that he is either Blake himself or
"a person of Blakean sensibility" (134). (D.V.E.)

Paley, Morton D. "A Victorian Blake Facsimile." *BIQ* 15 (1981):
24-27; illus.

The *Works* dated "1876" were published by Chatto and Windus
in 1878.

Pease, Donald. "Blake, Crane, Whitman, and Modernism: A Poetics
of Pure Possibility." *PMLA* 96 (1981): 64-85.

Milton is discussed in relation to the "modernist dilemma"
and Crane's attempt to resolve it.

Peterfreund, Stuart. "Blake and Newton: Argument as Art,
Argument as Science." *SECC* 10 (1981): 205-26.

Punter, David. "Blake and the Shapes of London." *Criticism*
23 (1981): 1-23.

Raine, Kathleen. *From Blake to A Vision.* (New Yeats Papers
17.) Dublin: The Dolmen Press; Atlantic Highlands, N.J.:
Humanities Press, 1979. Pp. 64. £4.50; $11.75 paper.

Rev. by Hazard Adams in *BIQ* 15 (1982): 187-88: "Raine
can accept much of Yeats's reading of Blake because her own
interpretive level is so lofty and abstract that she rarely
feels she must stoop to details of the text and never to
questions of tone.... Unfortunately, at Raine's level the
'wisdom' of Swedenborg, Blake, Yeats, and Jung is all one."

Read, Dennis M. "'An Eminent but Neglected Genius': An Early
    Frederick Tatham Letter about William Blake." ELN 19 (1981):
    29-33.

Riede, David G. "The Symbolism of the Loins in Blake's Jeru-
    salem." SEL 21 (1981): 547-63.

    Sets out to demonstrate, with quotations from the Bible
and the Church Fathers, the "typological" function of Blake's
genital imagery, "physical identity" leading upward to
"eternal truth." Some examples, such as the apocalyptic
rending of the veil, are corroborated by Blake's own meanings
as well as by tradition. Others, such as the pictorial
image from Jerusalem 58 (see p. 553), remain stubbornly
resistant to the "eternal truths" proposed.
    Riede sometimes misreads Blake, and his wholesale confla-
tions and condensations which yield the same reductive
meanings do violence to the complexities of the verse.
(I.H.C.)

Salemi, Joseph S. "Emblematic Tradition in Blake's The Gates
    of Paradise." BIQ 15 (1981): 108-24; 36 illus.

    A valuable "systematic study of the plates in relation
to emblematic motifs." (D.V.E.)

Sherry, Peggy Meyer. "The 'Predicament' of the Autograph:
    'William Blake.'" Glyph 4 (1978): 131-55.

    A deconstructionist reading of Blake's autograph in
William Upcott's album.

Singh, Charu Sheel. The Chariot of Fire: A Study of William
    Blake in the Light of Hindu Thought. (SSEL, Romantic Re-
    assessment 104.) University of Salzburg, Austria, 1981.
    Pp. iv+194. $12.50.

Stempel, Daniel. "Blake, Foucault, and the Classical Episteme."
    PMLA 96 (1981): 388-407.

    In an approach uncommon in Blake studies, Stempel examines
Blake's "discourse" according to Foucault's model for the
generation of the structures of classical texts. Ultimately
he finds a resolution of the "classical dilemma" in both
of Blake's arts: "Representation and being are one. Word
and image simultaneously create and reflect that discourse
which is the order of being."
    A dense, often difficult, but important essay. (I.H.C.)

Storch, Margaret. "Blake and Women: 'Nature's Cruel Holiness.'"
   AI 38 (1981): 221-46.

   "Women are benevolent only if they are under male domina-
   tion," concludes this study of Blake as a closet chauvinist
   beaten by his mother for his childhood visions--'tis pity.
   (T.L.A.)
   Based on serious misreadings of the finales of *Milton* and
   Jerusalem and on a psychological assumption that denies
   the possibility of social criticism, i.e., that what the
   poet describes as "the predicament of contemporary man" is
   primarily "his own mental condition" (241). Pity, indeed.
   (D.V.E.)

Summerfield, H. "Blake and the Names Divine." *BIQ* 15 (1981):
   14-22; illus.

   "Passing through non-dualism and a quasi-Gnosticism,"
   Blake "reaches his final position about 1800. Confronted
   with an apparent contradiction at the heart of this position, a grossly inconsistent use of the name Jehovah,
   critics have tended to be evasive or perfunctory." Summerfield dares to discover, finally, "a daring theology rooted
   in Boehme." (D.V.E.)

Summerfield, H. "Blake's *Pity*: An Interpretation." *CLQ* 17
   (1981): 34-38.

Vaughan, Frank A. "Blake's Illustrations to Gray's 'The Bard.'"
   CLQ 17 (1981): 211-37.

Welburn, Andrew J. "Blake's Cosmos: Sources and Transformations." *JEGP* 80 (1981): 39-53.

Westbrook, Mike. *Bright as Fire: Settings of William Blake.*
   Europa Records, Orlando, Fla., 1981. $8.98.

   Rev. by Anthony J. Harding in *BIQ* 15 (1981): 97-98.

Worrall, David. See *BRH* Blake Issue (above).

Wright, John. "Magnifying Blake's Books." Four-page exhibition pamphlet, 1981, available from the author at the University of Michigan, Ann Arbor.

   How we can create visions for ourselves by holding a
   glass to Blake's plates--as Blake himself may have done
   "if ... he anticipated by twenty years or more Wheatstone's
   discovery of similar effects and invention of the stereo-
   scope...."

See current issues of *Blake: An Illustrated Quarterly* for "minute particulars" not listed here.

See also Potts, Starobinski ("General 2. Environment"); Culler, Engell, Lobb ("General 3. Criticism"); Duncan, Neales, Pressly ("English 2. Environment"); Lenoski, Raine, Wesling ("English 3. Criticism").

Reviews of books previously listed:

DUNBAR, Pamela, *William Blake's Illustrations to the Poetry of Milton* (see *RMB* for 1980, p. 74), rev. by Michael Mason in *TLS*, Feb. 13, 1981, p. 169; by Marcia Pointon in *BM* 123 (May 1981): 313-14 as "a major contribution"; by Peter Quennell in *Apollo* 114 (1981): 136-37; ERDMAN, David V., John E. Grant, Edward J. Rose, and Michael J. Tolley, eds., *William Blake's Designs for Edward Young's Night Thoughts* (see *RMB* for 1980, p. 75), rev. by David Bindman in *BM* 123 (May 1981): 312-13, who finds some of the drawing "painfully inept" and is apprehensive that the promised commentary will deal "exhaustively with the minutiae of every single illustration"; by Andrew Lincoln, in *TLS*, June 5, 1981, p. 646; by Karen Mulhallen in *TWC* 12 (Summer 1981): 157-61 as "a major event in the history of art"; by Peter Quennell in *Apollo* 114 (1981): 136-37; by Daniel Traister in *ABC* (March-April 1981): 60-73 (with Robert Halsband's *The Rape of the Lock and Its Illustrations 1714-1896*, and studies of the art of E.H. Shepard, Rockwell Kent, and Maurice Sendak); FAIRCHILD, B.H., *Such Holy Song: Music as Idea, Form, and Image in the Poetry of William Blake* (see *RMB* for 1980, p. 76), rev. by Martha Winburn England in *SiR* 20 (1981): 545-49; by Stuart Peterfreund in *TWC* 12 (1981): 167-69; by James A. Winn in *BIQ* 15 (1981): 94-96; GALLANT, Christine, *Blake and the Assimilation of Chaos* (see *RMB* for 1979, p. 73), rev. by Anne K. Mellor in *JEGP* 78 (1979): 442-43; by James Swearingen in *Clio* 11 (1982): 209-11; GEORGE, Diana Hume, *Blake "and" Freud* (see *RMB* for 1980, p. 77), rev. by Alicia Ostriker in *TWC* 12 (1981): 161-64 as "gracious" and "free of jargon and polemic" yet "as full of controversial matter as a pie is of berries"; KLONSKY, Milton, *Blake's Dante* (see *RMB* for 1980, p. 79), rev. by Tom Phillips in *TLS*, Feb. 6, 1981, p. 169; KLONSKY, Milton, *William Blake: The Seer and His Visions* (see *ELN* 17, Supp., 49), rev. by Gerda S. Norvig in *BIQ* 15 (1982): 184-86; by Tom Phillips in *TLS*, Feb. 13, 1981, p. 169; RAINE, Kathleen, *Blake and the New Age* (see *RMB* for 1980, p. 81), rev. by Christine Gallant in *TWC* 12 (1981): 164-67

as distorting and "dated in ... fundamental ways"; by Martin
K. Nurmi in *BIQ* 15 (1981): 51-52 ("It seems to me very unfortunate that Raine feels she must deny Blake's originality
as much as she does"); by Julie Howe Stewart in *JR* 61 (1981):
445-47; SIMPSON, David, *Irony and Authority in Romantic
Poetry* (see *RMB* for 1980, p. 63), rev. by Gavin Edwards
in *BIQ* 15 (1982): 179-83 as "a splendid vindication of
theoretically informed and explicit textual analysis," yet
open to criticism.

Review articles:

Dörrbecker, Detlef W. "Fuseli, the Swiss, and the British:
Some Recent Publications." *BIQ* 15 (1981): 53-56.

Punter, David. "War and the Uses of War." *BIQ* 15 (1982): 189-
92.

A review essay based on the collection of *British War
Poetry in the Age of Romanticism: 1793-1815*, ed. Betty T.
Bennett (New York: Garland Publishing, 1976: see *ELN* 15,
Supp., 17).

An eloquent protest at the failure of historians and
literary critics to take war into account as "the major
constituent of experience" for most British people between
1793 and 1815. For instance, "it is the wars of the romantic age which provide ... a shape for those connections
between aggression and commerce which Blake makes so powerfully," and the war poetry which habitually made these
connections can provide "a constellation of popular writing
within which to situate his acts of mysterious demystification." The prevalent ideology generated "two separate
streams of imagery ... the French commit assault, the
British protect and nurture their colonies like offspring
or ... distant nieces." Blake himself "finds it very difficult ... to put this severed world together." There is
desire in *America*; a set of economic truths applied to
"Asia"; but *Europe* is "the most puzzling of geographies,
an apparent fairyland where, nonetheless, the displaced
sense of threat is a palpable absence. The land fit for
Englishmen to live in ... is a still point, at which change
can be forever avoided." (D.V.E.)

BURKE

Freeman, Michael. *Edmund Burke and the Critique of Political Radicalism*. University of Chicago Press, 1981. Pp. 250.

Rev. in *Inquiry*, March 30, 1981, pp. 26-27.
Unimpressive. (D.V.E.)

Janes, Regina. "Edmund Burke's Indian Idyll." *SECC* 9 (1980): 3-14.

"Like many other builders of utopias ... Burke does not want to live in his."

Troy, Frederick S. "Edmund Burke and the Break with Tradition: History vs. Psychohistory." *MR* 22 (1981): 93-132.

We need a biography of Burke. (R.A.B.)

See also Weaver ("English 2. Environment"); Ferguson ("English 3. Criticism"); Minnick and Dörrbecker ("Blake").

BYRON

Auld, William, trans. *Bajron: Don Juan*. Manchester: Esperantaj Kajeroj, 1979. Pp. 72. £2.00.

Rev. by Marjorie Boulton in *N&Q* 28 (1981): 85-86.
An Esperanto translation of Canto I only, called felicitous.

Burnett, T.A.J. *The Rise and Fall of a Regency Dandy: The Life and Times of Scrope Berdmore Davies*. London: John Murray, 1981. Pp. 256. £9.50.

Rev. by Doris Langley Moore ("Palmy Days in Piccadilly") in *TLS*, Sept. 25, 1981, p. 1094.

Byron Journal 9 (1981).

Reprints the articles by Clark, Kelsall, and Stürzl from the SSAA volume listed below under Stürzl. Contains also R.J. Dingley, "'I had a Dream....' Byron's 'Darkness'" (20-33), asserting that "there is more, however, to the opening of *Darkness* than a general statement about the equivocal nature of dreams"; Adeline R. Tintner, "Henry James and Byron: A Victorian Romantic Relationship" (52-63), an informed review of James's fascination with the Byron myth; John S. Gatton, "Portraits of a Doge: Delacroix's Reading of Byron's *Marino Faliero*" (74-84), a significant iconographical study that

makes a valuable contribution to studies of Romanticism;
Ian Scott-Kilvert, "Byron and Giorgione" (85-88), a note
on the reference in *Beppo*; Cedric Hentschel, "Unquiet Graves:
Allegra and Peachey" (89-92)--R.i.P.; and review notices
of recent SSEL volumes on Byron. (T.L.A.)

Clark, Irene Lurkis. "Byron's *Don Juan* and Moore's 'The Two
Penny Post-Bag.'" *N&Q* 28 (1981): 401-03.

  Two of Byron's squibs refer in a minor way. (T.L.A.)

Clubbe, John. *Byron's Natural Man: Daniel Boone & Kentucky*.
Lexington, Ky.: The King Library Press, 1980 [1982]. Pp.
vii+36. $60.00.

  A note in the form of an edition limited to 115 copies
for associates and friends of the University of Kentucky
libraries by Professor Clubbe, who teaches at the University.
Canto VIII: 60-68 of *Don Juan* is subject here, and careful
scholarship discovers the source of Byron's Boone in Frances
Wright's *Views of Society and Manners in America* (1821), given
to the poet by the artist West, who for the good fortune of
all was born in Lexington, Kentucky, as well. (T.L.A.)

de Almeida, Hermione. *Byron and Joyce through Homer: Don Juan
and Ulysses*. Columbia University Press, 1981. Pp. x+233.
$20.00.

  This is a daring book, and one which Byron--as the so-
called poet of the dare--would have appreciated. But for
critics of Byron's *Don Juan* (and this review deliberately
scants the work on Joyce) the valid perceptions here set
forth urgently require a context--*Don Juan in Context*, one
is tempted to say. Though McGann's work comes into the notes
in a minor way, the rethinking of Byron's epic there
occasioned makes no contribution. We are told that "also
the studies by George Ridenour and Robert Gleckner" help
out, but this is also a by-your-leave. Byron criticism in
this work means Boyd backed up by M.K. Joseph; just as the
author's sense of epic is largely from Brian Wilkie, and
of the meaning of Greek culture from Werner Jaeger. Montaigne and the continental tradition also make a contribution to the study of Byron. But it is the triad of Boyd,
Wilkie, and Jaeger that most frames the critical contribution made here, and it is the English side of Byron's epic
which is most scanted accordingly--and particularly by
complete omission of the influence of Scott. While this
approach succeeds in freeing the poem for fore-and-aft
analysis by means of comparison it is, I think, less than

faithful to Byron's own consciousness of purpose. As de
Almeida tells us: "My inquiry will examine whether Byron's
and Joyce's writing does indeed belong in one literary line ...
whether *Don Juan* and *Ulysses* might come close to being epic
equivalents, each functioning for the post-Kantian era in
much the same way as Homer's epics did for early Greek
civilization...." Whatever direct objection may be taken
by classicists to this statement, Byron critics will worry
about the necessities of forced comparison. In the end,
however, all is well: "One could say that it [*Don Juan*]
is to nineteenth-century Europe what *Tom Jones* is to eighteenth-century England: a mirror like a comedy, a voyage
like an epic.... One could even continue the formula and
add that *Ulysses* ... treating its content at once epically
and with mimicry, serves the twentieth century the same
way. This would not imply that the three counter-epics are
identical, but that they function congruently with regard
to the centuries which fostered them: as keys to the eras'
primary concerns, and ironical commentaries on the ages'
sentiments. *Yet even here the suggestive paralleling breaks
down* to highlight the problems inherent in placing influences,
distinguishing precedents, and marking periods" (167-68,
italics added). All to the good we will think, and we will
learn something of value: "Because of their function as the
consciences of the dispossessed world that followed Kant,
Don Juan and *Ulysses* must run composite tests to validate
their own contents, destroying much of the past as they
propose to summarize it, and remaining poised always to
fasten on or seize as exemplary whatever strains through
their layered debris" (174). This is to win a dare by losing
it, but in the course of the gamble de Almeida's approach
suffers a decline in methodology. First, we are told that
Byron learns from Montaigne, Rabelais, Ariosto, and the
comic-epic novelists from Cervantes through Sterne--this
misses Grierson's early work on *Don Juan* and *Don Quixote*
and does not remember that Byron called Scott "the Ariosto
of the North." Second, approach is early undercut by method
with the following claim: "He [Byron] may have been too
self-conscious to overtly call attention to the thicket of
Homeric parallels in his poem. But his signals are clear.
We cannot fall prey to the poet's ambivalence toward the
Greek's legendary influence and so miss his intention to
use Homer's wandering tale as his pattern for *Don Juan*.
Nor can we let the poet's parodic echoes of epic convention
blind us to the serious, intended, Odyssean parallels in
his poem. These latter, which will be shortly listed in de-

tail, signal distinctly enough Byron's epic intent in *Don Juan*—and his chosen model" (13). Now this is a question of who is preying on whom, and it raises a third objection for those who speculate that *Don Juan* will be wrenched both ways: "Having seen the sham of unnature and inhumanity that is society, having reached behind culture to nature, and beneath nature to a brutishness that undermines all, Byron and Joyce can see no further and nothing further" (113). Method here makes it seem that approach was all for nought, that Byron only copies Homer and does so to be a modern nihilist as Joyce is seen to be. This we may doubt, and it may be that de Almeida's own final doubts are virtuous—but "I leave the thing a mystery" for those to come. (T.L.A.)

Emerson, Sheila. "Byron's 'One Word': The Language of Self-Expression in *Childe Harold* III." *SiR* 20 (1981): 363-82.

"Byron's art may free expression from the circle of mortality, but it leaves the sting in language that recoils upon itself" is the conclusion of this well-thought-out study of Byron on Romanticism and the problem of language (which takes Rousseau and *Childe Harold* III as its twin centers). For Emerson the issue of words/things is central (as it was for Byron)—but she gets the key quotation from *Don Juan*, and (while correctly casting doubt on the Mirabeau attribution as Woodring did) she needs to find the earlier use and its implication in *Marino Faliero* discussed in *SiR* 13 (1974): 1-13. See Heinzelman below for another indication that Byron's thinking on the word will be important for future studies. (T.L.A.)

Founders Memorial Library. *Celebrating Our Millionth Volume: Poems on Various Occasions by George Gordon, Lord Byron.* Northern Illinois University, 1980. Pp. 24. "A Keepsake" (i.e., free while they last?).

Includes a facsimile of seven pages of *Poems* and an essay on its "Occasion" by Charles W. Hagleman, Jr.

Garber, Frederick. "The Energies of the Exotic in Byron and Delacroix." *Literature and the Other Arts.* (Proceedings of the 9th Congress of the International Comparative Literature Association, 3.) Innsbruck, 1979. Pp. 113-17; illus.

The point of Byron's *Oriental Tales* "is to create a context for the mind which is as rich, vital and deadly as the mind itself." The tonalities of Delacroix's exoticism "emerge, not from a rendering of the self-consuming mind but from a fascination with the amalgam of grace and fanaticism ... uniting classical poise and Romantic exuberance."

Garner, Stanton. "Lord Byron and Midshipman Chamier in Turkey."
    KSJ 30 (1981): 37-46.

    Investigates Frederick Chamier's *The Life of a Sailor*
(1832) for a memoir of Byron's three-month cruise (1810)
aboard the *Salsette* that shows the poet less than Byronic
as he swims the Hellespont imitating Leander. (T.L.A.)

Grant, Robert J. "La Bruyère and Young as Sources in *Don Juan*."
    N&Q 28 (1981): 399-401.

Heinzelman, Kurt. "Byron's Poetry of Politics: The Economic
    Basis of the 'Poetical Character.'" *TSLL* 23 (1981): 361-88.

    Heinzelman begins with a bravura application of the thesis
of his *The Economics of Imagination* (see *RMB* for 1979, p.
20) and gets caught by Byron in the process. The result is
an understanding that finds in Byron not simply the economi-
cally frustrated child/heir clinging to the mother at the
absent father's *expense*, but also a poet who could use an
economic metaphor with wit, subtlety, and both historical
and moral point--though Heinzelman is better on economics
than on political morality. Byron had Hanson and Zambelli
do a lot of his worrying--it's in the nature of aristocracy,
one may think. More important, this essay (see Emerson above)
falls under the spell of the "words are things" issue raised
in an earlier essay on "*Marino Faliero*: Byron's *Poetry* of
Politics," despite the fact that Heinzelman disregards
Woodring's discussion of the Mirabeau attribution while
elsewhere making use of *Politics in English Romantic Poetry*.
(T.L.A.)

Hogg, James, ed. *The Hannover Byron Symposium: 1979*. (SSEL,
    Romantic Reassessment, 80:2.) University of Salzburg,
    Austria, 1981. Pp. 197. $13.50.

    This I take to be the companion volume to *The Constance
Byron Symposium: 1977* (see *RMB* for 1979, p. 84) which is
number 80 in the continuing series. (But whether it's two
for one I can't ascertain.) Contents: Gerd Birkner, "The
Platonic Tradition and Literary Innovation in Byron's
Poetry" (3-22); Heide N. Rohloff, "The Disturbing Challenge
of Fact: Lord Byron and Romanticism" (23-116); Bernhard
Reitz, "'To die as honour dies'--Politics of the Day and
Romantic Understanding of History in Southey's, Shelley's
and Byron's Poems on Napoleon" (117-40); Armin Geraths,
"A Frog's Eye View of the Romantics: Clare and Byron as
Outcast Observers of Their Times" (141-64); Roger Hausheer,
"Byron and the Philosophical Foundations of the European

Romantic Revolt" (165-97). The Constance Byron Symposium
broke new ground for the *SSEL* series, making a valuable
contribution by introducing the work of new German scholars,
and of the last crop reviewed, only the German-authored
volume escaped the perils of Romantic Reassessment (which
can remind us of how Byron wants Assyrian pronounced in
Beppo). Of the Hannover Symposium, the critics are younger,
their English excellent and witty (though typographical
errors mar here and there), and their theme unified and
valuable--for with an exception this is a volume on Byron
and the philosophical currents of his day. In the Birkner
essay for Platonism read Shaftesbury then Whig then Byron:
"Shaftesbury's notion that the autonomy of the individual
grows out of a contemplation of nature which creates a consciousness of naturalness and entirety in the observer can
be distinguished from the intense, eruptive forms in which
Byron's subjectivity manifests itself.... At last Byron's
melancholy allows itself to be understood as the consequence
of the standard of self-sufficiency being now placed on the
experienced reality which should manifest itself in itself."
In Rohloff's work for Romanticism read Platonism then Lovejoy then Heraclitus then: "In fact, the peculiar issue which
prevents Byron from being tangled in hopeless contradictions ... lies in his indebtedness to the Heracleitan cos-
mology that, based upon a cyclic concept of change and
balance within the universe, was suited to unite and embrace
the different attitudes towards Nature and the ambivalence
existing in Nature herself." In the Reitz essay read from
politics to history to prophecy to Napoleon as fallen prophet:
"To call Shelley's understanding of history 'dialectical'
and Byron's 'historicistic" may seem an application of terms
which the poets themselves were never aware of. Though Hegel
was a contemporary of the poets, Shelley was not a follower
of his, and historical accuracy forbids calling Byron a
disciple of Ranke. But in spite of this the use of the
terms 'dialectical' and 'historicistic' seems justified.
What was to become after Hegel and Ranke the great opposition of the dialectical and the historicistic approach to
historical understanding was potentially present in the
Romantic period and had only to be given terminology." (This
is a very wise point that I regret having simplified in
summary.) Gerath's frog is really Clare who is here mostly
The Fool of Edward Bond's contemporary drama; but even here
the philosophical context emerges: "The step from Kant's
view to Hegel's view corresponds to the step in English
Romanticism from Wordsworth to Byron, from consonance to
dissonance." In Hausheer's work the *foundation* is Fichte

and then Max Weber and then: "'It is the fate of an entire cultural epoch, that has eaten of the Tree of Knowledge, to be compelled to recognize that we cannot read off the *meaning* of the world even from the most highly sophisticated results of our investigations of it; but rather that we must be in a position to create this meaning ourselves' ... these words of Max Weber's ... sum up the problem of an age, and, as I hope to show, might have been written especially to fit Byron." Whether or no these essays fit, their attempts are of value and interest. (T.L.A.)

Jones, Emrys. "Byron's Visions of Judgment." *MLR* 76 (1981): 1–19.

While good on Byron's footnotes and on Quevedo, the essay claims the first-time discovery of the relationship of Byron's satire to the Apocolocyntosis of Seneca (you will not learn here that this translates as the apotheosis of a pumpkin head): "As soon as one looks at Seneca's *Ludus* with Byron's *Vision* in mind, it seems inescapable that Byron must have known it and that, with whatever lack of conscious awareness, he used it for his own poem." This is all rather hard to take (and considering the journal it appears in), for as late as 1963, Gilbert Highet was telling his students to compare the works and had by then told others in print. Highet believed that Byron was fascinated by Seneca's joke about Claudius's palsy--his hand only stopped shaking when he gave the command for execution--but Highet himself could not document the connection which in fact can be documented when one is aware both of the continuing use of Seneca's work in models available to Byron, and of other scholarship. (T.L.A.)

Kirkland, Richard I., Jr. "Byron's Reading of Montaigne: A Leigh Hunt Letter." *KSJ* 30 (1981): 47–51.

The letter published in the *New Monthly Magazine* (Jan. and March numbers of 1827) entitled "Passages Marked in Montaigne's Essays by Lord Byron" is by Hunt and of definite interest. (T.L.A.)

Kushwaha, M.S. *Byron and the Dramatic Form.* (SSEL, Poetic Drama & Poetic Theory, 50.) University of Salzburg, Austria, 1980. Pp. xii+209. $13.50.

This year's laurel for Byron studies goes to Dr. Kushwaha, who has written a very intelligent and much needed study. Working abroad, he has still managed to keep abreast of current Byron scholarship; he writes with clarity and

humility, and what he writes is the most stimulating and
useful analysis of Byron's plays that has appeared since
Chew. His dedication to the memory of Ernest J. Lovell, Jr.
is fulfilled by the value of this study. First of all,
Kushwaha wants us to take Byron as a dramatist--not a poet
writing plays. Second, he knows almost everything about
English production in this time. Then he knows what was
actually put on the boards, and blessedly he does not scant
Byron's work at Drury Lane. For once and all time we suspect
that we are reading about a playwright called Byron. When it
comes to the plays themselves, the approach favors a graph-
ing of dramatic action that does help to expose Byron's
intent. One wishes that Kushwaha could tell us more about
Byron's theatrical experiences in Italy (Elledge was stronger
on this point), and sometimes his earnestness misses a
point: it is clear that Byron was thinking about *Marino
Faliero* in 1818, despite the two-year wait for composition
to begin. But this is an honest work, and--though it will
not be the last word on Byron's dramas--it is a fresh word
that teaches much. (T.L.A.)

Maner, Martin. "Pope, Byron, and the Satiric Persona." *SEL*
20 (Autumn 1980): 557-73.

Marchand, Leslie A., ed. *Byron's Letters & Journals*. Vol. XI:
Aug. 1, 1823-April 9, 1824. *For Freedom's Battle*. London:
John Murray; Harvard University Press, 1981. Pp. 243. $15.00.

  Rev. by Doris Langley Moore in *TLS*, April 24, 1981, pp.
453-54; by Peter Porter in *New Statesman*, June 5, 1981, pp.
22-23.
  Volume XII to follow will provide the comprehensive index
to Leslie Marchand's magnificent masterwork; so that Vol. XI
gives us Byron's last words. As well as the letters from the
Scrope Davies find, additions and corrections to earlier
volumes, and corrections of letters from Moore's *Life* are
given here--and alongside the normally included careful
biographical appendices that we have come to expect. In ten
years of current labor and a lifetime's scholarship, Marchand has added some 1700 letters to the 1198 of Prothero's
edition. The accomplishment is awesome--and the more so
because Marchand has not memorialized Byron, but humanized
his subject for all time. This is what we hear in the last
words of the last letter: "Of all these proceedings here,
health--politics--plans--acts and deeds--&c. good or otherwise Gamba or others will tell you--truly or not truly
according to their habits--"--*truly* indeed. (T.L.A.)
  Vols. IX and X rev. by Andrew Rutherford in *DUJ* 43 (1981):

143-44; Vol. IX by Frederick W. Shilstone in *SHR* 15 (1981):
79-81; Vol. X by Charles E. Robinson in *TWC* 12 (1981): 176-
77.

Ogle, Robert B. "The Metamorphosis of Selim: Ovidian Myth in
The Bride of Abydos II." *SiR* 20 (1981): 21-31.

A slow, extremely careful, and very valuable rethinking
of Gleckner's rich work on this tale, which adds much by
grounding Byron's work in the Hero and Leander myth out of
Ovid, in his swimming of the Hellespont, and in the hints
(they were *hints* from Horace) that Byron spread about for
scholars like Ogle who can tell us that Byron owned the
Sandys translation. Again what Woodring called the "palimp-
sest" of Byron's historical imagination (what I have called
casually the three-layered approach involving past, present,
and prophecy) is at work in this brilliant understanding
of Byron's consciousness. (T.L.A.)

Pritchard, William H. "Byronic Epistles." *HudR* 34 (1981):
569-78.

Pritchard's summary review of Marchand's *Byron's Letters
& Journals* (through Vol. XI) is delicately premised: "But
enough plaudits have been handed Mr. Marchand's beautifully
engineered editorial operation to make it unnecessary for
a non-Byron scholar like me to add mine; I should like instead to share my sense of the letters as expressions of
the masterful personality of their author." The preference
is for Byron on his own poems and other authors, with
neglect of the sticky realities of political aphorism.
(T.L.A.)

Rapf, Joanna E. "The Byronic Heroine: Incest and the Creative
Process." *SEL* 21 (1981): 637-45.

This essay takes Erica Jong's decision to preface *Fear of
Flying* with stanzas from *Don Juan* as a starting point,
passes into a review of Byron's heroines, and turns at last
to Byron's poetic and an insightful conclusion: "If Byron
comes down to us today as a male chauvinist, disdainful of
women who do mathematics and write novels, it should only
remind us again of the complexity of human psychology and
of the fact that the ideal and the real rarely, if ever,
meet in our non-edenic world." Of course reality here comes
to sound very much like a political decision--and Rapf
needs to check her sources against *RMB* on occasion. (T.L.A.)

Stürzl, Erwin A., and James Hogg, eds. *Byron: Poetry and Politics.* (SSAA [Salzburger Studien zur Anglistik und Amerikanistik], 13.) University of Salzburg, Austria, 1981. Pp. x+427. $18.50.

Being the proceedings of the Seventh International Byron Symposium, Salzburg, 1980, and the contents can only be called mouthwatering: "Byron & the *Republic*: The Platonic Background to Byron's Political Ideas" by Bernard Blackstone; "Aspects of the Myth of Natural Liberty in Byron's Poetry" by Ernest Giddey; "Byron's Idea of Democracy: An Investigation into the Relationship Between Literature and Politics" by Jurgen Klein; "Byron and the Poets of the Austrian Vormarz" by Erwin A. Stürzl; "Byron's Politics and the History Plays" by D.M. de Silva; "The Byronic Hero and the Revolution in Ireland: The Politics of *Glenarvon*" by Malcolm Kelsall; "Political Choices: *The Prophecy of Dante* and *Werner*" by J. Drummond Bone; "Casti's *Animali Parlanti*, the Italian Epic and *Don Juan*: The Poetry of Politics" by P.G. Vassallo; "Tales and Politics: *The Corsair, Lara,* and *The White Doe of Rylstone*" by Peter J. Manning; "Strange Political Bedfellows: Inkel and Wordswords [sic] in Iberia" by Gordon K. Thomas; "'The Politics of Paradise,' 'Transcendental Cosmopolitics,' and Plain Politics in Byron's *Cain* and Keats's *Hyperion*" by Wolf Z. Hirst; "Charles Baudelaire: Facets of Byron's French Legacy" by Philip F. Clark; "Poe's Vote for Byron: The Problem of Its Duration" by Katrina E. Bachinger; "Truth-Telling as Politics: Byron and Pound" by John Lauber; "*Beppo*: A Caricature of Utopia" by Koichi Yakushigawa; "Byron's Theatre: Private Spleen, or Cosmic Revolt: Theatrical Solutions--Stanislavsky to Grotowski" (note the fashionable double-colon title) by Boleslaw Taborski; and the last word: "Byron's Vacillating Attitude Towards Napoleon" by James Hogg. All of which point to the missing article, please indulge your reviewer's fancy--he typed this out remember, "Byron as Frankenstein's Monster: A Deconstructionist Approach" by M.R. Kurtz. Too late for inclusion, we may expect this next year. Of the seventeen essays included, the influence studies (the Vormarz school, Casti, Baudelaire, Poe, and Pound) are uniformly interesting and each better on the non-Byron side of the equation with Lauber's the best. Taborski's essay on dramatic method is more than useful--in some ways it is an influence study that will stimulate further work. Hogg is very useful for his synthesizing collations. Yakushigawa is sensitive about *Beppo* (which he has well in hand), but I find Patricia Ball (nowhere cited in the volume) better and in advance here. Hirst is better on Keats than on Byron--but his sense

of philosophic parallels is rich. It is a bit of a surprise
to find Manning so good on Wordsworth, and his reminders of
what else was being written at the time of Byron's poems are
extremely necessary. Kelsall's argument on *Glenarvon* knows
its Irish politics, but the novel is a morass that fails
to support. Bone and de Silva disappoint: the first is perceptive but short, the second long and somewhat dated. That
leaves us with Blackstone, Giddey, and Klein as the spine
of the volume's understanding of Byron's politics. Blackstone is the most perceptive, particularly because he distinguishes politics and justice—following Godwin—though he
is concerned with the Greek ideal state. Klein is very strong
on the relation of the democratic ideal and republican
society, making discriminations that Byron made himself.
Giddey does a good job grounding Byron's politics in poetic
imagery. But there are lapses in the volume as a whole:
Scott, Crane Brinton, Mme de Staël, Drinkwater, and the
Countess of Oxford were apt students and shapers of Byron's
politics (let me not forget Alfieri) and none come into
play in this volume. Some years ago, I called an essay on
Marino Faliero "Byron's '*Poetry* of politics'" (*Letters &
Journals*, V, 205), and while I find it strange that this
phrase from the letters is not reprinted here (nor do we
learn if the phrase is the source of the volume's title), the
important point has to do with what Byron meant by his stressed
"*Poetry*." Blackstone correctly points out that Byron distinguishes poetry and politics in an early letter, and we may
also remember his insistence that *Marino Faliero* is not
political. He claimed that the play was *historical* ("read
the history and judge"), and his "*Poetry*" in its context
clearly means *revolution*. What this volume needs to tell us
is the nature of the structure by which contemporary politics manifest historical revolution. (T.L.A.)

Trueblood, Paul G., ed. *Byron's Political and Cultural In-
    fluence in Nineteenth-Century Europe: A Symposium.* Atlantic
    Highlands, N.J.: Humanities Press; London: Macmillan, 1981.
    Pp. xx+210. $30.00; £15.00.

    Rev. by Doris Langley Moore in *TLS*, April 24, 1981, pp.
    453-54.
    Not seen.

Tyne, James L. "Terrestrial and Transcendental Man as Viewed
    by Swift and Byron." *EnlE* 8 (1977): 22-37.

    "Swift's lopsided depiction of man's amphibian nature is
    undeniably far more memorable than Byron's, but because
    the latter pays almost equal attention to man's 'Promethean

spark' and to his pedestrian 'clay,' his portrayal of a
complex humanity is invariably a kinder and a more finely
balanced one than the Dean's"--concludes this study of what
is called the Rabelaisian connection. (T.L.A.)

Watkins, Daniel P. "Violence, Class Consciousness, and Ideology
in Byron's History Plays." *ELH* 48 (1981): 799-816.

See also Garber, Hammond, Lobb ("General 3. Criticism");
Wellens ("English 1. Bibliography"); Harvey, Hogg, Twitchell
("English 3. Criticism"); Zoberman ("French 2. Mérimée");
Heinrich-Heine-Institut, Düsseldorf, ed. ("German 3. Heine");
Bourke ("German 3. Hoffmann").

Reviews of books previously listed:

LESSENICH, Rolf P., *Lord Byron and the Nature of Man* (see
RMB for 1980, p. 88), rev. by Ian Scott-Kilvert in *YES* 11
(1981): 306-07; MANNING, Peter, *Byron and His Fictions*
(see *ELN* 17, Supp., 72), rev. by Angus Easson in *N&Q* 28
(1981): 266-68; by Frederick W. Shilstone in *CP* 14 (1981):
75-78; by Leon Waldoff in *JEGP* 80 (1981): 144-47; McGANN,
Jerome J., ed., *Lord Byron: The Complete Poetical Works*,
Vol. I (see *RMB* for 1980, p. 89), rev. by W.R. in *CritQ*
23 (1981): 92-93; by Lorna Sage in *TLS*, Jan. 23, 1981,
pp. 71-72; Vols. I and II rev. by Alice Levine in *TWC* 12
(1981): 178-80.

CARLYLE

Bell, Alan. "Thomas Carlyle and the London Library." *TLS*,
May 29, 1981, pp. 611-12.

DeBruyn, John. "Thomas Carlyle and Sir Arthur Helps." *BJRL*
64 (1981): 61-86.

Hafter, Monroe Z. "Heroism in Alas and Carlyle's *On Heroes*."
MLN 95 (1980): 312-34.

The influence of Carlyle's *Heroes* lecture series on
Leopoldo Alas.

King, Margaret F., and Elliot Engel. "The Emerging Carlylean
Hero in Bulwer's Novels of the 1830s." *NCF* 36 (1981): 277-
95.

Mattheisen, Paul F. "Tennyson and Carlyle: A Source for 'The Eagle.'" *VN* 60 (1981): 1-3.

  Book III of *Sartor Resartus* contributes to Tennyson's verse fragment.

Sonstroem, David. "The Double Vortex in Carlyle's *On Heroes and Hero Worship*." *PQ* 59 (1980): 531-40.

Stein, Richard L. "Midas and the Bell-Jar: Carlyle's Poetics of History." *VN* 58 (1980): 5-9.

  "Carlyle works in a symbolic mode, plumbing surfaces for latent meanings, physical facts for metaphysical patterns. It is a method clearly poetic, dealing in what Hayden White has recently termed 'metahistory,'" concludes this useful reminder that White wrote in 1973 about what Byron and Scott had in mind 150 years earlier. (T.L.A.)

Sussman, Herbart. *Fact into Figure: Typology in Carlyle, Ruskin, and the Pre-Raphaelite Brotherhood*. Ohio State University Press, 1979. Pp. xix+158. $11.00.

  Rev. by Florence S. Boos in *VS* 24 (1981): 375-76. Not seen.

Tarr, Roger L., ed. "'The Guises': Thomas Carlyle's Lost Renaissance History." *VS* 25 (1981): 7-80.

  A project abandoned in 1855, carefully edited from the manuscript and published here for the first time. The editor's introduction goes to p. 12; the rest is Carlyle. The manuscript has been edited not only *verbatim* but *literatim* as well, and preserves all the revisions and corrections and crossed-out portions, so that it is very hard to read, though useful to study. Carlyleans will love it, and others will ask to be excused. (B.C.H.)

Trevor-Roper, Hugh. "Thomas Carlyle's Historical Philosophy." *TLS*, June 26, 1981, pp. 731-34.

Weaver, Frederick Stirton. "Thomas Carlyle on Dr. Francia: The Functional Role of the Carlylean Hero." *I&L* 3 (1980): 105-15.

See also Arac ("General 3. Criticism"); Bell ("English 1. Bibliography"); Green ("English 3. Criticism"); Kuczynski ("German 2. General").

Reviews of books previously listed:

SANDERS, Charles Richard, *Carlyle's Friendships and Other Studies* (see *ELN* 17, Supp., 77), rev. by Peter Morgen in *ES* 62 (1981): 84-85; SANDERS, C.R., and K.J. Fielding, eds., *The Collected Letters of Thomas and Jane Welsh Carlyle*, Vols. 8-9 (see *RMB* for 1980, p. 92), rev. by A.J.S. in *CritQ* 23 (1981): 94.

CLARE

Dendurent, H.O. *John Clare: A Reference Guide*. Boston: G.K. Hall & Co., 1978. Pp. xiv+136.

  Rev. by John Barrell in *RES* 32 (1981): 114-15.

Neumeyer, Peter. *Homage to John Clare: A Poetical and Critical Correspondence*. Salt Lake City: Peregrine Smith, Inc., 1979. Pp. x+91. $5.95.

  Rev. by L.J. Swingle in *WHR* 35 (1981): 293-95.

COLERIDGE

Avni, Abraham. "Coleridge and Ecclesiastes: A Wary Response." *TWC* 12 (1981): 127-29.

Bentley, G.E., Jr. "Coleridge, Stothard, and the First Illustration of 'Christabel.'" *SiR* 20 (1981): 111-16.

Bernstein, Gene. "The Recreating Secondary Imagination in Coleridge's 'The Nightingale.'" *ELH* 48 (1981): 339-50.

  "Deconstruction" by the secondary imagination of conventional nature imagery and the literary and mythological tradition; recreation through Coleridge's direct experience of nature and the transformation of Hartley's tears into joy. The child's "sense of wonder" is the "recreative genius" in the poet.

Blackstone, B. "A Koranic Echo in *The Ancient Mariner*?" *N&Q* 28 (1981): 313.

Coen, Rena N. "Cole, Coleridge and Kubla Khan." *Art History* 3 (1980): 218-28.

  The influence of Coleridge's poetry on Thomas Cole's painting.

Coleman, Deirdre. "A Horrid Tale in *The Friend*." *TWC* 12 (1981): 262-69.

Corrigan, Timothy J. "Coleridge, the Reader: Language in a Combustible Mind." *PQ* 59 (1980): 76-94.

On Coleridge's use of different languages as "subtle but powerful coding systems to determine what and for whom literature means."

Dingley, R.J. "Coleridge and the 'frightful fiend.'" *N&Q* 28 (1981): 313-14.

Gill, Richard. "'The Rime of the Ancient Mariner' and 'Crime and Punishment': Existential Parables." *P&L* 5 (1981): 131-49.

Harris, Wendell V. *The Omnipresent Debate: Empiricism and Transcendentalism in Nineteenth-Century Prose*. Northern Illinois University Press, 1981. Pp. ix+369. $22.50.

Harris takes on the formidable task of exploring "the philosophical implications" of the "modes of thought" of Samuel Taylor Coleridge and James Mill "as they extend into practical issues." Taking an approach different from that of most Coleridge scholars (among them Appleyard, Barfield, and Jackson) Harris seeks to investigate Coleridge's distinction between Reason and Understanding, concluding that Carlyle was correct when he said that the distinction amounts "to the sublime secret of believing by the reason what the understanding has been obliged to throw out as incredible" (46).

While Harris lists the new *Collected Works of Samuel Taylor Coleridge* under the general editorship of Kathleen Coburn, his footnotes cite the 1853 *Complete Works* edited by W.G.T. Shedd. I question whether Harris has profited from the recent scholarship on Coleridge. Also, I am dismayed by the major typo on p. 79 which quotes "repetition in the infinite [sic] mind of the eternal act of creation in the Infinite I AM."

Harris's expertise and sympathy seem to this reviewer to be on the side of the empiricists. (J.M.D.)

Havens, Michael Kent. "Coleridge on the Evolution of Language." *SiR* 20 (1981): 163-83.

"Coleridge ... treats language as the prime witness to the historical evolution of consciousness."

Jackson, J.R. de J., ed. *Logic*. (The Collected Works of Samuel
Taylor Coleridge, 13.) (Bollingen Series 75.) London: Routledge & Kegan Paul; Princeton University Press, 1981. Pp.
lxvii+420; 4 illus. $32.50.

This is the first complete publication of one of Coleridge's
least-known works, from a manuscript which after his death
was sequestered by his disciple Joseph Henry Green and during
the later nineteenth century changed hands three times without being associated with its true author. Although from a
philosophical standpoint the *Logic* is said to be "essentially
a popularization of [Kant's] *Critique of Pure Reason*," some
passages of which are translated without alteration, Coleridge himself intended it to be of practical use to young
men preparing for "the bar, the pulpit, and the senate."
(The manuscript was written by two such young men, Coleridge's
private students during the 1820s, who served as his amanu-
enses.) His concern with the psychology of language should
be of special interest to present-day readers. As so often,
his motives for joining the linguistic and epistemological
debates of his day were theological.
The standard of editing in the Collected Coleridge continues to be high. In addition to his Introduction and the
usual Chronological Table, Jackson includes other relevant
manuscript material in a series of appendixes and concludes
with a helpful Analytical Outline of Coleridge's main arguments. (I.H.C.)

Korn, Frederick. "An Unreported Poem by S.T. Coleridge." *N&Q*
28 (1981): 310-13.

"The Teacher's Office," printed some time in the nineteenth century and apparently genuine, but never reprinted
in any of the standard editions and thus unknown. It is long
(44 lines) and very bad, but it has its unintentional moments,
like the teacher's prayer at the opening: "Ask for an understanding heart, to rule in godly fear/ The feeble flock of
which the Lord hath made thee overseer." The surviving printed
copy was discovered at Florida State University. (B.C.H.)

Levere, Trevor H. *Poetry Realized in Nature: Samuel Taylor
Coleridge and Early Nineteenth-Century Science*. Cambridge
University Press, 1981. Pp. 271. $39.95.

To be reviewed next year.

Little, Geoffrey, and Elizabeth Hall. "Coleridge's 'To the
Rev. W.L. Bowles': Another Version?" *RES* 32 (1981): 193-96.

McGann, Jerome J. "The Meaning of 'The Ancient Mariner.'"
    CritI 8 (1981): 35-67.

As a result of the addition of the gloss in 1817, "The
Ancient Mariner" became an "imitation of a culturally re-
dacted literary work," as in theories of the ballad and the
Higher Criticism. Coleridge's readers continued the process
of textual evolution by interpretations according to their
"specific cultural views." McGann, however, does not pursue
the analogy more fully, from the relative to the progressive.
In effect, he would freeze the meaning of the poem (as
"religious," "Christian," "redemptive") at the level of
interpretation reached in the later nineteenth century.
The anxiety of influence is invoked to account for dissenting
readings since then; Coleridge's own interpretations are
dismissed as "special" and "peculiar" to him; the names
of Robert Penn Warren, Maud Bodkin, and even John Livingston
Lowes are never mentioned. The most glaring omission is
that of the very existence of the Latin epigraph from Thomas
Burnet, which was added at the same time as the gloss and
which from its authoritative position at the head of the
poem warns of ambiguity and the danger of error. (See the
essay by this reviewer in *SiR* 4 [1965]: 81-103.)

McGann's aim is to deliver the "Mariner" from hermeneutics
to history (p. 67). Because it does not confront but merely
evades the "antithetical" evidence of the epigraph and the
questions of more than one kind which that raises, his vale-
diction here is both incomplete and premature. (I.H.C.)

Milton, Mary Lee Taylor. *The Poetry of Samuel Taylor Coleridge:
    An Annotated Bibliography of Criticism, 1935-1970.* New York:
    Garland Publishing, 1981. Pp. xix+251. $30.00.

A full, chronologically arranged bibliography of all
items in English commenting on Coleridge's poetry that
appeared in print between 1935 and 1970. The argument of
each article is neatly abstracted in a few sentences or so.
Books devoted to Coleridge's poetry receive proportionately
longer entries, which are uniformly clear and informative.
A welcome addition to the bibliography is the introductory
section, "Major Issues in Coleridge Criticism," comprising
essays on "The Ancient Mariner," "Kubla Khan," and "Christabel" that organize the criticism of each poem according
to recurrent interpretive problems and orientations. There
is an index of authors and an index of poems with topical
subdivisions. (J.C.C.)

Peterfreund, Stuart. "Coleridge and the Politics of Critical
    Vision." *SEL* 21 (1981): 586-604.

    "The very critical endeavour undertaken by Coleridge, both
    in the poetry and the prose, is to keep the critical vision
    in a position of parity with, or priority to, the political
    vision," by focusing on "operant, procedural systems of
    truth."

Pierce, Donald. "'Kubla Khan' in Context." *SEL* 21 (1981):
    565-83.

    The "context" is broadly autobiographical: the landscape
    around Ottery St. Mary, the night Coleridge spent outdoors
    at the age of eight, and his reading (here, Purchas and
    Andrew Baxter).

Pradham, S.V. "Pleasure from the Activity of One's Own Mind:
    Coleridge's *Marginalia*." *DR* (Spring 1981): 143-53.

Roe, Nicholas. "Robespierre's Despotism and a Word Coined by
    Coleridge." *N&Q* 28 (1981): 309-10.

    He coined "to despotize" in 1794, five years earlier than
    the *OED* says he did.

Sitterson, Joseph C. "'Unmeaning Miracles' in 'The Rime of
    the Ancient Mariner.'" *SAR* 46 (1981): 16-26.

    The poem's supernatural machinery, especially in parts
    five and six, deliberately invites and frustrates allegorical
    interpretation, in order to emphasize the mystery at the
    heart of reality.

Sultana, Donald, ed. *New Approaches to Coleridge: Biographical
    and Critical Essays*. London: Vision Press, 1981. Pp. 246.
    £12.95.

    Brief review by A.N. Wilson in *TLS*, March 27, 1981, p.
    358.
    Papers by Alethea Hayter on the rejection of *Zapolya* and
    Coleridge's relation to Maturin; by Geoffrey Carnall on
    Coleridge as a comic figure in Hazlitt's essays; by Eric
    Anderson on his friendship with Scott; by Marion Lochhead
    on Coleridge and Lockhart; by Margo von Romberg on Cole-
    ridge and Frere's Aristophanes; by Kathleen Wheeler on his
    friendship with Tieck; and "an extremely erudite essay"
    by Sultana on "Coleridge's Political Papers in Malta."
    Not seen.

Tapscott, Stephen. "Pandemonium in Xanadu." *RP&P* 5,ii (1981):
23-40.

   Numerous antecedents of *Kubla Khan* in *Paradise Lost*.

Wallace, C. Miles. "Coleridge's Theory of Language." *PQ* 59
(1980): 339-52.

   An exploration of the theory in the perspectives of
   psychology and metaphysics, through its "practical applications," and in Coleridge's discussions of logic, poetry,
   and symbolism. "The extraordinary interrelatedness of all
   things so often celebrated in Coleridge's poetry and his
   prose proclaims exactly that idea inherent in his linguistics:
   the One Life within us and abroad."

Wallace, C.M. "The Function of Autobiography in *Biographia
Literaria*." *TWC* 12 (1981): 216-25.

Wellens, Oskar. "A Coleridgean Borrowing from the *Critical
Review*?" *N&Q* 28 (1981): 308-09.

Zall, P.M. "The Cool World of Samuel Taylor Coleridge: Charles
Mackay Visits Samuel Rogers and William Wordsworth." *TWC*
12 (1981): 113-15.

Zall, P.M. "The Cool World of Samuel Taylor Coleridge:
Elizabeth Inchbald; or, Sex & Sensibility." *TWC* 12 (1981):
270-73.

See also Engell, Grady, Hammond, Lobb, Reed ("General 3.
   Criticism"); Wellens ("English 1. Bibliography"); Reardon
   ("English 2. Environment"); Buckler, Havens, Hogg, McFarland,
   Troy, Twitchell ("English 3. Criticism"); Hayden, Newlyn
   ("Wordsworth"); Wieden ("German 3. Schiller").

Reviews of books previously listed:

   COBURN, Kathleen, *Experience into Thought: Perspectives
   in the Coleridge Notebooks* (see *RMB* for 1980, p. 94), rev.
   by Laurence S. Lockridge in *TWC* 12 (1981): 148-49; by Mary
   Wedd in *ChLB* 35 (1981): 62-64; COOKE, Katherine, *Coleridge*
   (see *RMB* for 1979, p. 91), rev. by Keith Hanley in *CritQ*
   23 (1981): 88; by K.M. Wheeler in *RES* 32 (1981): 341-42;
   CRAWFORD, Walter B., ed., *Reading Coleridge* (see *RMB* for
   1979, p. 91), rev. by C.R.W. in *ChLB* 36 (Oct. 1981): 81-12;
   DEKKER, George, *Coleridge and the Literature of Sensibility*
   (see *ELN* 17, Supp., 79), rev. by J.R. de J. Jackson in *ECS*

(Fall 1981): 97-99; EVEREST, Kelvin, *Coleridge's Secret Ministry: The Context of the Conversation Poems, 1795-1798* (see *RMB* for 1980, p. 95), rev. by W.J.B. Owen in *RES* 32 (1981): 233-35; HILL, John Spencer, ed., *Imagination in Coleridge* (see *ELN* 17, Supp., 80), rev. by George Dekker in *YES* 11 (1981): 302-03; KESSLER, Edward, *Coleridge's Metaphors of Being* (see *RMB* for 1979, p. 93), rev. by Daniel P. Deneau in *SHR* 15 (1981): 78-79; by Paul Magnuson in *SiR* 20 (1981): 121-26; LOCKRIDGE, Laurence S., *Coleridge the Moralist* (see *ELN* 16, Supp., 58), rev. by Alan Brinkley in *BPhilos* 27 (1980): 246; by Paulino Lim, Jr., in *ES* 62 (1981): 390-91; PYM, David, *The Religious Thought of Samuel Taylor Coleridge* (see *RMB* for 1979, p. 94), rev. by Stephen Prickett in *YES* 11 (1980): 303-04.

CRABBE

Bareham, T., and S. Gatrell. *A Bibliography of George Crabbe.* Hamden, Conn.: Archon Books/Shoe String Press, 1978. Pp. vii+194.

Rev. by A.J. Sambrook in *YES* 11 (1981): 288-90.

McGann, Jerome J. "The Anachronism of George Crabbe." *ELH* 48 (1981): 555-72.

Wade, Michael. "Object as Image in Crabbe's Portrait of Catherine Lloyd." *FMLS* 17 (1981): 337-50.

"... while avoiding the trap of a sentimental condone-ment, we feel that 'charitable sympathy' which has been impressed upon us by the creative rigour with which Crabbe's objects have been given the power of imagery...." An instructive explication that suggests we are to balance satiric and sympathetic responses. (J.C.R.)

DARLEY

Cooper, Robyn. "The Growth of Interest in Early Italian Painting in Britain: George Darley and the *Athenaeum*, 1834-1846." *JWCI* 43 (1980): 201-20; 5 illus.

The influence of Darley's art reviews and art criticism.

DE QUINCEY

Lindop, Grevel. *The Opium-Eater: A Life of Thomas DeQuincey*. London: Dent, 1981. Pp. 433. £12.00.

   Rev. by Duncan Fallowell in *S*, Aug. 8, 1981, pp. 18-19; by Lorna Sage in *Observer Review*, July 26, 1981, p. 28, as a story told by Lindop with patience and tact.

See also Reed ("General 3. Criticism").

Review of book previously listed:

   DENDURENT, H.O., *Thomas De Quincey: A Reference Guide* (see *RMB* for 1979, p. 99), rev. by Stuart M. Tave in *YES* 11 (1981): 305-06.

EDGEWORTH

See Kelly ("Opie").

GALT

MacGillivray, Alan. "Galt in the Schools." *SLJ* 7 (1980): supp. 13, pp. 62-73.

   Useful for those wishing to teach Galt. (T.L.A.)

Scottish Literary Journal. All Galt Number. *SLJ* 8,i (1981): 1-68.

   Ian A. Gordon, "Galt and Constable: Two New Galt Attributions" (5-9) identifies two essays in the *Edinburgh Gazetteer* (1822) with manuscript evidence and skill; in Keith A. Costain, "The Community of Man: Galt and Eighteenth-Century Scottish Realism" (10-29) Stewart, Smith, Reid, and Hutcheson lead to the valid conclusion: "Galt's own fiction exemplifies his belief that art must deal with the empirically observed 'living and local of the actual world,' and thus it emphasizes man's social nature"; J.D. McClure, "The Language of *The Entail*" (30-51) is not about linguistics but about dialect and its relationship with theme: "By the concluding chapters of *The Entail*, the world which Galt represents by English speech has supervened, and the other is increasingly remote and strange. That nearly all the Scots-speaking characters in the book are dead by this

stage is not accidental, but is a deliberate device to
suggest the passing of a way of life; and if it results
in the loss of the novel's most interesting and attractive
figures, there is no help for this. Galt is ... trapped
by his own linguistic symbolism"; finally, Patricia J.
Wilson, "*Ringan Gilhaize*: The Product of an Informing Vision"
(52-68) uses Galt's nonfiction to explode intentional
fallacy in approaches to the novels. (T.L.A.)

Whatley, Christopher A., ed. *John Galt: 1779-1979*. Edinburgh:
Ramsay Head, 1980. Pp. 212. £6.25.

   Rev. by Henri Gibault in *SLJ* 8 (1981): supp. 15, pp. 113-
16.
   This is a useful point of departure for major reassessment; the critics are: Chitnis, Whatley, Ward, Simpson,
Campbell, MacQueen, Wilson, Costain, McClure. (T.L.A.)

GODWIN

Myers, Mitzi. "Godwin's *Memoirs* of Wollstonecraft: The Shaping
of Self and Subject." *SiR* 20 (1981): 299-316.

   Argues that "Godwin's memoir is an unusual hybrid, one
which unites Wollstonecraft's notion of herself, Godwin's
reading of her character, and his analysis of that character's impact on himself and his philosophy. Moreover, these
variant species of life-writing mesh within a narrative
framework structured both by Godwin's basic philosophical
assumptions and his proclivities for romantic fiction."

Tysdahl, B.J. *William Godwin as Novelist*. Atlantic Highlands,
N.J.: Humanities Press, 1981. Pp. 205.

   A brief but workmanlike account, noting how carefully
Godwin considered narrative techniques that would reinforce
his political philosophy; how manfully he struggled against
novel structures that could undermine his social criticism;
noting also the inner personal struggle between the Calvin-
ist and the atheist, "a tension ... richly reflected in the
novels."
   On the whole, a valuable survey, though sometimes Tysdahl
runs too fast to notice significant overtones. For example,
he points out Godwin's skill with the epistolary genre,
in *Italian Letters*, noticing the self-revelation of "the
poor lover" writing to his "amiable Mathilda"--but over-
looking the cool wit of her reply, which should be a classic
putdown of male condescension, surely not unintended by the
author.

Tysdahl offers several well-pointed comparisons between
Godwin's imaginative writing and the novels, and poems, of
contemporaries and followers. Discussing *Caleb Williams* as
written in the 1790s, a time of "flux" which "did not provide any firm basis for long narratives," he notes the
better fortune of Wordsworth and Coleridge, some of whose
"best poems can be read as responses to challenging changes
in the intellectual climate" (73).

Damon and Delia, Godwin's first novel but only discovered
late in 1978, is given a postscript chapter. (D.V.E.)

See also Hammond, Novak ("English 3. Criticism").

Reviews of book previously listed:

LOCKE, Don, *A Fantasy of Reason: The Life and Thought of
William Godwin* (see *RMB* for 1980, p. 102), rev. by Betty T.
Bennett in *SiR* 21 (1982): 110-13; by Winifred F. Courtney
in *ChLB* 33 (1981): 17-19 with deservedly high praise; by
Burton R. Pollin in *KSJ* 30 (1981): 213-16 with errata and
praise.

THE GOTHIC NOVEL

Frank, Frederick S. "Polarized Gothic: An Annotated Bibliography of Poe's 'Narrative of Arthur Gordon Pym.'" *BB* 3
(July-Sept. 1981): 117-27.

Hennelly, Mark M., Jr. "*Melmoth the Wanderer* and Gothic
Existentialism." *SEL* 21 (1981): 665-79.

MacAndrew, Elizabeth. *The Gothic Tradition in Fiction*. Columbia
University Press, 1979. Pp. 289. $18.50.

Rev. by Coral Ann Howells in *English* 30 (1981): 185-90;
by Robert Lance Snyder in *SAR* 46 (1981): 97-101; by G.R.
Thompson in *MFS* (Winter 1980-81): 714-19.

Paulson, Ronald. "Gothic Fiction and the French Revolution."
ELH 48 (1981): 532-54.

In the 1790s the Gothic served as "a metaphor with which
some contemporaries in England tried to come to terms with
what was happening across the Channel." Section headings
indicate the topics covered: "Rebel/Tyrant"; "Crowd and
Cabal"; "Sentimental Response and Sexual Energy"; "The
Retrospect of Frankenstein."

Saliba, David R. *A Psychology of Fear: The Nightmare Formula of Edgar Allan Poe.*

> Rev. by Howard Kerr in *SSF* 4 (Fall 1981): 473-74.

See also Feder, Garber, Weber ("General 3. Criticism");
   Aers, Twitchell ("English 3. Criticism"); Wilt ("Austen").

Composite review:

Martin, Stoddard. *TLS*, Sept. 18, 1981, p. 1077.

> Reviews *An Edgar Allan Poe Companion*, by J.R. Hammond, and
> *The Unknown Poe*, ed. Raymond Faye, raising questions as to
> how strong an influence "the Shelley-Godwin circle" had on
> Poe, citing also the derivation of Poe's aesthetic theory
> from Coleridge.

HAZLITT

Allentuck, Marcia. "William Hazlitt's *Spirit of the Age* and
   Sir William Allan: An Unpublished Commentary." *KSJ* 30
   (1981): 29-33.

> Allen's copy of *The Spirit of the Age*, now in the Lilly
> Library, contains interleaved notes that object to Hazlitt's
> prejudiced opinions and that give additional details on the
> life and works of Sir James Mackintosh.

Anderson, Floyd Douglas, and Andrew A. King. "William Hazlitt
   as a Critic of Parliamentary Speaking." *QJS* 67 (1981): 47-
   56.

> "Despite his anti-rhetorical bias, Hazlitt is still a
> great rhetorical critic."

Jones, Stanley. "'Bad English in the Scotch Novels.'" *Library*,
   6th series, 3 (1981): 202-16.

> An impressive marshalling of circumstantial evidence
> pointing to Hazlitt as the author of an 1825 *Examiner*
> article attacking Scott's carelessness in grammar and
> style. Jones's article should be required reading as a
> demonstration of how scrupulous and energetic research,
> combined with sheer craftsmanship, can make the difference
> between pedantic niggling and stimulating scholarship.
> (R.M.R.)

Jones, Stanley. ["Hazlitt's Essay 'On Individuality.'"] *RES* 32 (1981): 197.

  Updating of Jones's remarks in his 1977 *RES* article.

Keynes, Geoffrey, Kt. *Bibliography of William Hazlitt.* Second ed. revised. (St Paul's Bibliographies.) University Press of Virginia, 1981. Pp. xx+152; illus. $32.50.

  Considerably revised since the 1931 edition; completely reset. The annotation is amplified; the entries now include additions from the National Union Catalog and a checklist of American editions.

Mahoney, John L. *The Logic of Passion: The Literary Criticism of William Hazlitt.* Revised ed. Fordham University Press, 1981. Pp. x+125. $17.50; $8.00 paper.

  This is essentially the book published in the SSEL series in 1978 and briefly reviewed in the *RMB* for that year (*ELN* 17, Supp., 85). It has benefited from minor stylistic revision, some supplementation and correction in the references and bibliography, and--more significantly--from being supplied with a pleasant format and an index--all of which combine to make the work a convenient and readable statement of Hazlitt's position in Romantic criticism. It partakes of some of his gusto. (J.E.J.)

Patterson, Charles I., Jr. "Hazlitt's Criticism in Retrospect." *SEL* 21 (1981): 647-63.

See also Engell, Lobb ("General 3. Criticism"); Butler ("English 3. Criticism"); Albrecht ("Keats"); Denier ("French 2. Stendhal").

Review of book previously listed:

  KINNAIRD, John, *William Hazlitt: Critic of Power* (see *ELN* 17, Supp., 85), rev. by J.H. Alexander in *YES* 11 (1981): 294-96.

HOOD

Korn, Frederick. "An Unpublished Letter by Thomas Hood: Hannah Lawrence and *Hood's Magazine.*" *ELN* 18 (1981): 192-94.

HUNT

Roe, Nicholas. "Leigh Hunt and Wordsworth's Poems." *TWC* 12
(1981): 89-91.

Corrects a minor matter of chronology in Moorman.

Thomas, Donald. "Leigh Hunt and 'The Prince on St. Patrick's
Day.'" *Library* 3 (1981): 145-49.

Reviews *Examiner*-instigated sedition charges against the
Hunts, concluding with the text of the editorial that brought
Hunt to Horsemonger Lane Gaol. (T.L.A.)

See also Kaier ("Reynolds").

INCHBALD

See Zall ("Coleridge").

KEATS

Albrecht, W.P. "The Tragic Sublime of Hazlitt and Keats."
SiR 20 (1981): 185-201.

"For Keats, the sublime cannot exist apart from empirical
reality. It simply heightens this reality into essential
beauty, regardless of any unpleasant materials reality may
include." Albrecht allows that Keats doesn't use the word
"sublime" carefully or consistently but, invoking the names
of Thomas Weiskel and Stuart Ende, he elaborates a definition (derived mainly from Hazlitt) that suits the poet as
well as can be expected. The real interest here is Albrecht's
art, not Keats's. (R.M.R.)

Aske, Martin. "Magical Spaces in 'The Eve of St. Agnes.'"
EiC 31 (1981): 196-209.

This straight-faced discussion of "the function of doors"
and "the dialectic of inside and outside" says nothing about
the poem that has not been said before less absurdly. (R.M.R.)

Becker, Michael G., Robert J. Dilligan, and Todd K. Bender,
eds. *A Concordance to the Poems of John Keats*. New York &
London: Garland Publishing, 1981. Pp. xv+719. $140.00.

In what essentials does this new Keats Concordance, based
on the Stillinger edition of 1978, differ from the Concordance of 1971, based on Forman's edition of 1907? In substance it contains, of course, all the 1978 corrected readings. More than that, each line of poetry (or title or note
by Keats) is immediately followed by a keyed note of variant,
cancelled, or emended readings, with sources indicated. And
thanks to advances in computerized typesetting, virtually
all typographical distinctions are observed. "By the end of
the century," says Dilligan's Technical Preface, "it is
most likely that computer technology will dominate textual
studies and become the primary means by which we preserve,
publish, and transmit our literary heritage. The techniques
used for this *Concordance* are an attempt to contribute to
this work...."

At first glance, the tight-packed entries, reduced to about
6-point type and all run together under each word-heading,
seem daunting; but trial has proved them legible and usable.
(D.V.E.)

Borck, Jim Springer. "Keats and the Drunken Landlord at Burns's
  Cottage." *KSJ* 30 (1981): 33-37.

  Another account of "the great bore."

Burnett, Leon. "Heirs of Eternity: An Essay on the Poetry of
  Keats and Mandel'shtam." *MLR* 76 (1981): 396-419.

  The poets are alike in their attraction to ancient Greek
  culture and, more specifically, in their use of insect
  images as analogies for the poetic construction of self-
  enclosed worlds.

Dulek, Ron. "Keats's Young Man-Poet; Shakespeare's Public-
  Private Man." *CLAJ* 24 (1980): 203-08.

  A discussion of similarities between "When I Have Fears"
  and Sonnet 30, most of which would be obvious to the casual
  reader. (R.M.R.)

Duncan-Jones, E.E. "Moore's 'A Kiss à l'Antique' and Keats's
  'Ode on a Grecian Urn.'" *N&Q* 28 (1981): 316-17.

Fitzpatrick, Margaret Ann. "The Problem of 'Identity' in
  Keats's 'Negative Capability.'" *DR* (Spring 1981): 39-51.

Goslee, Nancy M. "Plastic to Picturesque: Schlegel's Analogy
  and Keats's *Hyperion* Poems." *KSJ* 30 (1981): 118-51.

Reading English Romantic poetry in the light of German critical theory is becoming fashionable--a good thing. Here is one example of the fruitfulness of the approach, a plausible case that A.W. Schlegel's views on cultural history had some influence on Keats, perhaps through Hazlitt. (R.M.R.)

Gradman, Barry. *Metamorphosis in Keats*. New York University Press, 1980. Pp. xx+140. $13.95.

Gradman observes in Keats's narrative verse a recurrent situation in which a character is brought, by a discernible three-phase process, from a state of discontent to some higher level of consciousness. This "metamorphosis pattern" is seen to be of central importance in Keats's art and in his theory of art. One could quarrel with Gradman by objecting that his term "metamorphosis" is so comprehensive as to be synonymous with blander words like "change" or "transformation," since it can apply to just about any mental or physical alteration (e.g., Madeline's loss of her virginity), while it fails to accommodate the literal metamorphoses in *Lamia*. But one is reluctant to criticize overmuch a thesis that has provided Gradman with occasion for some quite stimulating readings of the narrative poems (as well as "Ode to a Nightingale") that will sharpen anyone's perception of them. He allows his theory to conflict with his good sense only in connection with *Lamia*, to which he reacts with a curious moral repugnance, but the lapse doesn't seriously unbalance a very able essay in criticism. (R.M.R.)

Hearn, Ronald B., et al., eds. *Keats Criticism Since 1954: A Bibliography*. (SSEL, Romantic Reassessment, 83:3.) University of Salzburg, Austria, 1981. Pp. 52. $13.50.

The open-ended title leaves it to the user to discover for himself that this brief bibliography lists articles through 1977 and books through 1978; he also discovers that coverage actually begins in 1953. What the user does not discover is why this bibliography was published at all.

The long list of "Articles in Learned Journals" is copied, one finds, from our own *RMB*, without acknowledgment and, what is of more consequence, without our critical annotations. So the reader is presented with a title like "Indication of Keats" (which should be "Indications," by the way--a typical mistranscription) with no hint that it refers to the poet's relations with Hunt. An even more awkward omission is the year of publication for periodicals like *TLS* and the *Listener*. It wasn't necessary for the annual *RMB* always to specify the year, but it should have occurred to the present compilers to supply it, since in a list

covering 24 years "TLS, January 17" isn't enough guidance.
Another limitation is the omission of articles published
in 1964--by inadvertence, it seems, rather than policy. All
of which raises the question, why would anyone use this list
when the original *RMB*, more complete, accurate, and helpful,
is available at a nearby library?

Not borrowed from us is another list, "Articles in Popular
Magazines," containing only 20 items for the 24-year period.
To the compilers this suggests that Keats's hold on the
popular imagination is "apparently not a very strong one."
They might have done better to consult something more than
the *Reader's Guide to Periodical Literature* (evidently their
sole source), something, for instance, that covers British
journals. An odd situation results in which W.F. Buckley's
National Review is called "popular" while *New Statesman* and
Spectator, because *RMB* lists them, are classified as "learned."

The list of dissertations on Keats might be welcome as a
handy guide at least for doctoral candidates, but, though
it is called "absolutely complete," it includes only those
theses whose titles contain the word "Keats." So (to choose
at random) G. Bernstein's "Structuralism and Romantic Myth-
making," which has a good deal to say about Keats, doesn't
get listed. The "Books" section likewise contains only works
whose titles refer to Keats. Chapters about him in more
general works are not mentioned; for example, there is no
reference to Harold Bloom's *The Visionary Company*. In fact,
Bloom's name appears nowhere in this survey of Keats criticism since 1954.

Enough. At a time when good books and articles are going
unpublished for financial reasons, it is distressing to see
a publisher throwing away money on things like this. (R.M.R.)

Hirst, Wolf Z. *John Keats.* (Twayne's English Authors Series,
    No. 334.) Boston: G.K. Hall, 1981. Pp. 194.

This is a useful book. Working conscientiously within the
limits of his assignment Hirst has produced a study of Keats's
verse admirable for its balance and thoroughness. One finds
considerable attention given to prosody, for example, as
well as to poems like "Isabella" and "The Eve of St. Mark"
that often are neglected in such surveys. Hirst's broad
knowledge of the history of Keats criticism reveals itself
in a thoughtfully annotated bibliography and in endnotes
reporting scholarly disputes over particular poems, as well
as in his own readings of the poetry, in which he usually
tries to reflect the critical consensus. His occasional
quarrels with the consensus, since they are clearly indicated
as such, add to the interest of the book without lessening

its usefulness as a reliable introduction for students (it
would also serve admirably to introduce them to the art of
literary scholarship) and as an informed report on the state
of Keats criticism at the start of the present decade.
(R.M.R.)

Holstein, Michael. "His Soul's Decree: *Poems* (1817) and Keats's
Poetic Autobiography." *ES* 62 (1981): 324-34.

An interesting attempt to read the volume as a unified
work, but the notion that the book is a kind of prophetic
autobiography, predicting the poet's ultimate identity and
accomplishment, is a bit strained; even Holstein appears to
lose interest in it before he's through. (R.M.R.)

Little, Geoffrey. "Serving Mammon: Keats's Reply to Shelley."
RP&P 5,ii (1981): 41-43.

Traces the images of Keats's Aug. 1820 letter to Shelley
("an artist must serve Mammon" and "'load every rift' ...
with ore") to *Paradise Lost*, Book I.

Luria, Maxwell. "Miss Lowell and Mr. Newton: The Record of
a Literary Friendship." *HLB* 29 (1981): 5-34.

One letter to Newton comments on the biography of Keats.

McNally, Paul. "Keats and the Rhetoric of Association: On
Looking into the Chapman's Homer Sonnet." *JEGP* 79 (1980):
530-40.

An important article, demonstrating that much of the poem's
power results from an ingenious use of metonymy and synes-
thesia combined in single images. McNally has an eagle eye.
(R.M.R.)

Richardson, Joanna. *Keats and His Circle*. London: Cassell,
1980. Pp. 126; illus. £8.95.

An attractive assembly of portraits, worth seeing if only
for a previously unpublished photograph of Fanny Brawne
Lindos that helps one understand Keats's fascination.
(R.M.R.)

Richardson, Joanna. *The Life and Letters of John Keats*.
London: Folio Society, 1981. Pp. 176. £7.85.

Rev. by Anthony Storr in *S*, Aug. 1, 1981, p. 19.
Largely a selection from the letters.

Stillinger, Jack. "Another Early Biographical Sketch of
  'Young Keats.'" *ELN* 18 (June 1981): 276-81.

  It appeared in an 1839 collection of medical biographies.
No new information.

Swaminathan, S.R. *The Still Image in Keats's Poetry.* (SSEL,
  Romantic Reassessment, 98.) University of Salzburg, Austria,
  1981. Pp. x+406; 35 plates. S12.50.

  This is a study of Keats's images of silence and repose
as they reveal a steadily intensifying quest for an ideal
stasis in a peaceful, timeless realm beyond the present
world. This essentially religious pursuit finally clarifies
as a death wish, a desire for escape into eternal union with
the Divine.
  Keats's mystical death wish would be an unpromising subject
even if Swaminathan did not allow two tangential enthusiasms
to distract his attention. One is his interest in proving
that much of Keats's inspiration came from the pictorial
arts. Picking up where Ian Jack (*Keats and the Mirror of
Art*) prudently left off, he asserts the "probable" influence
of well over one hundred paintings, offering in most cases
no convincing evidence that Keats ever saw them. The other
distraction is the author's obsession with Mary Magdalene.
Not only does he make her the actual heroine of "The Eve
of St. Agnes," he finds her in just about every other poem
Keats wrote, disguised as Psyche, La Belle Dame, Thea,
Autumn, Meg Merrilies, et al. She may even be, he thinks,
the "persona" of the Nightingale ode. And where Mary Magdalene is, Christ is not far away--in the guise of Porphyro,
Apollo, and even Cuthbert de St. Aldebrim. That last word,
"Keats's archaism meaning 'holy old sea,' is probably an
allusion to Galilee as the Holy Sea." That's an example of
a Swaminathan "probably" and of his *modus operandi* in
general.
  There are some good things in this book, but not enough
to ballast a flight of critical fancy so turbulent that most
readers will bail out long before the end. (R.M.R.)

Ting, Nai-tung. "Chatterton and Keats: A Reexamination." *KSJ*
  30 (1981): 100-17.

  Provocative and persuasive when arguing Chatterton's
influence on certain vowel-patterns in Keats's verse; more
routine and less convincing when discussing borrowed imagery.
But one sees more clearly that the influence was real and
how it worked. (R.M.R.)

Walsh, William. *Introduction to Keats.* London and New York: Methuen, 1981. Pp. 141. $13.95; $6.00 paper.

Having promised to use only "the lightest of biographical scaffolding" to support a study which will be "emphatically literary-critical in means and emphasis," Walsh surprises us by devoting only about one-third of the book to examination of the poetry. The rest is given over to admiration of the letters and a more general discussion of Keats's mental development as "the most brilliant example in literature of the education of a sensibility." Although he sometimes seems more attracted by Keats's moral character than by his poetry, his critical comments are usually acute, especially with regard to the early verse where his tone is just right. The blind spots include *Hyperion* and *Lamia*. Finally, the book is what it pretends to be, a useful introduction for students, and one which advanced scholars could read with profit as a very thoughtful reassessment of Keats's accomplishment. A bonus of pleasure comes from Walsh's ability to write English in a vigorous style, seasoned with good phrases. (R.M.R.)

White, R.S. "Shakespearean Music in Keats's 'Ode to a Nightingale.'" *English* 30 (1981): 217-29.

A useful list of verbal and tonal Shakespearean allusions in the "Ode." Notes 14 examples of the "persuasive indebtedness." (J.C.R.)

See also Booth, Engell, Lobb, Schoenholtz ("General 3. Criticism"); Owings ("English 1. Bibliography"); Hogg, Twitchell ("English 3. Criticism"); Kaier ("Reynolds"); Henel ("German 3. Brentano").

Reviews of books previously listed:

SHARP, Ronald A., *Keats, Skepticism, and the Religion of Beauty* (see *RMB* for 1979, p. 104), rev. by Ray Fleming in *MLN* 95 (1980): 1433-37; by Donald H. Reiman in *KSJ* 30 (1981): 201-03; by Robert M. Ryan in *JEGP* 80 (1981): 259-62; by Stuart M. Sperry in *SiR* 20 (1981): 126-28; by Leon Waldoff in *ELN* 18 (1981): 217-19; STILLINGER, Jack, ed., *The Poems of John Keats* (see *ELN* 17, Supp., 90), rev. by Ronald Sharp in *Review* 2 (University Press of Virginia, 1981), pp. 127-36.

LAMB

Aaron, Jane. "'We are in a manner *marked*': Images of Damnation in Charles Lamb's Writings." *ChLB* 33 (1981): 1-10.

Emphasizes Charles Lamb's share in his sister's social ostracism, especially as a theme in his dramatic works, the farces of 1808 and 1825 and his two tragedies, and in many of his essays.

Dalling, Graham. "Enfield in the Time of Charles Lamb." *ChLB* 34 (1981): 1-34.

Lamb's letters are "a useful source of information" on the state of the town during his stay there.

Huxstep, Madeline. "Fear of the Gallows." *ChLB* 36 (1981): 1-7.

The state of Law and Order during Lamb's lifetime.

Monsman, Gerald. "Charles Lamb's 'Enfranchised Quill': The Two First Essays of Elia." *Criticism* 23 (1981): 232-45.

Watters, Reginald. "Thomas Manning (1772-1840): 'An interesting man, but nothing more.'" *ChLB* 33 (1981): 10-17.

An account of the eccentric friend of Charles Lamb "who travelled in China and produced nothing."

Wickham, D.E. "Thomas Massa Alsager (1779-1846): An Elian Shade Illuminated." *ChLB* 35 (1981): 1-62.

Reviews of book previously listed:

MARRS, Edwin W., Jr., *The Letters of Charles and Mary Lamb*, Vol. III (see *ELN* 17, Supp., 92), rev. by Peter Morgan in *ES* 62 (1981): 83-84; Vols. I-III rev. by Hans-Jochen Schild in *Anglia* 99 (1981): 250-52.

LANDOR

See Owings ("English 1. Bibliography"); Newlyn ("Wordsworth, W.").

Review of book previously listed:

PROUDFIT, Charles L., *Landor as Critic* (see *RMB* for 1979, p. 107), rev. by Keith Hanley in *CritQ* 23 (1981): 89-90.

LEWIS

Carnochan, W.B., and D.W. Donaldson. "The Presentation Copy
   of 'Monk' Lewis's 'Oberon's Henchman.'" *BC* 30 (1981): 346-
   59; illus.

   The character of this precocious poem, written as early
   as 1800, published in 1808, is found to lie "as much in
   local allusion as in witchcraft and fairy lore."

See also Lewis ("English 3. Criticism"); Zimansky ("Shelley,
   P.B."); Romero ("German 3. Hoffmann").

MOORE

Tessier, Thérèse. *The Bard of Erin: A Study of Thomas Moore's
   Irish Melodies, 1808-1834.* (SSEL, Romantic Reassessment,
   110.) University of Salzburg, Austria, 1981. Pp. 231. $13.50.

   A translation of the author's doctoral dissertation (1976),
   whose confused style and frequent mixed metaphors make for
   difficult reading. (One reader of my copy quit at p. 50!)
   And at best this is a starting point on the lyrics in
   question, useful for its collection of commentary and its
   work on the settings. But even in these matters problems
   arise on the order of the discussion of Byron's interest
   in the songs: fifteen lines long and with no mention of the
   Hebrew Melodies whatsoever--despite obvious borrowings on
   Byron's part. (T.L.A.)

See also Clark ("Byron"); Duncan-Jones ("Keats"); *L'Année
   balzacienne* ("French 2. Balzac").

OPIE

Kelly, Gary. "Amelia Opie, Lady Caroline Lamb, and Maria
   Edgeworth: Official and Unofficial Ideology." *ArielE* 12
   (Oct. 1981): 3-24.

PEACOCK

Reviews of book previously listed:

   BUTLER, Marilyn, *Peacock Displayed: A Satirist in His Context* (see *RMB* for 1979, p. 109), rev. by Carl Dawson in

SiR 20 (1981): 260–62; by Avrom Fleishman in *ELN* 18 (1981):
310–12; by Alice Green Fredman in *KSJ* 30 (1981): 210–13; by
Stuart M. Tave in *NCF* 35 (1981): 547–51; by William Walling
in *TWC* 12 (1981): 172–74.

POE

See Frank, Martin, Saliba ("The Gothic Novel"); Ringe ("Scott");
Wuthenow ("German 3. Fouqué"); Pitcher, Trautwein, Von der
Lippe, Wolff ("German 3. Hoffmann").

RADCLIFFE

Gori, Stefano. "Il brano introduttivo a *The Italian or the
Confessional of the Black Penitents* de Ann Radcliffe." *RLMC*
33 (1980): 263–69.

See also Lewis ("English 3. Criticism"); Butler ("Wollstonecraft").

REYNOLDS, J.H.

Clubbe, John. "The Reynolds-Dovaston Correspondence." *KSJ* 30
(1981): 152–81.

　　Prints eight letters (1808–1813) from John Hamilton
Reynolds and his mother, Charlotte Cox Reynolds, to John
F.M. Dovaston. Clubbe supplies useful background information on the correspondents as well as on Ralph Rylance, a
frequent subject of these letters. (C.E.R.)

Kaier, Anne. "John Hamilton Reynolds: Four New Letters." *KSJ*
30 (1981): 182–90.

　　New information supplied by Reynolds to Leigh Hunt, 24
Feb. 1815; to William Jerdan, 25 Aug. 1820; to [? Pierre F.
Laporte], 31 Aug. 1833; and to George Cruikshank, 19 April
1847.

ROGERS

McClary, Ben Harris. "Alaric Watts on Samuel Rogers: An
Unpublished Personal Remembrance." *BRH* 84 (1981): 121–25.

See also Zall ("Coleridge").

SCOTT

Alexander, J.H. "The Treatment of Scott in Reviews of the English Romantics." *YES* 11 (1981): 67-86.

Brown, Cedric C. "Sir Walter Scott, Robert Belt, and *Ivanhoe*." *SLJ* 8,ii (1981): 38-43.

  Reproduces from manuscript Scott to Belt, 29 Jan. 1829, on the writing of historical romance--a letter that will be quoted. (T.L.A.)

Cottom, Daniel. "Violence and Law in the Waverley Novels." *SiR* 20 (1981): 65-84.

  "At every period of history described in these works the progressive elements of civilization are distinguished from the anachronistic on the basis of their commitment to the increasing sublimation of violent conflict within formal regulations, especially the written regulations of law."

Downs, Norton. "Sir Walter Scott and Oral History." *N&Q* 28 (1981): 321-22.

Finley, Gerald. *Landscapes of Memory: Turner as Illustrator to Scott*. London: Scolar Press, 1980. £30.00.

  Rev. by Graham Reynolds in *Apollo* 114 (1981): 68-69.

Garside, P.D. "Scott's Political Speech." *SLJ* 7,ii (1980): 12-30.

  Manuscript evidence put to work with care and thought illumines the myth of Scott the Orator of the anti-reform speech made in Jedburgh in 1831. (T.L.A.)

Johnson, R.V. "An Assurance of Continuity: Scott's Model of Past and Present in *Quentin Durward*." *SoRA* 13 (1980): 79-96.

  A careful, appreciative reading, finding in *Quentin Durward* an imaginative grasp of history usually associated only with the Scottish novels.

Millgate, Jane. "Scott and the Dreaming Boy: A Context for *Waverley*." *RES* 32 (1981): 286-93.

Mitchell, Jerome. "Scott's Use of the Tristan-Story in the Waverley Novels." *Tristania* 6,i (1980): 19-29.

  Scott's "debt to medieval romance was immense." We are offered here "just the tip of the iceberg."

Müllenbrock, Hans-Joachim. "Die Entstehung des Scottschen historischen Romans als Problem der Literaturgeschichtsschreibung." *Anglia* 99 (1981): 355-78.

Priestman, Donald G. "Old Battles Fought Anew: The Religious and Political Ramifications of Scott's *Old Mortality*." *TWC* 12 (1981): 117-21.

Raleigh, John Henry. "Scott and Pushkin." Pp. 11-47 in Samuel I. Mintz, Alice Chandler, and Christopher Mulvey, eds., *From Smollett to James: Studies in the Novel and Other Essays Presented to Edgar Johnson*. University Press of Virginia, 1981.

Ringe, Donald A. "Poe's Debt to Scott in 'The Pit and the Pendulum.'" *ELN* 18 (1981): 281-83.

Shaw, Harry E. "Scott, Mackenzie, and Structure in *The Bride of Lammermoor*." *SNNTS* 13 (1981): 349-66.

Smith, D.J. "Sir James and Sir Walter: Scott and James of Douglas." *SLJ* 8,ii (1981): 24-37.

   Scott as weaver of family myth, and useful for its collation. (T.L.A.)

Stein, Richard L. "Historical Fiction and the Implied Reader: Scott and Iser." *Novel: A Forum on Fiction* 14 (1981): 213-31.

Wilson, A.N. *The Laird of Abbotsford: A View of Sir Walter Scott*. Oxford University Press, 1980. Pp. xvi+197. $24.95.

   Rev. by Kenneth Curry in *TWC* 12 (1981): 174-75.

Wilt, Judith. "Steamboat Surfacing: Scott and the English Novelists." *NCF* 35 (1981): 459-86.

   Shows how Scott provided much crucial material for later novelists, many of whom sneered at their Great Original. Very interesting. (B.C.H.)

Wright, Beth Segal. "Scott's Historical Novels and French Historical Painting 1815-1855." *ArtB* 63 (1981): 268-87.

Wrobel, Arthur. "Use and Abuse of Sir Walter Scott: Nathaniel Beverley Tucker's *The Partisan Leader*." *AN&Q* 19 (Sept. 1980): 7-9.

Examines the influence of *Waverley* on this 1836 novel about
a Southern secession, offering support to Mark Twain's claim
that Scott was responsible for the Civil War.

See also Bell ("English 1. Bibliography"); Ehrenpreis, Harvey
("English 3. Criticism"); Jones ("Hazlitt"); Finley ("Turner");
Mower, Wright ("French 1. General"); Del Litto ("French 2.
Stendhal"); Johnston ("German 3. Heine"); Pitcher ("German
3. Hoffmann").

Reviews of books previously listed:

BROWN, David, *Walter Scott and the Historical Imagination*
(see *RMB* for 1980, p. 113), rev. by Donald A. Low in *RES*
32 (1981): 231-33; CORSON, James C., ed., *Notes and Index
to Sir Herbert Grierson's Edition of the Letters of Sir
Walter Scott* (see *RMB* for 1979, p. 111), rev. by David
Hewitt in *SLJ* 8 (1981): supp. 15, pp. 109-13, as "superb"
but with complaints of the index; by Donald A. Low in *RES*
32 (1981): 338-39.

Composite reviews:

Roper, Derek. *YES* 11 (1981): 296-98.

Reviews J.H. Alexander's *Two Studies in Reviewing* (see *ELN*
16, Supp., 67) and his *The Reception of Scott's Poetry by
His Correspondents, 1796-1817* (see *RMB* for 1980, p. 112).

Sutherland, Kathryn. *CritQ* 23 (1981): 84-85.

Reviews Wilson, *The Laird of Abbotsford* (see *RMB* for 1980,
p. 118) and Reed, *Sir Walter Scott: Landscape and Locality*
(see *RMB* for 1980, p. 115).

SHELLEY, MARY

Clubbe, John. "Mary Shelley as Autobiographer: The Evidence
of the 1831 Introduction to *Frankenstein*." *TWC* 12 (1981):
102-06.

Countering Rieger's judgment that Mary Shelley's 1831 Introduction to *Frankenstein* is "an almost total fabrication,"
Clubbe reexamines the evidence, determines that her recollection of the genesis of the novel is essentially accurate,
downplays Polidori's influence on the novel, and concludes
that Mary Shelley conceived the novel in a dream during the

night of 20 or 21 June--i.e., after Polidori had begun his
story and just before Byron and Shelley departed on 22 June
for their tour round Lake Geneva. (C.E.R.)

Conger, Syndy McMillen. "A German Ancestor for Mary Shelley's
Monster: Kahlert, Schiller, and the Buried Treasure of *Northanger Abbey*." *PQ* 59 (1980): 216-32.

Dean, Dennis R. "Mary Shelley and Gideon Mantell." *KSJ* 30
(1981): 21-29.

   The Mantell collection at the Alexander Turnbull Library
yields four Mary Shelley letters (two previously unpublished)
to Mantell as well as a journal with references to Mary
Shelley. Mantell, a physician and distinguished naturalist,
read *Frankenstein* in 1823, first corresponded with Mary
Shelley in 1839, and lived near her on Chester Square from
1846 to 1851.

Gross, Dalton, and Mary J.H. Gross. "Joseph Grimaldi: An Influence on *Frankenstein*." *N&Q* 28 (1981): 403-04.

Murray, E.B. "Changes in the 1823 Edition of *Frankenstein*."
Library 3 (1981): 320-27.

   This improves Rieger's collation of the 1818 and 1831
letterpress by noting 114 changes from 1818 in 1823. A case
is made for Godwin as the source of these changes; however,
Murray indicates "must have been the case" for Mary's use
of 1823 as copytext for 1831--an assertion that must be
hedged. (T.L.A.)

Schopf, Sue Weaver. "'Of what a strange nature is knowledge!':
Hartleian Psychology and the Creature's Arrested Moral Sense
in Mary Shelley's *Frankenstein*." *RP&P* 5,i (1981): 33-52.

   Another undistributed middle in logic. Schopf should have
been content to demonstrate that the pattern of the Monster's
development resembles Hartley's scheme for man's intellectual
and moral development. Mary Shelley probably read Hartley's
Observations on Man (both Godwin and Shelley owned copies),
but Schopf's argument for *direct* influence, in the absence
of any direct evidence, misrepresents the creative process
and undervalues Mary Shelley's common sense. Mary certainly
knew enough, without the aid of a Hartleian guidebook, to
structure the Monster's education in the manner we have it
in the novel. (C.E.R.)

Sherwin, Paul. "*Frankenstein*: Creation as Catastrophe." *PMLA*
    96 (1981): 883-903.

Worth reading, but too long and tedious or contrived in
parts. Most of the essay faults the previous Freudian and
psychoanalytical critics of the novel; these critics, Sherwin
claims with some bravado, have misread the text much in the
manner that Frankenstein misread his monster. Sherwin then
argues that Frankenstein's "catastrophe of origination,
engendering a creative self that anxiously pursues an impossible desire and an artifact that both represents and eclipses
the creator, serves as a paradigm of the genesis of any
sublime artwork" (Abstract). (C.E.R.)
    The critical wit of the contrived parts succeeded with
some readers. (D.V.E.)

Vasbinder, Samuel H. "A Possible Source of the Term 'Vermicelli'
    in Mary Shelley's *Frankenstein*." *TWC* 12 (1981): 116-17.

Unconvincing argument that Mary Shelley's reference to
Darwin's experiments with "vermicelli" comes from her (or
Byron and Shelley's) recollection of Darwin's remarks on
"*confera fontinalis*" in a note to *The Temple of Nature*.
Vasbinder should have consulted *The Annotated Frankenstein*
(p. 4) for Leonard Wolf and Desmond King-Hele's suggestion
that Darwin's first note to *The Temple of Nature* is a more
likely source, especially because of a reference to "*vorti-
cella*" coming to life after being dried. (C.E.R.)

Ziolkowski, Theodore. "Science, Frankenstein, and Myth." *SR*
    89 (1981): 34-56.

Reviews of books previously listed:

BENNETT, Betty T., ed., *The Letters of Mary Wollstonecraft
Shelley*, Vol. I (see *RMB* for 1980, p. 118), rev. by William
Keach in *EiC* 32 (1982): 87-88; by Edwin W. Marrs, Jr., in
KSJ 30 (1981): 203-07; by Hartley S. Spatt in *WHR* 35 (1981):
188-90; GILBERT, Sandra M., and Susan Gubar, *The Madwoman
in the Attic: The Woman Writer and the Nineteenth-Century
Literary Imagination* (see *RMB* for 1979, p. 113), rev. by
Betty T. Bennett in *KSJ* 30 (1981): 207-10; by Julia Prewitt
Brown in *SiR* 30 (1981): 132-36; by Katherine Frank in *PQ* 59
(1980): 381-83; by Eva Simmons in *EiC* 31 (1981): 249-58;
LEVINE, George, and U.C. Knoepflmacher, eds., *The Endurance
of Frankenstein: Essays on Mary Shelley's Novel* (see *RMB*
for 1979, pp. 114-15), rev. by Betty T. Bennett in *KSJ* 30
(1981): 207-10; by Benjamin Franklin Fisher IV in *ELN* 19
(1981): 67-68; by Coral Ann Howells in *English* 30 (1981):
185-90.

SHELLEY, P.B.

Baker, John Ross. "Poetry and Language in Shelley's *Defence of Poetry*." *JAAC* 39 (1980/81): 437-49.

  "This essay might have been called 'Making Sense in Shelley's *Defence*,'" writes Baker at the start, making a triple-entendre that eventually generates a wise conclusion: "Finally, we must suppose, only an empirical faithfulness to his own art allows him to depart so far from what he clearly would like to be able to say about artistic media." Useful but not conclusive. (T.L.A.)

Becht, Ronald E. "Shelley's *Adonais*: Formal Design and the Lyric Speaker's Crisis of Imagination." *SP* 78 (1981): 194-210.

Behrendt, Stephen C. "The Exoteric Species: The Popular Idiom in Shelley's Poetry." *Genre* 14 (1981): 473-92.

  "Shelley's choice of the wor[d] 'exoteric' [to describe "poems in the deliberately simplified style and overtly topical idiom of 'Song to the Men of England' or 'Similies for Two Political Characters of 1819'"] and the observable style and function of the exoteric poems, indicate the poet's keen awareness of both the hortatory purpose for which he wrote and the restrictions the limited sophistication of his intended audience would impose upon his performance."

Brisman, Leslie. "Mysterious Tongue: Shelley and the Language of Christianity." *TSLL* 23 (1981): 388-417.

Carothers, Yvonne M. "*Alastor*: Shelley Corrects Wordsworth." *MLQ* 42 (1981): 21-47.

Cronin, Richard. *Shelley's Poetic Thoughts*. New York: St. Martin's Press, 1981. Pp. xii+263. $22.50.

  Rev. by A.N. Wilson in *TLS*, April 17, 1981, p. 442, briefly.
  Language, syntax, verse form, and genre--these are not merely vehicles for a poem's meaning; they are, or should be, expressions of that meaning. By such standards, Cronin refreshingly evaluates most of Shelley's major poems by analyzing the artistry of the expressions. In Chapter 1 ("Language and Genre"), Cronin summarizes eighteenth- and nineteenth-century language theories, argues that Shelley's best poems "achieve an awareness of the conservative force of language and engage in a self-conscious struggle against it," and reminds us that "of all Romantic poets Shelley was

the most committed to the use of established genres" at the
same time that he subverted or modified those genres. Genre
more than language or syntax dominates most of the subsequent analysis. For example, in Chapter 2, *The Mask of
Anarchy* is discussed in terms of the ballad and the masque
("Shelley's reversal of the conventional masque action is
pointed and precise"). In Chapter 3, *Alastor* is placed in the
context of Virgil's tenth eclogue (the elegy for Gallus);
Laon and Cythna, in the context of Landor's and Southey's
"epic journalism"; and *Julian and Maddalo*, in the context
of Horace's, Pope's, Coleridge's, and even Crabbe's *sermo*,
epistle, or conversation poem. Not content only to describe,
Cronin evaluates Shelley's various achievements: in *Julian
and Maddalo*, a poem "about the aesthetics of belief," the
"language of Julian and Maddalo and the language of the
madman both express modes of thought and feeling, so that
the theme of the poem becomes the contrast between its
styles. This is why *Julian and Maddalo* [where "language is
thought"] is so evidently a better poem than either *Alastor*
or *Laon and Cythna* [where language "merely contains thought"]."
As would be expected, *Prometheus Unbound* and *Adonais* are
given extended treatment here, but we also encounter close
readings of *The Witch of Atlas* ("everything in the poem
is at the mercy of language"), *The Triumph of Life* ("a
sequence of carefully constructed uncertainties"), *Hymn to
Intellectual Beauty* (which fails to reconcile its "three
languages: a religious language borrowed from orthodox
Christianity, a declamatory language borrowed from the
eighteenth-century ode, and a language borrowed from Wordsworth"), *Ode to the West Wind* ("the firm, onward-moving
rhythm of its syntax expresses the harmonious process of
the seasonal cycle"), and *With a Guitar, to Jane* ("witty in
a distinctly seventeenth-century manner"). As a close reader,
Cronin finds "Bion wails" in "Albion wails" in stanza 17
of *Adonais* and "carnations" in "incarnations" in stanza 20;
and he sensitively remarks that "Hope's pronouns are carefully chosen" in the "Ye are many—they are few" line in
The Mask of Anarchy: "the people occupy one side of the
line, the government occupies the other—Shelley sits on
the dash." In short, Cronin's book offers much instruction,
although readers might object to a few hasty, unsupported
readings (e.g., the "rude" shape that Asia sees in Act II
is "the poet in his bardic, prophetic role"), and readers
should object to a half-dozen apparently unrevised places
where Cronin repeats a point without developing it (see,
e.g., pp. 245-46 where he tells us four times within a few
lines that both Shelley's guitar and Shakespeare's Ariel

were imprisoned in a tree). Finally, Cronin may have attempted
too much here: he does not fully treat any one of the categories of analysis (language, syntax, verse form, and genre),
but he does deftly use each where warranted to increase our
appreciation of Shelley's art. (C.E.R.)

Duffy, Edward. "Shelley, the Trinity, and the Enlightenment."
ELN 19 (1981): 41-44.

Few have been satisfied by the standard gloss on Shelley's
remark that "the three forms into which Plato had distributed
the faculties of mind underwent a sort of apotheosis, and
became the object of worship of Europe" (*Defence of Poetry*).
Here Duffy finds a more meaningful explanation in Gibbon's
remarks on Plato's three forms becoming the Trinity. The
exact source in Plato, however, is still waiting to be found.
(C.E.R.)

Foot, Paul. *Red Shelley*. London: Sidgwick & Jackson, 1981.
Pp. 293. £12.95.

Rev. by David Bromwich in *TLS*, July 17, 1981, pp. 805-06;
by P.M.S. Dawson in *CritQ* 23,iv (1981): 77-79; by Molly
Tibbs in *ContR* 238 (June 1981): 332-33; by Nicolas Walter
in *New Statesman*, May 15, 1981, pp. 18-19.
Not seen, but the reviews seem justly severe. Bromwich
points out, in a concise and meticulous survey of Shelley's
politics, many incidental flaws in Foot's interpretations,
his most serious distortion being the "pernicious casuistry"
of turning *Prometheus Unbound* inside out to make Shelley
an advocate of popular revolutionary violence, of the curse
of vengeance! (D.V.E.)

Hall, Jean. *The Transforming Image: A Study of Shelley's Major
Poetry*. University of Illinois Press, 1980. Pp. 176. $12.95.

Rev. by William Keach in *EiC* 32 (1982): 85-86; by A.N.
Wilson in *TLS*, March 17, 1981, p. 358.
This is a good but not a great book. Gracefully written,
it reads Shelley's major poetry in terms of "transformation"
rather than transcendence. By this, Hall means that Shelley
after *Alastor* no longer directed his vision to a tran-
scendent ideal that ultimately frustrated the poet and his
protagonists; rather, Shelley *envisioned* the world, transforming it, at least during the moment of the poem, into
an image of his ideal self. In terms of this thesis, Shelley's
major poetry is essentially about poetry or the poetical
process. Transformations of images, subjects, genres, worlds,
and voids abound in this book, and Hall occasionally obscures

or omits reference to those certain transcendentals in
Shelley's major poetry under consideration. These poems
include *Alastor*, "Hymn to Intellectual Beauty," "Mont Blanc,"
"Ode to the West Wind," *Prometheus Unbound*, *Epipsychidion*,
Adonais, and *The Triumph of Life*. Of these, *Epipsychidion*
is given the most illuminating analysis. In the first section
(11. 1-189), Shelley haltingly uses "sheer lyricism" to
describe Emily. In the second section, he uses an autobiographical narrative to "understand [the] contextual property
of his language.... He does not take the revelations of his
language literally, as he had attempted to do in the first
section.... He begins to realize that truth is not detachable
from its manner of expression; and that conversely, one's
mode of expression actually can create truths" (113). In the
final section (11. 288-591), Shelley "transforms" the autobiographical narrative into a "Romantic nature lyric" and
creates "a landscape infused with the soul of its maker."
According to Hall, "Imagining an island paradise becomes
yet another way of formulating the material that has been
the subject matter of all three sections of the poem: the
striving of the imagination to embody its ideal" (119).
(C.E.R.)

Hogle, Jerrold E. "Shelley's Fiction: The 'Stream of Fate.'"
KSJ 30 (1981): 79-99.

   Hogle does not defend Shelley's inept or incomplete plotting in *Zastrozzi*, *St. Irvyne*, "The Assassins," or "The
Coliseum"; rather, he explains it in terms of Shelley's
desire to reflect the human mind by repeated images or
circular plotting. Shelley's attempts at cause and effect
or progressive conflict or linear plotting are never sufficient to give the more traditional temporal or spatial
order to these narratives. (C.E.R.)

Holmes, Richard, ed. *Shelley on Love: An Anthology*. University
of California Press, 198[1]. Pp. 247. $16.95.

   With selections from Shelley's prose, letters, and poetry
(*Alastor*, *Julian and Maddalo*, *Epipsychidion*), this anthology
is divided into six parts, each with an introduction: "Childhood"; "First Love"; "Second Marriage"; "Platonic Harmonies";
"Italian Discords"; and "Eternal Image." Holmes copyrighted
this anthology and had it printed in Great Britain in 1980;
and it was then first published in 198[1] by the University
of California Press—to what end I cannot say. If Holmes
and California are able to attract the general reader and
thereby introduce Shelley to a larger audience, I applaud

their effort. However, with the exception of providing the
complete text of Shelley's translation of Plato's *Symposium*,
this anthology will not serve the scholar. Holmes does not
always clearly indicate the source of his texts; he tells
us he silently modernizes the spelling; a comparison of the
short extracts (p. 232) from Shelley's letters on *Epipsychidion* with their source in Jones's edition of letters
reveals that Holmes silently makes at least six other alterations within eighteen lines--including omitting a word;
Holmes dates "On Love" c. 1815, despite evidence to the
contrary; and he is not always accurate with dates and ages.
Even the general reader will not benefit from the arrange-
ment and selection of the texts. Dates, titles, and contexts
of each selection appear not in headnotes (where they would
help the reader) but buried in the separate introductions
and endnotes. And Holmes wastes two and one-half pages
printing the three cancelled Prefaces to *Epipsychidion* when
these pages could have been used to complete the text of
the poem: he prints only ll. 73-592; ll. 1-72 and ll. 593-
604 would have completed the text. (C.E.R.)

Keach, William. "Obstinate Questionings: The Immortality Ode
and *Alastor*." *TWC* 12 (1981): 36-44.

Using four prominent as well as some fainter echoes of
the Ode in *Alastor*, Keach neatly argues that Shelley's poem
is "centrally about the failure of both protagonist and
narrator to sustain through 'natural piety' a condition
of 'beloved brotherhood'" with Nature. Keach thus modifies
Wasserman's reading by arguing that the "Wordsworthianism
of Shelley's narrator never was the simple pantheistic
nature-worship" of someone reconciled to the natural world.
(C.E.R.)

Lucas, Timothy R. "The Old Shelley Game: Prometheus and Pre-
destination in Burgess' Works." *MFS*, Autumn 1981, pp. 465-
78.

Milne, Fred L. "The Eclipsed Imagination in Shelley's 'The
Triumph of Life.'" *SEL* 21 (1981): 681-702.

Rieder, John. "Shelley's 'Mont Blanc': Landscape and the
Ideology of the Sacred Text." *ELH* 48 (1981): 778-98.

Robinson, Charles E. "Shelley to the Editor of the *Morning
Chronicle*: A Second New Letter of 5 April 1821." *KSMB* 32
(1981): 55-58.

More evidence of Shelley's interest in the Greek Revolution.

Rubin, Merle R. "Shelley's Skepticism: A Detachment Beyond Despair." *PQ* 59 (1980): 353-73.

Sperry, Stuart M. "Necessity and the Role of the Hero in Shelley's *Prometheus Unbound*." *PMLA* 96 (1981): 242-54.

Responding to Shelley's dramatic "failure" to represent Prometheus's moral and intellectual regeneration, Sperry argues that Shelley did not abandon the principle of Necessity after *Queen Mab*; rather, Necessity informs the drama wherein Prometheus is "only a link in a larger chain of causality."

Tetreault, Ronald. "Shelley at the Opera." *ELH* 48 (1981): 144-71.

Tetreault, Ronald. "Shelley's Folio Plato." *KSJ* 30 (1981): 17-21.

Identifies one of Shelley's editions of Plato as the Basel folio of 1534/1556, cited in a memorandum on the back cover of one of his Pisan notebooks.

Ware, Tracy. "A New Miltonic Echo in Shelley's *Defence*." *ELN* 19 (1981): 120-21.

The echo is from *The Reason of Church Government*.

Woodman, Ross. "The Androgyne in *Prometheus Unbound*." *SiR* 20 (1981): 225-47.

After some initial and inertial confusion and despite an occasionally strained definition, this essay successfully uses the androgyne to illuminate "Shelley's revolutionary ideal in both its optimistic and despairing aspects." Woodman does not merely rehearse the male/female images in the drama; rather, he uses the androgynous union of Prometheus and Asia in their enchanted cave to gloss difficult relationships in *Prometheus Unbound* (e.g., between Asia and Earth), to interrelate Shelley's drama with such other poems as *Epipsychidion* and *Song of Apollo*, and to explore both Shelley's ontology and his legislative aesthetic: "As [Shelley] copies [in *Prometheus Unbound*] the dictation of his feminine soul, anima, or Muse, the moral reformer, in turn, follows his footsteps, copying the poet's creation 'into the book of common life' which the actual events of history even further distort." (C.E.R.)

Zimansky, Curt. "*Zastrozzi* and *The Bravo of Venice*: Another
    Shelley Borrowing." *KSJ* 30 (1981): 15-17.

See also Crow, Hammond, Lobb ("General 3. Criticism"); Aers,
    Butler, Hogg, Lenoski, Reiman, Twitchell ("English 3. Criti-
    cism"); Little ("Keats").

Reviews of books previously listed:

    ABBEY, Lloyd, *Destroyer and Preserver: Shelley's Poetic
    Skepticism* (see *RMB* for 1980, p. 121), rev. by Bernard A.
    Hirsch in *JEGP* 80 (1981): 425-29 (favorable); by Jerrold E.
    Hogle in *TWC* 12 (1981): 183-86; by Daniel Hughes in *SiR* 20
    (1981): 262-67; by William Keach in *EiC* 32 (1982): 82-85;
    by L.J. Swingle in *KSJ* 30 (1981): 194-96; BROWN, Nathaniel,
    Sexuality and Feminism in Shelley (see *RMB* for 1979, p. 117),
    rev. by Stuart Curran in *SiR* 20 (1981): 383-87; by Carl H.
    Ketcham in *ELN* 18 (1981): 219-23; by Susan M. Levin in *KSJ*
    30 (1981): 198-201; DAWSON, P.M.S., *The Unacknowledged
    Legislator: Shelley and Politics* (see *RMB* for 1980, p. 122),
    rev. by William Galperin in *JEGP* 80 (1981): 423-25; by Daniel
    Hughes in *SiR* 20 (1981): 262-67; by Gerald McNeice in *TWC* 12
    (1981): 181-83; by P.S. in *CritQ* 23 (1981): 93; by John F.
    Schell in *CollL* 8 (1981): 197-98; DUFFY, Edward, *Rousseau in
    England: The Context for Shelley's Critique of the Enlighten-
    ment* (see *RMB* for 1980, p. 124), rev. by John Clubbe in *KSJ*
    30 (1981): 196-98; by Carl H. Ketcham in *ELN* 18 (1981): 219-
    23; WEBB, Timothy, *The Violet in the Crucible: Shelley and
    Translation* (see *ELN* 16, Supp., 72), rev. by Rolf Breur in
    Anglia 99 (1981): 253-56.

SMITH

Reviews of book previously listed:

    BELL, Alan, *Sidney Smith* (see *RMB* for 1980, p. 128), rev. by
    John Clive in *ASch* 50 (1981): 416-19, enthusiastically; by
    Sam Pickering in *SR* 89 (1981): lxxxviii-xc.

SOUTHEY

Baine, Rodney M. "The Southey-Sargent Copy of Lewis and Clark's
    Travels." *HLB* 29 (1981): 450-52.

Southey's copy of the *Travels* (now in the Arnold Arboretum Library at Harvard) testifies to his "diligence" in preparing an anonymous review for *The Quarterly Review* in 1815. "Upon almost every page are his neat, almost feminine hooks, swastikas, occasional question marks, and *nota benes*." The review has been largely ignored by Southey scholars. (R.A.B.)

Curry, Kenneth. "The Text of Robert Southey's Published Correspondence: Misdated Letters and Missing Names." *PBSA* 75 (1981): 127–46.

Corrects dates for nearly one hundred letters appearing in two nineteenth-century editions of the correspondence, and supplies many of the names omitted by the editors.

Good, James M. "William Taylor, Robert Southey, and the Word 'Autobiography.'" *TWC* 12 (1981): 125–27.

See also Wellens ("English 1. Bibliography").

Review of book previously listed:

BERNHARDT-KABISCH, Ernest, *Robert Southey* (see *ELN* 17, Supp., 122), rev. by Chrystal Tilney in *ChLB* 33 (1981): 19–21, severely.

TAYLOR, WILLIAM

See Good ("Southey").

TURNER

Brown, David. "Turner's Lost Exhibits of 1799: Some New Evidence." *BM* 123 (April 1981): 227–28; 1 illus.

Chubb, William. "Turner's 'Cicero at his Villa.'" *BM* 123 (July 1981): 417–21; 4 illus.

Finley, Gerald. *Landscape of Memory: Turner as Illustrator to Scott*. London: Scolar Press, 1980. Pp. 272; 108 illus. £30.00.

Rev. by Evelyn Joll in *BM* 123 (April 1981): 244.

Marks, Arthur S. "Rivalry at the Royal Academy: Wilkie, Turner, and Bird." *SiR* 20 (1981): 333-62.

Mayoux, J.-J. "Turner à Paris." *QL* 358 (Nov. 1-15, 1981): 16-17.
    A Turner exhibition in Paris.

Wilton, Andrew. *Turner and the Sublime.* British Museum Publications, 1980. Pp. 192; 140 illus. (32 in color). £12.95; University of Chicago Press, 1980. $15.95 paper.

    Rev. by John Gage in *TLS*, Jan. 30, 1981, pp. 119-20; by Evelyn Joll in *Apollo* 114 (1981): 138.

Reviews of books previously listed:

GAGE, John, ed., *Collected Correspondence of J.M.W. Turner, with an Early Diary and a Memoir by George Jones* (see *RMB* for 1980, p. 38), rev. by Marcia Pointon in *BJA* 21 (1981): 77-79; by Andrew Wilton in *Apollo* 113 (1981): 56-59; WILTON, Andrew, *The Life and Work of J.M.W. Turner* (see *RMB* for 1980, p. 47), rev. by Luke Herrmann in *BM* 123 (May 1981): 314-15.

Composite review:

Errington, Lindsay. *Art History* 4 (1981): 232-33.

    Reviewing Gerald Finley, *Landscape of Memory: Turner as Illustrator to Scott*, and Andrew Wilton, *Turner and the Sublime*. See above under names of authors.

WOLLSTONECRAFT

Butler, Marilyn. "The Woman at the Window: Ann Radcliffe in the Novels of Mary Wollstonecraft and Jane Austen." Pp. 128-48 in Janet Todd, ed., *Gender and Literary Voice* (*Women and Literature*, Vol. 1, new series). New York: Holmes and Meier Publishers, Inc., 1980.

    Not seen.

Eisenstein, Zillah R. *The Radical Future of Liberal Feminism.* New York: Longman, 1981. Pp. xi+260. $17.95.

    Eisenstein analyzes the philosophy of liberal feminism which arose in seventeenth-century England, and counteracts the popular notion that liberalism is without ideology by tracing its growth through the philosophies of John Locke and Jean Jacques Rousseau.

Wollstonecraft responds to a transitional society in which women are no longer integrally involved in productive economic activity by recommending that women cultivate reason in order to be rational wives and mothers in the private sphere. This cultivation of reason will also foster independence. Despite her demand that women should also reap the benefit of the new thinking, Wollstonecraft fails to see that women cannot harvest the fruits of liberal individualism in their social and political reality if they are denied the public sphere. How Eisenstein factors into her engrossing study Wollstonecraft's notions in the second *Vindication* about the need for women to vote, pursue careers, and enter political life remains an open question.

In its serious treatment of Wollstonecraft as a thinker who must be located in the eighteenth-century philosophical tradition, this book makes a stimulating and sizable contribution toward a fully-fledged intellectual history of Mary Wollstonecraft. (M.F.)

Faderman, Lillian. *Surpassing the Love of Men: Romantic Friendship and Love Between Women from the Renaissance to the Present*. New York: William Morrow and Company, Inc., 1981. Pp. 496. $10.95.

Faderman documents the history of romantic friendship between women in literature from the sixteenth to the twentieth century. That Wollstonecraft experienced and cherished such friendships is evident from her early correspondence with Jane Arden and her desire to be an integral part of the Blood household. Godwin characterized her love for Fanny Blood as the "ruling passion of her mind." This relationship, Faderman suggests, formed her personality, although modern biographers still try hard to avoid any discussion of Wollstonecraft's love for other women. Wollstonecraft's inability to achieve the close relationships with women which she desired partly accounts for her melancholy and negative outlook throughout her life. This absorbing, carefully documented study is one of the most important works of feminist literary criticism to appear this decade. (M.F.)

Hamalian, Leo, ed. "Journey Through Sweden." Pp. 15-26 in Leo Hamalian, ed., *Ladies on the Loose*. New York: Dodd, Mead, & Company, 1981. $11.95.

Locates Mary Wollstonecraft in a tradition of adventurous, unconventional women such as Hester Piozzi, Lady Hester Stanhope, and Lady Mary Wortley Montagu who travelled to escape the confines of their society. Excerpted Letter V shows the intensity of Wollstonecraft's feelings and response to nature. The continual anthologizing of Wollstonecraft's works suggests that she has finally arrived. (M.F.)

McCormack, Kathleen. "George Eliot: Wollstonecraft's 'Judicious Person With Some Turn for Humour.'" *ELN* 19 (1981): 44-46.

Eliot's marginalia in her copy of *A Vindication of the Rights of Woman.*

McGuinn, Nicholas. "George Eliot and Mary Wollstonecraft." Pp. 188-205 in Sara Delamont and Lorna Duffin, eds., *The Nineteenth-Century Woman: Her Cultural and Physical World.* New York: Barnes and Noble, 1978.

How was *A Vindication of the Rights of Woman* received by nineteenth-century Englishwomen, since the work is predominantly moderate in tone by the standards of Mary Wollstonecraft's own time? Women should be rational wives and chastity must prevail. Female education conduces to that end. Ergo, her work could be mistaken for a "long-forgotten treatise by Hannah More."

Since Wollstonecraft does not identify the cause of female emancipation with the struggle of the working class, her radical contemporaries such as William Thompson complained of her "narrow views." Only the notoriety of her life and especially the fact that Godwin's *Memoirs of the Author of A Vindication of the Rights of Woman* coincided with the Kingsborough scandal in which Wollstonecraft's former pupils were deeply implicated brought *A Vindication* into disrepute. Thus, Wollstonecraft's supporters were forced into a defensive position, with women reluctant to defend her publicly. George Eliot broke that silence in 1855, but uncharacteristically toned down her style in order to avoid comparisons between Wollstonecraft's life and her own. Under cover of the feminist perspectives of Margaret Fuller and Wollstonecraft, Eliot contributes a personal feminist statement and retains her reputation "for moderation and impartiality," although her outburst in the seventh paragraph contrasts sharply with the essay's overall tone. She distances herself to win the reader's confidence, stresses the moderate views of *A Vindication*, and carefully avoids its radical dimension.

Eliot rescues *A Vindication* from fifty years of public obscurity but, like Dorothea Brooke, humiliates herself intellectually to do so. (M.F.)

Myers, Mitzi. "Godwin's *Memoirs* of Wollstonecraft: The Shaping of Self and Subject." *SIR* 20 (1981): 299-316.

The *Memoirs* are "a congeries of romantic attitudes, their shaping of self and subject in terms of internal and private aspects a paradigm of romantic biography and, to some extent, of confessional autobiography as well." Thus Godwin seeks to unfold Wollstonecraft's character in the *Memoirs* just as he described individual case studies in his romances.

Having learned from Wollstonecraft the importance of feelings, Godwin used the memoirs to come to terms with his grief and his loss. By emphatically entering her personality in this way, he assimilated the emotional lessons she taught him; minute particulars and psychological details counted for more than historical abstractions.

His emendations for the second version of the *Memoirs* reveal that he burrowed more deeply into her actions and their motivations, thereby enabling him to work out his own vision of human possibility. Although imperfect and even distorted, the *Memoirs* stand as Godwin's tribute to his mentor in human feelings. An invigorating, carefully argued hypothesis. (M.F.)

Peters, Margot. "Biographies of Women." *Biography* 2,iii (1979): 201-17.

Using gender as a basis for interpreting women's lives is not a new approach, but the contemporary understanding, emphasis, and interpretation of gender do constitute one.

Concentrating on Charlotte Brontë, and secondarily on Mary Wollstonecraft, Peters contrasts different approaches to their subjects by biographers in the last 120 years. Charles Kegan Paul tries to reestablish Mary Wollstonecraft's respectability and "social normality" by distorting the facts, Gabrielle Long (George R. Preedy), applying a traditional psychological approach, castigates Mary Wollstonecraft's character and works with a "schoolmistressly didacticism," while Margaret George is "confused about her subject's sexual status."

The third set of Ralph Wardle and Eleanor Flexner adopts a more traditional historical approach, stressing the shape of their subject's life according to Taine's dictates of race, milieu, and time. More recently, biographers such as Flexner, Clare Tomalin to some extent, but particularly Emily Sunstein follow the "biological absolute": the writer is explained by the life.

Peters questions the notion that the universal feminine experience makes more difference to a writer than race, environment, and time. As a case in point, Peters views Sunstein's emphasis on the "probable biological rhythms that influenced Wollstonecraft's behavior," as a position

which inevitably leads to the conclusion that only women
can understand and therefore write about women. She also
rejects a genetic or an environmental determinist approach
to biography, arguing by contrast that individuals possess
an attitude *toward* these forces, and *toward* gender, and are
not simply or only acted upon. (M.F.)

Todd, Janet. "Reason and Sensibility in Mary Wollstonecraft's
   The Wrongs of Woman." *Frontiers* 5,iii (1980): 17-20.

   In *A Vindication of the Rights of Woman*, Wollstonecraft
challenges the entrenched idea that reason is the province
of dominant men and sensibility of irrational, inferior
women. Although at first glance she seems to have altered
her point of view in *The Wrongs of Woman* by extolling the
sensibility of the heroine, Maria, in fact the plot of the
novel rather than Maria's words yields the same message.
Maria's difficulties stem from an excessive cultivation of
sensibility, not from the societal oppression of women, as
Maria herself argues. Jemima carries the book's moral weight
because the feelings she finally develops are grounded in
reason whereas Maria, beguiled by sensibility, remains
deceived by Darnford. A neatly worked out thesis which suggests why Wollstonecraft viewed *The Wrongs of Woman* as "A
Vindication of the Rights of Woman, Part 2." (M.F.)

Wexler, Alice. "Emma Goldman on Mary Wollstonecraft." *Fems* 1
   (1981): 113-33.

   Goldman chose Wollstonecraft as the subject of her 1911
lecture because her anarchism was founded less on an identification with the masses than on an identification with
history's rebels and martyrs, such as Wollstonecraft herself.
Goldman highlights the Wollstonecraft who, like Goldman
herself, opposed authority and sought a transformation in
consciousness, both a pioneer of modern womanhood and a
tragic Romantic heroine (another role in which Goldman saw
herself cast). A few years later, Ruth Benedict portrayed
Wollstonecraft as less heroic, less tragic, and less radical,
and emphasized the limits of Wollstonecraft's challenge,
particularly in domestic life.
   The different approaches to Wollstonecraft illuminate the
distance between the generations, cultures, and class backgrounds of Goldman and Benedict. Where Goldman's feminism
was Romantic, radical, and revolutionary, Benedict's was
practical, liberal, and reformist. In reinventing Wollstonecraft, Wexler finds Goldman and Benedict reinventing themselves. (M.F.)

See also Cleary ("French 2. Staël").

Reviews of books previously listed:

  TODD, Janet, *Women's Friendship in Literature* (see *RMB* for
  1980, p. 131), rev. by Marilyn Butler in *EiC* 31 (1981): 246-
  49; WARDLE, Ralph M., ed., *Collected Letters of Mary Wollstonecraft* (see *RMB* for 1979, p. 123), rev. by Gordon S.
  Haight in *YR* 69,i (1979), 112-18, along with Volume IV of
  The Letters of Virginia Woolf.

WORDSWORTH, DOROTHY

Gunn, Elizabeth. *A Passion for the Particular: Dorothy Words-
  worth--A Portrait.* London: Gollancz, 1981. Pp. 320. £12.50.

    Rev. by A.N. Wilson in *S*, Feb. 14, 1981, p. 21: "cliché-
  ridden and confused."

Homans, Margaret. *Women Writers and Poetic Identity: Dorothy
  Wordsworth, Emily Bronte, and Emily Dickinson.* Princeton
  University Press, 1981. Pp. x+260. $14.95.

    Rev. by Suzanne Juhasz in *ELN* 19 (1981): 143-45 as "an
  important and elegant contribution to feminist scholarship";
  by Edna Longley in *TLS*, May 29, 1981, p. 613, along with
  Aliki and Willis Barnstone, *A Book of Women Poets* (Schocken
  Books), rather severely.
    Has chapters on Dorothy Wordsworth, Emily Brontë, and
  Emily Dickinson. The chapter on Wordsworth has its moments,
  but also a good deal of exaggeration and an overemphasis (in
  my view) on psychologizing, e.g., "Separating nature from its
  maternal characterization, turning Mother Nature back into
  nature, ought to alleviate one of the major difficulties experienced by a woman writing in the Romantic tradition. But
  although Dorothy may recognize the importance of making this
  separation, this recognition does not open the way to an un-
  troubled or prolific poetics" (100). It is no service to
  Dorothy's exquisite sensibility to load it down with such
  stuff, nor to claim that "her potential for language and vision
  appears to have been just as great as her brother's, as far as
  such faculties can be measured" (41). Nonsense! (B.C.H.)

WORDSWORTH, WILLIAM

Betz, Paul F., ed. *"Benjamin the Waggoner" by William Wordsworth.* Cornell University Press, 1981. Pp. xii+356. $39.50.

This is the fifth title in the Cornell Wordsworth series,
and it is in every way a worthy companion to its predecessors.
This volume has an introduction tracing the history of the
composition of the poem, which turns out to be rather more
complex than had been thought, followed by "reading texts"
of *Benjamin the Waggoner* MS. 1 (1806) and *The Waggoner* as
first printed in 1819. These two texts are on facing pages
(like De Selincourt's *Prelude*), which makes comparison shop-
ping easy. The 1819 text has actually not been seen since
that date, for the poet went on tinkering with it until as
late as 1849. These tinkerings are preserved carefully in
an *apparatus criticus* at the foot of the 1819 *Waggoner* pages.
In keeping with the Cornell series, a number of transcriptions, with facing photographic reproductions, follow the
"reading" texts; these include transcriptions of MS. 2 (MS.
1, the basis of the reading text, is clear and apparently
very free of emendation, and thus does not require any photographs or transcriptions--which is at first confusing to
the reader, and then seen to be perfectly logical), and of
MS. 3 (1812). The transcription of MS. 2 (1806) is accompanied
by an *apparatus criticus* which records those places where
MS. 1 differs from MS. 2; the line numbers supplied in the
transcript are keyed back to the "reading text," which was
based on MS. 1. Again, this only appears to be confusing,
reversing, as it does, the usual chronology of text and
critical apparatus; all is clear when using the actual book,
at least if you pay attention to what you are about. Other
transcriptions include jottings for much later revisions
(e.g., 1836). Two appendices are included, one with transcriptions and photographs of Coleridge's proposed revisions
to MS. 1, the other concerned with T.J. Wise and the chronology of MS. 2. Betz is too tactful to quite come out and say
so, but it would seem that De Selincourt edited this poem
for the Oxford edition with perhaps less care than some
other texts. At any rate, Betz is the first to mention
Coleridge's contribution, though his handwriting is unmistak-
able, and unmistakably present in the photographs shown of
manuscripts known to have been used by De Selincourt.
Similarly (though this is a harder matter to gauge) De
Selincourt "incorrectly attributes both manuscripts [1 and
2] to Sara Hutchinson (*PW* II, 498)" when, in fact, they are
in Mary Wordsworth's hand (footnote, p. 15). We learn a
number of interesting details from all this textual tender-
loving-care, not the least interesting of which is that the
original title of Wordsworth's poem, as of 1806, was probably "Benjamin the Waggoner and his Waggon" (p. 42, *app. crit.*),
which has a fine, defiant ring of stubborn materiality about
it. The later stages of composition and revision, after 1819,

are frankly less interesting to follow, and are recorded
with an almost maddening minuteness—not the fault of the
editor, but of the ideals of present-day scholarship. I do
have to add that I find Wordsworth's final version of 1849
(De Selincourt's text) the most interesting version of the
poem as a poem, when all is said; but I suspect that this is
a minority view, and it in no way detracts from the significance or achievement of this admirable edition. (B.C.H.)

Bindman, David. "Sir Francis Chantrey, 1781-1841." *TLS*, Jan.
30, 1981, p. 110.

Review of exhibition in the National Portrait Gallery;
Chantrey's bust of Wordsworth illustrated.

Brinkley, Robert A. "The Incident in the Simplon Pass: A Note
on Wordsworth's Revisions." *TWC* 12 (1981): 122-25.

Bushnell, John P. "'Where is the Lamb for a Burnt Offering?':
Michael's Covenant and Sacrifice." *TWC* 12 (1981): 246-52.

Cosgrove, Brian. "Wordsworth and the Arcadian Imagination."
DUJ 42 (1980): 37-43.

Several poems, early and late, are used to demonstrate a
persistent critique of the tendency of an immature imagination to create poetic refuges from reality.

Darlington, Beth, ed. *The Love Letters of William and Mary
Wordsworth*. Cornell University Press, 1981. Pp. 265. $19.95.

Rev. by Claire Tomalin in *TLS*, Oct. 30, 1981, p. 1255.
This is it—the thirty-one new letters (fifteen by the
poet, sixteen by his wife) written in July and Aug. 1810
(nos. 1-7) and April-June 1812 (8-31). They were discovered
by accident in 1977 and have caused quite a stir, because
they really are passionate love letters from the man whom
Shelley called "solemn and unsexual" (perhaps, à la Bloom,
poets have to prove they are strong by unsexing their poetic
fathers). Wordsworthians will be very glad to have these
letters, since sexual passion is a current talisman of
authenticity, and Wordsworth's capacity in this regard has
been dismissed by a persistent minority of readers ever
since Shelley's time. They are edited here with taste, discernment, and just the right fullness of detail, making
this book a rarity in being appropriate for a general audience
as well as for scholars. We are given a preface, an introduction, and a short commentary before the text of each
letter itself. In addition, there are two maps and twenty-

two illustrations. These include miniatures, found with the
letters, by an unidentified artist, which are thought to be
of Thomas and Catherine Wordsworth, the poet's two children
who died at tragically early ages. Their countenances are,
I believe, otherwise unrecorded. Catherine was the subject
of Wordsworth's great sonnet, "I turned to share my transport," and it seems almost beyond the realm of scholarly
good fortune that we should now, and for all time, know
what she looked like. Let one excerpt take the place of any
further commentary: "Your beloved letter my William I never
can be enough grateful to thee for--O William! I really am
too happy to move about on this earth, it is *well* indeed
that my employments keep me active about other things or I
should not be able to contain my felicity--Good Heavens!
that I should be adored in this manner by thee thou first &
best of Men" (79-80). The publication of this book is an
important event in English literature. (B.C.H.)

Darlington, Beth, ed. *My Dearest Love: Letters of William and
Mary Wordsworth, 1810*. Printed at the Scolar Press for the
Trustees of Dove Cottage, 1981. Pp. 81. Pre-publication
prices, £450.00 and £250.00; distributors, Blackwell Rare
Books, Oxford.

  Rev. enthusiastically by Jonathan Wordsworth in *TWC* 12
(1981): 210, 273-75.
  Not seen; but evidently the letters are printed in facsimile.

Devlin, D.D. *Wordsworth and the Poetry of Epitaphs*. London:
Macmillan, 1980. £12.00.

  Rev. by Karin Horowitz in *EiC* 32 (1982): 74-81 dismissively.

Elder, John C. "John Muir and the Literature of Wilderness."
MR 22 (1981): 375-86.

  A brief discussion of Wordsworth which suggests that he
was not Muir. (R.A.B.)

Erdman, David V. "The Man Who Was Not Napoleon." *TWC* 12 (1981):
92-96.

  More about the real John Oswald and his possible connection
with Wordsworth. The evidence is circumstantial and speculative, but there are enough bits and pieces to make the
suggestion of *some* kind of connection persuasive. Oswald
in *The Borderers* is an almost certain example; and it looks
as though Wordsworth just may have contemplated a much more

radical involvement with the revolutionary cause, in the
fall of 1792, than the later record officially suggests--
perhaps even a hare-brained scheme of invasion of the British
Isles. (B.C.H.)

Essick, Robert N. "Wordsworth and Leech-Lore." *TWC* 12 (1981):
100-02.

Gates, Barbara T. "Wordsworth's Mirror of Morality: Distortion
of Church History." *TWC* 12 (1981): 129-32.

Haney, David P. "The Emergence of the Autobiographical Figure
in *The Prelude*, Book I." *SiR* 20 (1981): 33-63.

Studies the rhetoric of Book I in order to display the
"textual problems in relation to which the autobiographical
figure emerges." Argues that "autobiography functions here
in a way that is precisely 'figural.'"

Hayden, John O. "The Road to Tintern Abbey." *TWC* 12 (1981):
211-16.

Hayden, John O. "Wordsworth and Coleridge: Shattered Mirrors,
Shining Lamps?" *TWC* 12 (1981): 71-81.

Hodgson, John A. *Wordsworth's Philosophical Poetry, 1797-1814*.
University of Nebraska Press, 1980. Pp. xxi+216. $17.50.

Rev. by Peter J. Manning (mixed) in *TWC* 12 (1981): 151-53;
by David Profumo in *TLS*, Feb. 20, 1981, p. 209, as "rewarding" for those who know the poems.
This is a study, not so much of Wordsworth's poetry, as
of the ideas found in the poetry, and, as such, it runs a
certain risk of exteriority, of mere paraphrase. The author
presents "a history of Wordsworth's metaphysical beliefs
from *The Borderers* to *The Excursion*," and in the course of
this history he follows the development of what he calls
Wordsworth's "emblematizing" (as opposed to symbolic) vision.
He sees Wordsworth's career as going through four distinct
stages: 1797-1798, 1798-1804, 1804-1805, and "after 1805."
His career represents "a patterned, dialectical progression
through his interacting hopes for and anxieties about man's
proper relation to ultimate Power, hopes and anxieties
particularly centering on notions of godhead and of immortality." The four stages of growth comprise "an initial,
optimistic embracing of a metaphysical creed which seems to
offer a satisfying interpretation of man's nature and fate;
a reactive dissatisfaction, as some aspects or consequences

of the original creed gradually appear after all to be in-
adequately consolatory for or unacceptably false to human
experience; a defensive, compensatory response, whereby
Wordsworth strives to cope as best he can with these limitations of his creed; and finally a revisionary, corrective
response, whereby he modifies the very assumptions of his
original creed to accord with his new estimate of his
metaphysical needs."

The author is perceptive in his vision of Wordsworth's
skepticism on the way to a more orthodox faith, and he sees
the *Prelude* as a "great triumph of humanistic thought." The
use of "humanistic" in this sense to mean "skeptical" or
"not Christian" rather than in its richer sense as in the
phrase, "Renaissance humanism," may be deplorable, but with
all that is being said about the other Romantics and their
skepticisms of late, it is perhaps time that a similar quality
of mind were recognized in Wordsworth. If the book has a
weakness, it is that the ground has been covered before,
from slightly different perspectives. But the prose style
is readable and there are a number of local insights along
the way that are more rewarding, perhaps, than the central
thesis of the study. (B.C.H.)

Jackson, Geoffrey. "Nominal and Actual Audiences: Some Strategies of Communication in Wordsworth's Poetry." *TWC* 12 (1981):
226-31.

Jarvis, R.J. "The Five Book *Prelude*: A Reconsideration."
JEGP 80 (1981): 528-51.

Concludes, in sharp disagreement with Jonathan Wordsworth,
that "it seems certain that there was never a completed
version of the *Prelude* in five Books and we cannot now manu-
facture one ... we must not be tempted into hypothesising a
distinctive and identifiably finished five-Book *Prelude*
inviting analysis of a kind that would be inappropriate in
view of the disabling textual facts." All the facts, however,
may not be in. (B.C.H.)

Kelley, Paul. "Wordsworth and Pope's *Epistle to Cobham*." *N&Q*
28 (1981): 314-15.

Apparently the imagery of dissection (we murder to, etc.)
comes from this poem, which Wordsworth quotes at the end of
the preface to *The Borderers*, but it is surely an exaggeration to claim the *Epistle* as "a seminal influence" on the
whole period 1794-1797. (B.C.H.)

Kelley, Theresa M. "The Economics of the Heart: Wordsworth's Sublime and Beautiful." *RP&P* 5,i (1981): 15-32.

Kishel, Joseph F. "Wordsworth and the Grande Chartreuse." *TWC* 12 (1981): 82-88.

Larkin, Peter. "Wordsworth's 'After-Sojourn': Revision and Unself-Rivalry in the Later Poetry." *Sir* 20 (1981): 409-36.

  Examines the "three 'temperaments'--the counter-sublime, sufficient mutuality, and prevenience--whose presence can be felt among the myriad occasions of Wordsworth's late poetry [and which] are not so much positions or intentions as ways in which his language attempts to minister to itself as capable inheritor of his poetic past."

Luther, Susan. "Wordsworth's *Prelude*, VI. 592-616 (1850)." *TWC* 12 (1981): 253-61.

Magnuson, Paul. "The Genesis of Wordsworth's Ode." *TWC* 12 (1981): 23-30.

Marsden-Smedley, Hester. "Beginning at Racedown." *TWC* 12 (1981): 141-42.

  A lecture given at the Bicentennial celebrations in 1970 and printed here for the first time. The author grew up at Racedown, which her family (the Pinneys) built in the eighteenth century. There are some details about Wordsworth in this short but charming piece which have never been recorded before. (B.C.H.)

McGovran, James Holt, Jr. "'Alone Seeking the Visible World': The Wordsworths, Virginia Woolf, and *The Waves*." *MLQ* 42 (1981): 265-91.

McNulty, J. Bard. "Self-Awareness in the Making of 'Tintern Abbey.'" *TWC* 12 (1981): 97-100.

Newlyn, Lucy. "'In City Pent': Echo and Allusion in Wordsworth, Coleridge, and Lamb, 1797-1801." *RES* 32 (1981): 408-28.

Newlyn, Lucy. "Wordsworth, Coleridge, and 'The Castle of Indolence' Stanzas." *TWC* 12 (1981): 106-13.

Peterfreund, Stuart. "*The Prelude*: Wordsworth's Metamorphic Epic." *Genre* 14 (1981): 441-72.

"Wordsworth combines the ideas of internalization and metamorphosis with the idea of the progression of genres."

Rehder, Robert. *Wordsworth and the Beginnings of Modern Poetry.*
Totowa, N.J.: Barnes & Noble, 1981. Pp. 245.

   Rev. by Lachlan Mackinnon in *TLS*, June 19, 1981, p. 704.
   Not seen.

Robinson, Jeffrey C. "The Immortality Ode: Lionel Trilling and
Helen Vendler." *TWC* 12 (1981): 64-70.

Ross, Donald, Jr. "Poems 'Bound Each to Each' in the 1815
Edition of Wordsworth." *TWC* 12 (1981): 133-40.

Ruoff, Gene W. "'Fields of Sleep': The Obscurities of the Ode,
I-IV." *TWC* 12 (1981): 45-51.

Schofield, Mary Anne. "Wordsworth and the Philadelphia *Port
Folio.*" *ELN* 18 (1981): 187-91.

Schopf, Sue Weaver. "Wordsworth's Exploration of Geriatric
Psychology: Another Look at the Narrator of 'The Thorn.'"
ELN 19 (1981): 33-40.

Schulman, Samuel E. "The Spenser of the Intimations Ode."
TWC 12 (1981): 31-35.

Sherry, Charles. *Wordsworth's Poetry of the Imagination.*
Oxford: Clarendon Press, 1980. Pp. 148. $19.50.

   Rev. (guardedly) by Frances Ferguson in *TWC* 12 (1981):
   149-51.
   This book is an attempt to apply the Platonic theory of
   anamnesis, as set forth especially in *Phaedrus*, *Phaedo*,
   Meno, and *Philebus*, to the process of visionary experience
   in Wordsworth. "Memory" here differs from "recollection";
   the latter is a deeper term, much like anamnesis, and refers
   to the soul's *awareness* of an earlier vision of a deeper
   level of reality, a "remembering to remember" the imperial
   palace whence we came. In the author's words, "In this study
   I wish to explore the hypothesis that the source of the
   imagination and of what is divine in its visitations is the
   child's anamnestic view of the world as it is represented"
   in the Ode (7). "Recollection," on this reading, is "the
   discovery of the significance of what is revealed in the
   visitation of the imagination"; "recollection, seen in relation to the experience of the visitation of the imagination,

becomes the repetition of a repetition of an originary experience, and by such repetition recollection raises that
experience to conscious significance as the basis of the
poet's vision of the link between the divine and the mortal"
(8). I have reversed the order of these two quotations from
p. 8 deliberately, to show what I believe is the strength,
as well as the weakness, of this study. The book begins with
what is basically a good idea, and a simple one--"recollection" is a "discovery" of "significance," an understanding
of the meaning of meaning--and obfuscates it in a quite un-
necessarily elaborate terminological tangle, derived from
the phenomenological criticism of the last twenty years.
There are some useful insights to be had, for example, the
threefold division which the author sees in the poet's records
of the "visitations of the imagination": first, a "usurpa-
tion of the outward senses"; second, a "newly acquired perception of things"; third, "recollection," which "brings
the other two to completion by discovering in them the
significance they inherently bear, that is, that they were
divine intimations" (21-22). Now this account is obviously
true, or true enough; no one writing about the poetry of
the imagination in Wordsworth, at least since A.C. Bradley
in 1909, would be likely to dispute this account. So what's
new? Very little; at bottom, the essay represents what oft
was thought, but never so complexly expressed before. The
use of modern philosophers, for example, Heidegger, though
it may constrict the intellectual arteries, is probably more
competent here than the various excursions into Christian
metaphysics (the statement that many of Wordsworth's
"analogies for expressing the relation of the finite to
the divine, infinite totality encompassing it" actually
"come from St. Augustine" is not true, either historically--
they are older than the fourth century--or in terms of
literary "influence," and which sense the author means to
convey by "come from," p. 20, is in any case unclear).
Finally, this book seems to me full of portentous truisms,
thus: "There is in Wordsworth's poetry an interplay between
mind and nature which is expressed as a narrative of the
mind's coming to a conscious discovery of its powers" (94).
Again: "The development of the poet's mind from infancy to
the time recorded at the end of *The Prelude* is linked to
the reciprocating interplay of the soul and the natural and
historical world which it encounters" (73). Once more: "It
is not from the immediate vision of a natural scene that
the recollective recognition constituting the fundamental
character of the imagination comes, but from the image of
that scene remembered, over which the mind broods" (112).

The interesting, though debatable, notion that the imagination is much the same as *anamnesis* obscures the fact that
what this sentence is really saying is that we brood about
our *memories* of experience, and not the experience itself,
something which no one could doubt for a moment who paused
to think about the matter. I hope I am not just being a cur-
mudgeon (*Webster's*: "an avaricious, grasping fellow; niggard;
churl"). (B.C.H.)

Smith, K.E. "Love in *The Borderers*." *DUJ* 43 (1981): 97-102.

   The play's presentation of human love is a response to
Godwin's dramatization and investigation of human love in
Political Justice.

Spivak, Gayatri Chakravorty. "Sex and History in *The Prelude*
   (1805), Books Nine to Thirteen." *TSLL* 23 (1981): 324-60.

   Annette Vallon *rediviva*, this time through Derridean
spectacles, darkly. "As a feminist reader of men on women,
I thought it useful to point out that, in the texts of the
Great Tradition, the most remotely occluded and transparently
mediating figure is woman" (sic). We get dashes of Heidegger,
Feuerbach, Marx, "laissez-faire capitalism," castration, and
the "anti-Vietnam War Movement" (again, sic). The author
finds Emile Legouis to have been "sexist and politically
reactionary" in his account of *l'affaire Annette*; Herbert
Read's evaluation of same was "thoroughly sentimental,"
while Wordsworth's was "increasingly brutal." This article
is not for the faint of heart, nor (in Arnold's phrase)
"the disinterested lover of poetry." (B.C.H.)

Springer, Carolyn. "Far from the Madding Crowd: Wordsworth
   and the News of Robespierre's Death." *TWC* 12 (1981): 243-45.

Stempel, Daniel. "Wordsworth and the Phenomenology of Textual
   Constitution." *P&L* 5 (1981): 150-75.

Ward, William S. "Laying Bricks and Squaring a Circle: Wordsworth and Two of His Literary Friends--Barron Field and
   Thomas Noon Talfourd." *TWC* 12 (1981): 12-22.

Williams, Anne. "The *Intimations Ode*: Wordsworth's Fortunate
   Fall." *RP&P* 5,i (1981): 1-13.

Woolford, John. "Wordsworth Agonistes." *EiC* 31 (1981): 27-40.

   Ties the "Was it for this" passage of *The Prelude* with
Samson ("For this did th'Angel twice descend? For this/

Ordain'd thy nurture holy?"), rather than with *Paradise Lost*,
and the present opening of *Prelude* I with the opening of
Samson, down to "The breath of Heav'n fresh blowing," l. 10.
The author sees Samson as a type of failed vision for both
Wordsworth and Coleridge. Valuable. (B.C.H.)

Wu, Qian-zhi. "Another Possible Influence on Wordsworth's
Lyrical Ballads." *TWC* 12 (1981): 269-70.

   "Oh, dear, what can the matter be?" on a line in "Goody
Blake and Harry Gill."

See also Lobb, Reed ("General 3. Criticism"); Wellens
   ("English 1. Bibliography"); Aers, Buckler, Butler, Hopkins,
   McFarland, Reiman, Twitchell, Wesling ("English 3. Criticism");
   Zall ("Coleridge"); Roe ("Hunt"); Carothers, Keach ("Shelley,
   P.B.").

Reviews of books previously listed:

AVERILL, James, *Wordsworth and the Poetry of Human Suffering*
(see *RMB* for 1980, p. 133), rev. by William Galperin in
Criticism 23 (1981): 185-87; BAKER, Jeffrey, *Time and Mind
in Wordsworth's Poetry* (see *RMB* for 1980, p. 135), rev. by
James A. Butler in *TWC* 12 (1981): 153-54; BEER, John, *Wordsworth and the Human Heart* (see *RMB* for 1979, pp. 125-26),
rev. by Lucy Newlyn in *RES* 32 (1981): 227-31; BEER, John,
Wordsworth in Time (see *RMB* for 1980, p. 135), rev. by Lucy
Newlyn in *RES* 32 (1981): 227-31; FRIEDMAN, Michael H., *The
Making of a Tory Humanist: William Wordsworth and the Idea
of Community* (see *RMB* for 1979, p. 129), rev. by William H.
Galperin (mixed) in *JEGP* 80 (1981): 257-59; by William Heath
in *SiR* 20 (1981): 117-21; by W.J.B. Owen in *YES* 11 (1981):
300-02; HILL, Alan G., ed., *The Letters of William and
Dorothy Wordsworth, V: The Later Years, Part II, 1829-1834*
(see *RMB* for 1980, p. 137), rev. by Beth Darlington in *TWC*
12 (1981): 146-48; SHAVER, Chester L., and Alice C. Shaver,
Wordsworth's Library: A Catalogue (see *RMB* for 1979, p. 133),
rev. by James A. Butler in *ELN* 18 (1981): 301-04.

Review articles:

Hunter, Jefferson. "The Court-Suit Laureates." *HudR* 34 (1981):
135-40.

   Discussing Wordsworth and Tennyson. For the former, Hunter
draws on Hunter Davies, *William Wordsworth* (Atheneum, 1981;
$17.95).

Logan, Stephen. *N&Q* 28 (1981): 344-48.

A review of the Alan G. Hill edition of *The Letters of William
and Dorothy Wordsworth*, V: *The Later Years, Part II* (see *RMB*
for 1980, p. 137). On the basis of a random comparison between printed text and manuscript letters, Logan reveals a
quite high frequency of textual error, silently introduced
changes or omissions, and an apparent reliance on previous
printed texts rather than on the manuscripts themselves.
Tactfully presented, but disturbing, to say the least.
(B.C.H.)

FRENCH

(Compiled by Mary Ellen Birkett, Smith College; Alfred
G. Engstrom, University of North Carolina; Eugene F.
Gray, Michigan State University; Jon B. Hassel, Uni-
versity of Arkansas; James S. Patty, Vanderbilt Uni-
versity; Albert B. Smith, Jr., University of Florida;
Emile J. Talbot, University of Illinois at Urbana-
Champaign)

1. GENERAL

Albertone, Manuela. *Una Scuola per la Rivoluzione: Condorcet
e il dibattito sull'istruzione 1792-1794*. Naples: Guida
Editori, 1979. Pp. 247. L6,700.00.

Rev. by Horst Dippel in *JMH* 53 (1981): 729-31.

Allen, J.S. "French Romanticism and the Origins of Popular
Literature in Paris, 1820-40." *JPC* 15,iii (1981): 132-43.

Allen, James Smith. *Popular French Romanticism: Authors,
Readers, and Books in the 19th Century*. Syracuse University
Press, 1981. Pp. xiii+290. $20.00.

Rev. by Barbara T. Cooper in *NCFS* 10 (1981-82): 175-76;
by F.W.J. Hemmings in *TLS*, May 15, 1981, p. 540; by Warren
Roberts in *AHR* 86 (1981): 1101-02.
This seems to be the first major application by an American
scholar of the sociology of literature to French Romanticism.
Using, for the most part, a statistical approach, Allen
examines the evolution of the book trade, the technology of
book production, censorship, demographics, literacy, urbaniza-
tion, economic conditions, and politics in the years 1820-
43. He makes a number of good points: a demographic bulge,
peaking around 1830, quite literally produced *les Jeune-
France*; a new, unsophisticated readership arose in the 1840s,
provoking a decline in Romanticism; history emerged as a
popular genre; among urban low-brows, older peasant folkways
and their literary equivalents (e.g., the *Bibliothèque bleue*)

gave way to new forms such as the melodramas staged by the
boulevard theaters.

Allen is less convincing in his larger argument. Works,
traits, and trends are sometimes labeled "Romantic" in a
rather simplistic way. Literary phenomena are divided into
"elitist" and "popular" without adequate definition or reference to an adequate sample.

The sprinkling of minor factual errors, the examples of
poor English and incorrect French, do not, fortunately,
seriously detract from the value of the information Allen
has accumulated and most of the generalizations he extracts
from it. Though imperfect, his book is suggestive, and opens
the way to other such studies. (J.S.P.)

Arquié-Bruley, Françoise. "Un precurseur: le comte de Saint-
    Morys (1782-1817), collectionneur d''antiquités nationales.'"
    GBA 97 (Feb. 1981): 61-77; 13 illus.

    Part II of a two-part essay. For Part I, see *RMB* for 1980,
    p. 145.

Athanassoglou, Nina. "Under the Sign of Leonidas: The Political
    and Ideological Fortune of David's *Leonidas at Thermopylae*
    under the Restoration." *ArtB* 63 (1981): 633-49.

    On "the emblematic role of David's *Leonidas at Thermopylae*
    as a memento of Liberal values during the Restoration."

Baticle, Jeannine, and Cristina Marinas, eds. *La Galerie espa-
    gnole de Louis-Philippe au Louvre 1834-1848.* (Notes et Docu-
    ments des Musées de France, 4.) Paris: Musées nationaux,
    1981. Pp. 312. Fr. 100.00.

Baude, Michel, and Marc-Mathieu Münch, eds. *Romantisme et
    religion: théologie des théologiens et théologie des écrivains.*
    Colloque interdisciplinaire organisé à la Faculté des Lettres
    de Metz les 20, 21, 22 octobre 1978 sous le patronage de
    la Société des Etudes romantiques. (Centre de Recherche
    "Littérature et Spiritualité" de l'Université de Metz.)
    Paris: Presses universitaires de France, 1980. Pp. 460. Fr.
    160.00.

    Rev. by J.-Cl. Fizaine in *ETR* 56 (1981): 455-59, and in
    Romantisme 33 (1981): 111-15; by Jacques Landrin in *IL* 33
    (1981): 214-15; by Robert J. Sealy, S.J., in *NCFS* 10 (1981-
    82): 130-31.

    The following articles are those most directly pertinent
    to the study of French Romantic literature: Paul Viallaneix,
    "Le Christ dans la fable romantique" (97-111); Hans Georg

Schenck, "Le romantisme et la déchristianisation de l'Europe"
(113-16); Laudyce Rétat, "L'Evangile éternel et la philosophie
de l'histoire au XIXe siècle (Sand, Michelet, Renan)" (117-
24); Robert Couffignal, "L'interprétation 'romantique' des
premiers chapitres de la Genèse biblique" (125-30); discussion (131-38); Marie-Antoinette Grunewald, "La théologie de
Paul Chenavard: palingénésie et régénération" (141-52);
Elisabeth Hardouin-Fugier, "Le catholicisme du *Poème de l'Ame*"
(153-60); Stéphane Michaud, "La notion de rédemption chez
quelques philosophes et écrivains en France et en Allemagne"
(163-76); Frank P. Bowman, "Frère-Colonna: exégèse biblique
et philosophie de l'histoire chez un théologien catholique
des années 1830" (177-84); Hermann Hofer, "La pensée mystique
et religieuse de Charles Nodier" (185-94); Jean-René Derré,
"Ballanche et Lamennais" (195-202); discussion (203-08);
Marc-Mathieu Münch, "Le panthéisme de J.D. Guigniaut" (209-
11); Jacques Vier, "La 'théologie' de Liszt et de la Comtesse
d'Agoult" (213-19); Claudine Lacoste, "Un substitut théologique: la nature dans *Jocelyn*" (221-27); discussion (229-30);
Jacques Viard, "Pierre Leroux, croyant. Prolégomènes à la
préface aux fables de Pierre Lachambeaudie" (233-60); Jean-
Pierre Lacassagne, "Le vocable 'religion' et ses synonymes
dans l'oeuvre de P. Leroux" (261-67); Eric Fauquet, "La
communion selon l'Eglise militante de Michelet" (269-74);
discussion (275-81); Ceri Crossley, "Idée de Dieu et nature
chez Quinet jusqu'en 1842" (283-90); Maurice Domino, "Religion
et révolution chez Edgar Quinet" (291-306); Max Milner,
"Baudelaire et la théologie" (307-17); discussion (319-22);
Nicolas Wagner, "Sur la diffusion de la 'théologie' romantique: Villegardelle, Cabet, Dezamy, et 'La Basiliade' de
Morelly" (325-36); Bernadette Bensaude-Vincent, Thérèse
Moreau, and Annie Petit, "Comte, Michelet: la femme consacrée"
(337-52); discussion (353-58); Michel Baude, "Le riche et
le pauvre selon J.-M. de Gérando" (359-67); Louis Le Guillou,
"Lamennais, guide spirituel" (369-75); André Monchoux, "La
polémique des années 1840 autour de V. Cousin et de Pascal"
(377-85); discussion (387-89); Jean Mongrédien, "Transformations et adaptation du texte liturgique de la messe par
certains compositeurs au début du XIXe siècle en France"
(393-99); Benoît Neiss, "De Dom Guéranger à Huysmans: le
renouveau de la pensée liturgique" (401-09); discussion
(411-15); Edgard Pich, "Race et religion. Considérations
méthodologiques sur le lieu commun" (419-25); Philippe
Berthier, "Théologie et poétique: le prêtre dans les romans
de Barbey d'Aurevilly" (427-37); Jean Foyard, "Images re-
ligieuses et déviation théologique chez Maurice Barrès"
(439-48); Jean Gaulmier, "Quelques mots en guise de conclusion" (451-55).

For treatment of individual articles, see the above-mentioned reviews. In general, this massive symposium offers scholarly works of high quality and great interest, though, in some cases, they deal with rather specialized topics. In any case, a number of the articles make important contributions to the never-ending study of the religious element in French Romanticism. (J.S.P.)

Bellemin-Noël, Jean. *Vers l'inconscient du texte*. (Ecriture.) Paris: Presses universitaires de France, 1979. Pp. 203. Fr. 59.00.

   Rev. by Françoise Lecomte in *LR* 35 (1981): 259-60. Among others, Mérimée and Gautier are treated.

Bertier de Sauvigny, Guillaume de. "The Bourbon Restoration: One Century of French Historiography." *FHS* 12 (1981): 41-67.

Biet, Christian, et al., eds. *XIXe siècle*. (Collection Textes et Contextes.) Paris: Magnard, 1981. Pp. 511. Fr. 87.00.

   Rev. by Jude Stefan in *NRF* 346 (Nov. 1, 1981): 120-22. The gaudy cover of this "manuel d'études littéraires," both anthology and literary history, warns that the book is nothing if not trendy, in content and in presentation. The lavish illustrations, for example, range from paintings by the great French artists of the nineteenth century to comic strips. Snippets of criticism are taken from writers of the period and from modern gurus (Lukács, J.-P. Richard, Barthes, etc.). While much of the contextual material (illustrations, charts, etc.) is welcome--on Berlioz, for example--one is put off by the messy effect and by a number of fairly serious errors: e.g., Musset's *Lorenzaccio* is accompanied by a reproduction of Mucha's poster for somebody's *Médée*; a photograph of Daudet is identified as being of Gautier. There is no denying that the total effect is lively and "dans le vent." (J.S.P.)

Block, Olivier. "Un philosophe épicurien sous Louis-Philippe." *JHP* 18 (1980): 433-43.

   On Jean André Rochoux (1787-1852), a doctor and also author of "opuscules et libelles philosophiques," especially *De l'épicurisme et de ses principales applications* (1831) and *Epicure opposé à Descartes* (1843). Block sketches Rochoux's life, connections, and ideas.

Bluche, François. "Quelques dates des costumes français du XVIIIe siècle." *GBA* 98 (Nov. 1981): 151-54; 5 illus.

Boime, Albert. "The Case of Rosa Bonheur: Why Should a Woman Want to Be More Like a Man?" *Art History* 4 (1981): 385-409.

Boime stresses Saint-Simonian influences (notably on her blend of Lesbianism and feminism), her "espousal of a variety of mystical and magical beliefs," her "commitment to the animal world ... founded on mystical ideals" (i.e., metempsychosis), and the influence of Lamennais, George Sand, and Flora Tristan.

Boime, Albert. *Thomas Couture and the Eclectic Vision*. Yale University Press, 1980. Pp. xxii+683.

Rev. by Marilyn R. Brown in *NCFS* 10 (1981-82): 167-70; by Paul Joannides in *Art History* 4 (1981): 332-34; by Denys Sutton in *Apollo*, April 1981, pp. 249-50.

Brunet, Etienne. *Le Vocabulaire français de 1789 à nos jours*. Préface de Paul Imbs. 3 vols. Geneva and Paris: Slatkine, 1981. Sw.Fr. 350.00.

Chanda, A.K. "The Young Man from the Provinces." *CL* 33 (1981): 321-41.

Examples of this literary type are taken from Balzac, Maupassant, Thackeray, Trollope, Dreiser, and Abraham Cahan. Its antecedents are found in the *pícaro*, Marivaux's Jacob, and Rousseau. The type is subdivided into the dreamer, the social climber, and the *parvenu*; other facets of the typology are the young man's rise and fall, the women in his life, his return "home," self-discovery. His modern descendant is the existential hero.

Chauleau, Liliane. *La Vie quotidienne aux Antilles françaises au temps de Victor Schoelcher (XIXe siècle)*. Paris: Hachette, 1979. Pp. 380. Fr. 36.00.

Rev. by Etienne Taillemite in *RH* 538 (1981): 487-89.

Ciureanu, Petre. "Altri autografi francesi nelle biblioteche e negli archivi d'Italia." *Bollettino dell'Istituto di Lingue Estere* 10 (1976): 175-88.

On pp. 180-88 gives texts of brief letters by various major Romantic authors.

Cleaver, Dale G. "Michallon et la théorie du paysage." *Revue du Louvre et des Musées de France* 31,v-vi (1981): 359-66.

One wonders if Michallon's *La Mort de Roland* (Salon of 1819) might have been a source of Vigny's "Le Cor."

Compagna, Luigi. *Alle origini della libertà di stampa nella
Francia della Restaurazione*. (Biblioteca di Cultura moderna,
820.) Bari: Laterza, 1979. Pp. viii+252. L10,000.

   Rev. by C. Cordié in *SFr* 24 (1980): 574-76.

Comte, Philippe. "*La Naissance d'Henri IV* de Devéria." *Revue
du Louvre et des Musées de France* 31,ii (1981): 137-41.

   On the genesis of the various versions of this once-famous
picture. The cult of Henri IV in the Restoration is evoked,
and Hugo's influence on the painting is discussed.

Crosland, Maurice. *Gay-Lussac, Scientist and Bourgeois*.
Cambridge University Press, 1978. Pp. 334.

   Rev. by Christophe Charle in *Annales* 36 (1981): 248-49.

Daniels, Barry V. "Ciceri and Daguerre: Set Designs for the
Paris Opera, 1820-1822." *ThS*, May 1981, pp. 69-90.

Daniels, Barry. "Mélodrame: la musique." *RHT* 33 (1981): 167-75.

   A study of the manuscript of Victor Ducange's *Calas* (1819)
and its "indications musicales." "On peut voir d'après cet
exemple que l'emploi de la musique est plus complexe qu'on
ne l'a souvent imaginé."

De Bellaigue, Geoffrey. "Vive la France!" *BM* 123 (Dec. 1981):
735-39; 4 illus.

   On patriotic responses in the various arts in France--
paintings, prints, women's coiffures, Sèvres porcelain--
to a naval encounter between France and Great Britain, June
17, 1778.

Delas, Daniel. "On a touché au vers! Note sur la fonction
manifestaire du poème en prose au XIXe siècle." *Littérature*
39 (1980): 54-60.

Devéria, Achille (?). *Diabolico-foutro-manie*. Présentation
de Jacques Duprilot. Geneva: Slatkine Reprints, 1981.

   According to the publisher's blurb, "Ce reprint remet
à l'honneur un genre d'illustrations, celui des 'diableries
de lithographies', bien oublié aujourd'hui, mais qui fit
fureur dans les premières années du règne de Louis-Philippe.
Ce recueil de 12 planches, en noir, fantaisie des plus
échevelées et des plus élaborées, constitue le nec plus
ultra d'un genre ô combien facétieux: Messire Satan dans
ses pompes et dans ses oeuvres."

Devries, Anik. "Sebastien Erard, un amateur d'art du début du XIXe siècle et ses conseillers." *GBA* 97 (Feb. 1981): 78-86; 1 illus.

Duncan, Carol. "Fallen Fathers: Images of Authority in Pre-Revolutionary French Art." *Art History* 4 (1981): 186-202; 13 illus.

Artists whose works are cited include Greuze, Vincent, Peyron, Regnault, Boilly, and David. Blake is mentioned also.

Foucart, Claude. "L'oeuvre de Raphaël: étapes et formes d'une critique littéraire." *RHL* 80 (1980): 1003-25 (discussion: 1026).

On the cult of Raphael in nineteenth-century French literature, especially in the Romantic period (notably in Balzac, Vigny, and Musset). The beginnings of a reaction in Rio and other Catholic writers are noted.

Frappier-Mazur, Lucienne. "La description mnémonique dans le roman historique." *Littérature* 38 (May 1980): 3-26.

Fried, Michael. *Absorption and Theatricality: Painting and Beholder in the Age of Diderot.* University of California Press, 1980. Pp. 249; 70 illus. $27.50; $11.50 paper.

Rev. by Francis Haskell ("Out of the Picture") in *NYRB*, June 25, 1981, pp. 42-44; by Garry Wills ("Clearing the Stage") in *NR*, April 18, 1981, pp. 34-36.

Fulcher, Jane. "Meyerbeer and the Society of Music." *MusQ* 68 (1981): 213-29.

On the evolution of Meyerbeer's critical reputation. This topic is related to the views of the Saint-Simoniens, Comte, and Fourier as to the role and place of music.

Galievsky, Béatrice. *De la Restauration à la fin du Second Empire. 1815-1870.* (La Chronothèque, 12.) Paris: Ed. d'Organisation, 1981. Pp. 1516. Fr. 14.00.

Géricault. (Tout.) Paris: Flammarion, 1981. Pp. 96. Fr. 20.88.

Gilroy, James P. *The Romantic Manon and Des Grieux: Images of Prévost's Heroine and Hero in Nineteenth-Century French Literature.* (English Series, 5.) Sherbrooke (Canada): Naaman, 1980. Pp. 157.

Gladwyn, Cynthia. "Madame Récamier: A Romantic French Salon."
Pp. 57-68 in Peter Quennell, ed., *Affairs of the Mind: The
Salon in Europe and America from the 18th to the 20th Cen-
tury.* Washington, D.C.: New Republic Books, 1980. Pp. 188.
$14.95.

Guibert-Sledziewski, Elisabeth. "Du Citoyen au Moi social:
évolution du civisme bourgeois en France d'après la thématique
du rapport Société/Individu (1830-1850)." *Romantisme* 34
(1981): 67-88.

Guillou, Jean-Claude. "L'appartement de Madame Sophie au
château de Versailles: formation et métamorphoses, 1774-
1790." *GBA* 97 (May-June 1981): 201-18; 5 illus.

Hallam, John Stephen. "The Two Manners of Louis-Leopold Boilly
and French Genre Painting in Transition." *ArtB* 63 (1981):
618-33.

An important but neglected *genre* painter (1761-1845).

Heller, Stephen. *Lettres d'un musicien romantique à Paris.*
Présenté et annoté par Jean-Jacques Eigeldinger. (Harmonique.)
Paris: Flammarion, 1981. Pp. 344. Fr. 104.42.

Rev. by April FitzLyon in *TLS*, Oct. 23, 1981, p. 1226.

Hellerstein, Erna, Olafson, et al., eds. *Victorian Women: A
Documentary Account of Women's Lives in Nineteenth-Century
England, France, and the United States.* Stanford University
Press, 1981. Pp. 534.

Rev. by Kathryn J. Crecelius in *NCFS* 10 (1981-82): 181-82.
French examples are George Sand, Flora Tristan, and Delphine Gay.

Héraclès, Philippe, comp. *Les Plus Beaux Poèmes romantiques.*
"Romantisme et nostalgie." Anthologie. Préface de Gonzague
Saint-Bris. Paris: Le Cherche-Midi, 1981. Pp. 191. Fr. 49.00.

Johnson, Lee. "'La Grosse Suzanne' Uncovered?" *BM* 123 (April
1981): 218-21; 7 illus.

Speculations on the identity of the model in a drawing
by Géricault.

Jullian, René. *Le Mouvement des arts du Romantisme au Sym-
bolisme.* (Evolution de l'Humanité.) Paris: Albin Michel,
1979. Pp. 590. Fr. 75.00.

Rev. by Joseph-Marc Bailbé in *RHL* 81 (1981): 472-73; by
Barbara Scott in *Apollo*, Jan. 1981, p. 62.

Juretschke, Hans. "Du rôle médiateur de la France dans la
propagation des doctrines littéraires, des méthodes historiques et de l'image de l'Allemagne en Espagne au cours du
XIXe siècle." Pp. 9-34 in Université de Lille III, Centre
d'Etudes ibériques et ibéro-américaines au XIXe Siècle,
*Romantisme, réalisme, naturalisme en Espagne et en Amérique
latine.* Colloque 2, 1975. Villeneuve d'Ascq: Publications
de l'Université de Lille III, 1978. Pp. 191.

Kelly, Michael. "Hegel in France to 1940: A Bibliographical
Essay." *JES* 9 (1981): 29-52.

The principal figures from the first half of the nineteenth
century are Comte, Cousin, Leroux, Quinet, and especially
Proudhon. A certain Charles Bénard was Hegel's first French
translator.

Lanyi, Gabriel. "Debates on Romanticism in Literary France
(1820-30)." *JHI* 41 (1980): 141-50.

On the difficulty the Romantics and their adversaries had
in defining Romanticism, thanks especially to the claims
made on them by politics. Lanyi identifies a number of
groups: liberal classicists, royalists, doctrinaires, liberal
Romanticists, royalist Romanticists.

Lanyi, Gabriel. "The Patriotic Principle of French Romanticism."
AJFS 17 (1980): 221-31.

The resistance to Romanticism and the movement's triumph
are shown as functions of the idea of patriotism. Lanyi
argues "that the condemnation of romanticism was unanimous
in the first years of the Restoration when it was perceived
as a national threat; that the new system gained recognition and supporters in France when the young royalist romantics managed to present the new movement as an expression
of French national and religious ideals; and finally, that
the liberals could not endorse romanticism until 1824, when
they formulated their own patriotic basis for romanticism,
compatible with their political doctrines."

Lawler, Peter Augustine. "Tocqueville on Slavery, Ancient and
Modern." *SAQ* 84 (1981): 466-77.

Le Bris, Michel. *Le Paradis perdu.* (Figures.) Paris: Bernard
Grasset, 1981. Pp. 374. Fr. 69.00.

Rev. by Jean Gillet in *QL* 354 (Sept. 1-15, 1981): 22.
Elucubrations on the genesis of Romanticism in the eighteenth century. The reader gets an idea of what he is in for
on the first page, as the author describes the shooting of
a scene of jungle combat in Coppola's *Apocalypse Now*.

Ledoux, Claude-Nicolas. *L'Architecture considerée sous le
rapport de l'art.* Paris: UHL (diffusion: Fischbacher),
1981. Pp. 238. Fr. 369.00.

Facsimile reprint of the edition of 1804.

Lelièvre, Renée. "Fantastique et surnaturel au théâtre à
l'époque romantique." *CAIEF* 32 (1980): 193-204.

See comment by Carlo Cordié in *SFr* 25 (1981): 172.

Main, Alexander. "Liszt's *Lyon*: Music and the Social Conscience." *NCM* 4 (1980-81): 228-43.

On the genesis and date of this "fiery five-and-a-half
minute allegro, imbued with ideas and rhetorical élan,"
which is dedicated to Lamennais and reflects his influence
on the composer.

Mansel, Philip. *Louis XVIII*. London: Bloud and Briggs, 1980.
Pp. 497. £18.95.

Rev. by Irene Collins in *TLS*, May 1, 1981, p. 494; by
Juliet Gardiner in *HT* 31 (Jan. 1981): 51.

Michel, Pierre. *Les Barbares 1789-1848. Un Mythe romantique.*
Presses universitaires de Lyon, 1981. Pp. 656. Fr. 150.00.

Misan, Jacques. "L'oeuvre de Silvio Pellico vue par les revues
françaises." *RLMC* 32 (1979): 85-102.

Complements the list of references given by Henri
Bedarida in *RLC* (1932). The period covered is 1820-42.
Most of the articles appeared unsigned, but Charles Didier,
Nodier, and Stendhal can be identified among the critics
of Pellico's works (Misan regards Didier's 1842 article in
the *RDM* as the most important).

Misan, Jacques. "Vincenzo Monti vu par la presse française
de son temps." *RLMC* 32 (1979): 165-80.

The period covered is 1807-30; the most important critics
involved are Sismondi and Stendhal.

Mower, David. "Antoine Augustin Préault (1809-1879)." *ArtB*
63 (1981): 288-307.

    In what is claimed as the "first survey in English" of
Préault's career, literary sources and parallels for his
sculptures are often cited: A. Barbier, Delavigne, Dumas,
Hugo, and Scott.

Muhlstein, Anka. *James de Rothschild: Francfort 1792-Paris
1868. Une métamorphose, une légende*. Paris: Gallimard, 1981.
Pp. 252. Fr. 70.00.

Newman, Edgar. "L'image de la foule dans la Révolution de
1830." *AHRF* 52 (1980): 499-509.

    Thanks to its sober, dignified, even "sublime" behavior
during that revolution, the crowd--hitherto seen as just
a mob--won a remaking of its image. Newman cites popular
illustrations as well as other evidence. Delacroix's image
(in *La Liberté guidant le peuple*) is, then, rather too
Romantic.

Nicolas, Anne. "L'esthétique impossible, les *Poétiques*
françaises du XIXe siècle." *Langue Française* 49 (Feb. 1981):
5-13.

Nouvel, Odile. *Papiers peints français, 1800-1850*. Paris:
Office du Livre/Vilo, 1981. Pp. 128. Fr. 265.00.

    Wallpaper, it should be remembered, often featured themes
from mythology, history, and literature.

Olivier-Martin, Yves. *Histoire du roman populaire en France
de 1840 à 1980*. Paris: Albin Michel, 1980. Pp. 301. Fr.
65.00.

    As befits the subject, this is a popular, highly readable
survey. Early chapters hark back to Pigault-Lebrun and
Victor Ducange, and paint in broad strokes the sociology
of this kind of literature (*cabinets de lecture*, rise of
the *roman-feuilleton*, etc.). For the late Romantic period
there is fairly extended treatment of Paul de Kock, Sue,
Soulié, and their *épigones*. Many novels are helpfully sum-
marized. All in all, a pleasant and mildly informative
read. (J.S.P.)

O'Neill, Mary. "Origins of Pictorial Designs for French Printed
Textiles of the First Half of the Nineteenth Century." *BM*
123 (Dec. 1981): 722-35; 26 illus.

Ozouf, Mona. "L'invention de l'ethnographie française: le
questionnaire de l'Académie celtique." *Annales* 36 (1981):
210-30.

On the questionnaire drawn up by the leaders of the
Académie celtique in 1805-06: its adequacy by modern standards, its conservatism, its originality.

Parent-Duchâtelet, Alexandre. *La Prostitution à Paris au XIXe
siècle*. Ed. by Alain Corbin. Paris: Editions du Seuil, 1981.
Pp. 224. Fr. 40.50.

New edition of a famous book originally published in 1836.

Peyre, Henri. "On the Sapphic Motif in Modern French Literature." *Dalhousie French Studies* 1 (1979): 3-33.

Phillips, Roderick. *Family Breakdown in Late Eighteenth-Century France: Divorces in Rouen, 1792-1803*. Oxford: Clarendon
Press, 1980. Pp. viii+244.

Rev. by Alan Forrest in *TLS*, April 10, 1981, p. 410.

Pickford, Cedric E., ed. *Mélanges de littérature française
moderne offerts à Garnet Rees*. (La Thésothèque, 7.) Paris:
Minard, 1980. Pp. x+289. Fr. 150.00.

Rev. by Henri Peyre in *FR* 55 (1981-82): 415-17.
According to the above review, this *Festschrift* contains
the following pertinent material: Charles Dédéyan on
Chateaubriand's *Mémoires d'outre-tombe*, J.C. Ireson on
Lamartine, Paul Ginestier on Hugo's theater (especially
his *Théâtre en liberté*), D.G. Charleton on Musset's *Con-
fession d'un enfant du siècle*, Alison Fairlie on Constant's
Adolphe, and A.H. Diverres on Paul Féval.

Pierron, Agnès. "Deburau." *L'Avant-Scène* 681 (Jan. 1, 1981):
39-42.

On Sacha Guitry's *Deburau* (1918), revived at the Théâtre
Edouard VII, with Pierre Bergé directing and Robert Hirsch
in the title role.

Poniatowski, Michel. *Louis-Philippe et Louis XVIII: autour
du journal de Louis-Philippe en mars 1815*. Paris: Librairie
académique Perrin, 1980. Pp. 541. Fr. 75.00.

Popkin, Jeremy D. "The Newspaper Press in French Political
Thought, 1789-99." *SECC* 10 (1981): 113-33.

Poulet, Georges. *Entre Moi et Moi. Essais critiques sur la conscience de soi.* Paris: José Corti, 1977. Pp. 281. Fr. 75.00.

> Rev. by Georges Cesbron in *LR* 35 (1981): 255-59.
> Cesbron indicates that pp. 1-38 are devoted to Romanticism.

Poulot, Dominique. "Les Musées à la gloire de l'Empire: notes pour une recherche." *GBA* 98 (Oct. 1981): 127-31; 1 illus.

Quemada, Bernard, ed. *Trésor de la langue française du XIXe et du XXe siècle (1789-1960).* T. VIII: *Epicycle-Fuyard.* Paris: Editions du CNRS (diffusion: Klincksieck), 1980. Pp. xx+1364. Fr. 494.40.

Renouvier, Charles. *Manuel républicain de l'homme et du citoyen.* Présenté par Maurice Agulhon. (Les Classiques de la Politique.) Paris: Garnier, 1981. Pp. 176.

Robinson, Christopher. *French Literature in the Nineteenth Century.* (Comparative Literature.) Newton Abbott: David and Charles; New York: Harper and Row, Barnes and Noble Import Division, 1978. Pp. 216. £6.95.

> Rev. by John A. Green in *Contemporary French Civilization* 3 (1978-79): 477-79.

Rose, R.B. "Nursery of Sans-Culottes: The Société Patriotique of the Luxembourg Section, 1792-1795." *BJRL* 64 (1981): 218-45.

Rosenberg, Pierre. "A Drawing by Madame Vigée-Le-Brun." *BM* 123 (Dec. 1981): 739-40.

Rosset, Clément. "Intérieurs romantiques." *NRF* 321 (Oct. 1, 1979): 108-13.

> On the Romantic yearning for "l'ailleurs"; examples used are from the latter part of the nineteenth century, notably Jules Verne.

Roudaut, Jean. *Ce qui nous revient. Autobiographie.* (Le Chemin.) Paris: Gallimard, 1980. Pp. 464. Fr. 94.75.

> Includes essays on *le roman noir*, Balzac, and Senancour.

Schneider, Marcel, ed. *La Symphonie imaginaire.* Paris: Editions du Seuil, 1981. Pp. 256. Fr. 60.00.

> Includes essays on Balzac, Gautier, and Nerval.

Shaw, Marjorie. "French Studies: The Romantic Era." *YWMLS* 40
(1978): 160-71; 41 (1979): 159-72.

Société d'Histoire de la Révolution de 1848 et des Révolutions
du XIXe Siècle. *Mille huit cent quarante huit (1848)*. Préface
de Maurice Agulhon. Paris: C.D.U.-SEDES, 1981. Pp. 290.
Fr. 121.84.

Stamm, Therese Dolan. *Gavarni and the Critics*. (Studies in
the Fine Arts: Criticism, 12.) Ann Arbor: UMI Research
Press, 1981. Pp. xii+216.

     Among the critics studied are Balzac and Gautier (the
others treated are Baudelaire, Champfleury, and the Goncourts).
In the chapter on Balzac, the author works with the often-
noted resemblance between the representation of reality
which the novelist and the artist each attempted in their
respective media. The chapter on Gautier centers on the
writer's interest in the *transposition d'art* and the inter-
relationships between literature and the visual arts. A
lengthy appendix, "The *Grisette* and the *Lorette*: Romantic
Imagery of the Courtesan," studies Gavarni's popular types,
"to investigate their meaning for the age from which he
drew them, and to explore the role they played in his art."

Sutton, Denys. "Cross-Currents in Nineteenth-Century French
Painting." *Apollo* 113 (1981): 244-54.

Tison-Braun, Micheline. *Poétique du paysage (Essai sur le
genre descriptif)*. Paris: A.-G. Nizet, 1980. Pp. 204. Fr.
88.00.

     Rev. by Bettina L. Knapp in *NCFS* 10 (1981-82): 163-64.
Examples from the major Romantic authors are numerous
in this general study of description: Chateaubriand (2
passages), Stendhal (1), Lamartine (1), Vigny (1), Hugo
(3), Gautier (1), Nerval (1).

Vaux de Foletier, François de. *Les Bohémiens en France au
XIXe siècle*. (Lattès-Histoire.) Paris: J.C. Lattès, 1981.
Pp. 256. Fr. 64.92.

Viallaneix, Paul, and Jean Ehrard, eds. *Aimer en France. 1760-
1860*. Actes du colloque international de Clermont-Ferrand.
(Publications de la Faculté des Lettres et Sciences humaines
de l'Université de Clermont-Ferrand II, Nouvelle série,
fascicule 6.) 2 vols. Clermont-Ferrand: Association des
Publications de la Faculté des Lettres et Sciences humaines
de Clermont-Ferrand, 1980. Fr. 112.14.

Rev. by Jacques Landrin in *IL* 33 (1981): 167.

The following articles are those most directly pertinent to the study of French Romantic literature: François Pupil, "Représentations de l'amour 'troubadour'" (57-68); Alain Montandon, "La représentation de l'amour dans la peinture romantique allemande" (69-80); Elisabeth Hardouin-Fugier, "Aimer à Lyon: *Virginitas* (vers 1850)" (81-90); discussion (91-96); Laurence Viglieno, "Le thème de l'éducation sentimentale' de Rousseau à Balzac" (131-40); Jacques-Philippe Saint-Gérand, "L'amour: érotisme, pornographie et normes littéraires (1815-1845)" (191-204); Jacqueline Guiot-Lauret, "Amour et tabous linguistiques dans quelques romans et nouvelles des années 1833-36" (205-15); Jean-Maurice Gautier, "Amours romantiques, amours frénétiques" (217-25); Joseph-Marc Bailbé, "Autour de *La Dame aux camélias*: présence et signification du thème de la courtisane dans le roman français (1830-1850)" (227-39); Lucienne Frappier-Mazur, "Le régime de l'aveu dans *Le Lys dans la vallée* (1ère partie)" (241-52); discussion (263-73); Jean Deprun, "'Pur amour' et 'supposition impossible' chez quelques mystiques français (1750-1850)" (323-29); Louis Devance, "L'éthique de la sexualité dans le socialisme romantique en France: de la loi du désir et du désir de loi" (367-76); Stéphane Michaud, "La prostitution comme interrogation sur l'amour chez les socialistes romantiques (1830-1840)" (377-88); François Marotin, "De l'amour en mariage ou l'enracinement dans l'absolu (aspects de la pensée proudhonienne)" (389-99); Jean Molino, "Le mythe de l'androgyne" (401-11); discussion (413-25).

Nearly every major French Romantic is mentioned at least in passing in these studies of love and sexuality in the period 1760-1860. It is symptomatic of Balzac's importance in this domain that he is the subject of the only paper (Frappier-Mazur's) devoted to a single writer working in the central genres.

Viollet, Alphonse. *Les Poètes du peuple au XIXe siècle.* Présenté par Michel Ragon. (Mémoire populaire.) Geneva: Slatkine Reprints, 1981. Pp. 380. Fr. 75.00.

Reprint of the edition of Paris, 1846.

Von der Lippe, George B. "La vie de l'artiste fantastique: The Metamorphosis of the Hoffmann-Poe Figure in France." *CRCL* 6 (1979): 46-63.

Weill, Georges. *Histoire du catholicisme libéral en France (1828-1908).* Geneva: Slatkine Reprints, 1979. Pp. ix+312.

Rev. by Emile Poulatin in *ASSR* 51,ii (1981): 301-02.
Reprint of the classic study, published in 1909, with
presentation by René Rémond.

Weisberg, Gabriel P. *The Realist Tradition: French Painting
and Drawing 1830-1900*. Cleveland: Cleveland Museum of Art
(distribution: Indiana University Press), 1981. Pp. 360.
$50.00.

Rev. by Neil McWilliam in *Art History* 4 (1981): 468-70;
by Charles Rosen and Henri Zerner in *NYRB*, Feb. 18, 1982,
pp. 21-26.

Wright, Beth Segal. "Scott and Shakespeare in Nineteenth-
Century France: Achille Devéria's Lithographs of 'Minna et
Brenda' and 'Les Enfants d'Edouard.'" *Arts Magazine* 55
(Feb. 1981): 129-33.

On the "complex interaction of Scott and Shakespeare, history
and fiction, Delaroche and Devéria, French lithography and
British engraving." (Casimir Delavigne's play is involved, too.)

Wright, Beth Segal. "Scott's Historical Novels and French
Historical Paintings." *ArtB* 63 (1981): 268-87.

Wright's study reveals that the period 1814-26 was one of
"increasing curiosity," that 1827-33 was the "period of the
most numerous pictorial explorations," and that 1834-41
showed an "abrupt decline." She deals mostly with book
illustrations (T. Johannot, etc.), but paintings by Horace
Vernet, Cogniet, Roqueplan, Barbot, and, of course, Delacroix are discussed.

Wrigley, Richard. "Pierre-François Delauney, Liberty and
Saint Nicholas." *BM* 123 (Dec. 1981): 745-47; 5 illus.

Yardeni, Myriam, ed. *Les Juifs dans l'histoire de France*.
Premier colloque international de Haïfa. Leyden: Brill,
1980. Pp. 233.

Rev. by Doris Bensimon in *ASSR* 51,ii (1981): 303.

Ziegler, Jean. "Auguste de Chatillon sculpteur et Baudelaire."
GBA 97 (Jan. 1981): 26-28; 2 illus.

See also entries above under "General"; also Issawi ("English
2. Environment"); Wright ("English 4. Scott"); Köhler, Von
der Lippe ("German 3. Hoffmann").

Reviews of books previously listed:

BELLET, Roger, ed., *La Femme au XIXe siècle* (see *ELN* 17, Supp., 113, and *RMB* for 1979, p. 138), rev. by Gianni Mombello in *RLMC* 33 (1980): 315-18; BETHLENFALVAY, Marina, *Les Visages de l'enfant dans la littérature française du XIXe siècle* (see *RMB* for 1979, pp. 138-39), rev. by Robert Gibson in *FS* 35 (1981): 350-51; by Martha O'Nan in *NCFS* 10 (1981-82): 131-32; by Bruno Vercier in *RHL* 81 (1981): 317-18; BOWMAN, Frank Paul, *Le Discours sur l'éloquence sacrée* (see *RMB* for 1980, pp. 147-48), rev. by Carlo Cordié in *SFr* 25 (1981): 171-72; by Henri Peyre in *French Forum* 6 (1981): 181-82; BRESSOLETTE, Claude, *L'Abbé Maret* (see *RMB* for 1980, p. 148), rev. by Mark A. Gobbert in *CHR* 67 (1981): 325-26; by F. Robello in *SFr* 24 (1980): 177; BROOKNER, Anita, *Jacques-Louis David* (see *RMB* for 1980, p. 149), rev. by Richard Cobb in *TLS*, Jan. 9, 1981, p. 26; by Francis Haskell in *BM* 945 (Dec. 1981): 749-50; BROWN, Frederick, *Theater and Revolution* (see *RMB* for 1980, p. 149), rev. by Alfred J. Bingham in *SHR* 15 (1981): 271-72; BUSHNELL, Howard, *Maria Malibran* (see *RMB* for 1980, p. 149), rev. by April FitzLyon in *TLS*, May 8, 1981, p. 526; by Charlotte Greenspan in *NCM* 4 (1980-81): 273-76; by Kenneth Stern in *Opera News*, Feb. 13, 1982, p. 36; COORNAERT, Emile, *Destins de Clio en France depuis 1800* (see *ELN* 17, Supp., 113), rev. by R.A. in *RHE* 76 (1981): 189; DEL LITTO, Victor, ed., *Le Journal intime et ses formes littéraires* (see *ELN* 17, Supp., 142), rev. by Hans Rudolf Picard in *ZFSL* 91 (1981): 54-59; FELMAN, Shoshana, *La Folie et la chose littéraire* (see *RMB* for 1980, p. 153), rev. by Robert C. Carroll in *MLN* 96 (1981): 897-905; by Gilbert D. Chaitin in *CL* 33 (1981): 389-92; by Christopher Prendergast in *FS* 35 (1981): 103-04; by Sylvie Tinter in *RR* 72 (1981): 363-66; FELTEN, Hans, *Französische Literatur unter der Julimonarchie (1830-1848)* (see *RMB* for 1980, p. 153), rev. by Udo Schöning in *Romanistische Zeitschrift für Literaturgeschichte/Cahiers d'Histoire des Littératures Romanes* 5 (1981): 360-61; GILLET, Jean, *Le "Paradis perdu" dans la littérature française de Voltaire à Chateaubriand* (see *ELN* 15, Supp., 86-87), rev. by Tanguy Logé in *LR* 35 (1981): 161-63; HOFFMANN, Léon-François, *Le Nègre romantique* (see *ELN* 12, Supp., 74), rev. by Tanguy Logé in *LR* 35 (1981): 253-54; KENNEDY, Emmet, *A "Philosophe" in the Age of Revolution: Destutt de Tracy and the Origins of "Ideology"* (see *RMB* for 1979, p. 147), rev. by Aram Vartanian in *JHP* 4 (1981): 512-15; KNAPP, Heinz Wilhelm, *Die französische Arbeiterdichtung in der Epoche der Julimonarchie* (see *RMB* for 1979, p. 147), rev. by Hartmut Stenzel in *GRM* 30 (1980): 468-71; KNECHT, Edgar, *Le Mythe*

du Juif errant (see *ELN* 17, Supp., 115), rev. by Marc-Mathieu
Münch in *RLC* 55 (1981): 127-29; KRÖMER, Wolfram, ed., *Die
französische Novelle im 19. Jahrhundert* (see *ELN* 13, Supp.,
70), rev. by Hans Felten in *RF* 92 (1980): 465-66; LOUGH,
John, *Writer and Public in France* (see *ELN* 17, Supp., 116),
rev. by I.H. Smith in *AUMLA* 54 (Nov. 1980): 264-65; MAY,
Georges, *L'Autobiographie* (see *RMB* for 1980, p. 158), rev.
by Valentini Brady-Papadopoulou in *MLR* 76 (1981): 646-47;
by J. Voisine in *RHL* 81 (1981): 336-37; McCARTHY, Mary,
Ideas and the Novel (see *RMB* for 1980, p. 158), rev. by
Phyllis Grosskurth in *TLS*, March 6, 1981, p. 252; PICHOIS,
Claude, *Littérature française*, T. 13 (see *RMB* for 1979,
pp. 149-50), rev. by Jean Gaulmier in *RHL* 81 (1981): 151-
53; PORTER, Laurence M., *The Literary Dream in French Romanticism* (see *RMB* for 1979, pp. 151-52, and *RMB* for 1980, p.
226), rev. by Carlo Cordié in *SFr* 25 (1981): 171; by Susan
Noakes in *SiR* 21 (1982): 114-17; PORTER, Laurence M., *The
Renaissance of the Lyric in French Romanticism* (see *ELN* 17,
Supp., 117), rev. by Louis Le Guillou in *RHL* 81 (1981):
305; by Beverly Seaton in *RR* 72 (1981): 244-45; RAUHUT,
Franz, and C. Gänssle-Pfeuffer, *Die klassizistische und
romantische Lyrik der Franzosen* (see *RMB* for 1979, p. 152),
rev. by Peter Eckard Knabe in *RF* 92 (1980): 305-07; RICHARD,
Jean-Pierre, *Microlectures* (see *RMB* for 1979, p. 153), rev.
by Jeannine Jallat in *Littérature* 42 (1981): 123-27; SCHNACK,
Arne, *Animaux et paysages dans la description des personnages
romanesques (1840-1845)* (see *RMB* for 1980, p. 163), rev.
by C. Cordié in *SFr* 24 (1980): 170-71; STANTON, Domna C.,
The Aristocrat as Art (see *RMB* for 1980, p. 164), rev. by
Priscilla R.P. Clark in *CL* 33 (1981): 392-94; by John Van
Eerde in *NCFS* 10 (1981-82): 179-81; STOREY, Robert F.,
Pierrot (see *RMB* for 1979, p. 155), rev. by Pauline Baggio-
Huerre in *MLJ* 65 (1981): 93-94; by Oscar G. Brockett in
MLR 76 (1981): 649-50; by William Williford in *MLQ* 50
(1980): 379-81; THEVOZ, Michel, *L'Académisme et ses fantasmes*
(see *RMB* for 1980, p. 165), rev. by Jean Lacoste in *QL* 340
(Jan. 16-31, 1981): 19; TROUSSON, Raymond, *Voyages aux
pays de nulle part* (see *ELN* 16, Supp., 87), rev. by Claudine
Leube in *O&C* 5,i (1980): 153-55; VAN BIESROCK, Hans-Rüdiger,
*Die literarische Mode der Physiologien in Frankreich (1840-
1842)* (see *RMB* for 1979, p. 139), rev. by Annelie Hegen-
barth-Rösgen in *RHL* 81 (1981): 150; WEMYSS, Alice, *Histoire
du Réveil (1790-1849)* (see *RMB* for 1980, p. 166), rev. by
Jean Bauberot in *ASSR* 50,ii (1980): 354; ZELDIN, Theodore,
France: 1848-1945, Vol. II (see *RMB* for 1980, p. 166), rev.
by Frederick Busi in *Contemporary French Civilization* 3
(1978-79): 325-27.

2. STUDIES OF AUTHORS

AGOULT

See Baude and Münch ("French 1. General").

Review of book previously listed:

DESANTI, Dominique, *Daniel ou le visage secret d'une comtesse romantique, Marie d'Agoult* (see *RMB* for 1980, p. 169), rev. by Mary Anne Garnett in *NCFS* 10 (1981-82): 187-88.

AMPERE

Prandi, Carlo. "Pour une lecture stylistique sur quelques lettres de J.-J. Ampère." *Bollettino dell'Instituto di Lingue Estere* 10 (1976): 9-16.

ARLINCOURT

Mansau, Andrée. "Le vicomte d'Arlincourt, un espagnoliste inversif." *SC* 23 (1980-81): 255-63.

Comparisons but mostly contrasts with Stendhal's *espagnolisme* and *romanticisme*.

AZAIS

Baude, Michel. *Pierre-Hyacinthe Azaïs, témoin de son temps d'après son journal inédit (1811-1844).* Lille: Atelier de Reproduction des Thèses, Université de Lille III; Paris: Honoré Champion, 1981. Pp. 1220. Fr. 158.87.

BALLANCHE

Derré, Jean-René. "Ballanche continuateur et contradicteur de J. de Maistre." *Revue des Etudes Maistriennes* 5-6 (1980): 297-316.

Lubac, Henri de, S.J. "Les méditations de Ballanche." Pp. 310-25 in *La Postérité spirituelle de Joachim de Flore*, t. I: *De Joachim à Schelling.* (Le Sycomore.) Paris: Lethielleux; Namur: Culture et Vérité, 1979. Pp. 414.

Joachim (ca. 1130-1202), Cistercian monk and mystical
theologian, stands at the head of a long line of thinkers
who have viewed history as a progressive spiritual evolution.
Ballanche is one of several early nineteenth-century figures
who belong among Joachim's progeny.

Michel, Arlette, ed. *OEuvres politiques*. (Les Classiques de
la Politique.) Paris: Garnier, 1981.

La Ville des expiations et autres textes. Présentation de
P. Michel. Presses universitaires de Lyon, 1981. Pp. 197.
Fr. 80.00.

Yarrow, P. "The House of Thebes in the Late Eighteenth Century."
Pp. 271-86 in D.J. Mossop, G.E. Rodmell, and D.B. Wilson,
eds., *Studies in the Eighteenth Century Presented to John
Lough by Colleagues, Pupils and Friends*. University of
Durham, 1978. Pp. 291.

Includes a page-and-a-half discussion of Ballanche's prose
epic, *Antigone* (1814).

See also Baude and Münch ("French 1. General").

BALZAC

L'Année Balzacienne 1980. Paris: Garnier, 1980. Pp. 381.

Contains: M. Andreoli, "La politique rationnelle selon
Balzac. Esquisse d'une description synchronique" (7-36);
A.M. Meininger, "Catilina, les conjurations orléanistes et
Jacquet" (37-46); J.L. Filoche, "*Le Chef-d'oeuvre inconnu*:
peinture et connaissance" (47-60); J.L. Seylaz, "Une scène
de Balzac: le transport de l'or dans *Eugénie Grandet*" (61-
68); A.M. Bijaoui-Baron, "L'ironie de Balzac dans la
Physiologie de l'employé" (69-76); A. Michel, "A propos
de poétique balzacienne: réalisme et illusions perdues"
(77-98); P. Mustière, "Guérande dans *Béatrix* ou l'extrava-
gance du lieu balzacien" (99-110); F. Van Rossum-Guyon,
"Aspects et fonctions de la description chez Balzac. Un
exemple: *Le Curé de village*" (111-36); A. Grandjean, "Le
charabia des Alsaciens dans *La Comédie humaine*: approche
linguistique" (137-46); R. Guise, "Les mystères de Pensées,
sujets, fragments" (147-62); T. Bodin, "Petites misères d'une
préface. A propos des *Petites misères de la vie conjugale*"
(163-68); L. Frappier-Mazur, "Parodie, imitation et circu-
larité: les épigraphes dans les romans de Balzac" (169-80);

M. Le Yaouanc, "Balzac et Thomas Moore (I. Une admiration de jeunesse)" (181-208); J. Malavié, "Balzac sous le feu d'un legitimiste avignonnais, Armand de Pontmartin" (209-38); C. Dédéyan, "Balzac dans *Le Littérateur universel*" (239-44); M.A. Ruff, "'Honoré de Balzac' par Henry James" (245-54); N. Felkay, "Autour de Balzac imprimeur" (255-69); N. Mozet, "Ce texte est-il de Balzac?" (269-78); P. Berthier, "Quelques almanachs de province à l'époque de Balzac" (279-94); N. Mozet, "Biographie et description: quand Balzac est-il allé à Saumur?" (295-96); A.M. Bijaoui-Baron, "Les origines de Léon Gozlan" (297-99); N. Felkay, "Autour de Mme Bechet: nouveaux documents" (300-04); R. Fortassier, "Proust et Balzac" (305-08); J. Sarment, "Impressions sorties des presses de Balzac et conservées à la maison de Balzac" (309). Reviews and bibliography.

Barbéris, Pierre. *Le Colonel Chabert de Balzac.* (Collection Textes pour Aujourd'hui.) Paris: Larousse, 1981. Pp. 126. Fr. 10.80.

Bersani, Leo. "Rejoinder to Walter Benn Michaels." *CritI* 8 (1981): 158-64.

Primarily a theoretical debate dealing with questions of desire and its complicity with a capitalistic economy of excess. Thought-provoking, although quite sketchy, with some interesting comments on *La Peau de chagrin.* Michael's response follows (165-71). (J.B.H.)

Bismut, Roger. "*Illusions perdues* et *Ruy Blas*, ou un aspect insoupçonné des rélations entre Balzac et Victor Hugo." *LR* 35 (1981): 235-45.

Discusses mutual borrowings: Hugo borrows from first part of *Illusions* for the play, then Balzac borrows from *Ruy Blas* for later episodes of *Illusions.*

Blanchard, Marc. *La Campagne et ses habitants dans l'oeuvre d'Honoré de Balzac.* Geneva: Slatkine Reprints, 1980. Pp. 510. Sw.Fr. 100.00.

Reprint of 1931 edition.

Blanchard, Marc. *Témoignages et jugements sur Balzac.* Geneva: Slatkine Reprints, 1981. Pp. 340. Sw.Fr. 70.00.

Reprint of the 1931 edition.

Bolster, Richard, ed. *La Vie de Balzac*. Racontée par Théophile
Gautier. Paris: La Pensée universelle, 1981. Pp. 128. Fr.
32.00.

Borowitz, Helen O. "Balzac's Unknown Masters." *RR* 72 (1981):
425-41.

   Rather wide-ranging background article which explores the
artistic and literary ideas which Balzac may have drawn
upon in writing the 1830 version of the *Chef d'oeuvre inconnu*
and suggests that Balzac's "unknown masters" were Cousin,
Gustave Planche, and Henri de Latouche.

Campagna, Andrew F. "Le journalisme et la vente de l'âme chez
Balzac: signes/signatures/signifactions." *NCFS* 9 (1981):
175-84.

   Interesting article which focuses on what happens to individual values and ideas in the society of *France révolu-
tionée* of 1830s and 1840s as described by Balzac, both
allegorically (*Melmoth*) and concretely (*Illusions*). Concludes
that alienation and loss of identity are not, for Balzac,
inherent in human nature but a function of a society based
on money. Although not a radically new interpretation, very
well presented. (J.B.H.)

Carl, Joachim. *Untersuchungen zur immanenten Poetik Balzacs*.
(Beiträge zur neueren Literaturgeschichte: Folge 3, Bd. 48.)
Heidelberg: Winter, 1979. Pp. 216.

Castex, Pierre-Georges, ed. *La Comédie humaine*. Tome XII:
*Etudes analytiques, ébauches rattachées à la Comédie humaine,
index, bibliographie générale et tables*. (Bibliothèque de
la Pléiade.) Paris: Gallimard, 1981. Pp. 1984. Fr. 220.00.

Chanda, A.K. "The Young Man from the Provinces." *CL* 33 (1981):
321-41.

   Beginning from Trilling's definition of the character
type: "young man from the provinces," article redefines
that character type drawing on many French, English, and
American nineteenth- and twentieth-century novels including
Le Père Goriot and *Splendeurs et misères*.

Chollet, Roland. "Balzac journaliste: le tournant de 1830."
IL 33 (1981): 56-58.

   Summary of his "thèse de doctorat d'état" defended June
26, 1980.

Dangelzer, Joan Yvonne. *La Description du milieu dans le roman français de Balzac à Zola.* Geneva: Slatkine Reprints, 1980. Pp. 290. Sw.Fr. 60.00.

Reprint of the 1938 edition.

Duchet, Claude, et al., eds. *Sociocritique.* Paris: Nathan, 1979. Pp. 224.

Rev. by M. Hays in *French Forum* 6 (1981): 189-91.

Flahaut, François. "Sur *S/Z* et l'analyse des récits." *Poétique* 47 (1981): 303-14.

Commentary on Barthes's *S/Z* with some corrections of interpretation and additional clarification of the castration theme.

Gale, John. "'Sleeping Beauty' as Ironic Model for *Eugénie Grandet.*" *NCFS* 10 (1981-82): 37-44.

Develops fully the relationship between the fairy tale and Balzac's novel in terms of narrative structure and sees an ironic contrast developed between the ahistorical model and the historically situated novel.

Heathcote, O.N. "Politics, Desire and Art in Balzac's 'Le Lys dans la vallée.'" In *Bradford Occasional Papers. Essays in Language, Literature and Area Studies.* Issue 1 (Autumn 1980). Bradford University, Modern Languages Center, 1980. Pp. 125.

Heitman, Klaus. *Der französische Realismus von Stendhal bis Flaubert.* Wiesbaden: Athenaion, 1979. Pp. 137. DM 14.80.

Rev. by F.W.J. Hemmings in *MLR* 76 (1981): 470-71.

Jameson, Frederic. "Realism and Desire: Balzac and the Problem of the Subject." Pp. 151-84 in his *The Political Unconscious: Narrative as a Socially Symbolic Act.* Cornell University Press, 1981. Pp. 320. $19.50.

Rev. by David G. Gross in *Genre* 14 (1981): 271-76.

Joseph, Jean R. "A la recherche de l'unité perdue: idéologie et thématique dans le *Curé de village* d'Honoré de Balzac." *RR* 72 (1981): 442-59.

Concentrating particularly on the character of Véronique, argues that the *Curé de village* is a unified, artistic whole.

Lacassin, Francis, ed. *La Comédie inhumaine*. T. I.: *Histoire véritable de la bossue courageuse*. (Les Maîtres de l'Etrange et de la Peur.) Paris: U.G.E., 1981. Pp. 272. Fr. 46.70.

Le Huenen, Roland, and Paul Perron, eds. *Le Roman de Balzac: recherches, critiques, méthodes, lectures*. Paris: Didier, 1980. Pp. 230. Fr. 120.00.

   Rev. by M. Van Schendel in *UTQ* 51 (1981–82): 112–24.

Ménard, Maurice. "Balzac et le comique dans *La Comédie humaine*." *IL* 33 (1981): 144–47.

   Summary of his "thèse de doctorat d'état" defended June 21, 1980.

Michel, Arlette. "A propos du pessimisme balzacien: nature et société." *Romantisme* 30 (1980): 13–28.

Mileham, James W. "Balzac's Seven of Probation." *RomN* 21 (1980–81): 161–64.

   Argues that Balzac was aware of and consciously used the biblical symbolism of the number 7 (seven months, seven years, etc.) to mark the "probationary" period of his characters.

Mozet, Nicole. "La Ville de province dans l'oeuvre d'Honoré de Balzac." *IL* 33 (1981): 198–205.

   Summary of her "thèse de doctorat d'état" defended June 6, 1980.

Muray, Philippe. "Le Syncrétinisation: Balzac, le XIXe siècle et la fornication de l'occulte." *Tel Quel* 89 (1981): 3–40.

Raynaud, Michel. *Figures de la nécessité. Etude sur l'espace urbain dans la première moitié du XIXe siècle*. Paris: A.R.D.U., 1979. Pp. 102.

   Rev. by A.-M. Bijaoui-Baron in *L'Année Balzacienne* 1980, p. 332.

Rossum-Guyon, Françoise van, and Michel van Broderode, et al. *Balzac et les parents pauvres*. C.D.U./SEDES, 1981. Pp. 230. Fr. 66.00.

   Rev. by Nelly Stéphane in *Europe* 59 (1981): 247.

Schendel, Michel van. "Balzac: de l'oeuvre au texte." *UTQ* 51 (1981-82): 112-24.

  Long review article of two books on Balzac by Roland Le Heunen and Paul Perron: *Le Roman de Balzac* and *Sémiotique du personnage romanesque*.

Senninger, Claude-Marie, ed. *Honoré de Balzac par Théophile Gautier*. Avec le texte de l'étude de Gautier, version publié dans *L'Artiste*. Paris: Nizet, 1981. Pp. 228. Fr. 85.00.

Stowe, William W. "Interpretation *in* Fiction: *Le Père Goriot* and *The American*." *TSLL* 23 (1981): 248-67.

Ulrich, Hans, et al., eds. *Honoré de Balzac*. Munich: Fink, 1980. Pp. 496. DM 19.80.

  Rev. by D. Bellos in *MLR* 76 (1981): 971-73.

Weber, Samuel. *Unwrapping Balzac. A Reading of La Peau de chagrin*. University of Toronto Press, 1979. Pp. 180. $20.00.

  Rev. by M. Kanes in *French Forum* 6 (1981): 281-82; by M.S. McCarthy in *FR* 54 (1980-81): 470-71.

See also Johnson ("General 3. Criticism"); Chanda, Foucart, Roudaut, Schneider, Viallaneix and Ehrard ("French 1. General"); Barbéris ("Chateaubriand"); Delon ("Staël"); Dalet, Del Litto (2) ("Stendhal"); Thoma ("Vigny").

Reviews of books previously listed:

BARDÈCHE, Maurice, *Balzac* (see *RMB* for 1980, pp. 170-71), rev. by J. Hassel in *NCFS* 10 (1981-82): 142-44; BAYARD, Pierre, *Balzac et le troc de l'imaginaire* (see *ELN* 17, Supp., 122), rev. by D. Bellos in *MLR* 76 (1981): 196-97; by P. Mustière in *RHL* 81 (1981): 306-08; CHANTREAU, Alain, ed., *Stendhal et Balzac II* (see *RMB* for 1979, p. 161), rev. by F.W. Saunders in *FS* 35 (1981): 347-48; DUCHET, Claude, ed., *Balzac et La Peau de chagrin* (see *RMB* for 1979, p. 161), rev. by D. Adamson in *FS* 25 (1981): 214-15; by D. Bellos in *MLR* 76 (1981): 196-97; by A. Lorant in *L'Année Balzacienne* 1980, pp. 318-23; EITEL, Wolfgang, *Balzac in Deutschland* (see *RMB* for 1980, p. 172), rev. by V. Neuhaus in *Arcadia* 16 (1981): 220-22; FESTA-McCORMICK, Diana, *Honoré de Balzac* (see *RMB* for 1979, p. 162), rev. by M. Kanes in *MLJ* 65 (1981): 429; by R. Merker in *FR* 54 (1980-81): 738; IMBERT, Patrick, *Sémiotique et description bal-*

zacienne (see *RMB* for 1980, p. 173), rev. by Owen Heathcote
in *NCFS* 9 (1980-81): 262-63; SUSSMANN, Hava, *Balzac et les
"débuts dans la vie"* (see *ELN* 17, Supp., 127), rev. by A.
Michel in *L'Année Balzacienne* 1980, pp. 329-30; WINGARD,
Kristina, *Les Problèmes des couples mariés* (see *RMB* for 1979,
p. 165), rev. by C. Smethurst in *FS* 35 (1981): 346-47;
ZELINCOURT, Gaston de, *Le Monde de la Comédie humaine* (see
RMB for 1979, p. 165), rev. by M. Lichtle in *L'Année Balzacienne* 1980, p. 333.

BARBEY D'AUREVILLY

Anzalone, John B. "Diabolic Decadence: Alastair, Illustrator
of Barbey d'Aurevilly." *BduB*, 1981-III, pp. 309-21.

Includes five of Alastair's illustrations for a luxury
edition in German of *La Vengeance d'une femme*.

Berthier, Philippe. "Barbey d'Aurevilly lecteur de Chateaubriand." *Société Chateaubriand, Bulletin* 22 (1979): 51-66.

Includes reproduction of Emile Lévy's portrait of Barbey
d'Aurevilly.

Chartier, Armand B. *Barbey d'Aurevilly*. (TWA Series, France.)
Boston: Twayne Publishers, 1977. Pp. 182.

Rev. by Gabrielle Turgeon in *NCFS* 7 (1978-79): 128-29.

OEuvres complètes. 17 vols. in 7 vols. Geneva: Slatkine Reprints
(diffusion: Paris, H. Champion), 1979. Pp. 5722. Sw.Fr.
3000.00.

Reprint of the edition of Paris, 1926-27.

Petit, Jacques, ed. *OEuvres romanesques complètes*. T. II.
(Bibliothèque de la Pléiade.) Nouvelle édition. Paris:
Gallimard, 1980. Pp. 1707. Fr. 99.70.

Contains: *Les Diaboliques*; *Une Histoire sans nom*; *Une
Page d'histoire*; *Ce qui ne meurt pas*; *Du dandysme et de
George Brummell*; *Mémoranda*; *Poèmes*; *Pensées détachées*.

Petit, Jacques, ed. *Un Prêtre marié*. (Folio, 1183.) Paris:
Gallimard, 1980. Pp. 476.

Rev. by A. Calegari in *SFr* 24 (1980): 591.

Petit, Jacques, ed. *Une Vieille Maîtresse*. Préface de Paul
Morand. (Folio, 1115.) Paris: Gallimard, 1979. Pp. 540. Fr.
16.00.

Tundo, L. "Barbey d'Aurevilly et Sainte-Beuve." *Francia* 18 (1976): 72-82.

See also Baude and Münch ("French 1. General").

BARBIER

See Mower ("French 1. General").

BAUDELAIRE

See Chase, Johnson, Reed ("General 3. Criticism"); Ziegler ("French 1. General"); Wuthenow ("German 2. General"); Henel ("German 3. Brentano"); Köhler ("German 3. Hoffmann").

BERANGER

Murdoch, Brian. "Poetry, Satire and Slave-Ships: Some Parallels to Heine's 'Sklavenschiff.'" *FMLS* 15 (1979): 323-35.

Poems by Cowper, Béranger, and Chamisso are compared to Heine's. Béranger's is "Les nègres et les marionettes" (before 1821), sometimes regarded as Heine's source (Murdoch regards the connection as "extremely tenuous"). But this is not just a study of influences and sources: the author has a point to make about various ways of handling satire in poetry.

BERLIOZ

Blavaud, Monique. *Hector Berlioz: visages d'un masque.* Lyon: Le Jardin de Dolly, 1981. Pp. 228. Fr. 77.60.

Heuze, Philippe. "Berlioz lecteur de Virgile d'après les deux premiers actes des *Troyens*." Pp. 365-73 in R[aymond] Chevallier, ed., *Influence de la Grèce et de Rome sur l'Occident moderne.* Actes du colloque ... Paris, Tours, des 14, 15, 19 décembre 1975. (Caesarodunum, 12.) Paris: Les Belles Lettres, 1977. Pp. 396. Fr. 150.00.

Macnutt, Richard, ed. *A Bibliography of the Musical and Literary Works of Hector Berlioz.* By Cecil Hopkinson. Second edition. Tunbridge Wells: Macnutt, 1980. Pp. 230. £38.00.

Rev. by Robert Jacoby in *Library* 3 (1981): 166-67.

Shilstone, Frederick W. "Berlioz' 'One Work': An Interdis-
ciplinary Approach to Romanticism." Pp. 85-97 in Malinda
R. Maxwell, ed., *Images and Innovations: Update '70's.*
Papers of the Southern Humanities Conference. Spartanburg,
S.C.: Center for the Humanities, Converse College, 1979.
Pp. 175.

Review of book previously listed:

CONRAD, Peter, *Romantic Opera and Literary Form* (see above,
p. 32).

BERTRAND, A.

Morell, Hortensia R. "El doble en *Gaspard de la nuit:* José
Donoso à la manière de Ravel, en imitación de Bertrand."
REH (University of Alabama) 15 (1981): 211-20.

Slott, Kathryn. "Le texte e(s)t son double. *Gaspard de la
nuit*: Intertextualité, parodie, autoparodie." *French Forum*
6 (1981): 28-35.

Vanhese Cocchetti, Gisele. "L'archaïsme stylistique dans
Gaspard de la Nuit." Micromégas 6 (1979): 1-21.

BONALD

Petyx, V. "Borghesia e proletario in Bonald." *Pensiero
Politico* 12 (1979): 410-31.

  See résumé by C. Cordié in *SFr* 24 (1980): 359.

See also Preece ("J. de Maistre").

BOREL

Borgheggiana, P.A. "L'opera poetica di Pétrus Borel." *Pisa:
Annali della Scuola Normale Superiore di Pisa* 9 (1979):
1325-42.

  Rev. by C. Cordié in *SFr* 24 (1980): 368.

Géniès, Bernard. "Pétrus Borel, le Lycanthrope." *QL* 301
(May 1-15, 1979): 16.

Reviews of books previously listed:

Critica degli spettacoli (see *RMB* for 1980, p. 180), rev.
by Jean-Luc Steinmetz in *RHL* 81 (1981): 794-96; POMPILI,
B., ed., *Opera polemica* (see *RMB* for 1980, p. 180), rev.
by Jean-Luc Steinmetz in *RHL* 81 (1981): 794-96.

CHARRIERE

Deguise, Alix. *Trois femmes. Le monde de Madame de Charrière.*
Geneva: Slatkine, 1981. Pp. 245. Sw.Fr. 30.00.

Herrmann, Claudine, ed. *Caliste ou lettres écrites de
Lausanne.* Paris: Des Femmes, 1981. Pp. 190. Fr. 40.00.

   In her preface to this admittedly feminist edition of
the novel, Herrmann claims that her author was guilty of
a fault which neither her age nor male critics could for-
give: she was intelligent and original.

Thompson, Patrice, et al., eds. *OEuvres complètes*, T. IX:
Romans, contes et nouvelles, II, 1798-1806. Amsterdam:
G.A. Van Oorschot, 1981. Pp. 901.

Reviews of books previously listed:

CANDAUX, Jean-Daniel, et al., eds., *OEuvres complètes*,
T. I-II, VII-VIII (see *RMB* for 1980, p. 180), rev. by
Kurt Kloocke in *RF* 92 (1980): 470-73; COURTNEY, C.P.,
*A Preliminary Bibliography of Isabelle de Charrière (Belle
de Zuylen)* (see *RMB* for 1980, p. 180), rev. by Margriet
Bruyn Lacy in *FR* 55 (1981-82): 272; by Dennis Wood in
FS 35 (1981): 452-53.

CHATEAUBRIAND

Ansalone, M.R., ed. *René.* Naples: Liguori, 1980. Pp. 114.

   Rev. by F. Robello in *SFr* 24 (1980): 577-78.

Aynesworth, Donald. "Autobiography and Anonymity." *FR* 52
(1978-79): 401-09.

   On Chateaubriand's atemporal self-differentiation in
the *Mémoires d'outre-tombe*: "By means of ellipsis, the
narrator acquires a second self in the mind of the reader.
The ego is divided thus, creatively, between several per-

sons: one who exists, one who remembers, one who writes,
and one who reads." Eluding spatial and temporal location,
the *Mémoires* acquire the "ténébreuse et profonde unité"
of Baudelaire's "Correspondances." In a sense, if the person emerging in the *Mémoires* is original, he "originates
in his prose and thereby exemplifies the primordial function
of written language in a human life."

Barbéris, Pierre. "Juillet comme banc d'essai ou trois réac-
tions et leurs suites." *Romantisme* 28-29 (1980): 257-78.

   Concerns Stendhal, Chateaubriand, and Balzac.

Decottignies, Jean, ed. *Les Sujets de l'écriture*. Les Presses
universitaires de Lille, 1981. Pp. 264. Fr. 83.20.

   Essays on the question "Qui parle?" in a literary text
include Georges Benrekassa's "Le dit du moi: du roman personnel à l'autobiographie. *René/Werther/Poésie et vérité/
Mémoires d'outre-tombe*."

Lebègue, Raymond. "Les avatars du voyage de Chateaubriand
en Amérique." *Revue des Travaux de l'Académie des Sciences
Morales et Politiques*, Sept. 1, 1977 [1979].

Lebègue, Raymond. "Introduction à la correspondance de
Chateaubriand." *RHL* 78 (1978): 617-24.

   On *Correspondance générale, I: 1789-1807*, ed. Béatrice
d'Andlau, P. Christophorov, and P. Riberette (see *ELN* 16,
Supp., 96).

Letessier, Fernand. "Un citoyen du Pays de Retz, correspondant
occasionnel de Chateaubriand." *AnBret* 85 (1978): 125-40.

   Identification of Simon-Auguste (or Augustin) Guilbaud
affords details on Chateaubriand's reputation in Brittany
in his last years and posthumously.

Painter, George D. "Chateaubriand and Proust: A Matter of
Affinities." In *Essays by Divers Hands being the Transac-
tions of the Royal Society of Literature*, n.s. 41 (1980).

Racault, J.M. "D'Atala à René ou la fin de l'utopie." *TLL*
17,ii (1979): 85-103.

Scanlan, Margaret. "*Le Vide intérieur*: Self and Consciousness
in *René*, *Atala*, and *Adolphe*." *NCFS* 8 (1979-80): 30-36.

Schumann, Maurice. "Chateaubriand et Hegel." *Revue des Travaux de l'Académie des Sciences Morales et Politiques*, 2ᵉ semestre 1977 [1979].

Villiers du Terrage, Marc de. "La Louisiane de Chateaubriand." *Revue de Louisiane/Louisiana Review* 9 (1980): 36-60; 162-81.

"The first in a series of reprints of rare or generally unavailable articles on Louisiana." Le Baron Marc de Villiers's article appeared in the *Journal de la Société des Américanistes de Paris* 16 (1924): 125-67. It is especially amusing on Chateaubriand's innocence concerning Indian words employed in his narratives. Author wonders where Chateaubriand found that the name Chactas meant "la voix harmonieuse" [one critic has suggested, rather, *tête-plate*] and notes that the nearest word to it in an Indian dictionary is *Chakwas*, which means *mal de gorge*.

See also Pickford, Tison-Braun ("French 1. General"); Berthier ("Barbey d'Aurevilly").

Reviews of books previously listed:

ANDLAU, B. d', P. Christophorov, and P. Riberette, eds., *Correspondance générale*. T. I: *1789-1807* (see *ELN* 10, Supp., 96), rev. by Fernande Bassan in *NCFS* 9 (1980-81): 130-31; by Roger Judrin in *NRF* 303 (April 1978): 110-12; COELHO, Alain, ed., *Pensées, réflexions et maximes* (see *RMB* for 1980, p. 181), rev. by M.R. Ansalone in *SFr* 24 (1980): 577; DENUX, Roger, *La Terrible Course de Chateaubriand* (see *RMB* for 1980, p. 181), rev. by Jacques Landrin in *IL* 33 (1981): 167; by René Pretet in *RDM*, July 1980, pp. 255-56; GILLET, Jean, *Le "Paradis perdu" dans la littérature française de Voltaire à Chateaubriand* (see *ELN* 15, Supp., 86-87), rev. by Tanguy Logé in *LR* 35 (1981): 161-63; LEBEGUE, Raymond, *Aspects de Chateaubriand* (see *RMB* for 1980, p. 182), rev. by F. Robello in *SFr* 24 (1980): 362; by Richard Switzer in *NCFS* 9 (1981): 260-61; by P.J. Whyte in *MLR* 76 (1981): 967-70; PAINTER, George D., *Chateaubriand, a Biography*. Vol. I (see *ELN* 16, Supp., 97), rev. by Christine Jordis in *NRF* 303 (April 1978): 112-15; PORTER, Charles A., *Chateaubriand: Composition, Imagination, and Poetry* (see *ELN* 17, Supp., 130), rev. by P.J. Whyte in *MLR* 76 (1981): 969-70; RIBERETTE, Pierre, ed., *Correspondance générale*, T. 2 (see *RMB* for 1980, pp. 182-83), rev. by M.R. Ansalone in *SFr* 24 (1980): 576-77; by Fernande Bassan in *NCFS* 9 (1980-81): 130-31; by Raymond Lebègue in *RHL* 81 (1981): 145-48.

CHENEDOLLE

Centre d'Art, Esthétique et Littérature, Université de Rouen.
Le Paysage normand dans la littérature et dans l'art.
(Publications de l'Université de Rouen, 68.) Paris: Presses
universitaires de France, 1980. Pp. 316. Fr. 95.00.

COLET

Chaudonneret, Marie-Claude. "Souvenirs de Louise Colet."
Revue du Louvre et des Musées de France 31,ii (1981): 129-
30.

    On portraits of Louise Colet bequeathed to the Musée
Calvet in Avignon.

COMTE

Berrêdo Carneiro, Paulo E., and Pierre Arnaud, eds. *Correspondance générale et confessions.* T. IV: *1846-1848.* (Archives
positivistes.) Paris and The Hague: Mouton, 1981. Pp.
cxiv+334. Fr. 190.00.

See also Baude and Münch, Fulcher, Kelly ("French 1. General").

CONSTANT

Bourgeois, René, ed. *L'Affaire Regnault.* (Publications de
    l'Université des Langues et Lettres de Grenoble.) Univer-
    sité de Grenoble, 1979. Pp. 161.

Brady-Papadopoulou, Valentini. "The Killing of the 'Mother'
    in Constant's *Adolphe.*" *Neophil* 65 (1981): 6-14.

    In the light of divers modern psychological theories
concerning the effects on the child of the mother's disap-
pearance, the author suggests ways of interpreting Adolphe's
behavior toward Ellénore.

Chicoteau, Christine. *Chère Rose: A Biography of Rosalie de
    Constant, 1758-1834.* (Europäische Hochschulschriften,
    Series XIII, n⁰ 65.) Bern, Frankfurt/Main, Las Vegas:
    Lang, 1980. Pp. 364.

De la liberté chez les modernes. Paris: L.G.F., 1980. Fr.
    26.80.

Delbouille, Paul. "Lettres inédites de Constant à ses grands-tantes Villars et Chandieu et à sa tante Nassau." Pp. 623-33 in Jean-Marie D'Heur and Nicoletta Cherubini, eds., *Etudes de philologie romane et d'histoire littéraire offertes à Jules Horrent à l'occasion de son soixantième anniversaire.* Liège: J.-M. D'Heur, N. Cherubini, 1980. Pp. xxiii+853.

Delbouille, Paul. "Remarques sur la technique narrative et le style de Constant dans son 'Cahier rouge.'" Pp. 159-71 in Gerhard Schmidt and Manfred Tietz, eds., *Stimmen der Romania. Festschrift für W. Theodor Elwert zum 70. Geburtstag.* Wiesbaden: B. Heymann, 1980. Pp. ix+725.

Fairlie, Alison. *Imagination and Language: Collected Essays on Constant, Baudelaire, Nerval, and Flaubert.* Cambridge University Press, 1981. Pp. 479. £30.00.

Rev. by Robert Gibson in *TLS*, Oct. 16, 1981, p. 1216.

Fairlie, Alison. "The Shaping of *Adolphe.* Some Remarks on Variants." Pp. 145-64 in Cedric E. Pickford, ed., *Mélanges de littérature française moderne offerts à Garnet Rees par ses collègues et amis.* (La Thésothèque, Réflexion et Recherche universitaire, 7.) Paris: Minard (Lettres Modernes), 1980. Pp. xiv+291.

Harpaz, Ephraïm, ed. *Recueil d'articles.* Vol. 3: *1820-1824.* (Travaux d'Histoire éthico-politique, 35.) Geneva: Droz, 1981. Pp. 362. Fr. 126.00.

Articles which appeared mainly in *Le Courrier Français.*

Hofmann, Etienne, ed. *Bibliographie analytique des écrits sur Benjamin Constant (1796-1980).* (Bibliothèque cantonale et universitaire de Lausanne.) Oxford: The Voltaire Foundation, 1980. Pp. viii+318. £16.00.

Hofmann, Etienne. *Les Principes de politique de Benjamin Constant.* Vol. I: *Etude.* Vol. II: *Texte.* (Travaux d'Histoire éthico-politique, 34.) Geneva: Droz, 1981. Pp. 424, 696. Fr. 360.00.

Rev. by Arlette Michel in *IL* 33 (1981): 214.

Rougemont, Denis de, ed. *De l'esprit de conquête.* (Documentum.) Lausanne: Favre, 1980. Pp. 96.

Sirot, Isabelle. "Biographie et roman." *Adolphe* de Constant."
   FSSA 9 (1980): 19-28.

Thompson, Patrice. *La Religion de Benjamin Constant. Les
   Pouvoirs de l'image.* (Critica e Storia letteraria, 2.)
   Pisa: Pacini, 1978. Pp. 621.

   Rev. by F.P. Bowman in *RHL* 81 (1981): 142-45.

Waridel, Brigitte, Jean-François Tiercy, Norbert Furrer,
   and Anne-Marie Amoos. *Bibliographie analytique des écrits
   sur Constant (1796-1980).* Lausanne: Institut Benjamin-
   Constant; Oxford: The Voltaire Foundation, 1980. Pp. 310.

Wood, Dennis. "Benjamin Constant's First Novel?" *TLS*, Feb.
   6, 1981, p. 151.

   On a manuscript in the Bibliothèque de Neuchâtel.

See also Pickford ("French 1. General"); Scanlan ("Chateaubriand"); Del Litto (2) ("Stendhal").

Reviews of books previously listed:

   HARPAZ, Ephraïm, ed., *Recueil d'articles* (see *ELN* 17,
   Supp., 131), rev. by K. Kloocke in *ZFSL* 90 (1980): 80-84;
   LOWE, David, *Constant, an Annotated Bibliography* (see *RMB*
   for 1980, p. 187), rev. by C.P. Courtney in *FS* 34 (1980):
   346; by B. Fink in *FR* 54 (1980-81): 599; by J. Landrin in
   IL 33 (1981): 81; MERCKEN-SPAAS, Godelieve, *Alienation
   in Constant's "Adolphe"* (see *ELN* 17, Supp., 132), rev. by
   I. Alexander in *MLR* 76 (1981): 195-96.

COURCHAMPS

McLendon, Will L. *Une Ténébreuse Carrière sous l'Empire et
   la Restauration: le comte de Courchamps.* (Bibliothèque de
   Littérature et d'Histoire, 16.) Paris: Minard (Lettres
   modernes), 1980. Pp. 208. Fr. 150.00.

   McLendon has virtually disinterred an interesting figure;
in any case, he has made possible the serious study of
the man and his work. Since the putative Count's life was
indeed a rather murky business and since his literature was
largely plagiarized, emphasis necessarily falls on the
biographical side and on the scandals provoked by his
mystifications. Even biographically, there are great gaps,

the intervals between scandals and controversies. McLendon
has reprinted numerous documents *in extenso* and often clogged
his narrative; but at least we now have the documents. Moreover, McLendon provides a sensible and sensitive discussion
of the more important literary questions raised by Courchamps's work and especially by the fantastic element in
his most famous work, the *Souvenirs de la marquise de Créquy*
(1834-35); he also studies the complex relations between
Courchamps and Sue, Sophie Gay, Janin, Nodier, Barbey
d'Aurevilly, and Jean Lorrain, most of whom plagiarized
him, and gives an account of Courchamps's flagrant plagiarisms from Potocki, the revelation of which broke Courchamps's
career. Two unknown tales by Courchamps are reprinted in
an appendix.

The overall impression of McLendon's book is choppy, as
a result of the mixture of themes and genres. But each
element is handled with skill and insight, and his book
adds to the list of Romantic *minores* whom serious students
of French Romanticism must take into account. (J.S.P.)

COURIER

See Crouzet ("Stendhal").

COUSIN

See Baude and Münch, Kelly ("French 1. General"); Borowitz
("Balzac").

CUSTINE

Review of book previously listed:

PIERROT, Roger, ed., *Lettres à Varnhagen d'Ense* (see *RMB*
for 1979, p. 179), rev. by Carlo Cordié in *SFr* 25 (1981):
172-73.

DAVID

Puttfarken, Thomas. "David's *Brutus* and Theories of Pictorial
Unity in France." *Art History* 4 (1981): 291-304.

See also Warner ("General 2. Environment").

Review of book previously listed:

BROOKNER, Anita, *Jacques-Louis David* (see *RMB* for 1980, p. 149), rev. by Celia Betsky in *NR*, May 30, 1981, pp. 38-40.

Composite review:

Haskell, Francis. *BM* 123 (Dec. 1981): 49-50.

Considers Anita Brookner, *Jacques-Louis David* (see *RMB* for 1980, p. 149), and Antoine Schnapper, *David--Témoin de son Temps* (Paris: Bibliothèque des Arts; pp. 315, 191 illus.; £37.00).

DELACROIX

Berthier, Philippe. "Des images sur les mots, des mots sur les images: à propos de Baudelaire et Delacroix." *RHL* 80 (1980): 900-15 (discussion: 916-20).

The focus is on Baudelaire's transformation of the visual images which Delacroix--already a very "literary" painter-- furnished him into the verbal art of his criticism.

Johnson, Lee McKay. "Baudelaire and Delacroix: Tangible Language." Pp. 11-64 in Lee McKay Johnson, *The Metaphor of Painting. Essays on Baudelaire, Ruskin, Proust, and Pater.* (Studies in the Fine Arts: Criticism, 7.) Ann Arbor: UMI Research Press, 1980. Pp. xiv+260.

The author uses Baudelaire's criticism to illustrate his thesis that along with Ruskin's, it "is based on the application of principles derived from visual art to writing."

Johnson, Lee. "La *Chanson de pirates* de Victor Hugo interpretée par Delacroix." *Revue du Louvre et des Musées de France* 31,iv (1981): 273-75.

Delacroix's *Pirates africains enlevant une jeune femme* (1853) is linked to a poem from *Les Orientales*. The author regards this relationship as "plus que probable," but his case may not be quite that strong. (J.S.P.)

Johnson, Lee. "Delacroix, Dumas and 'Hamlet.'" *BM* 945 (Dec. 1981): 717-21.

The questions discussed (provenance and authenticity) are primarily art historical but also involve the Dumas-Meurice *Hamlet* and Delacroix's possible acquaintance with it.

Johnson, Lee. *The Paintings of Delacroix: A Critical Catalogue 1816-1831.* Vol. I: *Texts.* Vol. II: *Plates.* Oxford: Claren-don Press, 1981. £80.00.

Rev. anon. in *GBA* 1354 (Nov. 1981): "Chronique des Arts," 16-17; by Jon Whitely in *BM* 945 (Dec. 1981): 750-51.

Lichtenstein, Sara. *Delacroix and Raphael.* (Outstanding Dis-sertations in the Fine Arts.) New York and London: Garland, 1979. Pp. 403. $40.00.

Rev. (unfavorably) by Peter Hecht in *Semiolus* 11 (1980): 186-95.

Sérullaz, Maurice. *Delacroix.* Milan: Mondadori; Paris: Fernand Nathan, 1981. Pp. 208. Fr. 139.20.

Contains a catalogue of 494 works (about half of Dela-croix's production). Probably best described as "haute vul-garisation."

Spector, Jack L. "The *Vierge du Sacré-Coeur*: Religious Poli-tics and Personal Expression in an Early Work of Delacroix." *BM* 937 (April 1981): 198-206.

The picture is said to blend the expression of the Restora-tion cult of the Virgin and foreshadowings of "the frank conflicts and sadistic delights of [Delacroix's] romantic masterpieces."

See also Warner ("General 2. Environment"); Garber ("General 3. Criticism"); Garber ("English 4. Byron"); Newman, Wright (2) ("French 1. General").

Composite review:

Spurling, John. *New Statesman*, Sept. 11, 1981, pp. 20-21.

Reviews Johnson, *The Paintings of Eugene Delacroix*, and Wellington, *The Journal of Eugene Delacroix.*

DELAVIGNE

See Mower, Wright (1) ("French 1. General").

DE LEON

David, Sylvain-Christian. "La Tragédie du Monde de Louis de
Léon. OEuvre méconnue d'un romantique breton." Europe 625
(May 1981): 91-98.

A brief introduction to de Léon (1818-1843) and his only
published work. The author relates him to the Romantics,
but especially to Sade and Maistre.

DESBORDES-VALMORE

Baudot, Marcel. "Marceline Desbordes-Valmore." Les Normands
de Paris 72 (1978): 17-18.

Nothing new. (A.B.S.)

Spaziani, M. Luisa. Da "Stello" a "Chatterton" e la poesia
di Marceline Desbordes-Valmore. Rome: Lo Faro, 1977.
L.5000.00.

DESCHAMPS (A.)

Cohen, Henry. "L'art de Pétrarquiser in Antoni Deschamps'
Etudes sur l'Italie." Italica 58 (1981): 102-13.

Analyzes Deschamps' translations of five sonnets from
the Canzoniere as a product of neoclassical and Romantic
influences.

DIDIER

See Misan (1) ("French 1. General").

DONDEY

Hassel, Jon B. "Philothée O'Neddy and the Poetics of the
Petit cénacle." NCFS 8 (1980): 218-27.

Two texts from Feu et flamme are analyzed to support
the contention that the Petit cénacle had greater cohesion
and a more serious literary and esthetic program than
generally believed, "a common belief in the enormous
privilege and power of Art, the ability of Art to tran-
scend the limitations of human existence and to create

another reality far from the constraints of the Society in which [the members] found themselves."

DUMAS

Bäckvall, Hans. "Alexandre Dumas père, introducteur d'italianismes en français." *MSpr* 75 (1981): 177-92.

Bäckvall, Hans. "Pièces de théâtre de Dumas représentées à Stockholm par des comédiens français." *SN* 52 (1980): 161-66.

Bassan, Fernande. "Lettres d'Alexandre Dumas père conservées à la Pierpont Morgan Library à New York." *BduB* (1981-II): 172-94.

The texts of 34 letters, mostly short, and most of them addressed to Mr. or Mrs. Vanloo.

Bassan, Fernande, ed. *Théâtre complet*. Vol. II, fasc. 7: *Antony*. (Bibliothèque introuvable.) Paris: Lettres Modernes (Minard), 1980. Pp. 114. Fr. 45.00.

Derche, Roland. "Nerval poète, vu par Dumas." Pp. 201-21 in Jean Richer, ed., *Cahiers de l'Herne 37*. Paris: L'Herne, 1980. Pp. 400. Fr. 148.00.

Dumas, Alexandre. *Oeuvres: XVIIe siècle*. Vol. I: *Les Trois Mousquetaires*. Paris: Club de l'Honnête Homme, 1981. Pp. xxi+320. Fr. 240.00.

La Guerre des femmes. Geneva: Favot, 1978. Pp. 357. Fr. 29.80.

Histoire de la vie politique et privée de Louis-Philippe. (Hommes et Destins.) Paris: Olivier Orban, 1981. Pp. 424. Fr. 85.00.

Le Page du duc de Savoie. (Les Grands Romans historiques.) 2 vols. Geneva: Favot, 1981. Fr. 31.30 each vol.

Ross, Michael. *Alexandre Dumas*. Newton Abbott: David and Charles, 1981. Pp. 297. £9.95.

Rev. by April FitzLyon in *TLS*, April 17, 1981, p. 447.

Schärer, Kurt. "'A Alexandre Dumas.' L'Auteur et son miroir." Pp. 223-36 in Jean Richer, ed., *Cahiers de l'Herne 37*. Paris: L'Herne, 1980. Pp. 400. Fr. 148.00.

Schopp, C. "Apollinaire et Dumas." *RLM* 576-81 (1980): 171-72.

Sigaux, Gilbert, ed. *Le Comte de Monte-Cristo.* (Bibliothèque de la Pléiade.) Paris: Gallimard, 1981. Pp. 1477. Fr. 160.00.

See also Mower ("French 1. General"); Johnson, L. (3) ("Delacroix").

Reviews of books previously listed:

ADLER, Alfred, *Dumas und die böse Mutter* (see *RMB* for 1980, p. 189), rev. by C. Cordié in *SFr* 25 (1981): 176-77; by M. Kesting in *RF* 92 (1980): 311-15; MUNRO, Douglas, ed., *Alexandre Dumas: A Bibliography of Works Translated into English* (see *RMB* for 1979, p. 178), rev. by F.W.J. Hemmings in *FS* 35 (1981): 79-80.

DURAS

Le Dantec, Denise. "Deux rééditions féministes." *QL* 308 (Sept. 1-15, 1979): 13-14.

An interview with Claudine Herrmann about her feminist-oriented editions of *Ourika* (see *RMB* for 1979, p. 179) and Madame de Staël's *Corinne.*

ESQUIROS

See Delon ("Staël").

FABRE D'OLIVET

Caïn de Lord Byron. Traduit en vers français et réfuté dans une suite de remarques philosophiques et critiques. (Esotérisme.) Geneva: Slatkine Reprints, 1981. Pp. 248. Fr. 65.00.

Reprint of the edition of Paris, 1823.

Gardy, Philippe. "'L'Enclos de l'or': Fabre d'Olivet et l'écriture de la langue maternelle." *Romantisme* 34 (1981): 3-29.

FEVAL

La Fée des grèves. (Bibliothèque technique.) Paris: Jean
  Picollec, 1981. Pp. 236. Fr. 55.94.

See also Pickford ("French 1. General").

FLAUBERT

Bem, Jeanne. Désir et savoir dans l'oeuvre de Flaubert. Etude
  de "La Tentation de Saint Antoine." (Langages.) Neuchâtel:
  La Baconnière, 1979. Pp. 303. Fr. 57.00.

  Rev. by B. Bart in French Forum 6 (1981): 282-84; by C.
Haroche in Europe 58 (May 1980): 247; by A. Israel-Pelletier
in NCFS 10 (1981-82): 150-51; by G. Memmi in O&C 5 (1980-
81): 125-26; by J. Neefs in QL 324 (May 1-15, 1980): 20;
by U. Schulz-Buschhaus in RF 92 (1980): 321-24; by T. Unwin
in MLR 76 (1981): 973-74.
  Flaubert's Tentation de Saint Antoine has defied classi-
fication, even been declared unreadable. But the author of
this welcome, albeit at times confusing, full-length study
considers the Tentation to be at the center of all that
Flaubert wrote. The Flaubert which emerges is not the
Realist writer of the Education sentimentale, but a writer
whose obsession with the Bible, God, and myth places him
squarely within the Romantic tradition, a poet and prophet,
precursor of Rimbaud's voyant.
  The existence of three versions of the Tentation poses
a problem which the author resolves by treating them as
one text (after Lévi-Strauss's treatment of the Oedipus
myth). She attempts to justify this controversial approach
by isolating eleven basic sequences (in a Greimasian
analysis) common to all three versions.
  The author's approach is essentially Freudian, via
Lacan, with doses of Sartre and Lyotard. The structuring
element of the work thus stems from a "roman familial,"
which in Flaubert's case becomes a "drame de l'artiste,"
i.e., the struggle in his quest for knowledge of the son
(the artist) with the father, keeper of the Logos. This
view is especially enlightening in the author's discussion

of the *épisode des dieux*. The author extends it to other
of Flaubert's works, in which one finds so many negative
representatives of the medical profession, reflections of
the castrating father. In spite of Flaubert's praise of
science in his correspondence, he chooses art over science
in his search for a type of knowledge which goes beyond
science.

Although some readers may consider this approach reduc-
tionist, deploring especially the renunciation of any
diachronic considerations, and despite some obscurity and
jargon (fortunately limited) and an annoying use of capitalization, the author presents stimulating insights into
Flaubert's creative imagination. (E.F.G.)

Unwin, Timothy. "Flaubert's First *Tentation de Saint-Antoine*."
   Essays in French Literature 16 (1979): 17-42.

A long, thoughtful article on Flaubert's pantheistic
vision, which, although inspired by Spinoza, goes beyond
Spinoza's strict rationalism by positing a mystical force
which is at the heart of phenomena and which must be in-
tuited rather than logically deduced. Whence Flaubert's
attack on dogma and doctrine. But the author sees a self-
defeating aspect in Flaubert's pantheism, which is skeptical
of its own doctrinaire statements, and he suggests that
this is perhaps the reason why Flaubert will subsequently
attempt to express his world view primarily in esthetic
terms. (E.F.G.)

Weinberg, Henry H. "Irony and 'Style Indirect Libre' in
   Madame Bovary." *CRCL* 8 (1981): 1-9.

See also Schoenholtz ("General 3. Criticism"); Jacobs ("Sand").

FOURIER

Nathan, Michel. *Le Ciel des Fouriéristes. Habitants des
   étoiles et réincarnations de l'âme.* Presses universitaires
   de Lyon, 1981. Pp. 210. Fr. 66.00.

An often amusing survey of the speculations about life
on other planets, reincarnations in outer space, and cos-
mogony produced by Fourier, his disciples, and by other
writers who were influenced by the Fourierist vision or
had similar dreams of their own (e.g., Hugo, the only
major literary figure treated at some length here). Fourier's
own droll ideas seem to have embarrassed some of his fol-

lowers, somewhat as did his utopian eroticism (*Le Nouveau Monde amoureux* lay unpublished until recently). Still, his and related views were widespread, embodied quite serious aspirations, and, at the least, make for interesting reading. The cover illustration from Grandville sets the tone perfectly. (J.S.P.)

Spencer, Michael. "A(na)logie de Fourier." *Romantisme* 34 (1981): 31-46.

Spencer, Michael. "Charles Fourier: Les Progrès de l'intempérie." *NRF* 341 (June 1, 1981): 169-77.

  Reprints a lost article by Fourier from the *Journal Politique et Littéraire du Département du Rhône* of July 11, 1816, which (so Fourier claimed) aroused a storm of comment and official displeasure.

See also Fulcher ("French 1. General").

GAUTIER

Berchet, Jean-Claude, ed. *Voyage en Espagne*. (Garnier-Flammarion, 367.) Paris: Flammarion, 1981. Pp. 445.

Berthier, Patrick, ed. *Voyage en Espagne*. Suivi de: *España*. (Folio, 1295.) Paris: Gallimard, 1981. Pp. 608. Fr. 20.50.

  Rev. by André Bourin in *RDM*, July 1981, pp. 413-17; briefly by G[érard] S[pitéri] in *NL* 2794 (July 2-9, 1981): 10.

Bulletin de la Société Théophile Gautier 3 (1981).

  Contents: Carmen Fernandez Sanchez, "*Mademoiselle de Maupin* et le récit poétique" (1-10); Marie-Claude Schapira, "Une relecture des *Nouvelles* de Théophile Gautier" (11-25); Paul Pelckmans, "Inconscience ou apothéose? Une lecture de *Jettatura*" (27-47); David Graham Burnett, "The Destruction of the Artist in Gautier's Early Poetry" (49-58); Joel Goldfield, "Les concepts de l'exotisme chez Théophile Gautier et Arthur de Gobineau" (59-88); Andrew Gann, "Une revue inconnue de Théophile Gautier: *La Revue du XIXe Siècle*" (89-96); Marianne Cermakian, ed., "Le Journal d'Eugénie Fort (suite)" (97-129); Claudine Lacoste, ed., "Six lettres inédites de Judith Gautier" (131-37); Jean Richer, ed., "La statuette de Fanny Elssler" (attribution

to Gautier of an article on the dancer) (139-41); Jean
Richer, "Notes et documents" (clarifications on a poem,
"Sur un album," and indications on "Secours accordés à la
famille Gautier") (143-44); Jean-Claude Romer, "Théophile
Gautier à l'écran" (10 films based on works by Gautier)
(145-46); Minako Imura, "Théophile Gautier au Japon" (147).
Also lists new books on Gautier (1) by Richer and (2) by
Voisin (reviewed in the present *RMB*) and recent editions of
works by Gautier (also in the present *RMB* and *RMB* for 1980).
Society news.

Burnett, David Graham. "Sexual Rhetoric and Personal Identity
in Théophile Gautier's 'Préface' to *Mademoiselle de Maupin*."
Pp. 38-45 in A. Maynard Hardee, ed., *Manifestoes and Movements*. (French Literature Series, VII.) [Columbia, S.C.]:
University of South Carolina, 1980.

Correction of item listed in *RMB* for 1980, p. 192.

Chambers, Ross. "Le poète fumeur." *AJFS* 16, Part II (1979):
138-51.

Stimulating as usual, Chambers studies the poetic representation of smoking and its relation to literary creativity
in works by Gautier, Baudelaire, Mallarmé, and Ponge.
Gautier's sonnet, "La Fumée," leads to the conclusion that:
"Fumer une cigarette ou créer un texte, chez Gautier, c'est
moins donner quelque chose au monde que recevoir un con-
tentement personnel en posant les frontières d'un monde à
soi" (144).

Eigeldinger, Marc, ed. *Récits fantastiques*. (Garnier-Flammarion.) Paris: Flammarion, 1981. Pp. 480. Fr. 17.75.

Rev. by Gérard Spitéri in *NL* 2812 (Nov. 13-17, 1981): 49.

Gaudon, Jean, ed. *La Morte amoureuse, Avatar et autres récits
fantastiques*. (Folio, 1316.) Paris: Gallimard, 1981. Pp.
505. Fr. 19.10.

In his preface, Gaudon focuses on the principal motifs
in Gautier's fantastic tales: temporal upset, succubuses,
animation of the dead, antipathetic figures of authority,
doubling of the personality. Gautier's tales are viewed
as "tragic," representing illusory hopes inevitably frustrated by "la résurgence brutale du temps réel" (43). This
view is correct for the stories collected here. Unfortunately, it fails to recognize the hopefulness of *Spirite*.
(A.B.S.)

Gothot-Mersch, Claudine, ed. *Emaux et camées*. En appendice:
   Albertus. (Poésie/Gallimard, 154.) Paris: Gallimard, 1981.
   Pp. 288. Fr. 20.10.

Hunt, Tony. "The Inspiration and Unity of *Emaux et camées*
   (1852)." *DUJ* 73,i (N.S. 42,i) (1980): 75-81.

   "The poems depict the attempt to recover a lost harmony
pursued through the tensions of animate and inanimate,
spirit and form, past and present, reality and dream" (81).
Hunt is apparently unfamiliar with the work of Richard B.
Grant and of P.E. Tennant, both of whom have discussed
Emaux et camées at length (see *ELN* 14, Supp., 82 and 83,
respectively). (A.B.S.)

Malinowski, Wieslaw. "La Vision du monde antique dans les
   nouvelles de Théophile Gautier." *Studia Romanica Posnaniensia*
   4 (1978): 45-52.

   Stresses Gautier's recourse to archaeology in setting the
scenes of certain tales, and offers suggestions as to the
function of scene: antiquity represented for Gautier an
escape from modern ugliness and banality; its artistic conceptions correspond to his aesthetic ideals. For Malinowski,
Gautier fails to make antiquity live because he cannot
bring his scenes to life; and he cannot do this because he
emphasizes archaeology at the expense of his narration.

Raymond, Marcel. "Gautier, Baudelaire et 'Les paradis arti-
   ficiels.'" Pp. 135-46 in *Romantisme et rêverie*. Paris:
   José Corti, 1978. Pp. 304. Fr. 84.00.

   The character of the imagery produced by drugs. The discussion, insofar as Gautier is concerned, turns on *Le Club
des hachichins*. *Romantisme et rêverie*, already listed in
RMB for 1979, p. 152, also contains "Gautier: la rêverie
et la vision picturale" (91-108). Raymond believes that
with the Romanticism of 1830, revery, instead of giving in
to the vague and the uncertain, tended to project tangible
forms. Gautier is a prime example of the new focus.

Richardson, Joanna, trans. *Mademoiselle de Maupin*. Harmonds-
   worth: Penguin, 1981. Pp. 348. £2.25.

Richer, Jean. *Etudes et recherches sur Théophile Gautier
   prosateur*. Paris: Nizet, 1981. Pp. 268. Fr. 120.00.

   Briefly rev. by P[ierre] E[nckell] in *NL* 2812 (Nov. 13-
17, 1981): 49.

Contains a few full-length studies and a large number of brief reports on research into the life and works of Gautier. There are three main headings: "Le Fantastiqueur inquiet," "L'Italie et l'Orient: rêve et réalité," and "Aspects de la constellation Gautier." Titles under this last, cryptic heading include: "La famille humaine ou les types au théâtre et dans le roman," "Gautier et Nerval," and "Gautier, Shakespeare, Rimbaud." Contains also "Pages de prose retrouvées de Théophile Gautier" (six unpublished reviews) and a section of plates. Some of Richer's pieces have already appeared elsewhere.

One finds disappointing Richer's failure to recognize English-language studies on Gautier and especially the Italian contributions of Cecilia Rizza (1) on Gautier as critic and (2) on *Italia* (see *ELN* 10, Supp., 94, and 14, Supp., 82). (A.B.S.)

Schapira, Marie-Claude. "Le jeu de l'amour dans les nouvelles de Gautier." Pp. 83-95 in Roger Bellet, ed., *La Femme au XIXe siècle: littérature et idéologie*. Presses universitaires de Lyon, 1978. Pp. 202.

Schnack, Arne. "Surface et profondeur dans *Mademoiselle de Maupin*." *OL* 36 (1981): 28-36.

Gautier, the putative artist of surfaces, is in fact a man tormented by anxiety regarding his deepest moral and psychic impulses. What these may be Schnack fails to specify.

Voisin, Marcel. "L'insolite quotidien dans l'oeuvre de Th. Gautier." *CAIEF* 32 (1980): 163-78.

Even everyday objects frequently revealed something strange to Gautier. Instances of reality represented as possessing "fantastic" qualities reflect his basic anguish before the fearful prospect of death.

Voisin, Marcel. *Le Soleil et la nuit: l'imaginaire dans l'oeuvre de Théophile Gautier*. Préface de Roland Mortier. Editions de l'Université de Bruxelles, 1981. Pp. 377. Bel.Fr. 700.00.

Prematurely listed (see *ELN* 13, Supp., 90) because (unjustifiably) announced by Minard in 1974, Voisin's book owes its belated publication to the (justifiable) critical favor it found at the Editions de l'Université de Bruxelles. In this synthesis based upon study of Gautier's entire available production, Voisin presents a very complex in-

dividual, richer by far than manuals and most previous
studies have acknowledged. Voisin's own reduction of Gautier's
imagination to a tension between "diurnal" and "nocturnal"
is deceptive, for he shows both forces to be multifaceted:
"Solaire est son tempérament hédoniste. Mais cette force
rabelaisienne fut difficilement conquise sur une fragilité
intime et la mélancolie, faille nocturne, signe toutes ses
joies. Solaire est son aspiration culturelle au classicisme
hellénique. Mais le 'mal du siècle' l'a marqué de son ombre
propice aux monstres et aux chimères. Solaire est son oeuvre
au style rutilant, à la fantaisie débridée. Mais que de
perles ne sont que larmes pudiques et gouttes figées d'une
eau de mort!... Au regard du réel, la fête, sans cesse
désirée, toujours démentie, ne peut être qu'instant privi-
légié ou spectacle illusoire de l'imagination. Et sur la
fragilité de toute oeuvre humaine, le style étale un 'voile
d'or', lumineux mensonge et tenace espérance. Gautier parie
pour le jour, pour le marbre, pour l'éternité mais il ne
cesse d'être rongé par l'angoisse du néant" (349-50).

Voisin's search for the "author-in-the-work" might appear
old-fashioned to some critics. *Le Soleil et la nuit* will
stand, nevertheless, as the most detailed explanation of
Gautier to appear in recent years. Its principal merits are
its refinements and elaborations of points made by earlier
readers, and especially its demonstration that *l'imaginaire*
in Gautier is something that cannot be summed up so neatly
as many have wished to do. (A.B.S.)

Voisin, Marcel. "Th. Gautier: l'Italie et la rêverie médi-
terranéenne." In Vol. III of *France et Italie dans la culture
européenne: mélanges offerts à Franco Simone.* 3 vols. Geneva:
Slatkine, 1980.

Voisin, Marcel. "Théophile Gautier précurseur de Jules Verne?"
In *Colloque d'Amiens (11-13 novembre 1977). Jules Verne
II: filiations, rencontres, influences.* (La Thésothèque,
5.) Paris: Minard (Lettres modernes), 1980. Pp. 109.

Wetherill, P.M. "Poésie/Peinture/Réalité. Prolongement d'une
conversation avec R.-L. Wagner." Pp. 118-27 in *Les Voies
étranges, échos d'une prison dorée, recueillis et offerts
au Professeur R.-L. Wagner par ses amis de Manchester.*
Manchester: n.p., 1977.

See also Bellemin-Noël, Schneider, Tison-Braun, Viallaneix
and Ehrard ("French 1. General"); Bolster, Senninger
("Balzac"); Grunewald ("Nerval"); Smith ("German 3. Hoffmann").

Reviews of books previously listed:

Giselle (see *RMB* for 1980, p. 193), rev. by J. Legrand in
ECl 49 (1981): 63; ROBICHEZ, Jacques, ed., *Mademoiselle de
Maupin* (see *RMB* for 1980, p. 194), rev. by Claude Duchet
in *Romantisme* 32 (1981): 122-24; *Un Trio de romans* (see
RMB for 1979, p. 184), rev. by Carlo Cordié in *SFr* 25 (1981):
179-80.

GAY

See McLendon ("Courchamps").

GIRARDIN (D. de)

Richardson, Joanna. "Madame de Girardin: The Tenth Muse."
   Pp. 71-83 in Peter Quennell, ed., *Affairs of the Mind: The
   Salon in Europe and America from the 18th to the 20th
   Century.* Washington, D.C.: New Republic Books, 1980. Pp.
   188. $14.95.

See also Hellerstein ("French 1. General"); Teissier ("Lamartine").

GOZLAN

See L'Année Balzacienne ("Balzac").

GUERIN, E. and M. de

Bonnardot, Dr. Jacques. "Monsieur Féli centaure?" *AmG* 139
   (1981): 166-68.

   A light-hearted refutation of Albert Roux's statement
that "En aucune façon Chiron ne peut représenter Lamennais."
Author's answer: "Et qui sait?"

Hirissou, Pierre. "A père anxieux fils indolent (éditorial)."
   AmG 139 (1981): 129-30.

   On a letter dictated by Joseph de Guérin to his son
Maurice.

Mistler, Jean (secrétaire perpétuel de l'Académie française). "Au Cayla chez Eugénie et Maurice de Guérin" (discours prononcé à l'Institut de France en 1980). AmG 138 (1981): 65-75; 139 (1981): 131-40.

Peyrade, Jean. "La vie quotidienne au Cayla au temps d'Eugénie de Guérin." AmG 139 (1981): 146-55 (à suivre).

Roux, Albert. "L'aventure spirituelle de Maurice de Guérin." AmG 137 (1981): 10-28; 138 (1981): 80-97.

Continuation and conclusion of author's long article begun in AmG 136 (in the Autumn-Winter issue of 1980). Shows de Guérin seeking spiritual refuge from the world in a search for l'invisible and l'inouï that recalls the search of Novalis, Nerval, and Rimbaud. The famous "Cahier vert" is thus seen as "le journal d'un poète hanté par le mystère de la vie." Author notes that after 1835 "Maurice trouvera d'autres refuges: le dandysme, l'art, puis la mort." The editors add to the article de Guérin's poem, "Le Crucifix" (written when he was 22), which provides a quite different emphasis.

Sabin, Guy. "Comment les Guérin ont fait souche au Cayla." AmG 137 (1981): 29-36.

Includes a "Généalogie probable des Guérins" (36).

Vest, James. "Le Château d'armes et le Manoir de Maurice de Guérin." AmG 139 (1981): 158-64.

GUIZOT

See Viallaneix (1) ("Michelet").

HUGO (V.)

Albouy, Pierre, ed. Odes et ballades. (Poésie/Gallimard, 141.) Paris: Gallimard, 1980. Pp. 478. Fr. 20.10.

Albouy, Pierre, ed. Les Orientales. Les Feuilles d'automne. (Poésie/Gallimard, 151.) Paris: Gallimard, 1981.

Babuts, Nicolae. "Hugo's La Fin de Satan: The Identity Shift." Symposium 35 (1981): 91-110.

Develops the idea "that Hugo's capacity to form bonds of
identity with the fallen archangel has its beginning in the
act of meditation, and that it is part of a prevailing creative behavior in which the poet assumes the identity of
the protagonist." The "identity-shift" occurred over the
quarter-century from 1830 to 1854 and may well have been
significantly influenced by the table-turnings during the
poet's exile.

Barrère, Jean-Bertrand. *Le Regard d'Orphée ou l'échange
poétique: Hugo, Baudelaire, Rimbaud, Apollinaire*. Paris:
Société d'édition d'enseignement supérieur, 1977. Pp. 272.

  Rev. by Suzanne Nash in *RR* 72 (1981): 116-18.

Bonjour, Alexandre, ed. *Hernani: drame*. (Univers des Lettres:
Etude critique illustrée. Texte intégral; 229.) Paris:
Bordas, 1979. Pp. 159. Fr. 9.50.

Boudout, Jean, ed. *Quatrevingt-treize*. (Classiques Garnier.)
Paris: Garnier, 1981. Fr. 53.50.

Brombert, Victor. "*Les Travailleurs de la mer*: Hugo's Poem of
Effacement." *NLH* 9 (1977-78): 581-90.

Cordié, C. "Hugo." *CeS* 70 (April-June 1979): 50-60.

  Rev. briefly by P.A. Borgheggiani in *SFr* 24 (1980): 366.

Daniels, Barry Vincent. "Victor Hugo on the Boulevard: *Lucrèce
Borgia* at the Porte-Saint-Martin Theatre in 1833." *Theatre
Journal* 32 (1980): 17-42.

Galey, Jean-Marie. *Les Tables tournantes: théâtre*. [Paris,
Théâtre de la Cité internationale, 20 janvier 1981 / Jean-
Marie Galey; d'après les procès-verbaux des séances de
spiritisme rédigés par Victor Hugo et ses proches ...]
(Collection Théâtre.) Paris: A. Michel, 1981. Pp. 87.
Fr. 20.37.

Gély, Claude. "Etude d'un poème de Victor Hugo: 'Je la revois.'"
IL 33 (1981): 137-40.

  Gély calls "Je la revois" (8 août 1852, en arrivant à
Jersey--in *Toute la lyre*) "cette nouvelle 'Tristesse d'Olym-
pio.'"

Grimaud, Michel. "Trimétrie et rôle poétique de la césure chez
Victor Hugo." *RR* 70 (1979): 56-68.

Journet, Réne, and Guy Robert. *Contribution aux études sur Victor Hugo. Les manuscrits B.N. n.a.fr. 24.787 et 24.788. Analyse et textes inédits.* (Annales Littéraires de l'Université de Besançon, 248.) Paris: Les Belles Lettres, 1980. Pp. 170.

Juin, Hubert (Préface de). *L'homme qui rit.* (10/18; série: Domaine classique, 1444-1445.) 2 vols. Paris: U.G.E., 1981. Fr. 52.40.

Juin, Hubert. *Victor Hugo. Tome I: 1802-1843.* Paris: Flammarion, 1980. Pp. 882.

Rev. by Victor Brombert in *TLS*, Aug. 7, 1981, p. 900; by Pierre Gamarra in *Europe* 626-627 (1981): 206-09; by Bernard Géniès in *QL* 343 (March 1-15, 1981): 20-21; by Pierre-Louis Rey in *NRF* 340 (May 1, 1981): 114-16.
Two more volumes planned.

Kaplan, Edward K. "Victor Hugo and the Poetics of Doubt: The Transition of 1835-1837." *French Forum* 6 (1981): 140-53.

Laster, Arnaud. *Pleins feux sur Victor Hugo.* Paris: Comédie française (diffusion: Garnier), 1981. Pp. 884. Fr. 69.95.

"10 dessins de Tim, 15 dessins de V. Hugo."

Laster, Arnaud, ed. *Victor Hugo: un poète.* (Folio junior: En poésie; 18.) Paris: Gallimard, 1981. Pp. 153. Fr. 8.40.

Lestringant, Frank. "Rémanence du blanc: a propos d'une reminiscence hugolienne dans l'oeuvre de Mallarmé." *RHL* 81 (1981): 64-74.

Suggests relation of Hugo's reference to the lily "que la blancheur défend" (in "Le Pont," the first poem in Book VI of *Les Contemplations*) to the same phrase in Mallarmé's "Brise marine" and seeks to demonstrate the revolutionary change in the concept of *whiteness* in Mallarmé's use of the word.

Leuilliot, Bernard, ed. *Han d'Islande.* (Folio, 1331.) Paris: Gallimard, 1981. Pp. 576. Fr. 22.00.

Meschonnic, Henri. "Ce que Hugo dit de la langue." *Romantisme* 25-26 (1979): 57-73.

Petrey, Sandy. *History in the Text: "Quatrevingt-Treize" and the French Revolution.* (Purdue University Monographs in Romance Languages, 2.) Amsterdam: John Benjamins B.V., 1980. Pp. 129. 40 Guilders.

Rev. by Richard B. Grant in *NCFS* 10 (1981-82): 144-45.

Robichez, Jacques. "L'incohérence des *Contemplations*." *O&C* 5,i (1980): 83-90.

Shows criticism for a century (from Hugo's contemporaries through Faguet, Lemaitre, Gide, Claudel, Valéry, to later French critics) accusing *Les Contemplations* of lacking taste, order, and consistency (Claudel even wrote: "Hugo est un grand poète, si on peut l'être sans intelligence, ni goût, ni sensibilité, ni ordre"). But the most admired of French literary critics today think otherwise and insist that the poems have their subtle consistency and go beyond taste and logic. Changing attitudes toward religion (partly influenced by Vatican II) and toward sexuality are seen as influencing new critical attitudes (one might add the particular influence of Surrealism) and as providing identification of heretofore largely unrecognized coherence and complexity in the whole of *Les Contemplations*.

Scaiola, Anna Maria. "'Oui, je suis la fille de Victor Hugo.' Su due forme di riproduzione mancata." *Micromégas* 6,i (1979): 111-18.

Strugnell, Anthony. "Contribution à l'étude du républicanisme de Victor Hugo: lettres inédites et oubliées à Jean-Claude Colfavru et autres." *RHL* 78 (1978): 796-809.

See also Comte, Mower, Pickford, Viallaneix and Ehrard ("French 1. General"); Bismut ("Balzac"); Johnson, L. (1) ("Delacroix"); Nathan ("Fourier"); Centre de Recherches de Littérature française ("Nodier").

Reviews of books previously listed:

AREF, Mahmoud, *La Pensée sociale et humaine de Victor Hugo dans son oeuvre romanesque* (see *RMB* for 1979, p. 187), rev. by C. Gely in *Romantisme* 25-26 (1979): 247; GAUDON, Sheila, ed., *Victor Hugo--Pierre-Jules Hetzel. Correspondance*, T. I (see *RMB* for 1979, p. 188), rev. by Pierre L. Horn in *NCFS* 9 (1980-81): 131-32; GLAUSER, Alfred, *La Poétique de Hugo* (see *RMB* for 1979, p. 188), rev. by Reinhard Kuhn in *MLN* 95 (1980): 1087-91; GOHIN, Yves, ed., *Quatrevingt-treize* (see *RMB* for 1979, p. 188), rev. by W.J.S. Kirton in *FS* 35 (1981): 459; GORILOVICS, Tivadar, *"La Légende de Victor Hugo" de Paul Lafargue* (see *RMB* for 1980, p. 199), rev. by C. Cordié in *SFr* 24 (1980): 366; PETROVSKA, Marija, *Victor Hugo:*

l'écrivain engagé en Bohème (see *ELN* 16, Supp., 104), rev.
by Douglass R. Hall in *SAR* 46 (1981): 92-94.

JACQUEMONT

Redman, Harry, Jr., and Andy P. Antippas. "'Letter on America'
by Victor Jacquemont." *The French-American Review* 2 (1978):
95-120.

JANIN

Landrin, Jacques. "Jules Janin et Molière." Pp. 171-94 in
Mélanges littéraires François Germain. Dijon: Section de
Littérature Française de la Faculté de Lettres et Philosophie
de Dijon, 1980. Pp. 330.

In this rather long summary of Janin's view of Molière,
the author shows that Janin's admiration for Molière as
comic writer was somewhat tempered by the feeling that plays
like *Le Tartuffe* and *Dom Juan* may have helped to bring
about the end of the ancien régime, for which Janin expressed
a certain nostalgia.

See also Viallaneix and Ehrard ("French 1. General"); McLendon
("Courchamps"); Bailbé ("Stendhal").

JASMIN

Rudberg, Gosta. "Jasmin: en folkpoet." *Bokvännen* 35 (1980):
16-18.

JOUBERT

Ward, Patricia A. "Joubert and Vico." *RLC* 55 (1981): 226-31.

Based on the underlinings and annotations in Joubert's
own copy of Vico's *Diritto universale* (1720-21). "Joubert's
interest in Vico confirms his own Christian Platonism.
Further, his annotations suggest that Vico was a possible
influence on his theory of *pudeur*. More importantly, the
interest Joubert showed in Vico's discussion of language
indicates again that the evolution of modern esthetic theory
is rooted in the rise of theories about language in the
eighteenth century."

Review of book previously listed:

WARD, Patricia A., Joseph Joubert and the Critical Tradition (see RMB for 1980, p. 204), rev. by Mary Ellen Birkett in NCFS 10 (1981-82): 145-46.

LAMARTINE

Chavkin, Allan, and Fritz Oehlschlaeger. "An American Publisher in Europe with Dickens, Lamartine, Landor, and Thackeray: Six Letters of James T. Fields to Edwin P. Whipple." Resources for American Literary Study 8 (1978): 61-72.

Clarac, Pierre. "Aspects de la vie politique de Lamartine (I)." RDM, June 1981, pp. 580-92.

Drawing heavily on Lamartine's correspondence with Mme Angebert, Clarac retraces the poet's political evolution from 1817 to 1848.

Dédéyan, Charles. Lamartine et la Toscane. (Bibliothèque du Voyage en Italie, 3.) Geneva: Slatkine, 1981. Pp. 212. Sw.Fr. 30.00.

Guyard, Marius-François, ed. Méditations poétiques. Nouvelles Méditations poétiques suivies de Poésies diverses. (Poésie/Gallimard, 145.) Paris: Gallimard, 1981. Pp. 471.

Köhler, Erich. "Alphonse de Lamartine: 'L'Isolement' versuch einer sozio-semiotischen Interpretation." Romanistische Zeitschrift für Literaturgeschichte/Cahiers d'Histoire des Littératures Romanes 5 (1981): 129-50.

Summary in French, pp. 151-52.

Krauss, Cristel. "Alphonse de Lamartine." Pp. 82-101 in Wolf-Dieter Lang, ed., Französische Literatur des 19. Jahrhunderts, I: Romantik und Realismus. Heidelberg: Quelle & Meyer, 1979.

Letessier, Fernand. "Une amitié peu connue de Lamartine: le pasteur Joseph Martin-Paschoud." Bulletin de la Société d'Histoire du Protestantisme Français 126 (1980): 567-602.

Teissier, Philippe. "Autographes lamartiniens de la Bibliothèque Nationale d'Autriche." RHL 81 (1981): 438-52.

Five previously unpublished short letters, written between 1830 and 1837, illustrating aspects of Lamartine's

relations with Eugène Sue, political thought, religious
evolution; also one undated long poem, "Le rêve d'une jeune
fille," lines 1-38 signed Lamartine, lines 39-112 signed
Delphine Gay de Girardin.

Verdier, Abel. "Sur l''Elégie sixième' de Lamartine." *RHL* 80
   (1980): 623-25.

   Verdier maintains that the poem consists of two texts,
arbitrarily joined together; in a note, pp. 625-26, Paul
Bénichou contests Verdier's position.

Voyage en Orient. (Les Introuvables.) 2 vols. Plan-de-la-Tour
   (Var): Editions d'Aujourd'hui, 1980. Fr. 216.00.

See also Baude and Münch, Bertier de Sauvigny, Pickford,
   Tison-Braun, Viallaneix and Ehrard ("French 1. General").

LAMENNAIS

L'Actualité de Lamennais. Colloque de La Tourette, 2-4 juin
   1978. Préface de Jean Lacroix. Strasbourg: Cerdix, 1981.
   Pp. 174.

   According to a brief notice by Louis Le Guillou in *CMen*
13 (1981): 59, this symposium contains the following articles: Pierre Guiral, "L'actualité de Lamennais"; Louis Le
Guillou, "Les vraies raisons de la condamnation de Lamennais
par le Saint-Siège"; Jacques Gadille, "Lamennais instituteur
de la démocratie"; Fernand Rude, "Les insurrections ouvrières
lyonnaises de 1831 et de 1834 et l'engagement de Lamennais";
Roger Payot, "Lamennais métaphysicien: *Le Système de philosophie*"; J.-R. Derré, "La théologie sociale de Gerbet";
M.-J. Le Guillou, "Lamennais à la lumière de Vatican II."

Cahiers mennaisiens 13 (1981).

   Contents: Louis Le Guillou, "*L'Avenir* et le clergé de
1830-1831" (1-11); François Marotin, "L'enterrement de
Lamennais vu par l'historien Charles-Louis Chassin" (12-24);
le père Maurice Pontet, S.J., "Lamennais et Dostoïevski.
A propos de la 'Légende du grand Inquisiteur'" (25-34);
Louis Le Guillou, "La Pologne et les mennaisiens en 1830"
(35-41); Peter Byrne, "Lamennais jugé par Pierre Leroux
en 1836" (42-49); Louis Le Guillou, "Lamennais, Manzoni
et le catholicisme social" (50-57); review (58-61); "La
vie de l'Association" (62); "Bibliographie mennaisienne"
(63).

The most intriguing of the above articles is le père Montet's *rapprochement* of Lamennais and Dostoevski; he makes a fair case for the Russian novelist's having been influenced by a passage from *Paroles d'un croyant*, then goes on to show how, despite this one encounter, the two writers were in fact moving in opposite directions in their spiritual evolution. (J.S.P.)

Lebrun, Jean. *Lamennais ou l'inquiétude de la liberté.* (Douze Hommes dans l'Histoire de l'Eglise.) Paris: Fayard-Mame, 1981. Pp. 281. Fr. 69.00.

   Rev. by Louis Le Guillou in *CMen* 13 (1981): 58-59; by Bernard Reymond in *ETR* 56 (1981).

Spindler, Frank MacDonald. "Francisco Bilbao, Chilen Disciple of Lamennais." *JHI* 41 (1980): 487-96.

   This is a valuable overview of Lamennais's influence on the Chilean democrat and anticlerical. Bilbao encountered Lamennais's work in 1839; he translated a number of the Frenchman's works, he interviewed him in Paris in 1845; they corresponded until Lamennais's death. In a nutshell, both were men of "God and Liberty." (J.S.P.)

See also Baude and Münch, Boime (1) ("French 1. General"); Bonnardot ("E. and M. de Guérin"); *Friends of George Sand Newsletter* 4,i ("Sand").

Reviews of books previously listed:

   OLDFIELD, J.J., *The Problem of Tolerance and Social Existence in the Writings of Félicité Lamennais 1809-1831* (see *ELN* 14, Supp., 89), rev. by C. Cordié in *SFr* 24 (1981): 171-72; RUBAT DU MÉRAC, M.-A., *Lamennais et l'Italie* (see *ELN* 17, Supp., 141), rev. by F. Robello in *SFr* 24 (1980): 578-79.

LATOUCHE

See Borowitz ("Balzac").

LEROUX

Caponigri, A. Robert. "European Influences on the Thought of Orestes Brownson: Pierre Leroux and Vincenzo Gioberto."

Pp. 100-24 in Leonard Gilhooley, ed., *No Divided Allegiance: Essays in Brownson's Thought*. Fordham University Press, 1980. Pp. xiii+193.

See also Baude and Münch, Kelly ("French 1. General"); *Cahiers mennaisiens* 13 ("Lamennais"); *Friends of George Sand Newsletter* 4,1 ("Sand").

Review of book previously listed:

LACASSAGNE, Jean-Pierre, ed., *La Grève de Samarez* (see *RMB* for 1979, p. 196), rev. by Emile Poulot in *ASSR* 51,ii (1981): 256.

LOAISEL DE TREOGATE

Bowling, Townsend Whelen. *The Life, Works and Literary Career of Loaisel de Tréogate*. Oxford: Voltaire Foundation, 1981. Pp. 254.

MAINE DE BIRAN

Aarnes, Asbjørn. "Maine de Biran et Jens Baggesen: une correspondance inédite." *OL* 35 (1980): 206-19.

Baertschi, Bernard. "L'*idéologie subjective* de Maine de Biran et la phénoménologie." *RTP* 113 (1981): 109-22.

Morin, Serge. "Disagreement and Communication among Various Philosophical Systems: A Biranian View." *JHP* 18 (1980): 287-98.

On Maine de Biran as the philosopher of experience. "His insight consists essentially in the realization that the conscious life of the self is the central point of reference for giving meaning to the basic 'metaphysical concepts,' as he calls them, or categories." Morin admits that the philosopher had difficulty communicating this insight.

MAISTRE (J. de)

Beauvois, Daniel. "Entre Diderot et Maistre: la conception de l'université en Europe orientale." *La Pensée* 208 (1979): 61-78.

Coe, Richard N. "Champfleury, Stendhal et Joseph de Maistre."
SC 24 (1981-82): 70-71.

On Champfleury's surprising preference for Maistre over
Stendhal, expressed in a "note intime" of about 1855.

Preece, Rod. "Edmund Burke and His European Reception." *The
Eighteenth Century* 21 (1980): 255-73.

Bonald, Maistre, Schlegel, Müller, and Gentz are the
authors treated. Both of the French writers, in their reactionary absolutism, are not in tune with Burke. "For de
Maistre liberty is a luxury. For Burke it is an essence
of responsible manhood...."

Schuh, Hans-Manfred. "Joseph de Maistre." Pp. 21-34 in Wolf-
Dieter Lange, ed., *Französische Literatur des 19. Jahr-
hunderts, I: Romantik und Realismus.* Heidelberg: Quelle
& Meyer, 1979. Pp. 305.

See also David ("De Léon"); Richer ("Nerval").

Reviews of books previously listed:

LUBAC, Henri de, *La Postérité spirituelle de Joachim de
Flore*, T. I (see *RMB* for 1980, p. 210), rev. by Jean Seguy
in *ASSR* 50,ii (1980): 305; by Jacques Solé in *RHEF* 66
(1980): 261-64; TULARD, Jean, ed., *Considérations sur la
France* (see *RMB* for 1980, p. 210), rev. by Robert Bonnard
in *QL* 347 (May 1-15, 1981): 10.

MAISTRE (X. de)

Review of book previously listed:

LOMBARD, Charles M., *Xavier de Maistre* (see *ELN* 16, Supp.,
107-08), rev. by P.J. Whyte in *FS* 35 (1981): 453-54.

MERCIER

Review of book previously listed:

HOFER, Hermann, *Louis-Sébastien Mercier précurseur et sa
fortune* (see *RMB* for 1979, p. 199), rev. by Tanguy Logé
in *LR* 35 (1981): 266-68.

MERIMEE

Avni, Ora. "Et la chose fut; 'La Vénus d'Ille' de Mérimée."
   Poétique 46 (April 1981): 156-70.

   Inspired by J.L. Austin's studies of speech acts, the
author examines the performative status of the "marriage"
between Alphonse de Peyrehorade and the statue, providing
a framework for discussion of the story rather than an
interpretation.

Chabot, Jacques. "Objet fantasmatique et conte fantastique
   dans 'Vision de Charles XI' de Mérimée." *CAIEF* 32 (1980):
   179-91.

Collingham, H.A.C. "Prosper Mérimée and Guglielmo Libri. An
   Account of Mérimée's Role in the *Affaire Libri*, with Five
   Unpublished Letters." *FS* 35 (1981): 135-47.

   Unpublished letters showing Mérimée's effort to reverse
Libri's conviction for theft of valuable manuscripts, with
the author's summary of the affair.

Hunt, Tony. "L'Ironie du regard: Mérimée's *Arsène Guillot*."
   FMLS 17 (1981): 351-60.

Lokis, La Vénus d'Ille. (Les Introuvables.) Plan-de-la-Tour
   (Var): Editions d'Aujourd'hui, 1977. Pp. 164. Fr. 38.00.

Schwartz, Helmut. "'Tamango' von Mérimée. Ein Beispiel für
   die Integrierung landeskundlicher Fragestellungen in den
   französischen Literaturunterricht der Sekundarstufe II."
   Praxis des Neusprachlichen Unterrichts 27 (1980): 172-79.

Siebers, Tobin. "Fantastic Lies: *Lokis* and the Victim of
   Coincidence." *KRQ* 28 (1981): 87-93.

   The author concentrates on the accusatory nature of the
professor's cryptogram and concludes that the professor
himself cannot be excluded as a suspect in Ioulka's death.

Unwin, Timothy. "Henry James and Mérimée: A Note of Caution."
   RomN 21 (1980-81): 165-68.

   "It remains difficult to assess the extent of Mérimée's
influence."

Vanhese Cicchetti, Gisèle. "Mérimée e la 'negazione freudiana.'"
   Micromégas 6 (1979): 175-76.

Zoberman, Pierre. "Mérimée et la pratique intertextuelle,
ou les mésaventures d'un récit." *French Forum* 6 (1981):
36-49.

   In this study of *La Double Méprise*, the author examines
the effects of allusions to Byron's "The Giaour" and
Molière's *Les Fourberies de Scapin*. Darcy's narrative,
seemingly inspired by the latter, thus loses its referen-
tial character. A comparison of the two narratives of the
text, Mme Dumanoir's and Darcy's, shows that "on passe de
l'héroïque au comique, de la vaillance au ridicule, du
Giaour à Scapin." These textual allusions are important,
for they determine the divergent directions which Darcy
and Julie follow after the scene at Mme Lambert's.
Convincing application of intertextuality. (E.F.G.)

See also Bellemin-Noël, Viallaneix and Ehrard ("French 1.
General"); *Présence de George Sand* 10 ("Sand"); Del Litto
(2) (3) ("Stendhal").

Reviews of books previously listed:

   FIORENTINO, Francesco, *I gendarmi e la macchia* (see *RMB*
   for 1979, p. 201), rev. by D. Ferri and P. Jeoffroy-
   Fuggianelli in *RHL* 81 (1981): 314-15; MALLION, Jean, ed.,
   Oeuvres (see *RMB* for 1979, p. 202), rev. by A.W. Raitt in
   FS 34 (1980): 350-51.

MICHELET

Borie, Jean. "Terres vierges." Pp. 23-62 in Jean Borie,
   Mythologies de l'hérédité au XIXe siècle. (Débats.) Paris:
   Galilée, 1981. Pp. 215. Fr. 58.00.

   Rev. by Hubert Juin in *QL* 347 (May 1-15, 1981): 9; by
   Alain Pagès in *Les Cahiers Naturalistes* 27 (1981): 210-
   11.
   On Michelet's view of woman, most succinctly defined by
   Borie as "naturalisme, religieux bien qu'anticlérical":
   woman incarnates ever-fertile nature (man is the naturalist,
   the scientist, the gynecologist).

Casanova, Robert. "La transcription des manuscrits de Michelet
   dans l'édition des *OEuvres complètes*." Pp. 166-69 in Louis
   Hay and Winfried Woesler, eds., *Die Nachlassedition/La
   Publication de manuscrits inédits*. Bern: Lang, 1979.
   Pp. 248.

Fauquet, Eric. "De l'utilité de la connaissance du fonds
   Michelet, pour sa consultation: Les 'Papiers Michelet.'"
   Pp. 67-75 in Hélène Verlet, ed., *Constitution d'un patrimoine:
   la Bibliothèque historique depuis l'incendie de 1871.* Catalogue de l'exposition. Hôtel de Lamoignon 12 juin-31 juillet
   1980. Paris: Imprimerie municipale, 1980. Pp. 87.

   A guide to the Michelet papers in the Bibliothèque
   historique de la Ville de Paris. (See also nos. 279-97 in
   the main body of the catalogue.)

Fauquet, Eric. "Sur la restitution d'après les manuscrits de
   l'auteur d'un texte ayant fait l'objet d'une édition post-
   hume." Pp. 170-72 in Louis Hay and Winfried Woesler, eds.,
   Die Nachlassedition/La Publication de manuscrits inédits.
   Bern: Lang, 1979. Pp. 248.

Kippur, Stephan A. *Jules Michelet: A Study of Mind and Sensibility.* State University of New York Press, 1981. Pp. xiv+
   269.

   Rev. by Oscar A. Haac in *NCFS* 10 (1981-82): 188-90; by
   Edward K. Kaplan in *FR* (1981-82): 414-15.
   Although the author, in his introduction, speaks of his
   book as "the first full-length biography of Jules Michelet
   in the English language," it is less a biography as usually
   defined than a chronological study of the historian's works
   and ideas. As such, it is usually very good, but adds little
   to earlier work by the great Michelet specialists. Then,
   too, it is really too brief to deal adequately with its rich
   and various subject, especially with the later phases of
   Michelet's work. For more detailed criticism, see the above
   reviews. (J.S.P.)

La Mer. (Romantiques.) Lausanne: L'Age d'Homme, 1981. Pp. 240.
   Fr. 56.15.

Mettra, Claude, and Alain Ferrari, eds. *Histoire de France.*
   Livres I à XVII: *Le Moyen-Age.* (Bouquins.) Paris: Robert
   Laffont, 1981. Pp. 1100. Fr. 59.60.

Olrik, Hilde. "Michelet et Lombroso ou le discours exorciste."
   RevR 15 (1980): 37-55.

   Comparing Michelet's *L'Amour* and Lombroso's *La Femme
   criminelle et la prostituée*, Olrik finds in both books the
   same view of feminine sexuality: "un même discours exorciste
   ... dont le but idéologique est de confiner la femme dans le
   cadre du foyer, dans son rôle de procréatrice conjugale, et
   qui, à ces fins, stigmatise tout écart à la norme en la
   qualifiant de prostitution."

Tripet, Arnaud. "Michelet, la 'Montagne' et le Piémont."
   Studi Piemontesi 8 (1979): 319-24.

   See résumé by C. Cordié in *SFr* 24 (1981): 365-66.

Viallaneix, Paul. "Michelet, la Réforme et les Réformés.
   Deuxième partie." *BSHPF* 126 (1980).

   Sequel to an article published in 1977 (see *ELN* 16, Supp.,
   111). The present article deals primarily with Michelet's
   personal relationships with numerous Protestants, including
   a number of pastors. The most illustrious names are those
   of Guizot and Sismondi, "deux pères."

Viallaneix, Paul, ed. *OEuvres complètes*. T. XVI: *1851-1854*.
   Paris: Flammarion, 1980. Pp. 732. Fr. 261.03.

   Contains *Légendes d'or (fragments)*, *Légendes démocratiques
   du Nord*, *Les Femmes de la Révolution*, and *Le Banquet ou
   l'unité de l'Eglise militante*, edited in exemplary fashion
   by a team of specialists under Viallaneix. (J.S.P.)

Williams, John R. "Jules Michelet and Medieval French Literature." *Res Publica Litterarum: Studies in the Classical
   Tradition* 2 (1979): 347-58.

   Williams makes a sweeping claim: "Probably no Frenchman in
   the first half of the nineteenth century contributed more
   to the enormous development of research in the Middle Ages
   and the texts themselves than Jules Michelet...." Moreover,
   he brought a "special blend of emotion and erudition ...
   to his judgments of French medieval literature." True, there
   are factual errors; there are limitations (sketchiness and
   a tendency toward sweeping generalizations; and Michelet
   accepts the Romantic distinction between folk poetry and
   artificial poetry). But his history of medieval French
   literature reveals surprising insight.

See also Baude and Münch ("French 1. General"); *Présence de
   George Sand* 10 ("Sand"); Delon ("Staël").

Reviews of books previously listed:

   BOUILLIER, Henry, *Portraits et miroirs* (see *RMB* for 1980,
   p. 212), rev. by Jean Seznec in *FS* 35 (1981): 108-10;
   TIEDER, Irène, *Michelet et Luther* (see *ELN* 16, Supp., 110-
   11), rev. by Michèle Monteil in *EG* 35 (1980): 484-85.

MUSSET

Allem, Maurice, ed. *Poésies complètes*. (Bibliothèque de la
   Pléiade.) Nouvelle éd. Paris: Gallimard, 1980.

Les Caprices de Marianne: comédie. (Collection du répertoire--
Comédie Française.) Paris: Comédie Française, 1980.

Charlton, D.G. "Musset as Moral Novelist: La Confession d'un
enfant du siècle." Pp. 29-46 in Cedric E. Pickford, ed.,
Mélanges de littérature française moderne offerts à Garnet
Rees. (La Thésothèque, 7.) Paris: Minard (Lettres modernes),
1980. Pp. 291.

Defends the novel as having broader moral implications
than usually recognized and as expressing these more co-
herently than critics have been willing to acknowledge.

Cordié, Carlo. "Musset." CeS 76 (Oct.-Dec. 1980): 87-95.

Reviews the past ten years of Musset scholarship.

Lejeune, H.-H. "Dans les pas de Musset." Contrepoint 36 (Feb.
1981).

La Mort d'Andrea Del Sarto, peintre florentin. Adapté par
Bernard Chartreux. Introduction par Jean-Pierre Vincent,
Ginette Herry et Roland Recht. Strasbourg: Théâtre National,
1979. Pp. 104. Fr. 15.00.

Selected texts from Musset. Some color plates.

Reboul, Pierre. "Une conspiration en 1537: révélateur de
Lorenzaccio?" Pp. 175-82 in Errements littéraires et
historiques. Presses universitaires de Lille, 1979. Pp.
330. Fr. 89.00.

Previously published among papers presented at a journée
d'étude devoted to Musset and sponsored by the Société
d'Etudes Romantiques (see ELN 17, Supp., 146).
Errements also contains: "Le poète contre la poésie"
(167-74), previously published in a special Musset number
of Europe (see ELN 16, Supp., 112); and "Sur cinq à six
marches de marbre rose" (155-65), which hypothesizes on
the composition of the poem "Sur trois marches de marbre
rose," and concludes that the final form of the poem (1848)
reveals a Musset unwilling to come to grips with the néant
of his existence.

See also Foucart, Pickford, Viallaneix and Ehrard ("French
1. General").

Review of book previously listed:

FABIG, Angelika, Kunst und Künstler im Werk Alfred de
Mussets (see ELN 17, Supp., 145), rev. by Pierre Laubriet
in RBPH 58 (1980): 730-33.

NAPOLEON

OEuvres littéraires. Nantes: Le Temps singulier, 1979. Fr.
35.00.

Tulard, Jean, ed. Lettres d'amour à Joséphine. Préface de Jean
Favier. Paris: Arthème Fayard, 1981. Pp. 464. Fr. 64.00.

NECKER DE SAUSSURE

See Montandon ("German 3. Jean Paul").

NERVAL

Cahiers Gérard de Nerval, no. 3 (1980): Langage et expression
chez Nerval.

Contents: Kurt Schaerer, "La tentation du drame chez
Nerval" (3-7); Gabrielle Malandain, "Message et échange
dans 'Angélique'" (8-11); Henri Bonnet, "'Othys' ou Nerval
entre les mots et les choses" (12-14); Daniel Couty,
"Aurélia: De l'impuissance narrative au pouvoir des mots"
(15-17); Monique Streiff-Moretti, "'L'autre discours'"
(18-21); Ned Bastet, "Un langage en liberté surveillée:
de quelques procédés d'écriture dans Aurélia" (22-30);
Jean Richer, "Le simulacre de mariage: de l'idylle au
drame" (31-32); Claude Faisant et Jean Richer, "Le dialogue
avec l'écho" [dans la version primitive de l'Imagier de
Harlem, Acte III, sixième tableau] (33-34); lettres, etc.
(35-43); Olivier Encrenaz, "Trois rôles de Jenny Colon en
1827 et 1834" (43-44); Jean Senelier, "Nerval inspiré par
Robert-Houdin (sur un fragment manuscrit de Pandora)"
(45-47); "Sur le portrait de Nerval par A. Lebour": I. Pierre
Miquel, "Notice descriptive" (48-49), II. Jean Richer,
"Quelques remarques" avec illustrations (49-52); Nécrolo-
gie ... In Memoriam: François Constans (avec un poème de
Constans, "Nervaliennes"), Jean Folie Desjardins, Gilbert
Rouger, Marie-Jeanne Durry (53-58); Bibliographie ner-
valienne 1978-80 (62-64).

Cophignon, Dr Janine. "Figures féminines dans l'oeuvre de
Gérard de Nerval: Tentative de reconstruction de l'image
maternelle." Revue Française de Psychanalyse 44 (1980):
15-46.

Interprets Nerval's whole history as a vain attempt to re-
create his lost mother from real, imaginary, and literary
figures. His mother's absence is thus "une blessure profonde
qui ne cicatrisa jamais" and animates his life, his works,
and his suicide.

Dinh Van, A. *L'Expression de l'imaginaire dans "Aurélia" de
Gérard de Nerval*. Strasbourg: Université des Sciences
Humaines, 1979-80. Pp. 153.

A doctoral thesis.

Dunn, Susan. *Nerval et le roman historique*. (Archives des
Lettres modernes, 193; Archives nervaliennes, 12.) Paris:
Minard (Lettres modernes), 1981. Pp. 194. Fr. 31.25.

Dupraz, Jean-Yves. "Valéry critique de Nerval." *French Forum*
6 (1981): 50-60.

Fairlie, Alison. *Imagination and Language. Collected Essays
on Constant, Baudelaire, Nerval and Flaubert*. Cambridge
University Press, 1981. Pp. 479. £30.00.

Rev. by Robert Gibson in *TLS*, Oct. 16, 1981, p. 1216.

Gascar, Pierre. *Gérard de Nerval et son temps*. Paris: Gallimard, 1981. Pp. 336.

Rev. by Alain Clerval in *NRF* 340 (May 1, 1981): 116-18;
by Robert Gibson in *TLS*, Oct. 16, 1981, p. 1216.

Gilbert, Claire. *Nerval's Double: A Structural Study*.
(Romance Monographs, 34.) University, Miss.: Romance Monographs Inc., 1979. Pp. 199. $19.00.

Rev. by Ora Avni in *RR* 72 (1981): 362-63; by Helen
Cassou-Yager in *NCFS* 9 (1981): 269-71; by Susan Noakes
in *SiR* 21 (1982): 117-18 as "a thorough and responsible
account of one of Nerval's most important themes."

Grunewald, Marie-Antoinette. "Théo, Gérard, Paul et autres--
ou de quelques amitiés romantiques." *Europe* 601 (1979):
103-22.

Haase, Donald P. "Nerval's Knowledge of Novalis: A Reconsideration." *RomN* 22 (1981-82): 53-57.

Cites further evidence of "the probable factual link
between Novalis and Nerval" and urges precise focus on
parallels in their works for possible new insights into
the development of the European Romantic tradition.

Jouve, P.J. "Gérard de Nerval." *Argile* (Paris) 17 (1978): 25-33.

Marchetti, Marilia. "La minute éternelle: notes de lecture sur 'Fantaisie.'" *Micromégas* 6,i (1979): 103-10.

On Nerval's poem of ca. 1831.

Rauhut, Franz. "Nervals *Horus*. Palastrevolution bei den Göttern als Zeitwende." *NM* 82 (1981): 75-88.

Author resumes 40 years of scholarship (1937-77) concerning Nerval's "Horus" in a companion article to his "'El Desdichado' von Nerval," which appeared in *ZFSL* 85 (1975): 97-127. The present study includes a valuable bibliography of 54 items.

Richer, Jean. "Présence de Joseph de Maistre dans l'oeuvre de Gérard de Nerval." *Revue des Etudes maistriennes* (Les Belles Lettres), no. 5-6 (1980).

Rieger, Dietmar. "Nerval poète politique. Ebauche d'une analyse critique de l'idéologie nervalienne." Traduction par Jean-Louis Vallin. *Romanistische Zeitschrift für Literaturgeschichte/Cahiers d'Histoire des Littératures Romanes* 2 (1978): 21-38.

Vouga, Daniel. *Nerval et ses chimères*. Paris: José Corti, 1981. Pp. 128.

See also Schneider, Tison-Braun ("French 1. General"); Fairlie (1) ("Constant, B."); Derche ("Dumas"); Malandain ("German 3. Hoffmann").

Reviews of books previously listed:

Cahiers de L'Herne, Gérard de Nerval (see *RMB* for 1980, p. 218), rev. by Jérôme d'Astier in *NRF* 333 (Oct. 1, 1980): 122-24; FELMAN, Shoshana, *La Folie et la chose littéraire* (see *RMB* for 1980, p. 220), rev. by Maurice Blackman in *NCFS* 8 (1979-80): 290-91; by Ross Chambers in *French Forum* 5 (1980): 74-78; by Sylvie Tinter in *RR* 72 (1981): 363-66; JEANNERET, Michel, *La Lettre perdue* (see *ELN* 17, Supp., 147), rev. by Ross Chambers in *French Forum* 5 (1980): 74-78; by Alison Fairlie in *MLR* 76 (1981): 472-73; by J.-C. Fizaine in *Romantisme* 27 (1980): 148-51; KNAPP, Bettina, *Gérard de Nerval: The Mystic's Dilemma* (see *RMB* for 1979, p. 210),

rev. by Ross Chambers in *NCFS* 9 (1981): 268-69; by Susan
Dunn in *FR* 54 (1980-81): 739; by Micheline Tison-Braun in
ECr 21 (1981): 98; PORTER, Laurence M., *The Literary Dream
in French Romanticism* (see *RMB* for 1979, p. 151), rev. by
Bettina Knapp in *NCFS* 9 (1980-81): 152-54.

NISARD

Malavié, Jean. "Correspondants de Désiré Nisard: hommages à
un monument de la critique classique, *L'Histoire de la littérature française*." *RSH* 176 (1979): 101-10.

    Gives the texts of a number of letters of tribute to Nisard
apropos of his *Histoire*, including one from George Sand
(Aug. 28, 1862).

NODIER

Centre de Recherches de Littérature française (XIXe et XXe
Siècles). *Charles Nodier*. Colloque du deuxième centenaire,
Besançon - Mai 1980. (Annales littéraires de l'Université
de Besançon, 253.) Paris: Les Belles Lettres, 1981. Pp. 275.
Fr. 120.00.

    Contents: Pierre-Georges Castex, "Nodier et l'école du
désenchantement" (9-16); Hermann Hofer, "Leurs pleurs tombent
dans la poussière: les ouvrages de jeunesse de Nodier" (17-
22); B.G. Rogers, "Les *Souvenirs de jeunesse*" (23-30); Emile
Lehouck, "Discours autobiographique et tradition romanesque
dans *Suites d'un mandat d'arrêt*" (31-39); Hans Peter Lund,
"Nodier et le roman de l'Histoire: *Les Philadelphes*, *Histoire
des sociétés secrètes de l'armée*" (41-55); Anne-Marie Roux,
"Naissances, chiffres et lettres, ou biographie, fiction et
écriture chez Nodier" (57-69); Béatrice Didier, "L'amour et
la grimace. L'écriture et le désir dans quelques contes de
Nodier" (71-78); Yves Vadé, "L'imaginaire magique de Charles
Nodier" (79-90); Jean Richer, "Têtes d'animaux dans *La Fée
aux miettes*: Michel et le bailli de l'Ile de Man" (91-96);
Marie-Sophie Lambert, "Trilby" (97-111); Jean-Claude Rioux,
"Les tablettes de *Jean Sbogar*, ou le voleur et la révolution" (113-32); Monique Gosselin, "Sur la poétique romanesque de *Jean Sbogar*" (133-52); Victor Hell, "Deux figures
de brigands: Karl Moor et Jean Sbogar" (153-61); Jean-Pierre
Picot, "Inès de Las Sierras, ou la comédie du trompe-l'oeil"

(163-82); Daniel-Henri Pageaux, "L'Espagne de Charles Nodier"
(183-97); Simon Jeune, "Le Roi de Bohême et ses sept châteaux:
livre-objet et livre-ferment" (199-210); Jacques-Remi Dahan,
"Nodier et la mort du livre" (211-22); Albert Kies, "La
bibliothèque de Charles Nodier" (223-28); Raymond Setbon,
"Charles Nodier - Victor Hugo, nouvelles glanes" (229-39);
D. Ligou, "La vision maçonnique de Charles Nodier" (241-53);
Céline Mathon-Baduel, "Nodier et les traditions populaires"
(255-63); Marie-Claude Amblard, "Compléments aux bibliographies des oeuvres de Nodier" (265-74).

This colloquy achieves, to a rare degree, the weight and
unity of discourse at which, at least by definition, all
such enterprises should aim. The papers fit together har-
moniously and cover the major facets of Nodier, the man and
the work, with nearly uniform excellence. Since the titles
of the individual articles mostly indicate the subjects
treated and suggest the approaches used, suffice it here to
point out a few of the highlights: first of all, the central
papers on Nodier's major fictions, the studies of *Jean
Sbogar* and *Inès de Las Sierras* being especially welcome
since these two works have been overshadowed of late by
Trilby, *La Fée aux miettes*, and *Smarra* (the last named,
however, little discussed in this volume); Jeune's treatment of the *Histoire du Roi de Bohême* and Dahan's "Nodier
et la mort du livre," both of which reveal in Nodier a sub-
versive force in the history of the book; Ligou's meticulous
investigation of Nodier's relationship with Freemasonry
(and other secretive movements); finally, Amblard's impressive list of additions to the known works of Nodier. If a
few of the articles are somewhat lightweight or trendy,
there are, nevertheless, no major blemishes on the whole.
Castex, in his brief preliminary paper, manages well to set
the tone for the volume by suggesting the complex form of
disillusionment which characterizes an author who becomes
ever more fascinating. (J.S.P.)

Richer, Jean, and Jean Senelier. "Charles Nodier. Remarques
et compléments bibliographiques." *SFr* 24 (1980): 93-102.

Corrections and additions to Bender's bibliography. Most
involve Nodier's contributions to periodicals.

Rogers, B.G. "*La Fée aux miettes* de Charles Nodier." *CAIEF*
32 (1980): 151-61.

On the fantastic and the supernatural in this story.

See also Baude and Münch ("French 1. General"); McLendon
("Courchamps"); Porter ("German 3. Hoffmann").

Reviews of books previously listed:

CORTEY, Teresa, *La Rêve dans les contes de Charles Nodier*
(see *RMB* for 1980, p. 224), rev. by Donald P. Haase in *RR*
72 (1981): 361; LUND, Hans Peter, *La Critique du siècle chez
Nodier* (see *RMB* for 1979, p. 213), rev. by Donald P. Haase
in *RR* 72 (1981): 361-62; by A.-M. Roux in *RHL* 81 (1981):
148-49; by Joachim Schulze in *ZFSL* 91 (1981): 77-81; PORTER,
Laurence M., *The Literary Dream in French Romanticism* (see
RMB for 1980, p. 226), rev. by J.A. Hiddleston in *French
Forum* 6 (1981): 279-80.

OZANAM

Review of book previously listed:

OZANAM, Didier, ed., *Lettres de Frédéric Ozanam*, T. III
(see *RMB* for 1979, p. 214), rev. by Sally T. Gershman in
CHR 67 (1981): 327.

PLANCHE

See Borowitz ("Balzac").

PONSARD

Himmelbach, Siegbert. "François Ponsard, poète du juste
milieu." *RHL* 81 (1981): 99-109.

POTOCKI

See McLendon ("Courchamps").

Review of book previously listed:

BEAUVOIS, Daniel, ed., *Voyages au Caucase et en Chine* and
Voyages en Turquie et en Egypte, en Hollande, au Maroc
(see *RMB* for 1980, p. 229), rev. by Michel Delon in *AHRF*
53 (1981): 317-21.

PROUDHON

Crapo, Paul B. "Proudhon's Conspiratorial View of Society."
JES 11 (1981): 184-95.

Proudhon's conspiratorial view links him to his Romantic
contemporaries. His obsession leads to the creation of a
personal mythology and makes of him an imaginative writer.
(Michelet, Quinet, Hugo, Chateaubriand, and Lamartine are
mentioned en passant as parallels.)

Crapo, Paul B. "Proudhon's Romantic Rebellion." SFR 5 (1981):
173-88.

Proudhon's need for role-playing is emphasized. His "metaphysical revolt" led him to identify himself with Prometheus,
Adam, Job, and especially Lucifer (and, by the same token,
to reject Jesus). He rejected Romantic values but "assumed
the guise of a rebel quite readily and with little critical
self-examination."

Rubin, James Henry. Realism and Social Vision in Courbet and
Proudhon. (Princeton Essays on the Arts, 10.) Princeton
University Press, 1980. Pp. xvii+177. $17.50; $8.95 paper.

See also Kelly, Viallaneix and Ehrard ("French 1. General").

Reviews of books previously listed:

GUÉRIN, Daniel, Proudhon oui et non (see RMB for 1980, p.
230), rev. by Maurice Agulhon in Annales 35 (1980): 1321-
22; HYAMS, Edward, Pierre-Joseph Proudhon (see RMB for
1979, p. 214), rev. by Alan Clark in AUMLA 54 (Nov. 1980):
270.

QUINET

Crossley, Ceri. "The Young Edgar Quinet and the Philosophy
of History." SFR 4 (1980): 405-15.

On the evolution of Quinet's philosophy of history in
the years 1827-33 (i.e., in the wake of his translation
of Herder). The main finding is that even in this brief
early period, we find discussion of the major questions that
preoccupied the author all the rest of his life: "the search

for a meaning in history, the relationship between history
and religion, the role of the individual, the centrality
of freedom, and the relationship between man and nature."

See also Baude and Münch, Kelly ("French 1. General"); Delon
("Staël").

Review of book previously listed:

BERNARD-GRIFFITHS, Simone, and Paul Viallaneix, eds., Edgar
Quinet, ce juif errant (see ELN 17, Supp., 150), rev. by
C. Crossley in FS 35 (1981): 80-81.

REMUSAT

Review of book previously listed:

DERRE, J.-R., ed., L'Habitation de Saint-Domingue (see ELN
17, Supp., 151), rev. by Brian Rigby in FS 35 (1981): 214.

SAINTE-BEUVE

Antoine, Gérald. "'Groupe,' 'école,' 'famille,' 'génération'
dans la critique de Sainte-Beuve." RHL 80 (1980): 737-48.

    Sainte-Beuve's use of these terms derives from contemporary
natural sciences, except for the alien term école, which
Sainte-Beuve dropped early in his career.

Butler, R. "La rencontre de Zola et de Sainte-Beuve." Les
Cahiers Naturalistes 27 (1981): 176-78.

    Suppositions regarding the date of the only meeting
between the two men, a five-minute encounter occasioned
when Zola delivered some unspecified documents to the
critic.

Canto, Monique. "L'invention de la grammaire." Critique 35
(1979): 707-19.

    The book on which Canto's article appears to be based--
Port-Royal--actually receives no attention at all. The
article focuses on seventeenth-century attempts to produce
a universal grammar.

Cordié, Carlo. "Sainte-Beuve." *CeS* 72 (Oct.-Dec. 1979): 71-80.

Reviews the past 25 years of Sainte-Beuve scholarship.

De Cesare, Raffaele. "Due lettere inedite di Sainte-Beuve a Cesare Cantù." Pp. 160-72 in *Studi di letteratura e di storia in memoria di Antonio Di Pietro*. (Vita e Pensiero.) Milan: Pubblicazioni della Università Cattolica, 1977. Pp. 405.

Summary of the Italian critic's (generally favorable) judgments of Sainte-Beuve. The letters have to do with (1) arrangements for an interview between the two men in 1843 and (2) Sainte-Beuve's receipt of a volume--unidentifiable, given present knowledge--sent him by Cantù.

Granarolo, Jean. "Du classicisme libéral de Sainte-Beuve à l'idéal virgilien de T.S. Eliot." Pp. 533-40 in R. Chevallier, ed., *Présence de Vigile*, Actes du Colloque des 9, 11 et 12 décembre 1976 (Paris E.N.S., Tours). Paris: Les Belles Lettres, 1978. Pp. 582.

Comparative study of Sainte-Beuve's idea of a "classic" (*causerie du lundi* of Oct. 21, 1850) and Eliot's (lecture of Oct. 16, 1944, at the inaugural meeting of the Virgil Society in London). Sainte-Beuve's notion is "liberal" because inclusive: a "classic" will be any author, whatever his race or century, whose work may figure in an ideal library of humankind. Eliot ranks classics on the bases of breadth of understanding and universality. In this perspective, Virgil is the classic par excellence.

Stiennon, Jacques. "'L'Excellent M. Amiable' de Sainte-Beuve." Pp. 637-42 in *Mélanges de philologie et de littérature romanes offerts à Jeanne Wathelet-Willem*. (Cahiers de l'A.R.U.Lg.) Liège: Marche Romane, 1978.

François-Antoine-Joseph Amiable, who presumably became a friend of Sainte-Beuve during the critic's visit to Belgium in 1848-49. Nothing for Sainte-Beuve scholarship.

See also Tundo ("Barbey d'Aurevilly").

Review of book previously listed:

CHADBOURNE, Richard M., *Sainte-Beuve* (see *ELN* 17, Supp., 151), rev. by Lucy M. Schwartz in *NCFS* 9 (1981): 265-66.

SAINT-MARTIN

Amadou, Robert, ed. *Louis-Claude de Saint-Martin. L'homme de désir*. Monaco: Editions du Rocher, 1979. Pp. 325. Fr. 60.00.
Rev. by Jean-Pierre Laurant in *ASSR* 50,ii (1980): 232.

Les Cahiers de Saint-Martin 3 (1980).

Contents: "Calendrier perpétuel" (a survey of Saint-Martin's influence 1803-70, by various hands); Béatrice Didier, "Senancour et Saint-Martin"; Jules Bruneau, "Saint-Martin l'illuminé" (1835); Eugène Stourm, "Etudes philosophiques sur Saint-Martin" (1837; presented by Frank P. Bowman); A. Faivre, ed., "Un *Catéchisme coën*."

Jacques-Chaquin, Nicole. "L'imaginaire et le discours théosophique ou les rêves de l'écriture chez Louis-Claude de Saint-Martin." *RSH* 182 (1981): 31-44.

SAINT-SIMON

Brand, Wolfgang. "Claude-Henri de Saint-Simon." Pp. 35-49 in Wolf-Dieter Lange, ed., *Französische Literatur des 19. Jahrhunderts, I: Romantik und Realismus*. Heidelberg: Quelle & Meyer, 1979. Pp. 305.

Bulcioli, Maria Teresa. *L'Ecole saint-simonienne et la femme. Notes et documents pour une histoire du rôle de la femme dans la société saint-simonnienne, 1828-1833*. (Etudes sur l'Egalité.) Pisa: Goliardica, 1980. Pp. 253.

Gennaoui, Josette, trans. *La Pensée politique de Saint-Simon: textes*. Introduction de Ghita Ionescu. (Bibliothèque sociale.) Paris: Aubier-Montaigne, 1979. Pp. 259. Fr. 69.00.

Locke, Ralph P. "Liszt's Saint-Simonian Adventure." *NCM* 4 (1980-81): 209-27.

On the evolution of the composer's relationship with Saint-Simonism. The residue of his involvement is said here to have been "a serious, if unfulfilled--perhaps unfulfillable--urge to find a new role for the artist in a society in which the artist had come to be treated more as a consumer symbol than as a serious expression of the spirit."

Rancière, Jacques. *La Nuit des prolétaires. Archives du rêve ouvrier*. (L'Espace du Politique.) Paris: Arthème Fayard, 1981. Pp. 451. Fr. 89.00

Reconstructs the world of Saint-Simonian workers in Paris
for the period 1830-40, using the writings of the workers
themselves.

Weill, Georges. *L'Ecole saint-simonienne, son histoire, son
influence jusqu'à nos jours*. Aalen (GFR): Scientia Anti-
quariat/Verlag, 1979. DM 80.00.

Reprint of a classic study originally published in 1896.

Weill, Georges. *Un précurseur du socialisme: Saint-Simon et
son oeuvre*. Aalen (GFR): Scientia Antiquariat/Verlag, 1979.
DM 55.00.

Reprint of a classic study originally published in 1894.

See also Boime (1), Fulcher ("French 1. General").

SAND

Atwood, William G. *The Lioness and the Little One: The Liaison
of George Sand and Chopin*. Columbia University Press, 1980.
Pp. 352. $16.95.

Rev. by April FitzLyon in *TLS*, Feb. 27, 1981, p. 222;
by Lesly S. Hermann in *NCFS* 10 (1981-82): 190-92; by Byron
Janis in *Friends of George Sand Newsletter* 4,i (1981): 43.
    Although this account of the liaison of Sand and Chopin
contains little new scholarship, it has the major virtue
of being extremely readable. Atwood's goal is to make the
humanity of these two artists come alive. He is generally
successful in evoking sympathy for the sensitive Chopin,
without turning him into a pathetic victim. It is, however,
admiration for Sand, her strength and motherly tolerance,
that most marks Atwood's work. She emerges from this tandem
biography the greater human being. (M.E.B.)

Balayé, Simone, ed. *Journal intime*. (Ressources.) Geneva:
Slatkine Reprints, 1981. Pp. 256. Sw.Fr. 60.00.

Reprint of the edition of Paris, 1926.

Bertiaux, Jean-Claude. "George Sand et le mythe de l'âge
d'or." Pp. 47-55 in Jean Bessière, ed., *Mythe-symbole-roman*.
Université de Picardie, Centre d'Etudes du Roman et du
Romanesque; Actes du Colloque d'Amiens. Paris: Presses
universitaires de France, 1980. Pp. 156. Fr. 35.00.

Boisdeffre, Pierre de. *L'Ile aux livres/Littérature et critique*. Paris: Seghers, 1980. Pp. 360. Fr. 48.50.

Mentions Sand in a first section entitled "Les Classiques d'hier et d'aujourd'hui."

Bourdet-Guillerault, Henri. *George Sand: ce qu'elle croyait*. Marseille: Rijois, 1979. Pp. 214.

Cahiers Ivan Tourguéniev-Pauline Viardot-Maria Malibran 3 (Oct. 1979). Special issue: "Hommage à George Sand."

Contents: G. Lubin, "Editorial" (9-10); A. Saunier-Seite, "George Sand" (11-18); J.-M. Bailbé, "George Sand et la Malibran" (19-24); M. L'Hôpital, "George Sand et ses amis Viardot" (25-42); S. Vierne, "George Sand, Pauline Viardot et la chanson populaire" (43-55); Th. Marix-Spire, "Vicissitudes d'un opéra-comique: 'La Mare au diable' de George Sand et de Pauline Viardot" (56-74); M. Beaulieu, "Deux lettres inédites de Pauline et Louis Viardot à George Sand à propos de la *Mare au diable* et de *Consuelo*" (75-81); L. Guichard, "Pauline Garcia et la musique dans *Consuelo* et *la Comtesse de Rudolstadt*" (88-103); H. Fuchs, "Ivan Tourguéniev et Madame Viardot: une amitié de quarante ans" (104-08); I. Silberstein, "Du nouveau sur les rapports de George Sand avec Ivan Tourguéniev et la famille de Pauline Viardot" (110-42); I Tourguéniev, "Quelques mots sur George Sand" (143-44); A. Zviguilsky, "Le triangle Tourguéniev-Sand-Viardot" (145-57); D. Vierny, "Souvenirs de George Sand, Pauline Viardot et Tourguéniev dans une collection parisienne" (159-62); M. Poupet, "Pauline Viardot à Nohant d'après les souvenirs inédits de Charles Duvernet" (163-67); M. Beaufils, "En souvenir des deux Aurore" (169-76); N. Solntsev, "En hommage à la dernière Sand: Aurore Sand inédite" (177-80); Y. Grès-Veron, "George Sand et le peintre Jules Véron" (181-86).

Courrier, Jean. "George Sand et Grenoble." *Trait d'Union* 31 (1981): 15-19.

Courtivron, Isabelle de. "Weak Men and Fatal Women: The Sand Image." Pp. 210-17 in George Stambolian and Elaine Marks, eds., *Homosexualities and French Literature: Cultural Contexts/Critical Texts*. Cornell University Press, 1979. Pp. 387.

Rev. by Anna Otten in *AR* 39 (1981): 511.

Dauphiné, James. "Ecriture et musique dans *Les Maîtres Sonneurs* de George Sand." *NCFS* 9 (1981): 185-91.

Examines how the myth of Orpheus determines presentation of the hero Joseph Picot and how the musical concepts of repetition, harmony, and counterpoint shape plot structure in this novel of peasant life.

Dunilac, Julien. *George Sand sous la loupe*. Geneva: Slatkine, 1979. Pp. 160.

Elle et lui. (Demain et son Double.) Paris: J.-M. Laffont, 1981. Pp. 320. Fr. 64.50.

Friends of George Sand Newsletter (Hofstra University), 3,ii (1980).

Contents: Gérard Roubichou, "Comme c'est triste, l'histoire!" (3-5); Francis Steegmuller, "Gustave Flaubert and George Sand's *Reply to a Friend*" (6-14); Claude Tricotel, "The Political Ideas of Gustave Flaubert and George Sand (An Extract from *Comme deux troubadours*)" (15-18); Sherry A. Dranch, "*Histoires, Mémoires* and *Confessions*: Sand, Flaubert and Jean-Jacques Rousseau" (19-21); Isabelle Naginski, "*The George Sand-Gustave Flaubert Correspondence*-Extracts" (22-23); Alex Szogyi, "An Interview with Françoise Gilot" (37-42); Georges Lubin, "George Sand and Women's Rights" (43-47); Joseph Barry, "Georges Lubin, ed., *Correspondance*, Vol. XIV" (48-49); Thelma Jurgrau, "Dan Hofstadter, ed. and trans., *My Life*" (50-51); Thelma Jurgrau, "Translation of an Extract from *Histoire de ma vie*" (51-55); Georges Lubin, "Chronologie" (56-57); "Miscellany" (58-68).
The bulk of this issue is devoted to displaying the irreconcilable differences between the two friends, Sand and Flaubert. In addition, Gilot discusses what it means to be an artist-woman, Lubin assesses Sand's contribution to the movement for women's rights in the nineteenth century, and Jurgrau gives an up-to-date translation of the first, deeply moving pages of her autobiography.

Friends of George Sand Newsletter (Hofstra University), 4,i (1981).

Contents: Thelma Jurgrau, "Editorial" (2-3); Nancy Rogers, "The Novelist as Teacher" (4-8); Georges Lubin, "George Sand et l'éducation" (9-12); George Bernstein, "George Sand as an Educated Woman in Her Time" (13-18); Bernadette Chovelon, "George Sand, professeur" (19-20); Thelma Jurgrau,

"Sand's Principles of Education" (21-23); Debra Lenowitz Wentz, "George Sand's *Contes d'une grand'mère* as an Educational Device" (24-31); John Allman, "George Sand at Palaiseau-1865 (A Poem)" (32-35); Peter Byrne, "George Sand, Marcie, Lamennais and *Le Monde*" (36-38); Georges Lubin, "En survolant le tome XV" (39-42); Byron Janis, "William G. Atwood, *The Lioness and the Little One*" (43); Peter Byrne, "Pierre Leroux, *La Grève de Samarez*" (44); "Miscellany" (45-59).

This issue treats George Sand and education from a number of viewpoints: the "schoolteacherly prose" style of her novels (Rogers), the kind of education she received (Lubin and Bernstein), the importance she attached to teaching her own children (Chovelon). Many of her principles of education derive from Rousseau (Jurgrau); many of the images in her *Contes d'une grand'mère* form an instructive network for children and adults alike (Wentz). In addition, Byrne finds the coherence of Sand's *Lettres à Marcie* to lie in the patterns of thought discernible from letter to letter; Lubin resumes the high points of her *Correspondance*, Vol. XV.

Iwasaki, Hiroshi. "Le côté de Madeleine: 'François le Champi' dans 'A la recherche du temps perdu.'" *Littérature* 37 (Feb. 1980): 86-99.

Jacobs, Alphonse, ed. *Gustave Flaubert et George Sand - Correspondance*. Paris: Flammarion, 1981. Pp. 608. Fr. 104.42.

First gathering into a single volume of previously dispersed letters.

Lacassagne, Jean-Pierre, ed. *Mauprat*. (Folio, 1311.) Paris: Gallimard, 1981. Pp. 480. Fr. 19.10.

Lacassin, Francis, ed. *Le Chêne parlant: contes et nouvelles*. (Les Maîtres de l'Etrange et de la Peur.) Paris: U.G.E., 1981. Pp. 241. Fr. 46.70.

Levin, Susan M. "George Sand in the Sign of Leo." *CLAJ* 23 (1979-80): 303-21.

Lubin, Georges. "George Sand et les Bonaparte. George Sand, cousine de Napoléon III? Un article inédit de George Sand ('Les Prétendants,' 11 janvier 1873)." *Souvenir napoléonien*, Jan. 1980.

Lubin, Georges, ed. *Correspondance*. T. XV: *Juin 1858-Juin 1860*. (Classiques jaunes.) Paris: Garnier, 1981. Pp. 1024.

Rev. by Jean-Hervé Donnard in *Présence de George Sand* 11 (1981): 53.

Lubin, Georges, ed. *Lélia*. (Les Introuvables.) 2 vols. Plan-de-la-Tour (Var): Editions d'Aujourd'hui, 1980. Fr. 165.00.

Lubin, Georges, ed. *Spiridion*. (Les Introuvables.) Plan-de-la-Tour (Var): Editions d'Aujourd'hui, 1980. Fr. 70.00.

Madácsy, Piroska. "George Sand és Magyarország." *Irodalom-történeti Közlemények* 83 (1979): 292-96.

Maillon, Jean, and Pierre Salomon, eds. *Les Maîtres sonneurs*. (Classiques jaunes.) Paris: Garnier, 1981. Pp. 640.

Mallet, Francine. *George Sand*. Paris: Grasset, 1981. Pp. 444. Fr. 94.89.

OEuvres complètes. 35 vols. Geneva: Slatkine Reprints, 1979-80. Fr. 4500.00.

Facsimile edition of the 103 volumes in the Paris editions of M. Lévy and Calmann-Lévy, 1863-1926.

Poli, Annarosa. "George Sand e la memoria involontaria: Ricordo del lago di Nemi." *Bollettino del Centro Interuniversitario di Ricerche sul Viaggio in Italia*, 1,ii (1980): 91-93.

Présence de George Sand 10 (1981):

Contents: Jean-Hervé Donnard, "Changement et continuité" (2-3); Claude Tricotel, "George Sand à la recherche des paysages: *Mademoiselle Merquem* et les voyages en Normandie" (4-11); Christian Abbadie, "A. Thiers, source littéraire du pyrénéisme de George Sand et de Michelet?" (12-14); Christian Abbadie, "Du nouveau sur George Sand, Mérimée et Carmen ... en Espagne!" (15-16); Claude Galtayries, "Un hiver à Majorque" (17-19); Michèle Hirsch, "Clopinet ou la vie sauvage" (20-25); Françoise Genevray, "Le personnage de Don Juan dans *Lélia* et le *Château des Désertes*" (26-31); Francine Mallet, "George Sand et la musique" (32-38); Françoise Clément, "Lecture et transposition plastique des *Maîtres sonneurs*" (39-40); "Chroniques" (41-48).
In the section of this issue devoted to "Voyages et paysages," Tricotel suggests that despite their realism, Sand's landscapes are subjectively determined, Abbadie cites at

length passages relating to the image of Spain in her works, Galtayries finds Sand rejecting the principles of tourism in favor of crystallizing socialist theories in *Un Hiver à Majorque*. In the section "Art et fiction," Hirsch gives a close reading of one of the stories in *Les Idées d'un maître d'école*, Genevray discovers that the identification that certain of Sand's characters make with Don Juan is often discontinuous and unstable, Mallet evokes her love of music, particularly in *Consuelo* and *La Comtesse de Rudolstadt*, Clément details an interdisciplinary project carried out by "une classe de troisième."

Présence de George Sand 11 (1981).

Contents: Jean Lavédrine, "Bilan et perspectives" (2-3); Jo Vareille, "George Sand, journaliste?" (4-5); Jo Vareille, "Aurore Dudevant débute au *Figaro*" (6-7); Jo Vareille, "Présentation de *Fanchette*" (8-9); George Sand, *Fanchette* (10-27); Jo Vareille, "Un rédacteur en chef, cet oiseau rare" (28-29); Jean-Hervé Donnard, "George Sand journaliste chez les Indiens peaux-rouges" (30-36); Georges Lubin, "La journaliste de 1848" (37-39); Roger Bellet, "La presse française de 1830 à 1876" (40-46); "Chroniques" (47-60).
In addition to the various facets of Sand's activities as journalist from 1831 to 1848 presented here, Bellet offers a panoramic history of the French press from 1830 to 1876.

Présence de George Sand 12 (1981).

Contents: Jean Lavédrine, "George Sand et la musique" (2-4); Marie-Claire Bancquart, "La musique et les *Maîtres sonneurs*: fusion et séparation" (5-12); Paul Pelckmans, "Fantastique et pédagogie: *L'Orgue du Titan*" (13-21); Béatrice Didier, "George Sand critique musical dans ses lettres" (22-28); Joseph-Marc Bailbé, "George Sand et Meyerbeer: essai de critique musicale" (29-33); Christian Abbadie, "Le thème du contrebandier" (34-45); Bernadette Chovelon, "George Sand et Pauline Viardot" (46-52); Thierry Bodin, "Balzac, George Sand et la musique" (53-59); Georges Lubin, "Les pianos de Nohant" (60-65); "Chroniques" (66-72).
An issue on George Sand and music combining a variety of approaches: thematic (Bancquart), anthropological (Pelckmans), textual (Didier, Bailbé), descriptive (Abbadie), biographical (Chovelon), comparatist (Bodin), historical (Lubin).

Rheault, Raymond, ed. *Mademoiselle Merquem*. Editions de l'Université d'Ottawa (Canada), 1981. Pp. 560. $21.00.

Sacken, Jeannee P. "Nature Imagery as Narrative Structure in George Sand's *Indiana*." *RomN* 21 (1980-81): 313-17.

The imagery of gardens, bird life, and atmospheric conditions reinforces the novel's development from psychological enslavement for its heroes, Ralph and Indiana, in Lagny, in Paris, and on the Ile Bourbon to their self-discovery, freedom, and happiness at Bernica.

Salomon, Pierre, and Jean Mallion, eds. *La Mare au diable; François le Champi*. (Classiques Garnier.) Paris: Garnier, 1981. Pp. 514. Fr. 74.00.

Salomon, Pierre, and Jean Maillon, eds. *La Petite Fadette*. (Classiques Garnier.) Paris: Garnier, 1981. Pp. 400. Fr. 61.00.

Schaeffer, Gérard. *Espace et temps chez George Sand*. Neuchâtel: La Baconnière; Paris: Payot, 1981. Pp. 154.

Studies of *Mauprat, Consuelo*, and *Laura, Voyage dans un cristal*.

Schulze, Wolfgang. "*François le champi*: Vorbild für *Henry Esmond*?" *Archiv* 216 (1979): 2-8.

Sivert, Eileen Boyd. "*Lélia* and Feminism." *YFS* 62 (1981): 45-66.

Derived from the French feminist criticism of Luce Irigary and Hélène Cixous, this interpretation stresses the problems of woman's recognition in a male society and of her struggle for self-definition within the confines of masculine discourse.

Standring, Enid M. "Rossini and His Music in the Life and Works of George Sand." *NCFS* 10 (1981-82): 17-27.

After examining George Sand's reactions to Rossini's music as expressed throughout her works, the author concludes that "if it is uncertain whether Sand knew Rossini as a friend, it would appear that, from as early as 1816, his music was a vital element in her life" (26).

Vest, James M. "Fluid Nomenclature, Imagery, and Themes in George Sand's *Indiana*." *SAR* 46 (1981): 43-54.

Veyriras, Paul. "Mazzini et la réhabilitation de George Sand en Angleterre (1837-47)." *Confluents* 1975,i: 117-28.

Vierne, Simone, ed. *Le Dernier Amour*. (Ressources, 106.) Geneva: Slatkine Reprints, 1980. Pp. 400. Sw.Fr. 24.00.

Reprint of the edition of Paris, 1878.

Vierne, Simone, ed. *Monsieur Sylvestre*. Geneva: Slatkine Reprints, 1980. Pp. 348. Sw.Fr. 22.00.

Reprint of the edition of Paris, 1866.

Waddington, Patrick. *Turgenev and George Sand: An Improbable Entente*. London: Macmillan, 1981. Pp. 146. £12.00.

Rev. by April FitzLyon in *TLS*, Nov. 6, 1981, p. 1310.

Wolfzettel, Friedrich. "George Sand's 'François le Champi': 'Familienroman' im sozialen Kontext." *NM* 82 (1981): 97-110.

Zalom, Marilyn. "They Remember *Maman*: Attachment and Separation in Leduc, de Beauvoir, Sand, and Cardinal." *Essays in Literature* 8 (1981): 73-90.

See also Baude and Münch, Boime (1), Hellerstein, Viallaneix and Ehrard ("French 1. General"); Malavié ("Nisard"); Raggi-Page ("Stendhal"); Werner ("Tristan").

Reviews of books previously listed:

BLOUNT, Paul G., *George Sand and the Victorian World* (see *RMB* for 1979, p. 219), rev. by Francis S. Heck in *Rocky Mountain Review* 34 (1980): 270-71; COURRIER, J., ed., *La Ville noire* (see *RMB* for 1979, p. 220), rev. by Alain Buisne in *RHL* 81 (1981): 153-54; *George Sand Papers: Conference Proceedings, 1976* (see *RMB* for 1980, pp. 234-35), rev. by James M. Vest in *French Forum* 6 (1981): 280-81; HOFSTADTER, Dan, trans., *My Life* (see *RMB* for 1979, p. 222), rev. by Thelma Jurgrau in *Friends of George Sand Newsletter*, 3,ii (1980): 50-51; LUBIN, Georges, ed., *Correspondance*, T. XII (see *ELN* 15, Supp., 127), rev. by L.J. Austin in *FS* 35 (1981): 81-84; LUBIN, Georges, ed., *Correspondance*, T. XIII (see *ELN* 17, Supp., 153), rev. by L.J. Austin in *FS* 35 (1981): 81-84; LUBIN, Georges, ed., *Correspondance*, T. XIV (see *RMB* for 1980, p. 236), rev. by L.J. Austin in *FS* 35 (1981): 81-84; by Joseph Barry in *Friends of George Sand Newsletter* 3,ii (1980): 48-49.

SCRIBE

Koon, Helene, and Richard Switzer. *Eugène Scribe*. (Twayne World
Authors Series, 547.) Boston: Twayne, 1980. Pp. 174.

Appropriately, this is a well-made account of the famous
(or infamous?) playwright's life and work: smooth and very
readable, filled with deft summaries of dozens of his plays.
After an initial chapter devoted to Scribe's life and theatrical career comes the core of the book, a study of the plays:
first, a summary of his dramatic system, then a series of
analyses of numerous individual plays treated by genre ("topical works," "literary-theatrical satires," farces, "serious
plays," "sentimental plays," social comedies, and history
plays, these latter two categories being accorded a full
chapter each). Then follows a chapter on Scribe's influence,
first in France, then abroad (here it is surprising to find
Kierkegaard among those who spread Scribe's influence).
Scribe's major collaborations with composers (Auber, Rossini,
Donizetti, Boieldieu, Meyerbeer, Halévy, Gounod, and Verdi)
are the subject of an especially welcome discussion, for
here, as throughout, the authors' summaries stress the
theatrical and even the moral and psychological values inherent in Scribe's texts. There are few factual errors (e.g.,
on p. 139, Mérimée's *Chronique du règne de Charles IX* is
ascribed to Vigny), but it is a serious distortion of the
theme of Hugo's play to say that "In *Ruy Blas* a bandit loves
a queen" (p. 155). Such flaws, however, are trivial when set
against a very good presentation of an author who certainly
worked well within the limits of the *littérature de consom-
mation* but who performed with flair and boundless drive.
(J.S.P.)

Review of book previously listed:

RUPRECHT, Hans-Georg, *Theaterpublikum und Textauffassung*
(see *RMB* for 1979, p. 226), rev. by Wolfgang Zimmer in *O&C*
5,i (1980): 151-53.

SENANCOUR

Didier, Béatrice, ed. *Isabelle*. Geneva: Slatkine, 1980. Pp.
304.

Monglond, André, ed. *Obermann*. (Les Introuvables.) Plan-de-
la-Tour (Var): Editions d'Aujourd'hui, 1980. Fr. 132.00.

See also Roudaut ("French 1. General"); *Les Cahiers de Saint-Martin* 3 ("Saint-Martin").

SISMONDI

King, Norman, and Jean-Daniel Candaux. "La correspondance de Benjamin Constant et de Sismondi (1801-1830)." *Annales Benjamin Constant* 1 (1980): 81-172.

Tableau de l'agriculture toscane. (Di Toscana: Excerpta di Diari, Corrispondenze e Memorie della Toscana.) Florence: Istituto regionale per la programmazione economica della Toscana, 1980. Pp. 6+xiv+371.

   Rev. by C. Cordié in *SFr* 24 (1980): 578.
   The facsimile of Sismondi's text is followed by an essay by Simonetta Bertolozzi Batignani, "Il Sismondi del *Tableau*" (331-69).

See also Misan (2) ("French 1. General"); Viallaneix (1) ("Michelet").

SOULIÉ

See Olivier-Martin ("French 1. General"); Tanguy Baum ("Sue").

STAEL

Cleary, John. "Madame de Staël, Rousseau, and Mary Wollstonecraft." *RomN* 31 (1981): 329-33.

   Mary Wollstonecraft's extreme hostility toward Mme de Staël's admiration for Rousseau in her *Lettres sur le caractère et les écrits de J.-J. Rousseau* of 1788 illustrates the two women's diametrically opposed views of intellectual responsibility and of their own sex.

Davis, Natalie Zemon. "Gender and Genre: Women as Historical Writers, 1400-1820." Pp. 153-82 in Patricia H. Labalme, ed., *Beyond Their Sex: Learned Women of the European Past.* New York University Press, 1980. Pp. 188.

Dehon, Claire L. "Corinne: une artiste héroïne de roman." *NCFS* 9 (1980-81): 1-9.

A description of traits characterizing the ideal artist,
as embodied by Corinne, followed by an examination of the
role of love in the life of the woman writer.

Delon, Michel. "La Saint-Barthélémy et la Terreur chez Mme
de Staël et les historiens de la Révolution au XIXème siècle."
Romantisme 31 (1981): 49-62.

Analogies between the sixteenth-century massacre and the
violence of the Reign of Terror allow Mme de Staël to interpret the French Revolution as an expression of a legitimate
desire for liberty, a desire that meets with failure. A
straightforward yet subtle presentation of the complex, often
ambivalent equation between religion and politics in the
*Considérations sur les principaux événements de la Révolution
française*. Followed by penetrating brief analyses of how the
positions taken by Balzac, Esquiros, Louis Blanc, Michelet,
and Quinet diverge from or develop out of those of Mme de
Staël. (M.E.B.)

Jacobi, Ruth. "Heines 'Romantische Schule': eine Antwort auf
Madame de Staël's 'De l'Allemagne.'" *HeineJ 1981*, pp. 140-68.

Jeune, Simon. "De Coppet à Bordeaux: un livre et ses ex-libris."
Revue Française d'Histoire du Livre, July-Sept. 1979.

Johnson-Cousin, Danielle. "Les 'leçons' de déclamation de
Germaine Necker: note sur le 'mystère' Clairon." *SVEC* 183
(1980): 161-64.

Links Mlle Clairon to the Neckers' interest in theater
and to Germaine's *début* as writer and actress in the years
1777-78.

Johnson-Cousin, Danielle P. "Madame de Staël 'vue' par John
Adams: deux lettres inédites de John Adams à Adrian Van der
Kemp." *NCFS* 9 (1981): 171-74.

Gives the text of letters containing brief indications
of Adams' admiration for the Neckers' daughter, whom he
never met.

Johnson-Cousin, Danielle. "The Reception of Madame de Staël's
De l'Allemagne in North America." Pp. 151-57 in Milan V.
Dimić and Juan Ferraté, eds., *Actes du VIIe Congrès de
l'Association Internationale de Littérature Comparée, I:
Littératures americaines: Dépendance, indépendance, inter-
dépendance*. (Lib. of CRCL, 2.) Stuttgart: Bieber, 1979.
Pp. 562.

Mercken-Spaas, Godlième. "Death and the Romantic Heroine:
   Chateaubriand and De Staël." Pp. 79-86 in Robert L. Mitchell,
   ed., *Pre-Text/Text/Context: Essays on Nineteenth-Century
   French Literature.* Ohio State University Press, 1980. Pp.
   291.

Pange, Victor de. *Le Plus Beau de toutes les fêtes: Madame de
   Staël et Elisabeth Hervey, duchesse de Devonshire, d'après
   leur correspondance inédite 1804-17.* Paris: Klincksieck,
   1980. Pp. 266. Fr. 168.00.

   Rev. by Anita Brookner in *TLS,* April 10, 1981, p. 411;
   by Arlette Michel in *IL* 33 (1981): 213.
   A meticulous compilation of 121 letters whose political
   orientation and stylistic concision constantly call for
   elucidation. This edition responds generously to these needs.
   De Pange supplies a wealth of invaluable background in the
   introduction to each letter. Conscientious footnotes, useful
   appendices, and interesting photographs complete, without
   overwhelming, the verve of the correspondents' insights into
   politics and society. A fine piece of scholarship that should
   prove indispensable for understanding the ties linking
   England and France in the early nineteenth century. (M.E.B.)

Tieck, Dorothea, trans. *Corinna oder Italien.* Munich: Winkler,
   1979. Pp. 617.

   Rev. by Maria Moog-Grünewald in *Arcadia* 16 (1981): 96-98.

See also Viallaneix and Ehrard ("French 1. General").

Reviews of books previously listed:

BALAYÉ, Simone, *Madame de Staël: lumières et liberté* (see
   RMB for 1979, p. 227), rev. by Jean Gaulmier in *RHL* 81 (1981):
   465-68; by Arno Kappler in *Arcadia* 15 (1980): 335-36; by
   Norman King in *MLR* 76 (1981): 190-95; by Eberhard Leube in
   RF 92 (1980): 307-11; by Lucia Omacini in *SFr* 24 (1980):
   126-27; by Daniel Roche in *RHMC* 28 (1981): 215-16; GUTWIRTH,
   Madelyn, *Madame de Staël, Novelist* (see *RMB* for 1979, p.
   228), rev. by Frank Paul Bowman in *MLQ* 41 (1980): 102-04;
   by Norman King in *MLR* 76 (1981): 190-95; by Eberhard Leube
   in *RF* 92 (1980): 307-11; JASINSKI, Béatrice W., ed., *Correspondance générale,* T. IV, 2e partie (see *RMB* for 1979,
   p. 229), rev. by Norman King in *MLR* 76 (1981): 190-95;
   by Joanna Kitchen in *FS* 35 (1981): 454-55; OMACINI, Lucia,
   ed., *Des cironstances actuelles qui peuvent terminer la
   révolution* (see *RMB* for 1979, p. 229), rev. by Jean Gaulmier

in *RHL* 81 (1981): 141; by Madelyn Gutwirth in *FR* 55 (1981-
82): 274-76; by Norman King in *MLR* 76 (1981): 190-95; TODD,
Janet, *Women's Friendship in Literature* (see *RMB* for 1980,
p. 244), rev. by Marilyn Butler in *EiC* 31 (1981): 246-49.

STENDHAL

Allen, Robert F. "Caractérisation affective de quelques ad-
jectifs-clefs dans *le Rouge et le noir* livre premier." *SC*
24 (1981-82): 23-32.

   Justifies Stendhal's frequent use of the adjectives
   extrême, *singulier*, and *affreux*.

Arrous, Michel. "Note sur la carrière politique de Félix
Faure." *SC* 23 (1980-81): 358-63.

   More details on the career of Stendhal's boyhood friend.

Attuel, Josiane. *Le Style de Stendhal: efficacité et romanesque.*
Paris: Nizet, 1980. Pp. 736.

   Rev. by V. Del Litto in *SC* 23 (1980-81): 375.

Attuel, Josiane. "Le style de Stendhal: une union de contraires."
SC 24 (1981-82): 1-22.

   An extract from the author's recent work (see above).
   Attuel sees the key to Stendhal's style in the harmoniza-
   tion and conjunction of the logical mode with the stylistic
   manifestations of *l'âme sensible*.

Autant-Lara, Claude. "Parm's Tchartreuse." *SC* 23 (1980-81):
311-24.

   A diatribe against the French television networks for
   their role in *l'affaire Chartreuse* (see below).

Autant-Lara, Claude. *Télémafia*. Nice: Editions Alain Lefeuvre,
1981. Pp. 292. Fr. 58.00.

   Claude Autant-Lara, the director of the film version of
   Le Rouge et le noir and the television version of *Lucien
   Leuwen* gives his account of *l'affaire Chartreuse*, the
   controversy over the assignment of a television production
   of *La Chartreuse* to an international group.

Bailbé, Joseph-Marc. "Jules Janin juge de Stendhal: du para-
doxe à l'improvisation." *SC* 23 (1980-81): 215-24.

Discussion of Janin's views on Stendhal as found in his review of *Le Rouge et le noir* and his prospectus for the 1853 edition of Stendhal's collected works. By the time he wrote the prospectus, Janin's appreciation for Stendhal had grown considerably, and he had a particular affection for *La Chartreuse de Parme*, which responded in a number of ways to his concept of the novel.

Booker, John T. "Retrospective Movement in the Stendhalian Narration." *RR* 72 (1981): 26-38.

Argues for "the undeniable presence of flashback and temporal overlap" in Stendhal's fiction and proposes that these are probably as common in the novels of Stendhal as in those of any traditional novelist. What is unique about them is that "they seem actually to support that general impression of presentness for which Stendhal's narration is so justly known." A solid piece. (E.J.T.)

Brotherson, Lee. "L'importance de Vergy dans *le Rouge et le noir*." *SC* 23 (1980-81): 325-36.

Vergy stands in contrast to Verrières, Besançon, and Paris as the privileged place of love, nature, and freedom. It may well be a reminiscence of Henri Beyle's boyhood visit to les Echelles.

Caramaschi, Enzo. "Stendhal, Taine, Barrès face aux Léonards de Milan." *SC* 23 (1980-81): 247-54.

Good comparative/contrastive study. (E.J.T.)

Chanda, A.K. "The Young Man from the Provinces." *CL* 33 (1981): 321-41.

Stendhal's Julien Sorel, *passim*.

Chantreau, Alain. "Deux lettres inédites de Stendhal: l'affaire Romanelli (Civitavecchia, avril 1835)." *SC* 23 (1980-81): 303-10.

Official letters from Stendhal as French consul relating to the quarantine of French ships.

Coe, Richard N. "Champfleury, Stendhal et Joseph de Maistre." *SC* 24 (1981-82): 70-71.

Champfleury preferred Joseph de Maistre over Stendhal.

Collet, Annie. "Une lettre de Matilde Dembowsky." *SC* 24 (1981-82): 66-69.

Reproduction of the first letter ever found by Matilde (who is seeking permission from the authorities to withdraw her sick son from school).

Comeau, Paul T. "The Love Theme and Monologue Structure in *Armance*." *NCFS* (1980-81): 37-58.

A competent plot-analysis emphasizing the role of monologue clusters. (E.J.T.)

Crouzet, Michel. "Littérature et politique chez Stendhal." *IL* 32 (1980): 102-07.

The author presents his *thèse de doctorat d'état, L'Ecrivain révolté ou le point de départ*. The thesis, which limits its study to the period prior to 1814, appears to be rich and varied in its insights. Crouzet sees "beylisme" as a coherent thought whose genesis he seeks to discover (in Rousseau, in the myth of Italy, in Henri Beyle's childhood, in ideology). (E.J.T.)

Crouzet, Michel. "Polémique et politesse ou Stendhal pamphlé-taire (II)." *SC* 23 (1980-81): 156-78.

Continuation of the author's article listed last year (see *RMB* for 1980, p. 247). Continued discussion of the richness of polemical manoeuvre in Stendhal (including vari-ous *rapprochements* with Courier). Crouzet analyzes the choice of polemical mask and the deliberate decision not to oppose anger with anger but rather with mild wit accompanied by self-deprecation. An excellent article. (E.J.T.)

Crouzet, Michel. *Stendhal et le langage*. (Bibliothèque des Idées.) Paris: Gallimard, 1981. Pp. 424. Fr. 135.00.

Dalet, Gilbert. "Rencontre dauphinoise de deux personnages de Balzac et de Stendhal." *SC* 23 (1980-81): 337-57.

Amable Rome and Victor Michel, both *dauphinois* who held positions of health officer and director respectively at the *dépôt de mendicité* in Grenoble, are probable models, one for Benassis in Balzac's *Le Médecin de campagne*, the other for Valenod in *Le Rouge et le noir*.

Daprini, Pierre B. "Le jardin d'Armide: refuge et imagination stendhalienne." *SC* 23 (1980-81): 225-42.

Discussion of the presence of the *jardin d'Armide* (from Tasso's *Gerusalemme Liberata*) in Stendhal's fiction and non-fiction where it appears as a paradigm for a privileged place where *sensibilité* and imagination can express themselves in isolation from the world. An intelligent essay. (E.J.T.)

Day, James T. "The Hero as Reader in Stendhal." *FR* 54 (1980-81): 412-19.

Studies Stendhal's heroes as readers and concludes that "the author's unequivocal message ... is consistently that reading and contemplation can produce a more exalted frame of mind than encounters with events and individuals before these are transformed into reading matter."

Del Litto, Victor. "Bibliographie stendhalienne. Année 1980." *SC* 24 (1981-82): 103-18.

Del Litto, Victor. *Essais stendhaliens*. Ed. Pierre-Georges Castex et al. Geneva: Slatkine, 1981. Pp. xx+486. Sw.Fr. 50.00.

This volume, assembled by friends of Victor Del Litto to mark his 70th birthday and his retirement from the Université de Grenoble, contains 37 articles by Del Litto, many of which had become inaccessible: "*La Vie de Henry Brulard*: Qui était Brulard" (3-12); "Le père de Stendhal et ses moutons" (13-25); "Pour le dossier de Chérubin Beyle" (27-30); "Le testament du docteur Henri Gagnon" (31-35); "La succession de l'oncle de Stendhal et la bibliothèque du docteur Gagnon" (37-46); "Nouveaux documents sur l'abbé Raillane, le précepteur honni de Stendhal" (47-71); "Le bataillon de l'Espérance" (73-84); "Louis-Joseph Jay, professeur de Stendhal" (85-94); "Louis Joseph Jay, fondateur du musée de Grenoble" (95-116); "Les réfugiés italiens à Grenoble en 1799 et 1800" (117-28); "Stendhal et le Dauphiné" (129-46); "Le texte d'une phrase de *La Vie de Henry Brulard*" (147-50); "Stendhal, le jeu et la loterie" (151-55); "Stendhal et l'Amérique" (157-63); "Pourquoi Stendhal n'a pas été 'épicier' à Marseilles" (165-78); "Un texte capital pour la connaissance de Stendhal: *Les Privilèges*" (179-98); "Une lettre inédite de Louis Crozet à Félix Faure" (199-206); "Stendhal, Félix Faure et Victor Michel à Vienne en 1809" (207-23); "Romain Colomb" (225-38); "Un amour de Stendhal: Giulia (iconographie inédite)" (239-48); "Une maîtresse de Stendhal: Alberthe de Rubempré (iconographie inédite)" (249-70); "Prosper Mérimée: 'H.B.'" (271-97); "Stendhal romancier réaliste?" (301-06); "Journal

élaboré et journal brut" (307-11); "Stendhal et Walter
Scott" (313-20); "Stendhal et le Corrège" (321-35); "Stendhal
et Cimarosa" (337-38); "Stendhal et Rubens" (339-43); "Stendhal, Constant et l'industrialisme" (345-47); "Un nouveau
plagiat de Stendhal" (349-60); "La province dans l'oeuvre
de Stendhal" (361-74); "Un livre peu connu de Stendhal:
Rome, Naples et Florence en 1817" (375-91); "*Il Forestiere
in Italia* ou Stendhal librettiste" (393-98); "L'article de
Balzac sur *La Chartreuse de Parme*" (399-435); "Stendhal et
Bologne" (439-45); "Stendhal et Venise" (447-55); "Arrigo
Beyle Milanese" (457-62). The articles are followed by a
bibliography of Del Litto's writings and preceded by testi-
monials by Pierre-Georges Castex, Georges Dethan, and Ernest
Abravanel. The volume is a fitting tribute to the man recog-
nized as the foremost authority on Stendhal. (E.J.T.)

Del Litto, Victor. "Mérimée et Stendhal." *SC* 23 (1980-81):
183-86.

Survey of references to Stendhal in the new Pléiade
edition of Mérimée's works.

Del Litto, Victor, ed. *OEuvres intimes*. Tome I. (Bibliothèque
de la Pléiade.) Paris: Gallimard, 1981. Pp. xxxix+1637.

Rev. by E. Abravanel in *SC* 24 (1981-82): 78-80.
This new Pléiade edition, which contains in the first
volume the *Journal* from 1801 to 1817, includes a number of
variants not previously available.

Delorme, Jeanne. "Correspondances en relisant Stendhal." *RLC*
55 (1981): 239-48.

In spite of its title, this essay is not on Stendhal but
rather on the striking similarities between Alfieri and
Montherlant.

Denier, Renée. "A propos d'un compte rendu anglais de *De
l'amour*." *SC* 23 (1980-81): 139-55.

Argues that the lengthy review of *De l'amour* which appeared
in the *New Monthly Magazine* in 1822 was probably written
by Hazlitt.

Devos, Willy. "Stendhal en Néerlandais. Bibliographie 1980."
SC 24 (1981-82): 102.

Doyon, André. "Cinq lettres inédites de Stendhal à sa soeur
Pauline (1810-1814)." *SC* 23 (1980-81): 293-302.

Beyle gives details about his career ambitions.

Doyon, André. "Henri et Pauline Beyle: histoire de 'la cara sorella' (d'après des documents inédits)." *SC* 24 (1981–82): 41–65.

The first part of a biography (the first) of Stendhal's sister, Pauline Beyle.

Felkay, Nicole. "Stendhal et l'imprimeur Henri Fournier." *SC* 23 (1980–81): 132–38.

Relationships between Stendhal and the printer of *Racine et Shakespeare No. II* and *D'un nouveau complot contre les industriels*.

Goetz, William R. "Nietzsche and *Le Rouge et le noir*." *CLS* 18 (1981): 443–58.

Proposes that it was Stendhal's depiction of society as an aggregate of power relationships and his depiction of Julien Sorel as a "masterful" character that explains Nietzsche's fascination with Stendhal and *Le Rouge et le noir*. Goetz sees a consonance of views between Stendhal and Nietzsche on the notion of the "true aristocracy." Both associate "true freedom" with a "true noble class" which cannot be found in the nineteenth century. Both rejected religion as unworthy of a superior man. More importantly, though, Goetz analyzes *Le Rouge et le noir* from a Nietzschean point of view to produce some fresh and insightful readings of the novel. An excellent essay. (E.J.T.)

Gohira, Takashi. "La signification du refus: une lecture d'*Armance*." *Revue de l'Université de Keio* (Tokyo) (1980): 213–33.

Gracq, Julien. *En lisant, en écrivant*. Paris: José Corti, 1981. Pp. 302. Fr. 56.20.

Stendhal *passim*.

Hamilton, James F. "Two Psychodramatic Scenes in Stendhal's *Armance*." *KRQ* 28 (1981): 121–30.

Argues that Octave's secret is that he loves two women, Armance and his mother, with equal passion, resulting morally in shame and guilt and physically in the dysfunction of impotence.

Hamm, Jean-Jacques. "Stendhal et l'autre du plagiat." *SC* 23 (1980–81): 203–14.

Attempts a theory of plagiarism within which it is possible
to see Stendhal's plagiarisms in his *Vie de Haydn* as part
of his search for the other, both the plagiarized Carpani
and Haydn possessing qualities which Stendhal much admired.

Histoire de la peinture en Italie. Préface inédite de V. Del
Litto. (Les Introuvables.) 2 vols. Plan-de-la-Tour (Var):
Editions d'Aujourd'hui, 1980. Pp. vii+348. Pp. 435. Fr.
160.00.

Jasenas, Eliane. "Stendhal et Baudelaire: la dédicace 'Aux
Bourgeois.' La problématique d'un texte." *NCFS* 9 (1981):
192-203.

Argues that Baudelaire's *dédicace*, "Aux bourgeois," is in
large part the consequence of his reflection on Stendhal's
D'un nouveau complot contre les industriels and can be understood only in reference to that pamphlet. Baudelaire
sided with the *classe pensante* as did Stendhal and accepted
the latter's irony while rejecting his indignant attitude
and turning his argument upside down.

Lansard, Colette. "Milan, patrie d'élection de Stendhal, vu
par un voyageur français en 1808." *SC* 23 (1980-81): 113-31.

The heretofore unpublished letters on Milan dating from
May and June 1808 by Honoré-Anthelme Passerat de la Chapelle.

Macropoulou, Maria. "Stendhal en Grèce. Bibliographie 1925-
1980." *SC* 24 (1981-82): 99-101.

Translations of Stendhal's works into Greek as well as
articles on Stendhal appearing in Greece.

Maquet, Albert. "Fantasmagorie stendhalienne chez Filippo
Tommaso Marinetti." *Marche Romane* 31 (1981): 5-20.

Stendhal's influence on Marinetti's *La Grande Milano
tradizionale e futurista* (written in 1943-44, published
posthumously in 1969).

McWatters, K.G., ed. *Chroniques pour l'Angleterre. Contributions à la presse britannique.* Publications de l'Université des Langues et Lettres de Grenoble, 1980. Pp. 310.

Rev. by René Bourgeois in *SC* 23 (1980-81): 264-65.
The first volume of a series destined to replace Marti-
neau's unreliable *Courrier anglais.*

Miller, D.A. "Narrative 'Uncontrol' in Stendhal." Pp. 195-264 in *Narrative and Its Discontents: Problems of Closure in the Traditional Novel*. Princeton University Press, 1981. Pp. 300.

Basing himself on the argument that novels are never fully or finally governed by closure, Miller discusses *Le Rouge et le noir* and *Lucien Leuwen*, demonstrating Stendhal's dislike of closure (as that which ends the possibility of play). In *Le Rouge* the narratable is seen to derive from the movement from daydream to plot. *Lucien Leuwen* is seen as a tentative willingness on the part of Stendhal to relish the patterns of plot for its own sake. *Lucien Leuwen*'s incompleteness does not derive from a poverty of imagination but from an inability to restrict imagination. A first-rate discussion of Stendhalian narration. Highly recommended. (E.J.T.)

Morcovescu, N. "Stendhal, un des maîtres véritables de Lucien Febvre." *AJFS* 16 (1979): 480-87.

Establishes, convincingly, that Stendhal was one of the *maîtres à penser* of the famous French historian Lucien Febvre and posits some aspects of Stendhal's work, such as his interest in groups, which would have interested Febvre. (E.J.T.)

Moutote, Daniel. *Egotisme français moderne. Stendhal, Barrès, Valéry, Gide*. Paris: S.E.D.E.S.-C.D.U., 1980. Pp. 381. Fr. 77.00.

The chapter on Stendhal, "L'expression de l'égotisme dans les romans de Stendhal," is a reprint of the essay published in *CAIEF* in 1974 (see *ELN* 13, Supp., 115).

Peytard, Jean. *Voix et traces narratives chez Stendhal: Analyse sémiotique de "Vanina Vanini."* Paris: Les Editeurs français réunis, 1980. Pp. 139.

Rich in its perspectives on opening/closure, sequences, narrative voice, and Stendhal's *écriture*. (E.J.T.)

Picard, Michel. "Le petit chaperon rouge et noir: lecture d'un passage de Stendhal." *Littérature* 43 (1981): 24-42.

Very close and detailed analysis of the scene relating the first meeting between Julien and Madame de Rênal.

Pollard, Patrick. "Color Symbolism in *Le Rouge et le noir*." *MLR* 76 (1981): 323-31.

Concludes that the major colors "provide the reader with
a message on three separate but interrelated levels of interpretation": red is associated with the color of objects
connected with the church; black, with the color of the
priest's frock. Red is associated with ecclesiastical pre-
ferment; black with ecclesiastical and social subordination.
Red is associated with energy, ambition, and passion; black
with melancholy and intelligence. "These are connected in
such a way that the opposition between low (black) and high
(red), between melancholy and passion, is constantly present."

Pons-Ridler, Suzanne. "Index et étude comparative des fré-
quences dans *le Rouge et le noir*, *la Chartreuse de Parme* et
la *Vie de Henry Brulard*." *SC* 24 (1981-82): 33-40.

Basing herself on computer analyses done by the CNRS, the
author compares noun frequencies in the three works.

Raggi-Page, Pierre. "Quand George Sand rencontra Stendhal."
SC 24 (1981-82): 76-77.

Reproduces the passage from Sand's *Histoire de ma vie* in
which she relates her meeting with Stendhal.

Rogers, Nancy E. "The Use of Eye Language in Stendhal's *Le
Rouge et le noir*." *RomN* 20 (1979-80): 339-43.

Studies "eye language" in Chapters VIII and IX of Book II
to show that "the flames of truth and power do, indeed,
shine in the eyes of a true *homme stendhalien*."

St. Aubyn, F.C. "Stendhal and Salome." *SFR* 4 (1980): 395-404.

Survey of "Stendhal's profound infatuation over more than
a quarter of a century with a portrait, or portraits, of
Salome." The author contends that this portrait "provided
his imagination with details of character and plot that,
at least in a minor but unusual way, helped him create
great novels."

Salamund, Georges. "A propos de Stendhal à Aix-les-Bains en
1837: le Barral de la 17e liste." *SC* 23 (1980-81): 179-81.

More information on the Barral family.

Sciascia, Leonardo. "Les trois âges de Stendhal." *QL* 357
(Oct. 16-31, 1981): 11-12.

Fragment from Sciascia's journal, 1969-79, which was not
published along with the other fragments in his *Noir sur*

noir. Contains reflections on Tomaso di Lampedusa's, Gide's, and Gramsci's comments on Stendhal.

Simons, Madeleine Anjubault. *Sémiotisme de Stendhal.* (Histoire des Idées et Critique littéraire, 186.) Geneva: Droz, 1980. Pp. 335.

Rev. by W.J. Berg in *NCFS* 10 (1981-82): 133-34; by G. Strickland in *MLR* 76 (1981): 970-71.

Sonnenfeld, Albert. "Ruminations on Stendhal's Epigraphs." Pp. 99-110 in Robert L. Mitchell, ed., *Pre-text/Text/Context: Essays on Nineteenth-Century French Literature.* Ohio State University Press, 1980. Pp. 291.

Although not indicated as such, this essay is largely an English version of the author's essay in French on the same subject (see *ELN* 17, Supp., 165).

Théodoridès, Jean. "Stendhal, la rage et le 'thème de la morsure.'" *SC* 23 (1980-81): 243-46.

Of minimal interest. (E.J.T.)

Théodoridès, Jean. "Sur une anecdote médicale d'*Armance* ou Stendhal lecteur de Collé." *SC* 24 (1981-82): 72-73.

Stendhal's probable source for the anecdote relating to *la pituite vitrée* was Collé's *Journal historique* (1807).

Tintner, Adeline R. "In the Footsteps of Stendhal: James' 'A Most Extraordinary Case' and *La Chartreuse de Parme.*" *RLC* 55 (1981): 232-38.

Argues that James's story—about a passionately loved nephew, fresh from the war, who loves a young girl—adapts important structural relationships from Stendhal's *Chartreuse.* Convincing. (E.J.T.)

Todorov, Tzvetan. "Reading as Construction." Pp. 67-82 in Susan R. Suleiman and Inge Crosman, eds., *The Reader in the Text: Essays on Audience and Interpretation.* Princeton University Press, 1980. Pp. 441.

Deals briefly with *Armance,* which Todorov sees as a perfect example of a text "where construction appears as one of the principal themes."

Viti, Robert M. "The Dual Role of Enclosed Space in *Lucien Leuwen.*" *RomN* 20 (1979-80): 344-48.

The author concludes that "enclosed spaces ... have a dual
function in *Lucien Leuwen*: they often represent constraint
and the absence of freedom to act for oneself; they also
translate concretely the experience of freedom, the freedom
to mature, to decide, and, most importantly for Stendhal,
the freedom to love."

Wahl, Pauline. "Stendhal's *Lamiel*: Observations on Pygmalionism."
Pp. 113-19 in Robert L. Mitchell, ed., *Pre-text/Text/Con-
text: Essays on Nineteenth-Century French Literature*. Ohio
State University Press, 1980. Pp. 291.

Proposes that *Lamiel* constitutes an inquiry into the
nature of pygmalionism by exploring the possibility of
liberty for the pupil in the first version of the novel
and the possibility of control for the teacher in the second
version.

Weiland, Christof. "Stendhal à la télévision: à propos d'une
dramatique russe tirée de *Rouge et noir*." *SC* 23 (1980-81):
364-66.

Sees the five-hour Soviet cinematic version of *Le Rouge
et le noir* as a successful adaptation.

See also Misan (1) (2), Viallaneix and Ehrard ("French 1.
General"); Barbéris ("Chateaubriand"); Coe ("J. de Maistre").

Reviews of books previously listed:

ALTER, Robert, *A Lion for Love* (see *RMB* for 1979, p. 230),
rev. by K.G. McWatters in *FS* 35 (1981): 77-79; BAYARD, P.,
Symptôme de Stendhal (see *RMB* for 1980, p. 246), rev. by
C. Cordié in *SFr* 25 (1981): 175; BOLL-JOHANSEN, Hans,
Stendhal et le roman (see *RMB* for 1979, p. 231), rev. by
P. Berthier in *RHL* 81 (1981): 470-72; by G. Strickland in
FS 35 (1981): 77; DEL LITTO, V., ed., *De l'amour* (see *RMB*
for 1980, p. 248), rev. by J.-J. Hamm in *SC* 23 (1980-81):
374; MATHIS, Ursula, *Wirklichkeitssich und Stil* (see *RMB*
for 1979, p. 235), rev. by R. Rie in *NCFS* 9 (1980-81):
132-33; SCHELLEKENS, O., ed., *Stendhal, le saint-simonisme
et les industriels* (see *RMB* for 1980, p. 253), rev. by Yves
Ansel in *RHL* 81 (1981): 468-69; by C. Cordié in *SFr* 24
(1980): 364-65; by J.-J. Hamm in *NCFS* 10 (1981-82): 135-36;
TALBOT, Emile, ed., *La Critique stendhalienne* (see *RMB* for
1979, p. 237), rev. by C. Smethurst in *MLR* 76 (1981): 706;
VIGNERON, Robert, *Etudes sur Stendhal et sur Proust* (see
RMB for 1979, p. 238), rev. by C. Cordié in *SFr* 24 (1980):
581-82; by V. Del Litto in *MP* 78 (1980): 198-200.

SUE

Atar Gull. (Classiques populaires reliés.) Paris: Garnier,
1981. Fr. 50.00.

Jean Cavalier ou les fanatiques des Cévènes. (Les Grands
Romans historiques.) 2 vols. Geneva: Favot, 1978-79. Fr.
29.00 each vol.

Le Juif errant. (Les Grandes OEuvres.) 3 vols. Paris: Hachette,
1980. Fr. 37.10 each vol.

   Facsimile of the 1883 edition, with drawings by A. Ferdin-
andus.

Tanguy Baum, Margrethe. *Der historische Roman im Frankreich
der Julimonarchie: eine Untersuchung anhand von Werken der
Autoren Frédéric Soulié und Eugène Sue*. (Bonner romanistische
Arbeiten, 9.) Franfurt/Main, Bern, Cirencester: Lang, 1981.
Pp. 197. Sw.Fr. 43.00.

Thiesse, Anne-Marie. "L'éducation sociale d'un romancier: le
cas d'Eugène Sue." *Actes de la Recherche en Sciences
Sociales* 32-33 (1980): 51-63.

See also Olivier-Martin ("French 1. General"); McLendon
("Courchamps"); Teissier ("Lamartine").

THEIS

Bied, Robert. "Un roman archéologique sous Louis XVIII."
LR 35 (1981): 59-89.

   Alexandre-Guillaume de Théis' *Le Voyage de Polyclète ou
Lettres romaines* (1821)--a picture of Roman life in the days
of Marius and Sulla, "époque de mutation culturelle dont
le choix permet à l'auteur, en reprenant un lieu commun
de la rhétorique des Anciens et des Modernes, d'opposer
le luxe et la perversion des jeunes générations à la
simplicité rustique et austère des Anciens." Bied treats
the work from many angles: Théis' sources, his use of the
epistolary form, style, the reception and influence of the
book, and others. He concludes that Théis is not yet writing
an historical novel in the Romantic manner but "l'expression stéréotypée de l'univers mental du bon notable
de la Monarchie Censitaire."

THIERRY

Récits des temps mérovingiens. (L'Arbre double.) Paris: Les
   Presses d'Aujourd'hui, 1981. Pp. 300. Fr. 52.00.

   Rev. by Jean Philippe Guinle in NRF 344 (Sept. 1, 1981):
   131-33.

TILLIER

Belle-Plante et Cornélius. Préface de Jules Renard. (Les
   Introuvables.) Plan-de-la-Tour: Editions d'Aujourd'hui,
   1977. Pp. 253. Fr. 65.00.

TRISTAN

Werner, Pascale. "Des voix irrégulières: Flora Tristan et
   George Sand, ambivalence d'une filiation." In Christine
   Dufrancatel et al., eds., *L'Histoire sans qualités*. (L'Espace
   critique.) Paris: Galilée, 1979. Pp. 224. Fr. 41.10.

See also Boime (1), Hellerstein ("French 1. General").

Review of book previously listed:

   MICHAUD, Stéphane, ed., *Lettres* (see RMB for 1980, p. 258),
   rev. by Arlette Michel in IL 33 (1981): 124.

VIGNY

Association des Amis d'Alfred de Vigny. Bulletin No. 11:
   1981-82. Pp. 80.

   Contents: Christiane Lefranc, "Vie de l'Association"
   (3-5); "Réponse de M. Léopold Sédar Senghor à M. Jacques
   Chirac, Maire de Paris" (5-8); Max Heilbronn, "Quatre lettres
   inédites de Vigny en provenance de Moscou" (9-13); Christiane
   Lefranc, "Une lettre inédite à Charles Fournier" (14-15);
   André Jarry, "Lettres et notes inédites de Vigny" (16-39);
   Simone Pirard et Marie-Christine Bécuwe-Pirard, "Généalogie:
   Vigny, ses parents, ses grands-parents et arrière-grands-
   parents" (40-41); Michel Cambien, "Les mémoires d'un poète:
   le sens d'une entreprise autobiographique; les systèmes
   conflictuels dans l'oeuvre d'A. de Vigny" (42-56); Jacques-
   Philippe Saint-Gérand, "Le coeur grammairien et l'esprit

sensible d'Alfred de Vigny: une lettre inédite de Napoléon
Landais à Vigny" (57-63); Alphonse Bouvet, "Sur le manuscrit de *Stello*" (64-69); Fernande Bassan, "Les représentations de *Chatterton* en dehors de la Comédie Française" (70-
79); Simone Pirard, "Renseignements pratiques" (80);
"Bibliographie" (80).

The bulk of this issue presents previously unpublished
manuscripts reflecting the circumstances--social, financial,
artistic--of Vigny's life from 1830 to 1850. The Pirards'
genealogical table and Bassan's study offer items of historical interest; Cambien also uses historical methods (dating
fragments of Vigny's texts) to consider whether or not his
Memoires belongs to the genre of autobiography.

Porter, Laurence M. "Body Language in Vigny's Theater." *NCFS*
7 (1979): 172-73.

Followed by comment by Robert T. Denommé and the author's
response, pp. 174-75.

Ratisbonne, Louis de, ed. *Journal d'un poète.* (Les Introuvables.)
Plan-de-la-Tour (Var): Editions d'Aujourd'hui, 1981. Pp.
324. Fr. 70.00.

Reprint of the edition of Paris, A. Lemerre, 1885.

Thoma, Heinz. "'Kunst als Ware': zum Verhältnis von politischer
Ökonomie und Literaturproduktion am Beispiel Balzacs und
Alfred de Vignys." *Romanistische Zeitschrift für Literatur-
geschichte/Cahiers d'Histoire des Littératures Romanes* 5
(1981): 39-60.

Résumé in French, pp. 61-62, of this study of Balzac's
*Correspondance, Lettre adressée aux écrivains du XIXe
siècle* and Vigny's *Journal d'un poète, Chatterton, De
Mademoiselle Sedaine et la propriété littéraire* in the
light of the theory of "art as merchandise."

Vivier, Robert. "'Fille de l'océan': a propos d'une apostrophe
ambiguë." Pp. 831-37 in Jean Marie d'Heur and Nicoletta
Cherubini, eds., *Etudes de philologie romane et d'histoire
littéraire offerts à Jules Horrent a l'occasion de son
soixantième anniversaire.* Tournai: Gedit, 1980. Pp. 853.

See also Baude and Münch, Cleaver, Foucart, Tison-Braun
("French 1. General"); Spaziani ("Desbordes-Valmore").

Reviews of books previously listed:

Les Pyrénees et l'Angleterre; Colloque Alfred de Vigny
(see *RMB* for 1979, p. 242), rev. by George R. Humphrey in
NCFS 9 (1981): 263–65; Relire "Les Destinées" de Vigny
(see *RMB* for 1980, pp. 263–64), rev. by Marija Petrovska
in *NCFS* 10 (1981–82): 156–58.

VILLEMAIN

Koppen, Erwin. "Abel-François Villemain." Pp. 70–81 in Wolf-
Dieter Lange, ed., *Französische Literatur des 19. Jahrhun-
derts, I: Romantik und Realismus*. Heidelberg: Quelle &
Meyer, 1979. Pp. 305.

VILLIERS DE L'ISLE ADAM

See Gendolla ("German 3. Jean Paul").

VOLNEY

Gaulmier, Jean, ed. *La Loi naturelle. Leçons d'histoire.*
(Classiques de la Politique.) Paris: Garnier, 1980. Pp.
164. Fr. 59.00.

WEISS

Lepin, Suzanne, ed. *Journal de Charles Weiss*. T. II. (Annales
littéraires de l'Université de Besançon, 257.) Paris: Les
Belles-Lettres, 1981. Pp. 425. Fr. 150.00 (bound).

For review of Vol. I, see *ELN* 12, Supp., 121.

GERMAN

(Compiled by John F. Fetzer, University of California,
Davis; Wulf Koepke, Texas A & M University; Winfried
Kudszus, University of California, Berkeley; Robert
Mollenauer, University of Texas, Austin; Jeffrey L.
Sammons, Yale University; Steven P. Scher, Dartmouth
College; Leonard Schulze, University of Texas, Austin)

1. BIBLIOGRAPHY

Allen, Robert R., ed. *The Eighteenth Century: A Current
Bibliography*. N.S. 1, for 1975. Philadelphia: American
Society for Eighteenth-Century Studies, 1978. Pp. 438.
$10.00 (Ln. $15.00).

Rev. by Alfred Anger in *Germanistik* 21 (1980): 9.

Bense, Max, and Elisabeth Walther. *Wörterbuch der Semiotik*.
Cologne: Kiepenheuer and Witsch, 1973. Pp. 137. DM 26.00.

Beyer, Horst. "Literarische Lexika und Einführungen aus dem
Bibliographischen Institut Leipzig." *Deutsch als Fremdsprache* 17 (1980): Sonderheft, 43-45.

Braak, Ivo. *Gattungsgeschichte deutschsprachiger Dichtung in
Stichworten. Teil 1a. Dramatik: Antike bis Romantik*. (Hirts
Stichwortbücher.) Kiel: Hirt, 1978. Pp. 269. DM 49.60.

Rev. by Walter Seifert in *Germanistik* 19 (1978): 386-37.

Braak, Ivo. *Gattungsgeschichte deutschsprachiger Dichtung in
Stichworten. Teil 2b. Lyrik: Vom Barock bis zur Romantik*.
Kiel: Hirt, 1979. Pp. 319. DM 24.80.

Rev. by Walter Seifert in *Germanistik* 20 (1979): 741-42.

*Deutsche Bücher: Referatenorgan germanistischer, belletristi-
scher und deutschkundlicher Neuerscheinungen* (vorm. *Het
Duitse Boek*) 11 (1981).

This review journal offers broad but apparently selective
coverage of recent critical works. Each quarter of Vol. 11
begins with an interview of a contemporary new writer.
Survey reviews in the concluding "Kurz Berichtet."

Deutsche Bücherei, ed. *Jahresverzeichnis der Hochschulschriften:
1978.* Jahrgang 94. Leipzig: VEB Verlag für Buch- und Biblio-
thekswesen, 1978.

Alphabetical listings by the university locations throughout the BRD and DDR; Verfasserregister; Verweisungen (name
changes); Sachregister; Inhaltsverzeichnis.

"Doctoral Dissertations 1980-81 [U.S. and Canada]." *Monatshefte*
73 (1981): 329-32.

Lists only dissertations completed in German departments
(not in comparative literature departments).

Franke, F.R. "Zeitschriftenschau." *Mitteilungen des deutschen
Germanisten-Verbandes* 27 (1980): 38-44.

Gebhardt, Walther. *Spezialbestände in deutschen Bibliotheken:
Bundesrepublik Deutschland einschliesslich Berlin (West).*
Im Auftrag der Deutschen Forschungsgemeinschaft. (Special
Collections in German Libraries.) Berlin, New York: de
Gruyter, 1977. Pp. xix+739. DM 148.00.

Rev. by Klaus Garber in *Germanistik* 19 (1978): 9.

*Germanistik: Internationales Referatenorgan mit biblio-
graphischen Hinweisen.* Jahrgang 22. 4 Hefte: Jan., April,
July, and Oct. Tübingen: Niemeyer, 1981.

For Romanticism see "II. Allgemeines"; "XVII. Allgemeines
zur Literaturwissenschaft"; "XVIII. Vergleichende Literaturwissenschaft"; "XXI. Deutsche Literaturgeschichte, Allgemeines"; "XXIX. Goethezeit (1770-1830)"; "XXX. Von der
Spätromantik bis zum Realismus (1830-1880)." Books but not
articles are reviewed. Articles and independent chapters
within *Sammelwerke* are cross-listed by epoch and author.
Heft 4 includes the annual index of authors and topics.

Hoffman, Charles W. "Survey of German Research Tool Needs."
Monatshefte 70 (1978): 239-53.

Peter, Klaus, ed. *Romantikforschung seit 1945.* (Neue wissen-
schaftliche Bibliothek 93.) Königstein: Verlagsgruppe
Athenäum/Hain/Scriptor/Hanstein, 1980. Pp. 380. DM 36.00.

Rev. by Gerhard Schulz in *Germanistik* 21 (1980): 138-39.

Walker, C.A.S. "The Romantic Era." *YWMLS* 42 (1980): 821-50.

Zeller, Otto. *Internationale Bibliographie der Rezensionen (IBR).* Vol. 11 (Pars 1 and 2, each in 3 vols.), 1981. Osnabruck: Felix Dietrich, 1981.

Review listings for each half-year are arranged in three volumes: A. Index of periodicals consulted; B. Classified subject index of book reviews; Index of book reviews, by reviewing authors.

Zeller, Otto. *Internationale Bibliographie der Zeitschriften- literatur aus allen Gebieten des Wissens (IBZ).* Vol. 17 (Pars 1 and 2, each in 6 vols.), 1981. Osnabruck: Felix Dietrich, 1981.

The article listings for each half-year are arranged in: A. Index of periodicals consulted (Periodica); B. Classified subject index (Index rerum); and C. Index of articles arranged by the names of authors (Index autorum).

2. GENERAL

Alperson, Philip. "Schopenhauer and Musical Revelation." *JAAC* 40 (1981): 155-66.

Bartel, Klaus J. *German Literary History 1775-1835: An Anno- tated Bibliography.* (German Studies in America, No. 22.) Berne, Frankfurt: H. Lang, 1976. Pp. 229. Sw.Fr. 41.00.

Rev. by Helmut Riege (negatively) in *Germanistik* 20 (1979): 301-02.

Becker-Cantarino, Bärbel. "Priesterin und Lichtbringerin: Zur Ideologie des weiblichen Charakters in der Frühromantik." Pp. 111-24 in Wolfgang Paulsen, ed., *Die Frau als Heldin und Autorin: Neue kritische Ansätze zur deutschen Literatur.* (Amherster Kolloquium zur deutschen Literatur, 10.) Bern, Munich: Francke, 1979. Pp. 291. Sw.Fr. 68.00.

Rev. by Peter Stein in *Germanistik* 21 (1980): 291-92.

Belgardt, Raimund. "Die konkrete Utopie: Zur Neuaneignung der literarischen Epochen Klassik und Romantik." *Jahrbuch Deutsch als Fremdsprache* 3 (1977): 168-92.

Belza, I. "Romantic Literature and Music." Pp. 503-41 in Sötér and Neupokoyeva, eds., *European Romanticism.* (see Sötér below).

Berger, Willy R. "Drei phantastische Erzählungen: Chamissos
Peter Schlemihl, E.T.A. Hoffmanns *Die Abenteuer der Silvester-
Nacht* und Gogols *Die Nase*." *Arcadia: Zeitschrift für verg-
leichende Literaturwissenschaft* 13 (1978): Sonderheft, 106-38.

Bolz, Norbert W. "Die Öffnung der Geschichte: Zur Subjekt-Objekt-Beziehung in der Frühromantik." Pp. 119-34 in Gisela
Dischner and Richard Faber, eds., *Romantische Utopie--
utopische Romantik*. Hildesheim: Gerstenberg, 1979. Pp. 358.
DM 28.00.

   Rev. by Jochen Hörisch in *Germanistik* 20 (1979): 801-02.

Bolz, Norbert W. "Über romantische Autorschaft." Pp. 44-52 in
Friedrich A. Kittler and Horst Turk, eds., *Urszenen: Literatur-
wissenschaft als Diskursanalyse und Diskurskritik*. Frankfurt:
Suhrkamp, 1977. Pp. 409. DM 34.00.

   Rev. by Manfred Frank in *Germanistik* 19 (1978): 333-34.

Brinker-Gabler, Gisela. "Wissenschaftlich-poetische Mittel-
alterrezeption in der Romantik." Pp. 80-97 in Ernst Ribbat,
ed., *Romantik: Ein literaturwissenschaftliches Studienbuch*.
(Athenäum Taschenbücher, 2149.) Königstein/Ts.: Athenäum
Verlag, 1979. Pp. 236. DM 19.80.

   See also Ribbat below.

Crimmann, Ralph P. *Literaturtheologie: Studien zum Vermittlungs-
problem zwischen Germanistik und Theologie, Dichtung und
Glaube, Literaturdidaktik und Religionspädagogik*. (Europäische Hochschulschriften, Reihe 1, Bd. 240.) Frankfurt,
Bern, and Las Vegas: Lang, 1978. Pp. 164. Sw.Fr. 37.00.

   Rev. by Peter Rusterholz in *Germanistik* 20 (1979): 368.
   The "Romantische Schule" is one of the five "historical"
schemes considered in the first part, which considers the
possibility of a relationship between literary scholarship
and theology.

Csapláros, István. "Der Widerhall der Polenbegeisterung
österreichischer und deutscher Dichter in der ungarischen
Literatur im Zeitalter der Romantik." *Germanica Wratislaw-
iensia* 34 (1978): 163-78.

Dessauer, Maria. *Märchen der Romantik: Mit zeitgenössischen
Illustrationen*. (insel taschenbuch 285.) Frankfurt: Insel
(Suhrkamp commission), 1977. Pp. 285. DM 18.00.

Goethe (*Das Märchen*), Tieck (*Eckbert*, *Elfen*), Novalis
(*Hyazinth und Rosenblütchen*, *Klingsohr*), Eichendorff (*Zauberei*,
Libertas), Brentano (*Klopfstock*, *Rosenblättchen*), Fouqué
(*Undine*), Arnim (*Melück*, *Maria Blainville*, *Majoratsherren*),
Chamisso (*Schlemihl*), Hoffmann (*Königsbraut*, *Goldner Topf*),
Hauff (*Kalif Storch*, *Zwerg Nase*, *Affe als Mensch*), Mörike
(*Schatz*, *Bauer und sein Sohn*).

Diefendorf, Jeffrey M. *Businessmen and Politics in the Rhine-
land, 1789-1834*. Princeton University Press, 1980. Pp. xiv+
400. $22.50.

Rev. by Eda Sagarra in *TLS*, March 6, 1981, p. 262.

Dischner, Gisela. "Gedanken-Spiele zum orphischen Narzißmus."
Pp. 270-300 in Dischner and Richard Faber, eds., *Romantische
Utopie--utopische Romantik*. Hildesheim: Gerstenberg, 1979.
Pp. 358. DM 28.00.

Rev. by Jochen Hörisch in *Germanistik* 20 (1979): 801-02.

Dischner, Gisela, and Richard Faber, eds., *Romantische Utopie--
utopische Romantik*. Hildesheim: Gerstenberg, 1979. Pp. 358.
DM 28.00.

Rev. by Jochen Hörisch in *Germanistik* 20 (1979): 801-02.

Elistratova, A. "Epistolary Prose in the Romantic Period."
Pp. 347-87 in Sötér and Neupokoyeva, eds., *European Romanticism*. (See Sötér below.)

Elistratova, A. "Romantic Writers and the Classical Literary
Heritage." Pp. 91-126 in Sötér and Neupokoyeva, eds.,
European Romanticism. (See Sötér below.)

Faber, Karl-Georg. *Deutsche Geschichte im 19 Jahrhundert:
Restauration und Revolution, von 1815 bis 1851*. Wiesbaden:
Akademische Verlagsgesellschaft Athenaion, 1979. Pp. 319.

Rev. by Paul R. Sweet in *AHR* 86 (1981): 156.

Faber, Richard. "Frühromantik, Surrealismus und Studenten-
revolte oder die Frage nach dem Anarchismus." Pp. 336-58
in Gisela Dischner and Faber, eds., *Romantische Utopie--
utopische Romantik*. Hildesheim: Gerstenberg, 1979. Pp. 358.
DM 28.00.

Rev. by Jochen Hörisch in *Germanistik* 20 (1979): 801-02.

Feilchenfeldt, Konrad. "Öffentlichkeit und Chiffrensprache in
  Briefen der späteren Romantik" [incl. discussion]. Pp. 125-
  54, 268-69 in Wolfgang Frühwald, ed., *Probleme der Brief-*
  Edition: Kolloquium der deutschen Forschungsgemeinschaft.
  Schloß Tutzing am Starnberger See 8-11 September 1975.
  (Deutsche Forschungsgemeinschaft. Kommission für germanis-
  tische Forschung, Mitteilung 2.) Boppard: Boldt, 1977. Pp.
  283. DM 20.00.

Finger, Ellis. "Detectives and Artists: Toward a Typology of
  the German Romantic Novel." *Neophil* 65 (1981): 424-35.

   The author sees a "recurring pattern," in German Romantic
   fiction, of "the unification of detective and artist in a
   single figure."

Firchow, Peter E. "Germany and Germanic Mythology in *Howards*
  End." *CL* 33 (1981): 50-68.

   Cites Novalis, the Schlegels, et al.

Frank, Manfred. "Die Dichtung als neue Mythologie: Motive und
  Konsequenzen einer frühromantischen Idee." *RG* 9 (1979): 122-
  40.

Frank, Manfred. *Das kalte Herz und andere Texte der Romantik:*
  Mit einem Essay von Manfred Frank ["Steinherz und Geldseele:
  Ein Symbol im Kontext"]. (insel taschenbuch 330.) Frankfurt:
  Insel (Suhrkamp commission), 1978. Pp. 367. DM 9.00.

   See Frank below.
   Andersen (*Die Schneekönigin*), Arnim (*Des ersten Bergmanns*
   ewige Jugend), Hauff (*Das kalte Herz*), Hawthorne (*Ethan*
   Brand), E.T.A. Hoffmann (*Die Bergwerke von Falun*; *Der Sand-*
   mann), G.H. Schubert (*Der Bergmann von Falun*), Tieck (*Der*
   Runenberg), R. Wagner (*Die Bergwerke von Falun*), and con-
   cluded by a survey of the motif in Western literature.

Frank, Manfred. "Das Motiv des 'kalten Herzens' in der roman-
  tisch-symbolistischen Dichtung." *Euphorion* 71 (1977): 383-
  405.

   See also Frank immediately above.

Freund, Winfried. *Die deutsche Kriminalnovelle von Schiller*
  bis Hauptmann: Einzelanalysen unter sozialgeschichtlichen
  und didaktischen Aspekten. (Wort, Werk, Gestalt.) Paderborn:
  Schöningh, 1975. Pp. 115. DM 6.80.

Rev. by Rainer F. Schönhaar in *Germanistik* 19 (1978): 751.
Discusses, among others, Schiller, Kleist, Brentano, E.T.A.
Hoffmann.

Garber, Frederick. "Nature and the Romantic Mind: Egotism,
Empathy, Irony." *CL* 29 (1977): 289-99.

Godet, Alain. "Hexenglaube, Rationalität und Aufklärung:
Joseph Glanvill und Johann Moriz Schwager." *DVLG* 52 (1978):
581-603.

Göres, Jörn, ed. *Deutsche Schriftsteller im Porträt. Bd. 3:
Sturm und Drang, Klassik, Romantik.* (Beck'sche schwarze Reihe
214.) Munich: Beck, 1980. Pp. 286. DM 24.00.

Rev. by Ludwig Uhlig in *Germanistik* 21 (1980): 135.

Greiner, Bernhard. *Welttheater als Montage: Wirklichkeits-
darstellung und Leserbezug in romantischer und moderner
Literatur.* (medium literatur 9.) Heidelberg: Quelle & Meyer,
1977. Pp. 160. DM 19.80.

Rev. by Ansgar Hillach in *Germanistik* 19 (1978): 359.
Refers to Bonaventura, Jean Paul, Novalis, and Wackenroder.

Haas, Gerhard. "Struktur und funktion der phantastischen literatur." *WW* 28 (1978): 340-56.

Hany, Arthur. *Die Dichter und ihre Heimat. Studien zum
Heimatverhalten deutsch-sprachiger Autoren im 18., 19. und
20. Jahrhundert.* Bern and Munchen: Francke Verlag, 1978.
Pp. 108. Sw.Fr. 16.80.

Rev. by Steffen Steffensen in *JEGP* 80 (1981): 113-15.
Not seen.

Heinrich, Gerda. "Autonomie der Liebe? Frühromantische
Liebesauffassungen." *NDL* 28 (1980): 83-110.

Heller, Agnes. *Die Seele und das Leben: Studien zum frühen
Lukács.* (suhrkamp taschenbuch wissenschaft, 80.) Frankfurt:
Suhrkamp, 1977. Pp. 326. DM 12.00.

Rev. by David H. Miles in *Germanistik* 19 (1978): 578-79.
(See also *ELN* 16, Supp., 134.)

Hermand, Jost, and Francis G. Gentry. "Neue Romantik? West-
Östliches zum Thema 'Mittelalter.'" *Basis: Jahrbuch für
deutsche Gegenwartsliteratur* 9 (1979): 122-48, 264-66.

Herzfelde, Wieland. "Über romantischen Realismus." *Sinn und Form* 31 (1979): 1065-70.

Hillach, Ansgar. "Die Einholung des Traums in das Leben mittels der Kunst: Über romantische und avantgardistische Esoterik anlaßlich Albert Béguins 'Traumwelt und Romantik.'" *LJGG* 18 (1977): 336-44.

Hopf, Helmuth. "Einige Gedanken zur romantischen Musikauffasung." Pp. 406-14 in Hopf and Jürgen Janning, eds., *Freundschaftliche Begegnungen eines Magister ludi. Festschrift für Eberhard Ter-Nedden zum 70. Geb. am 26. Sept. 1978*. Münster: Pädagogische Hochschule Westfalen-Lippe, 1978. Pp. 487.

Itô, Kazuhiko. "Das Absolute und der Geist der Sehnsucht: Fichte, Novalis und Hölderlin" [Jap.]. *Keisei* 38 (1974): 1-9.

Jost, François. *Introduction to Comparative Literature*. Indianapolis: Bobbs-Merrill, 1974. Pp. xiii+349. $9.95.

    Rev. by Hans Gerd Rötzer in *Germanistik* 20 (1979): 114. Discusses Romanticism as a supra-national concept.

Kambas, Chryssoula. "Walter Benjamins Verarbeitung der deutschen Frühromantik." Pp. 187-221 in Gisela Dischner and Richard Faber, eds., *Romantische Utopie--utopische Romantik*. Hildesheim: Gerstenberg, 1979. Pp. 358. DM 28.00.

    Rev. by Jochen Hörisch in *Germanistik* 20 (1979): 801-02.

Köpke, Wulf. "Die emanzipierte Frau in der Goethezeit und ihre Darstellung in der Literatur." Pp. 96-110 in Wolfgang Paulsen, ed., *Die Frau als Heldin und Autorin: Neue kritische Ansätze zur deutschen Literatur*. (Amherster Kolloquium zur deutschen Literatur, 10.) Bern and München: Francke, 1979. Pp. 291. Sw.Fr. 68.00.

    Rev. by Peter Stein in *Germanistik* 21 (1980): 291-92.

Kortländer, Bernd. "Die Landschaft in der Literatur des ausgehenden 18. und beginnenden 19. Jahrhunderts." Pp. 36-44, 52-53 in Alfred Hartlieb and Wallthor and Heinz Quirin, eds., *"Landschaft" als interdisziplinäres Forschungsproblem: Vorträge und Diskussionen des Kolloquiums am 7./8. Nov. 1975 in Münster*. (Veröffentlichungen des Provinzialinstituts für westfälische Landes- und Volksforschung des Landesverbandes Westfalen-Lippe, Reihe 1, H. 21.) Münster: Aschendorff, 1977. Pp. 97. DM 24.00.

Krogoll, Johannes. "Religion und Staat im romantischen Drama."
Vestigia: Jahrbuch des Deutschen Bibel-Archivs Hamburg 1
(1979): 59-94.

Kuczynski, Jürgen. *Studien zu einer Geschichte der Gesellschafts-
wissenschaften. Bd. 4: Zum Briefwechsel bürgerlicher Wissen-
schaftler.* Berlin: Akademie-Verlag, 1976. M 16.00.

Rev. by Uwe Schweikert in *Germanistik* 20 (1979): 15.
Correspondences of concern: Goethe/Carlyle, J. Grimm/
Dahlmann, A.v. Humboldt/Varnhagen.

Lajarrige, Jean. "La Jeune Pologne et la tradition romantique."
RLC 50 (1976): 153-68.

Lefevere, Andre. "German Translation Theory: Legacy and
Relevance." *JES* 11 (1981): 9-17.

Discusses Goethe and the Schlegels.

Lindner, Hermann. *Fabeln der Neuzeit: England, Frankreich,
Deutschland. Ein Lese- und Arbeitsbuch.* (Kritische Information, 58.) München: Fink, 1978. Pp. 422. DM 19.80.

Rev. by Theo Elm in *Germanistik* 20 (1979): 115.

Lützeler, Paul Michael. "'Kosmopoliten der europäischen Kultur':
Romantiker über Europa." Pp. 213-36 in Ernst Ribbat, ed.,
Romantik: Ein literaturwissenschaftliches Studienbuch.
(Athenäum Taschenbücher, 2149.) Königstein/Ts.: Athenäum,
1979. Pp. 236. DM 19.80.

See also Ribbat below.

Maehder, Jürgen. "Die Poetisierung der Klangfarben in Dichtung
und Musik der deutschen Romantik." *Aurora* 38 (1978): 9-31.

Malsch, Wilfried. "Klassizismus, Klassik und Romantik der
Goethezeit." Pp. 381-408 in Karl Otto Conrady, ed., *Deutsche
Literatur zur Zeit der Klassik.* Stuttgart: Reclam, 1977.
Pp. 460. DM 34.80. Collection listed previously (see *ELN*
17, Supp., 173).

Rev. by Ludwig Uhlig in *Germanistik* 19 (1978): 794-95.

Mann, Otto. *Die klassische und die romantische Auffassung
von dem Wesen und der Form der Dichtung.* (Beiträge zur
neueren Literaturgeschichte, F. 3, Bd. 40.) Heidelberg:
Winter, 1978. Pp. 82. DM 24.00.

Rev. by Joachim Müller in *Germanistik* 20 (1979): 92.
Kant, Hegel, Schelling, Fr. Schlegel, Novalis.

Meixner, Horst. "Figuralismus und Rollenspiel: Versuch über
den Gegenwartsroman zwischen Romantik und Realismus." Pp.
192-212 in Ernst Ribbat, ed., *Romantik: Ein literaturwissenschaftliches Studienbuch.* (Athenäum Taschenbucher, 2149.)
Königstein/Ts.: Athenäum Verlag, 1979. Pp. 236. DM 19.80.

See also Ribbat below.

Menhennet, Alan. *The Romantic Movement.* (Literary History of
Germany, part 6.) London: Croom Helm; Totowa, N.J.: Barnes
& Noble, 1981. Pp. 276. £15.95.

Rev. by Michael Hofmann in *TLS*, Dec. 18, 1981, p. 1474,
as "detailed and wide-ranging, fair-minded and not impersonal."
Focuses on German Romanticism.

Metzner, Joachim. *Persönlichkeitsstörung und Weltuntergang:
Das Verhältnis von Wahnbildung und literarischer Imagination.*
(Studien zur deutschen Literatur, Bd. 50.) Tübingen: Nie-
meyer, 1976. Pp. ix+286. DM 66.00.

Rev. by Ansgar Hillach in *Germanistik* 19 (1978): 352.
Analyzes Chamisso and Novalis in support of Levi-Strauss'
theory of myth.

Meyer-Krentler, Eckhardt. "Romantik als Verirrung: Zur Abwehr
romantischen Lebensgefühls in der 'bürgerlichen' Literatur
um 1800." Pp. 131-52 in Gerd Michels, ed., *Festschrift für
Friedrich Kienecker zum 60. Geburtstag: Gewidmet von seinen
Kollegen, Schülern und Mitarbeiten.* Heidelberg: Groos, 1980.
Pp. 295. DM 88.00

Miller, Norbert. "Das Erbe der Zauberflöte: Zur Vorgeschichte
des romantischen Singspiels." Pp. 99-121 in Günter Schnitzler,
ed., *Dichtung und Musik: Kaleidoskop ihrer Beziehungen.*
Stuttgart: Klett-Cotta, 1979. Pp. 308. DM 28.00.

Mounier, Jacques. *La Fortune des écrits de Jean-Jacques
Rousseau dans les pays de langue allemande de 1782 à 1813.*
(Publications de la Sorbonne, série "NS Recherches, Littéra-
tures," 38.) Paris: P.U.F., 1980. Pp. 342. Fr. 150.00.

Rev. by Lilian R. Furst in *CL* 33 (1981): 387-89.

Naumann, Dietrich. *Literaturtheorie und Geschichtsphilosophie.*
T. 1: Aufklärung, Romantik, Idealismus. (Sammlung Metzler,
Bd. 184.) Stuttgart: Metzler, 1979. Pp. xiii+147. DM 14.80.

   Rev. by Ludwig Uhlig in *Germanistik* 20 (1979): 702.

Nemoianu, Virgil. *Micro-harmony: The Growth and Uses of the*
Idyllic Model in Literature. (European University Papers,
Ser. 18, Vol 11.) Bern, Frankfurt, Las Vegas: Lang, 1977.
Pp. 152. Sw.Fr. 27.00.

   Rev. by Renate Böschenstein in *Germanistik* 21 (1980):
95-96.
   E.T.A. Hoffmann, Jean Paul, Goethe.

Neupokoyeva, I. "General Features of European Romanticism and
the Originality of Its Natural Paths." Pp. 11-49 in Sötér
and Neupokoyeva, eds., *European Romanticism.* (See Sötér
below.)

Pikulik, Lothar. *Romantik als Ungenügen an der Normalität:*
Am Beispiel Tiecks, Hoffmanns, Eichendorffs. Frankfurt:
Suhrkamp, 1979. Pp. 550. DM 38.00.

   Rev. by Waltraud Wiethölter in *Germanistik* 20 (1979): 473.

Pongs, Hermann. *Das Bild in der Dichtung. Bd. 4: Symbolik der*
Einfachen Formen. Marburg: Elwert, 1973. Pp. 418. DM 74.00.

   Rev. by Gonthier-Louis Fink in *Germanistik* 20 (1979):
715.
   Brentano, the Grimms, Hebel, Kleist.

Raible, Wolfgang. "Literatur und Natur: Beobachtungen zur
literarischen Landschaft." *Poetica* 11 (1979): 105-23.

Rasch, Wolfdietrich. "Zum Verhältnis der Romantik zur Auf-
klarung." Pp. 7-21 in Ernst Ribbat, ed., *Romantik: Ein*
literaturwissenschaftliches Studienbuch. (Athenäum Taschenbücher, 2149.) Königstein/Ts.: Athenäum, 1979. Pp. 236.
DM 19.80.

   See also Ribbat below.

Reed, Terence James. *The Classical Centre: Goethe and Weimar*
(1775-1832). (The Literary History of Germany, 5.) London:
Croom Helm; New York: Barnes & Noble, 1980. Pp. 271. £14.95.

   Rev. by Walter Dietze in *Germanistik* 21 (1980): 143-44;
by Robert Heitner in *GQ* 54 (1981): 95-96; by Christoph E.

Schweitzer in *JEGP* 80 (1981): 93-94.
Stresses Hölderlin, touches on Kleist and Jean Paul.

Rehm, Walter. "Der Todesgedanke in der deutschen Dichtung vom
Mittelalter bis zur Romantik." Pp. 177-81 in Hans Helmut
Jansen, ed., *Der Tod in Dichtung, Philosophie und Kunst.*
Mit 100 Abbildungen und 1 Tabelle. Darmstadt: Steinkopff,
1978. Pp. 254. DM 24.80.

  Rev. by Gerhard Kurz in *Germanistik* 20 (1979): 399.

Remak, Henry. "Exoticism in Romanticism." *CLS* 15 (1978): 53-65.

Remak, Henry H.H. "Functional Aspects of Exoticism in West
European Romanticism." Pp. 181-82 in Robert D. Eagleson,
ed., *Language and Literature in the Formation of National
and Cultural Communities.* Proceedings of the XIII Congress
of the Fédération Internationale des Langues et Littératures
Modernes and the XVII Congress of the Australasian Univer-
sities Language and Literature Association held at Sydney
Univ., 25 to 29 Aug. 1975. Sydney: Australasian University
Language and Literature Association, 1976. Pp. 274.

Ribbat, Ernst, ed. with intro. *Romantik: Ein literaturwissenschaftliches Studienbuch.* (Athenäum Taschenbücher, 2149.)
Königstein/Ts.: Athenäum, 1979. Pp. 236. DM 19.80.

  Listed without review in *RMB* for 1979, p. 256.
  Rev. by Heinz Hartl in *DLZ* 102, Nr. 7/8 (1981): 595-97;
by Wulf Koepke in *GQ* 54 (1981): 493-94.
  A collection of eleven studies on various aspects of
German Romanticism with a short introduction by the editor.
Most contributions deal with specific works of an individual
author, e.g., Novalis' *Heinrich von Ofterdingen* (R. Leroy
and E. Pastor), some poems by Clemens Brentano (K. Eibl),
Achim v. Arnim's *Isabella von Ägypten* (L. Völker), Eichendorff's stories (E. Schwarz); others are concerned with
more general aspects, like the relationship of Enlightenment and Romanticism (W. Rasch), the reception of the
Middle Ages by Romanticism (G. Brinker-Gabler), E.T.A.
Hoffmann's sense of history (H. Kraft), or the concept of
Europa of the Romanticists (P.M. Lützeler). The volume is
primarily designed for students. It provides some model
analyses and suggests a number of methodological and
historical approaches; it is not a reference book nor does
it attempt to synthesize the essence of "Romanticism."
Some contributions have the style of an introduction to
the subject, while others presuppose a high degree of familiarity with the author and previous research. The volume

is more convincing in its individual parts than as a whole. The contributions by Rasch, Ribbat (on Tieck), Brinker-Gabler, Meixner (on the novel between Romanticism and Realism), and Lützeler are the most significant ones. Egon Schwarz's Eichendorff essay is a reprint of previously published material. (W.K.)

Richter, Lutz. *Johann Gottfried Herder im Spiegel seiner Zeitgenossen: Briefe und Selbstzeugnisse.* Göttingen, Berlin: Vandenhoeck and Ruprecht and Union Verlag, 1978. Pp. 367. DM 34.00; M 15.00.

Rev. by Ludwig Uhlig in *Germanistik* 20 (1979): 485-86. Discusses Jean Paul.

Sammons, Jeffrey L. *Literary Sociology and Practical Criticism--An Inquiry.* Indiana University Press, 1977. Pp. 235.

Rev. by Kurt Binneberg in *Arcadia* 14 (1979): 305-08.

Saprykina, E. "Some Distinctive Features of the Romantic Theory of Drama." Pp. 183-207 in Sötér and Neupokoyeva, eds., *European Romanticism.* (See Sötér below.)

Schanze, Helmut. "'Es waren schöne glänzende Zeiten ...': Zur Genese des 'romantischen' Mittelalter-Bildes." Pp. 760-71 in Rudolf Schützeichel and Ulrich Fellmann, eds., *Studien zur deutschen Literatur des Mittelalters.* Mit 45 Abbildungen. Bonn: Bouvier, 1979. Pp. 810. DM 160.00.

Schlaffer, Hannelore. "Frauen als Einlösung der romantischen Kunsttheorie." *JDSG* 21 (1977): 274-96.

Schmidt-Dengler, Wendelin. *Genius: Zur Wirkungsgeschichte antiker Mythologeme in der Goethezeit.* München: Beck, 1978. Pp. 323. DM 48.00.

Rev. by Jochen Schmidt in *Germanistik* 21 (1980): 139-40. Especially Hölderlin.

Schulz, Gerhard, ed. with intro. *Jens Baggesen, ed.: Der Karfunkel oder Klingklingel-Almanach. Ein Taschenbuch für vollendete Romantiker und angehende Mystiker. Auf das Jahr der Gnade 1810. Faksimiledruck nach der Ausgabe von 1809.* (Seltene Texte aus der deutschen Romantik, Bd. 4.) Bern, Frankfurt, Las Vegas: Lang, 1978. Pp. 47 (text)+xii+186. Sw.Fr. 75.00.

Rev. by Leif Ludwig Albertsen in *Germanistik* 20 (1979):
475-76 ("Der Almanach stellt selber ein abstruses und ab-
surdes Sprachspiel dar, das die nihilistischen Konsequenzen
des romantischen Philosophiesalats wonnevoll (und frivol)
auskostet").

Segeberg, Harro. "Deutsche Literatur und Französische Revolu-
tion: Zum Verhältnis von Weimarer Klassik, Frühromantik und
Spätaufklärung." Pp. 243-66 in Karl Otto Conrady, ed.,
Deutsche Literatur zur Zeit der Klassik. Stuttgart: Reclam,
1977. Pp. 460. DM 34.80. Collection listed previously (see
ELN 17, Supp., 173).

Rev. by Ludwig Uhlig in *Germanistik* 19 (1978): 794-95.

Sötér, I. "Romanticism: Pre-history and Periodization." Pp.
51-89 in Sötér and Neupokoyeva, eds., *European Romanticism.*
(See Sötér below.)

Sötér, I., and Neupokoyeva, eds., and É. Rona, trans. *European
Romanticism.* Budapest: Adadémiai Kiadó, 1977. Pp. 540. DM
78.20.

Rev. by Ingeborg L. Carlson in *Germanistik* 20 (1979): 113-
14.

Swales, Martin. *The German Novelle.* Princeton University Press,
1977. Pp. xi+229. $19.00.

Rev. by Wolfgang Monath in *Germanistik* 20 (1979): 835-36.
Goethe (*Novelle*), Chamisso (*Schlemihl*).

Sziklay, L. "The 'Popular Trend' in the Romantic Literature
of Some Central-European Nations." Pp. 295-345 in Sötér
and Neupokoyeva, eds., *European Romanticism.* (See Sötér
above.)

Tiedemann, Rüdiger von. *Fabels Reich: Zur Tradition und zum
Programm romantischer Dichtungstheorie.* (Komparatistische
Studien, Bd. 8.) Berlin, New York: de Gruyter, 1978. Pp.
253. DM 92.00.

Rev. by Herbert Anton in *Germanistik* 19 (1978): 701.

Timm, Hermann. *Die heilige Revolution: Das religiöse Totalitäts-
konzept der Frühromantik. Schleiermacher-Novalis-Friedrich
Schlegel.* Frankfurt: Syndikat (Autoren- und Verlagsgesellschaft), 1978. Pp. 179. DM 24.00.

See also *RMB* for 1979, p. 259.
Rev. by Waltraud Wiethölter in *Germanistik* 20 (1979): 165.

Träger, Claus. "Des Lumières à 1830: héritage et innovation dans le romantisme allemand." *Romantisme* 28-29 (1980): 87-102.

Trautwein, Wolfgang. *Erlesene Angst--Schauerliteratur im 18. und 19. Jahrhundert: Systematischer Aufriß. Untersuchungen zu Bürger, Maturin, Hoffmann, Poe, und Maupassant.* (Literatur als Kunst.) Munich, Vienna: Hanser, 1980. Pp. 272. DM 36.00.

　　Rev. by Gunter Grimm in *Germanistik* 21 (1980): 301-02. Bürger (*Der wilde Jäger*), Hoffmann (*Der unheimliche Gast*).

Völker, Klaus. *Künstliche Menschen: Dichtungen und Dokumente über Golems, Homunculi, Androiden und liebende Statuen.* München: Dt. Taschenbuch Verlag, 1976. Pp. 401. DM 11.80.

Wawrzyn, Lienhard. *99 romantische Gedichte: Liebesleid und Natursehnsucht. Die Antiträume des Bürgers.* Mit einem Essay und Kurzbiographien. (Wagenbachs Taschenbücherei 37.) Berlin: Wagenbach, 1978. Pp. 191. DM 9.50.

Wilhem, Daniel. *Les Romantiques allemands.* Paris: Editions du Seuil, 1980. Pp. 190.

　　Rev. by Lou Bruder in *QL* 339 (Jan. 1-15, 1981): 13-14 ("... voici le romantisme allemand dédramatisé, quadrillé, apprivoisi.... Tout le Démonisme romantique se trouve ainsi évacué.").

Wilson, James D. "The Romantic Love Object: The Woman as Narcissistic Projection." *CLS* 15 (1978): 388-402.

Wuthenow, Ralph-Rainer. *Muse, Maske, Meduse: Europäischer Ästhetizismus.* (edition suhrkamp, 897.) Frankfurt: Suhrkamp, 1978. Pp. 367. DM 12.00.

　　Rev. by Jens Malte Fischer in *Germanistik* 19 (1978): 1084. German Romanticism is the source of a European aestheticism that binds such authors as Nietzsche, George, Hofmannsthal, and even H. Mann, but also Flaubert and Baudelaire, etc.

Ziolkowski, Theodore. *The Classical German Elegy.* Princeton University Press, 1980. Pp. xiv+344. $20.00.

　　Rev. by John M. Ellis in *MLQ* 42 (1981): 306-09 as "wildly implausible," "weak," "narrow"; by Klaus Weissenberger in *JEGP* 80 (1981): 390-92.

Ziolkowski, Theodore. *Disenchanted Images: A Literary Iconology*.
Princeton University Press, 1977. Pp. ix+273. $16.00.

Rev. by Walter Veit in *Germanistik* 20 (1979): 393-94.

See also Brown, Moran, Warner ("General 2. Environment");
Bubner, Hennebo, Kuhn, Rasch, Weinberg ("German 3. Goethe");
Sammons ("German 3. Heine"); Behler, Heller ("German 3.
Nietzsche").

Reviews of books previously listed:

BÉGUIN, Albert, *Traumwelt und Romantik: Versuch über die
romantische Seele in Deutschland und in der Dichtung Frank-
reichs* (see *ELN* 12, Supp., 122-23), rev. by Raymond Immerwahr
in *CG* 3/4 (1975): 353-56; BROWN, Marshall, *The Shape of
German Romanticism* (see *RMB* for 1980, pp. 271-72), rev. by
Hans Eichner in *Seminar* 16 (1980): 261-62; by Paul Michael
Lützeler in *JEGP* 80 (1981): 94-95; DOEBELE-FLÜGEL, Verena,
*Die Lerche: Motivgeschichtliche Untersuchung zur deutschen
Literatur, insbesondere zur deutschen Lyrik* (see *ELN* 17,
Supp., 173), rev. by Siegfried Sudhof in *Germanistik* 19
(1978): 716-17; HUGHES, Glyn Tegai, *Romantic German Litera-
ture* (see *RMB* for 1980, p. 272), rev. by Hans Eichner in
Germanistik 21 (1980): 136; by Richard Littlejohn in *JES*
(Sept. 1981): 225-26; KOZIELEK, Gerard, ed., *Mittelalter-
rezeption: Texte zur Aufnahme altdeutscher Literatur in der
Romantik* (see *ELN* 17, Supp., and *RMB* for 1979, p. 253),
rev. by Hartmut Beckers in *Germanistik* 19 (1978): 577;
MANNHEIM, Ralph, trans., *Tales for Young and Old* (see *RMB*
for 1979, p. 279), rev. by James R. Dowin in *AF* 98 (1980):
356-58; SCHUMACHER, Hans, *Narziß an der Quelle: Das romantische Kunstmärchen* (see *ELN* 17, Supp., 180), rev. by Elisa-
betta Bolla in *Germanistik* 21 (1980): 340-41; by Gerhard
Kluge in *LMFA* 13 (1980): 165-67; VAUGHAN, William, *German
Romantic Painting* (see *RMB* for 1980, p. 272), rev. by A.B.
Bird in *JES* 11 (1981): 298-301; by Jon Whitely in *Art History*
4 (1981): 228-31; VON EINEM, Herbert, *Deutsche Malerei des
Klassizismus und der Romantik, 1760 bis 1840* (see *RMB* for
1980, p. 272), rev. by Thomas Pelzel in *ArtB* 63 (1981):
688-90.

3. STUDIES OF AUTHORS

ARNIM, ACHIM VON

Huber, Hans Dieter. *Historische Romane in der ersten Hälfte des 19. Jahrhunderts: Studie zu Material und 'schöpferischem Akt' ausgewählter Romane von A.v. Arnim bis A. Stifter.* (Münchner Germanistische Beiträge, Bd. 24, and Münchner Universitätsschriften.) Munich: Fink, 1978. Pp. 148. DM 24.00.

Rev. by Charlotte Jolles in *Germanistik* 20 (1979): 472. Arnim's *Die Kronenwächter*.

Völker, Ludwig. "Naturpoesie, Phantasie und Phantastik: Über Achim von Arnims Erzählung *Isabella von Ägypten*." Pp. 114-37 in Ernst Ribbat, ed., *Romantik: Ein literaturwissenschaftliches Studienbuch.* (Athenäum Taschenbücher, 2149.) Königstein/Ts.: Athenäum, 1979. Pp. 236. DM 19.80.

Listed without a review in *RMB* for 1979, p. 262. See also Ribbat ("German 2. General").

See also Dessauer, Frank ("German 2. General"); Frühwald, Riley ("Brentano"); Boie, Neubauer, Seiverth ("Hoffmann").

Reviews of books previously listed:

RILEY, Helene M. Kastinger, *Achim von Arnim in Selbstzeugnissen und Bilddokumenten* (see *RMB* for 1979, pp. 261-62), rev. by Bernhard Gajek in *Germanistik* 20 (1979): 803; RILEY, Helene M. Kastinger, *Ludwig Achim von Arnims Jugend- und Reisejahre* (see *ELN* 17, Supp., 184-85), rev. by Heinz Härtl in *DLZ* 101, no. 5 (1980): 382-83.

ARNIM, BETTINA VON

See Nahrebecky ("Hoffmann").

BEETHOVEN

See Mühlher ("Hoffmann").

BÖRNE

Morita, Shigeru. "Börnes Anschauungen und seine Stellung in
    der Literaturgeschichte" (Japanese with German summary).
    DB 58 (1977): 16-25.

See also Schoeps ("Heine").

BONAVENTURA

Hoffmeister, Gerhart. "Bonaventura: *Nachtwachen* (1804/05)."
    Pp. 194-212 in *Romane und Erzählungen der deutschen Romantik:
    Neue Interpretationen*, ed. Paul Michael Lützeler. Stuttgart:
    Reclam, 1981.

    Reviews the history of the authorship problem and offers
    interpretive perspectives with excellent judgment and ad-
    mirable thoroughness in such a brief format. The best compact
    introduction to the *Nachtwachen* available to date. (J.L.S.)

Hunter-Lougheed, Rosemarie. "E.T.A. Hoffmann: Der Verfasser
    der 'Nachtwachen'?" *Akten des VI. Internationalen Germa-
    nisten-Kongresses, Basel, 1980. JIG*, Series A, Vol. 8,4
    (1980): 446-52.

    Adduces evidence from Hoffmann's biography and his diary
    from his quasi-exile in Plozk to support the argument that
    he might be the author. (J.L.S.)

Hunter-Lougheed, Rosemarie. "Der Mann in Kants Schuhen und
    Lessings Perücke: Eine unbekannte Quelle zu den 'Nacht-
    wachen von Bonaventura.'" *Aurora* 40 (1980): 147-51.

    Convincingly traces the figure who wears Kant's shoes
    along with other memorabilia of the great to an amusing,
    evidently real-life anecdote in the *Zeitung für die elegante
    Welt*. (J.L.S.)

See also Greiner ("German 2. General").

BRECHT

See Corkhill ("Kleist"); Donnenberg ("Schiller").

Behrens, Jürgen, et al., eds. *Clemens Brentano: Sämtliche Werke und Briefe*. Vol. 26: *Das bittere Leiden unsers Herrn Jesu Christi*, ed. Bernhard Gajek. Stuttgart: Kohlhammer, 1980. Pp. 466. DM 188.00.

This volume of the handsome and erudite historical-critical edition offers the reader the opportunity to peruse in one location Brentano's biographical synopsis of the stigmatic's life, his rendition of her visions of the Last Supper and Christ's Passion, together with some additional religious fragments (on Joseph of Arimathea and Longinus, for instance). A comprehensive index (with meaningful cross-references) enables the user to locate with ease people and places mentioned in the text. One looks forward with great anticipation to volume 27, which will contain a commentary together with the critical apparatus for this material previously accessible in a variety of sources and, because of its often cryptic substance, still in need of scholarly exegesis. (J.F.F.)

Behrens, Jürgen, et al., eds. *Clemens Brentano: Sämtliche Werke und Briefe*. Vol. 28, Part I: *Anna Katharina Emmerick-Biographie*, ed. Jürg Mathes. Stuttgart: Kohlhammer, 1981. Pp. 581. DM 188.00.

A highly illuminating volume which encompasses not only Brentano's early diary entries concerning his initial encounter with the nun in the Westphalian town of Dülmen (complete with original drawings by the poet to illustrate certain contentions), but his tentative working draft of a planned biography of the stigmatized woman (with the sections "Childhood and Early Youth," "Life in the Cloister," and "Last Days") together with sketches for the missing years as well as materials which were ultimately rejected for inclusion. The absence of an index as well as a commentary by the editor does not diminish the intrinsic value of this material for either the literary or the liturgical scholar, and this shortcoming should be obviated a few years hence when these meticulous helpmate tools do appear. (J.F.F.)

Bellmann, Werner. "Zur Wirkungsgeschichte von Brentanos *Lustigen Musikanten*." *JFDH* (1981): 338-42.

Fascinating marginalia revealing that a certain Dr. Nicolaus Meyer, whose poetic style was parodied at the close of *Godwi*, wrote a New Year's farce for the Bremen

theater based on Brentano's *Singspiel*. Deducing from the
playbill and the cast of characters the extent to which
Meyer altered the original text for his satirical purposes—
a resounding failure, apparently—Bellmann makes a plea
that any extant copy of the manuscript be placed at his
disposal, and one can only wish him luck in this enterprise.
(J.F.F.)

Brown, Marshall. "*Godwi* und die Krise der deutschen Romantik."
Pp. 301-12 in Gerhart Hoffmeister, ed., *Goethezeit: Studien
zur Erkenntnis und Rezeption Goethes und seiner Zeitgenossen:
Festschrift für Stuart Atkins*. Berne: Francke, 1981. Pp. 392.

Posing the daring postulate that the year 1800 marked
the watershed between early Romantic yearning to obliterate
distinctions between outer and inner worlds, between subjectivity (the private world of "time") and universality
(the public sphere of "space") because the asymptotic approach was no longer acceptable, Brown attempts to demonstrate this thesis with reference to *Godwi*, the structure
of which is felt to embody the transformation of Romanticism
from a kind of delimitation drive (*Entgrenzung*) to a new
form of self-limitation, with both forces hovering in a
sort of precarious equilibrium. The novel thus constitutes
a stage in the evolution of Romanticism, not in its dissolution, as has often been maintained. A tempting hypothesis
which is only partially undergirded by the analysis of the
novel itself. (J.F.F.)

Eibl, Karl. "Suche nach Wirlichkeit: Zur 'romantischen
Ironie' in Clemens Brentanos Dirnengedichten." Pp. 98-113
in Ernst Ribbat, ed., *Romantik: Ein literaturwissenschaftliches Studienbuch*. (Athenäum Taschenbücher, 2149.) König-
stein/Ts.: Athenäum, 1979. Pp. 236. DM 19.80.

Listed with a review by John F. Fetzer in *RMB* for 1979,
p. 265.
See also Ribbat ("German 2. General").

Eilert, Heide Christina. "Clemens Brentano: *Godwi* (1800/1802)."
Pp. 125-40 in Paul Michael Lützler, ed., *Romane und Erzählun-
gen der deutschen Romantik: Neue Interpretationen*. Stuttgart:
Reclam, 1981. Pp. 389.

Following a concise and cursory overview of the critical
literature on the novel since Kerr (1898), this essay
examines the work in its dialectical interplay between
subjective individualism and integration into society,
between the "self" and the "other," and traces the inevit-

able failure of this enterprise. Interesting, but hardly
innovative, are the attempts to link the female figures
with the vegetative sphere, to relate the ballad of the
prostitute Violette concerning the Lore-Lay's demise by
drowning to the death of Godwi's mother in a similar fashion,
and the well-documented alliance of art with sickness and
suffering. (J.F.F.)

Fetzer, John F. *Clemens Brentano*. Boston: Twayne Publishers,
1981. Pp. 179. $15.00.

   This introductory monograph in the standard Twayne format
focuses on the poet's place within the context of Romanticism
(as defined by Brentano himself), since this writer lived
through the entire period from its meteoric rise to prominence and dominance to its eventual eclipse and demise. The
opening and closing chapters, the biographically oriented
"Prelude" and the recapitulative "Postlude" respectively,
make oblique reference to Brentano's acknowledged literal
and literary musicality, a topic which has been treated
elsewhere by this critic and numerous others. The principal
thrust of the study, however, is an analysis of selected
key works (nine poems encompassing the entire chronological
scope and stylistic spectrum of his lyric productivity;
prose writings, including the novel *Godwi*, which, as one
can infer from the articles reviewed this year, is still
provoking critical interest; two major shorter pieces--the
Chronika and the *Kasperl und Annerl* novella--together with
the fairy tales of the Rhine and the *Gockel* complex; the
stage works, which for the most part are given short shrift
because of their unwieldiness, are limited to *Ponce* and
Die Gründung Prags). By dividing the analyses of each of
the larger works into four distinct sections--an examination of the components of the title, a content summary, a
survey of the scholarly literature, and an interpretive
commentary--this monograph seeks to fulfill the needs of
both the non-initiated reader as well as the specialist, a
utopian aim which runs the risk of satisfying neither
echelon completely. (J.F.F.)

Frühwald, Wolfgang. "Achim von Arnim und Clemens Brentano."
Pp. 145-58 in *Handbuch der deutschen Erzählung*. Düsseldorf:
Bagel, 1981.

   A two-pronged attempt is made to examine the shorter narrative prose of the *Wunderhorn* collaborators on both an individual basis and on the basis of common Romantic ground
and concepts (such as triadic historicism, the poeticiza-
tion of the world in the course of historical evolution,

the mediating role of poetry in these developments). In Arnim's case interesting light is shed on the real (biographical) roots of his often surrealistic tales, so that, for instance, in *Mistress Lee* Brentano's bizarre escapades with Auguste Bußmann are given literary expression in accordance with the Romantic penchant to discover in an individual instance a general model, to uncover in the concrete example or event the symbolic or mythic element. Very enlightening are the cooperative creations of Arnim and Brentano, beginning with their respective Melusine interpretations, their common techniques in the craft of fiction (the centrality of a specific song in the *Chronika* and in *Majoratsherren*), thematic ties between the *Schachtel mit der Friedenspuppe* and *Melück Maria Blainville*, internal correspondences in their respective works--especially in Brentano's *Wehmüller*--which offer eye-opening glances into the poet's workshop and the making of literature, and finally their mutual loss of resonance during the Restoration period only to be followed at the outset of the twentieth century by a resonant, dual-track resurrection. (J.F.F.)

Grob, Elisabeth. *Die verwilderte Rede in Brentanos Godwi und L. Sternes Tristram Shandy.* (Europäische Hochschulschriften, Reihe 1, Vol. 358.) Berne: Peter Lang, 1980. Pp. 97.

In spite of a tendency toward excruciating repetitiveness of certain contentions and phrases ("post hoc, ergo propter hoc," for instance, becomes a virtual leitmotif signaling the straightforward causal-chronological mode of narration) in support of the hypothesis that the narrative fabric of *Godwi* does not so much involve the transmission of metafictional facts (*informieren*) as it does the undermining of the belief that such information can be transmitted at all (*entgrenzen*), this investigation has some positive insights to offer. It is especially the *verwilderte Rede* which helps knock out the underpinnings of a naively communicative function of what is related in prose fiction by means of an immediate relativization of what has been said. Much here, however, is warmed-over Böckmann, but a new dimension is probed with regard to the self-referential quality of the language and the active role of the reader in ordering and integrating for himself what this recalcitrant fictional discourse has to offer. (J.F.F.)

Henel, Heinrich. "Brentanos Gedicht 'Sprich aus der Ferne': Dazu etwas über Keats und Baudelaire." Pp. 313-30 in Gerhart Hoffmeister, ed., *Goethezeit: Studien zur Erkenntnis und Rezeption Goethes und seiner Zeitgenossen. Festschrift für Stuart Atkins.* Berne: Francke, 1981. Pp. 392.

In this, one of his last interpretations, Heinrich Henel circumspectly builds an analysis of the poem which differs from Killy's "tautologies" and Lüder's "contradictory paraphrases" by the dimension of concepts found in Keats's ode "Fancy" and Baudelaire's "Correspondences." The former reveals the combinatory and compensatory powers of the imagination to heighten barren reality while the latter anticipates the modern practice (already manifest in Brentano) of metaphoric interchange and exchange--including the use and abuse of shopworn images. Very effective is the demonstration of how, in Brentano's hands, commonplace structural devices such as verbatim stanzaic repetition can evolve into "fulfilled forms" when they acquire semantic value, as well as the observation that Brentano is at best a qualified mysticist whose self-awareness obviated the requisite self-denial of the true mystic. (J.F.F.)

Riley, Helene Kastinger. "Kontamination und Kritik im dichterischen Schaffen Clemens Brentanos und Achim von Arnims." *CG* 13 (1980): 350-58.

This essay forms a splendid pendant and complement to that of Frühwald discussed above insofar as both critics investigate the shorter prose writings of the respective authors with an eye toward certain themes and techniques they held in common, if not as common property. Thus the static portrait of Annonciata in *Godwi* comes to life as a dancing Annonciata in Arnim's hands, while the long-standing misconception of Brentano's *Schachtel* as a parody of Arnim's *Melück* is modified to that of a re-working or free adaptation in the light of changing political constellations between 1812 and 1814. One key insight deserves mention: Brentano's *imitatio Arnimi* can indeed be considered the sincerest form of flattery, since it does not stem from a diminished capacity in imagination or creative impulse nor from crisis of language, but rather from the genuine desire to come to terms with and to tap the full poetic potential of ideas and images of a kindred spirit. (J.F.F.)

Rölleke, Heinz. "Brentano-Zitate bei Wilhelm Raabe." *JFDH* (1981): 365-69.

The super sleuth is again at work and this time the Sherlock Holmes of German Romanticism discovers previously overlooked parallelisms--or paraphrases--from *Kasperl und Annerl* and from the poem "Die Gottesmauer" in Raabe's novel of 1862, *Die Leute aus dem Walde*, as well as in several other works of the later writer who could lament how wretched it was

that "the entire machinery of Romanticism is falling into
disrepair" to the chagrin of those fiction writers who would
prefer to see this marvelous mechanism continue to function
as a kind of *perpetuum mobile*. (J.F.F.)

Rölleke, Heinz. "Gustav Mahlers 'Wunderhorn'-Lieder: Text-
grundlagen und Textauswahl." *JFDH* (1981): 370-78.

The perplexing and frustrating question of which of the
Wunderhorn editions was used by Mahler for his twenty-four
song settings is complicated enough, but is compounded by
the fact that the composer made slight alterations in the
text of each and every one of them to suit his musical taste,
ranging in scope from spelling and punctuation modifications
to full-fledged contaminations (the fusion of several versions
of a poem into one). The composer's sensitivity for what
constitutes the true folk quality of certain songs is nicely
juxtaposed with the sentimental and trite concept of other
musicians who try to prescribe what folk art should be.
(J.F.F.)

Schultz, Hartwig. *Der unbekannte Brentano*. Frankfurt: Freies
Deutsches Hochstift, n.d. Pp. 27.

The startling ignorance of the modern German-speaking world
for what *Des Knaben Wunderhorn* was—answers in a recent poll
ranged from a kind of ice cream cone to a fog warning device!—
leads Schultz to examine the many modes of misinterpretation
and misinformation surrounding this collection and its
collaborators' *modus operandi*. What follows depicts in succinct fashion the causes and effects of certain misconcep-
tions in Brentano's case: one-sidedly religious studies or
those focusing exclusively on the young poet to the detri-
ment of the later religious writer. Brentano's never-ending
hide-and-seek game with his audience, his ubiquitous satirical barbs against fossilized systems of behavior and thought,
and finally his persistent patterns of erotic imagery help
to establish overall coherence and consistency, so that a
more well-rounded writer emerges. Nothing startlingly new,
only a spartanly stated and clearly organized panorama of
the poet's checkered reception in the past and his ongoing
transvaluation. (J.F.F.)

Seidlin, Oskar. *Von erwachendem Bewußtsein und vom Sündenfall:
Brentano, Schiller, Kleist, Goethe*. Stuttgart: Klett-Cotta,
1979. Pp. 171.

See also Seidlin ("Kleist").
Rev. by Egon Schwarz in *GQ* 54 (1979): 119-20.

Contains revised and bibliographically updated versions of
Seidlin's incisive analyses of the "Jägerlied" (see *ELN* 15,
Supp., 153), *Die Gründung Prags* (see *ELN* 15, Supp., 153-54),
the *Gockel* fairy tale (see *ELN* 13, Supp., 138), and the
Melusine figure (see *RMB* for 1979, p. 270). It seems interesting that in a book dealing with the rise of consciousness
and fall of man, analyses of Brentano occupy over 100 of
the 171 pages. (J.F.F.)

Tunner, Erika. "Die 'denkende Klasse' und Clemens Brentanos
Emmerick-Schriften." *JFDH* (1980): 259-71.

A case is made for the influence of Brentano's religious
writings on the intellectual elite in France--something which
failed to happen in Germany. But aside from a few well-known
figures who were marginally acquainted with the Emmerick
papers--Huysmans, Claudel, Valéry--the case for influence
is built around the converted Jew, Max Jacob, who died in
1944, in a Nazi internment camp, and whose writing and thinking are shown to closely resemble those of his Romantic
predecessor. Very enlightening is the account of a 1969 French
radio play on the stigmatic. (J.F.F.)

See also Dessauer, Freund, Pongs ("German 2. General");
Holbeche, Seiverth ("Hoffmann").

Reviews of books previously listed:

ANTON, Bernd, *Romantisches Parodieren* (see *RMB* for 1980,
p. 279), rev. by Klaus Peter in *CG* 14 (1981): 184-86;
BEHRENS, Jürgen, et al., eds., *Clemens Brentano: Sämtliche
Werke und Briefe*, Vols. VI, VII, VIII, IX (see *ELN* 16, Supp.,
143; *ELN* 17, Supp., 187-88), rev. by John Fetzer in *GQ* 54
(1981): 224-26; by Heinrich Henel in *Monatshefte* 73 (1981):
465-69; BEHRENS, Jürgen, et al., eds., *Clemens Brentano:
Sämtliche Werke und Briefe*, Vol XVI (see *RMB* for 1980, p.
280), rev. by Joachim Müller in *DLZ* 102 (1981): 1062-65;
by Alfred Rieman in *Aurora* 41 (1981): 225-27; HUBER, Michael,
Clemens Brentano: Die Chronika des fahrenden Schülers (see
ELN 16, Supp., 146-47), rev. by Gerhard Schaub in *CG* 12
(1979): 165-69; LUEDERS, Detlev, *Clemens Brentano: Beiträge
des Kolloquiums* (see *RMB* for 1980, pp. 280-89), rev. by E.W.
Herd in *AUMLA* 56 (1981): 271-72; by Joachim Müller in *DLZ*
102 (1981): 1062-65; by Helene K. Riley in *CG* 14 (1981):
187-89; TUNNER, Erika, *Clemens Brentano* (see *ELN* 17, Supp.,
192-92), rev. by Pierre-François Moreaux in *NRF* 328 (1980):
117-20.

BÜCHNER

See Kuhn ("Goethe"); Seiverth ("Hoffmann").

Review of book previously listed:

BENN, David G., *The Drama of Revolt: A Critical Study of Georg Büchner* (see *ELN* 16, Supp., 157), rev. by David G. Richards in *JEGP* 79 (1980): 93-95.

BÜRGER

Wackermann, Erwin. "Frühe illegale Münchhausen-Ausgaben: Kleine Schritte zu einer Volksausgabe." *Philobiblon* 23 (1979): 266-78.

See also Trautwein ("German 2. General").

CHAMISSO

Baatsch, Henri Alexis, ed. and trans. *Voyage autour du monde 1815-1818*. Paris: Le Sycomore, 1981. Pp. 480.

Rev. by Jean-Marie Gibbal in *QL* 351 (July 1-15, 1981): 26-27.

Freund, Winfried. "Verfallene Schlösser--Ein gesellschafts-kritisches Motiv bei Kleist, E.T.A. Hoffmann, Uhland and Chamisso." *Diskussion Deutsch* 11 (1980): 361-69.

Langner, Ilse. "Adalbert von Chamisso." *NDH* 28 (1981): 100-16.

See also Berger, Dessauer, Metzner, Swales ("German 2. General").

DROSTE-HÜLSHOFF

See Heinrich-Heine-Institut, Düsseldorf, ed. ("Heine").

EICHENDORFF

Farquharson, R.H. "Poets, Poetry, and Life in Eichendorff's *Ahnung und Gegenwart.*" *Seminar* 17 (1981): 17-34.

Schwarz, Egon. "Der Erzähler Eichendorff." Pp. 163-91 in Ernst
  Ribbat, ed., *Romantik: Ein literaturwissenschaftliches
  Studienbuch.* (Athenäum Taschenbücher, 2149.) Königstein/Ts.:
  Athenäum, 1979. Pp. 236. DM 19.80.

  Listed with a review by John F. Fetzer in *RMB* for 1979,
  p. 276.
  See also Ribbat ("German 2. General").

Sims-Gunzenhauser, William D. "Eichendorff, Verlaine and the
  Secularization of Symbolist Poetics." *Neophil* 65 (1981):
  200-13.

See also Dessauer, Pikulik ("German 2. General"); Schindler
  ("Fouqué"); Heinrich-Heine-Institut, Riemen ("Heine");
  Seiverth, Wolff ("Hoffmann"); Köpke ("Jean Paul").

FICHTE

See Itô ("German 2. General"); Neubauer ("Hoffmann").

FOUQUÉ

Schindler, Karl. "Fouqués '*Die Familie Hallersee*' als Schlüssel-
  drama der Familie Eichendorff?" *Aurora* 38 (1978): 122-26.

Wuthenow, Ralph-Rainer, ed., with Meinhard Hasenbein. *Friedrich de la Motte Fouqué: Undine und andere Erzählungen. Mit
  der Rezension von Edgar Allan Poe.* (insel taschenbuch 311.)
  Frankfurt: Insel (Suhrkamp commission), 1978. Pp. 213.
  DM 7.00.

See also Dessauer ("German 2. General").

FREUD

See Ellis, Hertz, Lehmann, Schneider, Tatar ("Hoffmann").

GEORGE

See Speier ("Jean Paul").

GOETHE

Bubner, Rüdiger. *Hegel und Goethe.* (Euphorion, Beih. 12.)
  Heidelberg: Winter, 1978. Pp. 51. DM 18.00.

  Rev. by Klaus-Peter Philippi in *Germanistik* 20 (1979):
  171.
  Discusses the "Classic"-vs.-"Romantic" issue.

Gearey, John. *Goethe's Faust: The Making of Part I.* Yale University Press, 1981. Pp. 228. $19.00.

  Rev. by Idris Parry in *TLS*, Oct. 9, 1981, p. 1181.
  Schiller, acknowledging some problems with his play *Don
  Carlos* and attributing them in part to the four years it
  had taken him to write the piece, once remarked that a drama
  ought to be the fruit of a summer. What, then, is one to say
  about the problematic nature of *Faust I* and *Faust II* which
  took Goethe 60 years to write, with the composition of *Faust
  I* stretching over some 35 years and that of *Faust II* from
  about 1816 to the end of his life in 1832. Given the long
  incubation time of the work, it is no surprise that the
  academic debate about form, coherence, characters, central
  meaning, relationship between the two parts, has been formidable both in quantity and intensity. It is probably safe
  to say that no other work of German literature has been
  analyzed as exhaustively as Goethe's *Faust* for the last 150
  years. Could there possibly be anything new anyone could
  say?
  John Gearey's book is a surprise, a fresh and eminently
  sensible re-reading of the German classic by tracing the
  complex genesis of the play. Gearey's analysis is about the
  form of *Faust I* (and in part also of *Faust II*), but a new
  concept of form evolves from his analysis, that of an organism
  of art in its evolution, having absorbed at various stages
  the changing artistic, philosophical, and existential experiences of its author: "The meaning of the work grew as
  its author grew" (92). Whereas in *Werther* Goethe did not
  choose "to include in the novel what he had learned through
  writing it" (42), "there was no Goethe outside of Faust in
  the way that there was an author outside of Werther" (45).
  Gearey shows how Goethe conceived and provisionally shaped
  different Faust figures from the *Urfaust* to *Faust II* taking
  in features from the legendary magician, from his own
  Werther, his unfinished Mahomet and Prometheus (thereby
  completing them as Faust figures), connecting his already
  complex character with a social problem of his time: that
  of infanticide by unwed mothers, and further heightening

the complexity by infusing his figure with personal aspirations and disappointments, like the struggle for
harmony between his intellectual and sensual desires. The
result is a composite Faust figure that convinces not because
one central idea is being exemplified, but because the author
has endowed it with the authenticity of his own changing and
growing experience of life. It is quite possible that there
is no particular detail really new to a Goethe scholar, but
to weave the various threads from the literary tradition,
the contemporary social and intellectual ambience, and from
the author's biography together into a thoroughly convincing,
enlightening, and very readable study is a major achievement. (Walter Wetzels, University of Texas at Austin.)

Gille, Klaus F., ed. *Goethes Wilhelm Meister: Zur Rezeptions-
geschichte der Lehr- und Wanderjahre*. (Texte der deutschen
Literatur in wirkungsgeschichtlichen Zeugnissen, Bd. 3.)
Konigstein: Athenäum, 1979. Pp. xl+314. DM 68.00.

   Rev. by Ulrich Schödlbauer in *Germanistik* 20 (1979): 810.

Hennebo, Dieter. "Goethes Beziehungen zur Gartenkunst seiner
Zeit." *JFDH* (1979): 90-119.

Knepler, Georg. "Schuberts Goethelieder und Goethes Musik-
verständnis." Pp. 136-55 in Walter Dietze and Peter Goldam-
mer, eds.; Red.: Reiner Schlichting, *Impulse: Aufsätze,
Quellen, Berichte zur deutschen Klassik und Romantik*. 32
Abbildungen auf Tafeln, 3 Pläne in Rückenschlaufe. Berlin:
Aufbau-Verlag, 1978. Pp. 413. M 15.00.

Kuhn, Reinhard. *The Demon of Noontide: Ennui in Western
Literature*. Princeton University Press, 1976. Pp. 395.
£17.40.

   Rev. by Gert Mattenklott in *Germanistik* 19 (1978): 1072.
   Chapter on Goethe and analyses of Hölderlin, Jean Paul,
and Büchner.

Rasch, Wolfdietrich. *Goethes "Iphigenie auf Tauris" als Drama
der Autonomie*. Munich: Beck, 1979. Pp. 205. DM 19.80.

   Rev. by Fritz Hackert in *Germanistik* 20 (1979): 482-83.
   Discusses Iphigenie's confrontation with "restaurative
Romantik."

Weinberg, Kurt. *The Figure of Faust in Valéry and Goethe: An
Exegesis of "Mon Faust."* (Princeton Essays in Literature.)
Princeton University Press, 1976. Pp. 257. $18.50.

Rev. by Peter Boerner in *Germanistik* 19 (1978): 1087.
Faust as a "Romantic Genius."

See also Dessauer, Kuczynski, Lefevere, Nemoianu, Reed, Swales
("German 2. General"); Seidlin ("Brentano"); Fendri, Kaufmann
("Heine"); Geißler, Krolop ("Hoffmann"); Seidlin ("Kleist");
Toyoda ("Runge").

GRASS

See Raddatz ("Heine"); Krolop ("Hoffmann").

GRIMM, JACOB and WILHELM

Dammann, Günter. "Über Differenz des Handelns im Märchen:
Strukturale Analysen zu den Sammlungen von Christian W.
Günther, J.G. Münch und J. und W. Grimm." Pp. 71–106 in Walf-
gang Haubrichs, ed., *Erzählforschung: Theorien, Modelle und
Methoden der Narrativik.* 3, Mit einem Nachtrag zur Auswahl-
bibliographie in Erzählforschung 1 und 2. (Zeitschrift für
Literaturwissenschaft und Linguistik, Beiheft 8.) Göttingen:
Vandenhoeck & Ruprecht, 1978. Pp. 415. DM 78.00.

  Rev. by Ernst Weber in *Germanistik* 21 (1980): 85–86.
  Grimms and the *Kunstmärchen* of E.T.A. Hoffmann.

Denecke, Ludwig. "Das dynamische Konzept der Brüder Grimm."
Pp. 63–79 of Jürgen Kühnel, ed., *Mittelalter-Rezeption:
Gesammelte Vorträge des Salzburger Symposions "Die Rezeption
mittelalterlicher Dichter und ihrer Werke in Literatur,
bildender Kunst und Musik des 19. und 20. Jahrhunderts.*
(Göppinger Arbeiten zur Germanistik, Nr. 286.) Göppingen:
Kümmerle, 1979. Pp. 631. DM 88.00

Ernst, Synes. *Deutschunterricht und Ideologie: Kritische
Untersuchung der "Zeitschrift für den deutschen Unterricht"
als Beitr. zur Geschichte des Deutschunterrichts im Kaiser-
reich (1887–1911).* (Europäische Hochschulschriften, Reihe
1, Bd. 165.) Bern: H. Lang; Frankfurt: P. Lang, 1977. Pp.
290. Sw.Fr. 52.00.

  Rev. by Jürgen Hauff in *Germanistik* 21 (1980): 252.

Höck, Alfred. *Die Brüder Grimm als Studenten in Marburg.*
[Marburg]: Elwert, [1978]. Pp. 34. DM 4.80.

Laßberg, Joseph Freiherr von. "Fünf Briefe an Jacob und Wilhelm Grimm. [Submitted by] Volker Schupp." *Euphorion* 72 (1978): 277-301.

Mollenauer, Robert. "Kultur and Counter-Culture in the Grimms' *Kinder- und Hausmärchen.*" *Neophil* 65 (1981): 565-73.

Nutz, Maxmilian. "Die Macht des Faktischen und die Utopie: Zur Rezeption 'emanzipatorischer' Märchen am Beispiel von F.K. Waechters 'Tischlein deck dich und Knüppel aus dem Sack.'" *Diskussion Deutsch* 10 (1979): 397-410.

Psaar, Werner, and Manfred Klein. *Wer hat Angst vor der bösen Geiß? Zur Märchendidaktik und Märchenrezeption.* Braunschweig: Westermann, 1976. Pp. 308. DM 26.00.

   Rev. by Leander Petzoldt in *Germanistik* 20 (1979): 110.

Wyss, Ulrich. "Jacob Grimm (1785-1863)." Pp. 167-76, 335-36 in Horst Turk, ed., *Klassiker der Literaturtheorie: Von Boileau bis Barthes.* (Becksche schwarze Reihe, Bd. 192.) München: Beck, 1979. Pp. 374. DM 24.00.

   Rev. by Jürgen Söring in *Germanistik* 20 (1979): 377.

See also Kuczynski, Pongs ("German 2. General").

Review article:

Soeteman, C. "Jacob und Wilhelm Grimm." *Neophil* 62 (1978): 314-17.

HAUFF

See Dessauer, Frank ("German 2. General").

HAYDN

See Mühlher ("Hoffmann").

HEBEL

Hebel, Johann Peter. *Briefe: Sel. and intro. by Wilhelm Zentner. Mit Anmerkungen und Abbildungen.* Karlsruhe: Müller; Ebenhausen: Langewiesche-Brandt, 1976. Pp. 287. DM 24.00.

   Rev. by Wolfgang Hecht in *Germanistik* 19 (1978): 804.

Rusterholz, Peter. "Faktoren der Sinnkonstitution literarischer Texte in semiotischer Sicht: Am Beispiel von Hebels Kalendergeschichte: Die leichteste Todesstrafe." Pp. 78-124 in Wilhelm Köller and Kaspar H. Spinner, eds., *Zeichen, Text, Sinn: Zur Semiotik des literarischen Verstehens.* (Kleine Vandenhoeck-Reihe, 1436.) Göttingen: Vandenhoeck and Ruprecht, 1977. Pp. 165. DM 15.80.

See also Pongs ("German 2. General"); Neubauer ("Hoffmann").

HEGEL

Bubner, Rüdiger. *Hegel und Goethe.* (Euphorion, Beih. 12.) Heidelberg: Winter, 1978. Pp. 51. DM 18.00.

   Rev. by Klaus-Peter Philippi in *Germanistik* 20 (1979): 171.
   Discusses the "Classic"-vs.-"Romantic" issue.

Hinck, Walter. "Das lyrische Subjekt im geschichtlichen Prozeß oder der umgewendete Hegel: Zu einer historischen Poetik der Lyrik." Pp. 125-37, 149-51 in Hinck, *Von Heine zu Brecht: Lyrik im Geschichtsprozeß.* (suhrkamp taschenbuch 481.) Frankfurt: Suhrkamp, 1978. Pp. 154. DM 5.00.

Turk, Horst. "Hegel (1770-1831)." Pp. 122-32, 326-28 in Turk, ed., *Klassiker der Literaturtheorie: Von Boileau bis Barthes.* (Becksche schwarze Reihe, Bd. 192.) München: Beck, 1979. Pp. 374. DM 24.00.

   Rev. by Jürgen Söring in *Germanistik* 20 (1979): 377.

See also Mann ("German 2. General"); Zinke ("Heine"); Horster ("Hölderlin"); Ettelt, Fühmann ("Hoffmann").

HEIDEGGER

See Böckmann, Methagl, Murray, Ziegler ("Hölderlin").

HEINE

Bellmann, Werner, ed. *Heinrich Heine: Deutschland. Ein Winter-märchen.* (Universal-Bibliothek, No. 8150, Erläuterungen und Dokumente.) Stuttgart: Reclam, 1980. Pp. 205. DM 3.80.

A commentary with very elementary annotations, documents of genesis and reception, imitations, parallel passages from Heine and others, and a selected bibliography. No real problems of the poem are addressed. (J.L.S.)

Bodi, Leslie. "Heinrich Heine: The Poet as *Frondeur.*" Pp. 43-60 in *Intellectuals and Revolution: Socialism and the Experience of 1848*, ed. Eugene Kamenka and F.B. Smith. New York: St. Martin's Press, 1980. Pp. viii+165.

A general biographical account of Heine's reaction to the events of the Revolution of 1848, not overly precise but capturing his ambivalence and his posture as a "lonely guerilla." (J.L.S.)

Böhm, Hans. "'Bey einem Buch wie dieses, sollte dem Drucker jedes Comma heilig seyn.' Zur Edition der Lyrik in der Heine-Säkularausgabe." *Zeitschrift für Germanistik* 2 (1981): 88-95.

Editorial principles governing text and commentary of the poetry volumes in the East German edition. (J.L.S.)

Bourke, Thomas. "Heines Stimmungsbrechung." Pp. 211-85 in Bourke, *Stilbruch als Stilmittel: Studien zur Literatur der Spät- und Nachromantik. Mit besonderer Berücksichtigung von E.T.A. Hoffmann, Lord Byron und Heinrich Heine.* (Europäische Hochschulschriften, Series I, Vol. 297.) Frankfurt am Main, Bern, and Cirencester: Peter D. Lang, 1980. Pp. 357. DM 76.00.

See also Bourke ("Hoffmann").
With an unusually fine display of critical penetration and explication, the familiar stylistic breach in Heine's poetry is shown to derive from the opposition to the same used-up, untruthful lyrical language that Byron called "cant." The overall excellent and absorbing monograph deals with stylistic breach in general and in a progressive devel-

opment from Hoffmann to Heine as an intentional, increasingly
conscious attack on conventional horizons of poetic expecta-
tions, which were not fully overcome until quite modern times.
The comparison of Heine and Byron has never been treated so
perceptively, and the parallels of reception between Byron's
post-Romantic *Don Juan* and Heine's mature verse are striking
and thought-provoking. While Bourke somewhat underestimates
Heine's elegiac attachment to (Romantic) poesy as a lost
value in exile, he has achieved one of the most critically
skillful studies of Heine's poetry in recent times. The
author, who is Irish, also deserves credit for an eminently
precise, bright, and resourceful German style. (J.L.S.)

Brauner, Charles S. "Irony in the Heine Lieder of Schubert and
Schumann." *Musical Quarterly* 67 (1981): 261-81.

Addresses the question of whether the literary device of
irony can be reflected in music, and to what extent this may
or may not have succeeded in selected *Lied* settings. (J.L.S.)

Espagne, Michel. "La recherche du pontifex maximus. (Les
manuscrits de Kommunismus, Philosophie und Klerisei de H.
Heine.)." *Recherches Germaniques* 11 (1981): 62-86.

Using the model of Lebrave (see below), Espagne illustrates
the changes in a passage on Guizot between first publication
and the *Lutezia* version. The changes show the decay of Heine's
Young Hegelian hopes for a strong personality who would
reconcile philosophy and social reality. (J.L.S.)

Espagne, Michel. "Sur quelques manuscrits tardifs de Heine."
EG 35 (1980): 416-29.

A study of the manuscripts and deleted materials for the
late prefaces to the new German and French editions of *Zur
Geschichte der Religion und Philosophie in Deutschland* argues
that the genesis of the texts shows a continuity in Heine's
thought about religion that is obscured by the claims of
rupture in the final texts. (J.L.S.)

Fendri, Mounir. *Halbmond, Kreuz und Schibboleth: Heinrich
Heine und der islamische Orient.* (Heine-Studien, ed. Joseph
A. Kruse.) Hamburg: Hoffmann und Campe, Heinrich Heine
Verlag, 1980. Pp. 350. DM 78.00.

This very thorough study is divided into four topics: the
Moorish culture of medieval Spain; Persian literature and
its transmission via Goethe and the orientalizing German
poets and scholars of the time; Heine's view of Mohammed and

the Koran; and Heine's political reportage on the problems
of the contemporary Near East. Fendri shows that the poetic
vision of the Orient and the realities of the Near East
were two very different things for Heine, and it emerges
clearly that the former is one of Heine's most distinctly
Romantic elements. It also emerges once again, though Fendri
seems less aware of this, that Heine's appropriation of
literary influences was more extensive than intensive.
Although Fendri does not always exhaust English-language
resources, the study is well researched and contains some
valuable contributions, for example, on the pervasive influence of the *Arabian Nights* or on Heine's notable aloofness
from the Philhellenic enthusiasms of the 1820s. The fourth
section, on current events, is historically well founded.
Fendri is careful in judgment, especially in regard to the
connection of Heine's Jewish interests to these matters; he
is unafraid to point out where Heine's biases were conventional and unreflective, and he avoids speculation. (J.L.S.)

Fjodorow, A. "Block als Prosaautor in seinem Verhältnis zu
Heine." *KuL* 29 (1981): 641-46.

Certain parallels between Alexander Block and Heine reflect
affinities rather than influence from Heine's prose, of which
Block was rather critical. (J.L.S.)

Götze, Karl-Heinz. "Literarische Tradition und gesellschaftliche Humanität. Perspektiven der Transformation: Heinrich
Heine." Pp. 394-490 in Götze, *Grundpositionen der Literaturgeschichtsschreibung im Vormärz*. (Europäische Hochschulschriften, Series I, Vol. 343.) Frankfurt am Main, Bern, and
Cirencester: Peter D. Lang, 1980. Pp. 629. DM 128.00

Rev. by Bernd Kortländer in *HeineJ 1981*, pp. 191-93.
Heine's *Zur Geschichte der Religion und Philosophie in
Deutschland* and *Die Romantische Schule* are examined in
comparison with four other, rather disparate pre-1848
literary histories: the influential work of Wolfgang Menzel,
who evolved from moderate liberalism to an obscurantist and
repressive position; the long-popular reactionary school-
book of August Vilmar; the major scholarly achievement of
the time by G.G. Gervinus; and a minor essay by Wilhelm
Zimmermann from a petty-bourgeois democratic viewpoint.
Götze imposes upon these materials a strictly orthodox
Marxist class analysis, which in places is naive and irritating; nevertheless, the individual studies are learned
and instructive. The chapter on Heine is less original; though
not without insight, it exaggerates the value of Heine's

essays on Romanticism as literary history. The most interesting results are the parallels with Gervinus, whom Heine
thought a more elaborate but less gifted imitator. In fact,
the political affinity with Gervinus is greater than Götze
makes it out to be; with a customary confusion of rhetoric
with program, he portrays Heine as more of a radical democrat than he was, whereas his monarchist affects and sus-
picion of the lower classes' potential for anarchic violence
are not so different from Gervinus' classical bourgeois
liberalism. (J.L.S.)

Grésillon, Almuth. "Les variantes de manuscrit: critères et
degrés de pertinence." Pp. 179-89 in Louis Hay and Winfried
Woesler, eds., *Die Nachlassedition--La Publication de manuscrits inédits: Akten des vom Centre National de la Recherche
Scientifique und der Deutschen Forschungsgemeinschaft veranstalteten französisch-deutschen Editorenkolloquiums Paris
1977. (JIG,* Series I, Vol. 4.) Bern, Frankfurt am Main, and
Las Vegas: Peter Lang, 1979. Pp. 248.

　　Rev. by Walter Huge in *HeineJ 1981,* pp. 193-96.
　　Employs a *Lutezia* passage to present a model of a variant
apparatus distinguishing degrees of relevance. (J.L.S.)

Grésillon, Almuth, and Michaël Werner. "Dossier Heine." *Romantisme,* no. 30 (1980): 83-99.

　　A comprehensive report on the modern study of Heine with
particular emphasis on France, where, it appears, despite a
notable recent upsurge in scholarly work, Heine is not easily
available in translation or very prominent in education or
the public consciousness. The evaluative judgments are brief;
some are judicious, others less so. The commentary is un-
literary and rather narrowly focused on Heine's political
significance. A number of the bibliographical references
are incompletely given. Yale is said to be in Princeton,
an error Werner has made once before (*ELN* 15, Supp., 167).
While the article may be of some value to the uninformed
French reader, one has come to expect more thoughtful work
from Werner, at any rate. (J.L.S.)

Guski, Andreas. "Übersetzung und semantische Verschiebung:
Lermontovs Heine-Adaption *Na severe dikom.*" *Die Welt der
Slaven* 25 (1980): 109-34.

　　Lermontov's highly regarded translation of *Lyrisches Intermezzo* 33 ("Ein Fichtenbaum steht einsam") alters the
meaning of the poem to suit his own poetic and ideological
intentions. (J.L.S.)

Hay, Louis, and Michel Espagne. "I. Genèse du texte et études
comparées. II. Les Moissons de François Guizot: Histoire d'un
article de Heine." *RLC* 55 (1981): 5-29.

After a general discussion by Hay of problems and techniques
in the newly developed interest in genetic textual study,
Espagne deals in detail with a specific case, the revisions
over the years of an article on Guizot, eventually dated
May 6, 1843 (*Lutezia* LVIII). The revisions exhibit Heine's
changing political response over the years, to which Espagne
ascribes perspectives grown richer and more varied. His phrase,
"anticipation a posteriori, cette écriture au futur antérieur,"
is extendable to Heine's practice generally in such matters.
(J.L.S.)

Heinrich-Heine-Institut, Düsseldorf, ed. *Heine-Jahrbuch 1981*
[= *HeineJ 1981*]. Hamburg: Hoffmann und Campe, 1981. Pp. 253;
8 pls.

The current *HeineJ* is very scholarly; along with interpretive articles, it contains a substantial amount of basic
research, much of it with manuscript materials. Ulrich
Stadler derives from Heine's affinity to Don Quixote his
insight into the conflict of truth and beauty in his poetry,
by which its modern relevance might be rescued. With a wide
range of literary examples, Alfred Opitz shows how animal
images reflect social consciousness and ideological perspectives; Heine's employment of eagle and rat images exhibits
ambivalence and limits in his socio-political outlook. Though
the argument is burdened by inelastic Marxist notions of
the evils of the bourgeoisie, it is nevertheless illuminating
and stimulating, and at least refrains from overestimating
Heine's revolutionary posture. Winfried Freund argues that
Heine developed the tradition of the Gothic ballad in the
direction of parody in order to undermine patterns of political, religious, and sexual repression in the consciousness
of readers. The well-written essay seems to me to overlook
the autobiographical dimension of some of these poems and
the genuinely Gothic facet of Heine's imagination, and it
is marked here and there by ideological wishful thinking.
The interpretation of the deplorable post-1848 poem "Kobes
I." is painfully apologetic and falsely claims that Heine
was a partisan of republican solutions. An excellent article
by an art historian, Werner Hofmann, shows how Heine's art
criticism, with its organicist allegiances, the primacy of
the "supernatural" idea over realistic content, and the
attraction to color as an expression of sensualist joy,
failed to perceive the lineaments of the future of painting

in his time. Helmut Koopmann argues that the "Gedanken und
Einfälle" are not just scraps and memoranda, as they have
been presented in all Heine editions, but organized groups
of literary aphorisms in bound notebooks intended for the
promised posthumous volume of the Campe edition. René
Anglade has found in Heine's personal copy of the Renduel
translation of the *Reisebilder* of 1834 two manuscript pages
of corrections for the Lévy edition of 1856. The manuscripts
are reproduced and the changes tabulated; some of the corrections were accepted, others not. The material shows graphical-
ly how Heine collaborated in the translation process. Christa
Stöcker's detailed study of the manuscript materials for the
Elementargeister shows how Heine revised and self-censored
the original text from which the French version was translated
for the subsequently published German version. In a significant analysis of the *Geständnisse* manuscripts and paralipomena, Michel Espagne shows how the "metabolism" of older
and newer texts exhibits the process of Heine's self-inter-
pretation and the reorganization, in the light of current
events, of his basic ideas.

Among smaller contributions, Werner Bellmann corrects the
commentary in Briegleb's edition on Heine's encounter with
the artisan-communist Weitling, which must have occurred in
Hamburg in 1844, not 1843. Heinz Wetzel finds affinities
between Heine's youthful Byronic poem "Götterdämmerung" and
Thomas Mann's *Tonio Kröger*. Kurt Abels comments on a cartoon
that applied Heine's "Belsatzar" to Franz Josef Strauss's
situation in the 1980 elections. Herbert Clasen and Swantje
Naumann report on plans for a Heine monument in Hamburg and
the debates they have generated. Berndt Kortländer reviews
a joint conference on literary popularity of the Heine,
Droste-Hülshoff, and Eichendorff Societies, certainly a
welcome initiative and perhaps a symptom of an emerging
peace process in German literary studies. Running bibliography as usual; the review section is expanded beyond specific monographs on Heine to more general literary studies.
(J.L.S.)

Johnston, Otto W. "Literary Influence as Provocation: Sir
Walter Scott's Impact on Heinrich Heine and the Young
Germans." *SLJ* 12 (1980): 73-84.

Johnston argues that Heine's bitter attack in the *Englische
Fragmente* changed Scott from a literary model to a provocation for the Young German generation. This is a real subject, but it is not well presented here. Inflated and in
some degree inaccurate claims are made for the revolutionary
social purpose of Young German writing. There is a dearth

of evidence, except for brief references to Gutzkow and to
Wienbarg (who was anything but an anti-nationalist, as the
imprecise argument implies). The article is written in an
irritating style more reminiscent of gonzo journalism than
scholarly discourse. (J.L.S.)

Kaufmann, Hans. "Poesie und Prosa bei Heine." *Zeitschrift
für Germanistik* 2 (1981): 69-87.

A general introduction to a Heine reader locates him as
the successor of Goethe and the predecessor of Marx, and
focuses on the interpenetration of poetry and prose, beauty
and world. (J.L.S.)

Klinkenberg, Ralf H. *Die Reisebilder Heinrich Heines: Vermitt-
lung durch literarische Stilmittel.* (Europäische Hochschulschriften, Series I, Vol. 394.) Frankfurt am Main and Bern:
Peter D. Lang, 1981. Pp. xx+249. DM 82.00.

With a theory maneuvering between Ingarden and Iser, and
a method derived from Preisendanz, the monograph argues
that the *Reisebilder* can be made to communicate to pupils
by attention to their specifically literary stylistic elements, and the pedagogical purpose should be to help the
pupil become a literary reader. The focus on literary interpretation as the key to Heine's texts is unusual and welcome,
and Klinkenberg's interpretive results are generally, if
not always, satisfactory, though somewhat elementary. But
the analysis of rhetorical devices, of which the interpretation mainly consists, tends to atomize the tone and rhythm
of the texts and in some places to deambiguate them. Furthermore, the actual interpretive part of the monograph fills
only 85 pp.; the rest is theory, an account of genesis and
reception of the *Reisebilder* useful only to the most uninformed teacher or pupil, and no fewer than 1,008 reference
notes. What might have been a compact interpretive demonstration comes upon us as an unedited, typewritten dissertation at an outrageous price. Except for one 14-year-old
paper of my own, incorrectly cited, there are no non-German-
language items in the bibliography. (J.L.S.)

Komar, Kathleen L. "The Structure of Heine's 'Harzreise':
Should We Take the Narrator at His Word?" *GR* 56 (1981):
128-33.

An interesting and largely persuasive analysis contrasts
the negative, oppressive dreams in the text with the more
positive poems, showing Heine seeking a victory in aesthetic
form over "what the social critic cannot redeem in the real

world." There is a partial reconciliation at the end, but
the gap between harmonizing poesy and the recalcitrant,
oppressive world remains open and acknowledged. The scholarly
references are not quite up to date, perhaps owing to the
creeping pace of the academic publication process. (J.L.S.)

Koopmann, Helmut. "Heines sogenannte 'Gedanken und Einfälle':
Versuch einer Neubewertung." Pp. 206-11 in Louis Hay and
Winfried Woesler, eds., *Die Nachlassedition--La Publication
de manuscrits inédits: Akten des vom Centre National de la
Recherche Scientifique und der Deutschen Forschungsgemeinschaft veranstalteten französisch-deutschen Editorenkolloquiums Paris 1977. (JIG*, Series I, Vol. 4.) Bern, Frankfurt
am Main, and Las Vegas: Peter Lang, 1979. Pp. 248.

Rev. by Walter Huge in *HeineJ 1981*, pp. 193-96.
A briefer prestudy to Koopmann's article in the current
HeineJ. See above, under Heinrich-Heine-Institut. (J.L.S.)

Kopelew, Lew. *Ein Dichter kam von Rhein: Heinrich Heines Leben
und Leiden*. Translated from Russian by Helga Jaspers and
Ulrich H. Werner. Berlin: Severin und Siedler, 1981. Pp.
510; 35 illus. DM 38.00.

The circumstance that the author of this new popular
biography is a prominent Soviet dissident, whose long history
of courage and humaneness has eventuated in his expatriation,
is likely to bring the book considerable attention. While
Kopelev's great-heartedness and balanced judgment are evident
in it, the book has otherwise little to recommend it. In form
it is compact of quotations from Heine and the anecdotal
material concerning him, augmented with imaginatively re-
constructed conversations and fictionalized situations.
Nearly every anecdote and legend known to the tradition must
have been woven into it; it is out of touch with contemporary
scholarship, full of errors, and uncritical of evidence.
Unfortunately it is another in that long line of popular
biographies that have more obscured our vision of Heine than
clarified it. (J.L.S.)

Kruse, Joseph A., et al. *Heine in Paris 1831-1856*. Düsseldorf:
Droste Verlag, 1981. Pp. 178.

This illustrated catalogue to an anniversary exhibition
contains essays by Kruse on Heine's move to France, his
life in Paris, and the conditions of his private life; by
Pierre Grappin on Heine in Paris; by Michael Werner on
Parisian political and social life; by Bernd Kortländer
on Parisian literature and the press; by Ursula Lehmann on
the arts; and a compendium of Heine's comments on Paris

compiled by Heidemarie Vahl. While a brave attempt is made to shore up the conventional view of Heine as a mediator between Germany and France and as a "world citizen," the details show once again that he remained a stranger in Paris, impervious rather than receptive to experience. (J.L.S.)

Kruse, Joseph A., et al. *Heinrich Heine und seine Zeit 1797-1856*. Düsseldorf: Heinrich-Heine-Institut, 1980. Pp. 124.

This illustrated exhibition catalogue makes no effort at essayistic explication, as the previous item does, and contains nothing that will be new to the informed student, but provides a number of attractive pictures and illustrations. (J.L.S.)

Lebrave, Jean-Louis. "Vers une édition automatique de manuscrits." Pp. 216-23 in Louis Hay and Winfried Woesler, eds., *Die Nachlassedition--La Publication de manuscrits inédits: Akten des vom Centre National de la Recherche Scientifique und der Deutschen Forschungsgemeinschaft veranstalteten französisch-deutschen Editorenkolloquiums Paris 1977*. (*JIG*, Series I, Vol. 4.) Bern, Frankfurt am Main, and Las Vegas: Peter Lang, 1979. Pp. 248.

Rev. by Walter Huge in *HeineJ 1981*, pp. 193-96.
A suggestion for solving the problem of arranging genetic variants in Heine's prose texts by computer. (J.L.S.)

Motte-Haber, Helga de la. "'Es flüstern und sprechen die Blumen ...': Zum Widerspruch zwischen Lied als romantischer Kategorie und musikalischer Gattung." *LiLi* 9, no. 34 (1979): 70-79.

An analysis of Schumann's setting of *Lyrisches Intermezzo* 45 in *Dichterliebe*, Op. 48. (J.L.S.)

Nabrotzky, Ronald H. "Karl Marx als Heinrich Heines politischer und poetischer Mentor: Die Legende von Marx' Mitarbeit an Heines 'Wintermärchen.'" Pp. 129-40 in *Sprache und Literatur: Festschrift für Arval L. Streadbeck zum 65. Geburtstag*, ed. Gerhard P. Knapp and Wolff A. von Schmidt, with Heinz F. Rahde. Bern, Frankfurt am Main, and Las Vegas: Peter Lang, 1981.

Gives examples of exaggerated claims in East German cultural propaganda for Marx as the presiding genius of the *Wintermärchen*, even though, as Nabrotzky points out, some socialist and Marxist commentators saw from the beginning that the poem

grew out of Heine's long-standing concerns and owed little
to the association with Marx. (J.L.S.)

Nationale Forschungs- und Gedenkstätten der klassischen
deutschen Literatur in Weimar and Centre National de la
Recherche Scientifique in Paris, eds. *Heinrich Heine Säkular-
ausgabe*. Vol. 4: *Tragödien. Frühe Prosa 1820-1831*, ed. Karl
Wolfgang Becker and Fritz Mende. Berlin and Paris: Akademie-
Verlag and Editions du CNRS, 1980. Pp. 270. DM 23.00 (sub-
scription price).

Vol. 4 of the East German edition contains the text of
Almansor, William Ratcliff, both versions of the *Briefe aus
Berlin, Über Polen*, and the essays up to the move to Paris,
including the introduction to *Kahldorf über den Adel*, as
well as the strange unpublished piece on Wit von Dörring.
(J.L.S.)

Prawer, S.S. "Heine and the Photographers." *GL&L* N.S. 34 (1980):
64-73.

An elegant little article shows how Heine reacted to the
invention of the daguerreotype with reservations, using it
as a metaphor for an unmediated reproduction of nature un-
refined by the meaningfully selective and personal sensibility of the artist. (J.L.S.)

Prawer, S.S. "Heine's Portraits of German and French Jews on
the Eve of the 1848 Revolution." Pp. 353-83 in *Revolution
and Evolution 1848 in German-Jewish History*. (Schriftenreihe
wissenschaftlicher Abhandlungen des Leo Baeck Instituts,
39.) Tübingen: J.C.B. Mohr (Paul Siebeck), 1981.

As part of a larger study in progress of Heine's charac-
terizations of Jewish personalities, Prawer concentrates
on the treatment of Lassalle, Felix Mendelssohn, the Jewish
notables prominent at the time of the Damascus pogrom--the
Foulds, Rothschild, and Crémieux--and Ludwig Markus. With
his customary perspicacity, Prawer exhibits the subtlety
and wit with which Heine nuances personal and physical
characteristics, linking them to his own ongoing self-com-
mentary as well as to larger historical issues. At times
Prawer goes rather far in extenuating Heine's frequent mean-
spiritedness and ethical carelessness of expression--e.g.,
in his anti-Jewish remarks. Heine was a caricaturist, as
Prawer freely admits; he was not a portraitist, for that
requires an empathy into other human selves that he largely
lacked. (J.L.S.)

Prawer, Siegbert. "Der Komet als Licht des Exils: Heines
Porträt seines Zeitgenossen Eduard Gans." Pp. 347-68 in
*Goethezeit: Studien zur Erkenntnis und Rezeption Goethes
und seiner Zeitgenossen. Festschrift für Stuart Atkins*, ed.
Gerhart Hoffmeister. Bern and Munich: Francke, 1981. Pp. 392.

An informative review of Heine's relations with and references to Eduard Gans, showing clearly that Heine displaced
his own bad conscience about his apostasy to Judaism onto
his view of Gans. (J.L.S.)

Raddatz, Fritz J. *Von Geist und Geld: Heinrich Heine und sein
Onkel, Bankier Salomon. Eine Skizze. Mit sechs Radierungen
von Günter Grass.* Cologne: Bund-Verlag, 1980. Pp. 99. DM 42.00.

Fritz J. Raddatz' talent for chic self-promotion on modest
resources of information and insight is impressive. From his
careless Heine "essay" of 1977 (see *ELN* 16, Supp., 163),
Raddatz recycles some of the commentary, indiscriminately
drawn from anecdote and gossip, on Heine's relationship
with his rich uncle and the Rothschilds. The text, which is
wastefully printed in huge 18-point type, eventuates in a
banal sermon on the oppression of the life of the mind by
the power of money and the misery of German writers, so often
driven into exile. Grass's six etchings, all previously
published, are, as usual, very skilled and quite hermetic;
their relevance to Raddatz' argument is obscure, especially
since Grass is surely one of the most successful and wealthi-
est of writers and artists in today's world. (J.L.S.)

Riemen, Alfred. "Heines und Eichendorffs literarhistorische
Schriften." *ZDP* 99 (1980): 532-59.

A comparison of Heine's and Eichendorff's literary-histori-
cal essays shows that they focused on similar literary issues
and events, though from opposite evaluative and ideological
positions. Both are convinced that the struggle between
Christianity and "materialism" is crucial to their time,
both transfer aspects of late Romanticism to early Romanticism, both see the opposite side as a conspiracy, and both
perceive and judge through pre-established priorities. Since
Heine is the only opponent Eichendorff mentions by name,
there is good reason to think that his reactionary, Catholic
literary history was expressly directed against Heine.
(J.L.S.)

Sammons, Jeffrey L. "Heine and His Age: Literary Dissidence
in Nineteenth-Century Germany." *Yale University Library
Gazette* 55 (1981): 165-76.

An introductory lecture to an anniversary rare-book exhibit stressing the literary dissidence of Heine and his contemporaries.

Schoeps, Julius H. "Aron Bernstein über Heinrich Heine: Ein Kapitel Heine-Rezeption in der Zeit des Vormärz." Pp. 143-48 in *Juden in Deutschland: Zur Geschichte einer Hoffnung. Historische Längsschnitte und Einzelstudien.* (Veröffentlichungen aus dem Institut Kirche und Judentum, ed. Peter von der Osten-Sacken, Vol. 11.) Berlin: Selbstverlag Institut Kirche und Judentum, 1980. Pp. 224. DM 10.50.

Aron Bernstein, who later made a name for himself as the author of novellas with Jewish themes, published at age 23 an essay, reacting to Börne's attack on Heine, charging Heine's younger critics with ingratitude, since they were his essayistic pupils. The defense of Heine himself is rather left-handed, and Schoeps's introduction somewhat naive. (J.L.S.)

Ueding, Gert, with Bernd Steinbrink. *Hoffmann und Campe: Ein deutscher Verlag.* Hamburg: Hoffmann und Campe, 1981. Pp. 615; 56 illus.

For the first time we have a well-researched, fully documented study of the two-hundred-year history of Heine's publishing house. The section devoted to Benjamin Gottlieb Hoffmann and the origins of the firm in the Enlightenment is the most interesting part of the book. The judicious chapters on Heine's publisher Campe bring little that is new to the well-informed reader, although, unlike Edda Ziegler's study (see *ELN* 16, Supp., 165), they deal in some detail with Campe's other authors. The systematic near-ruination of the firm by Campe's son and its gradual recovery to its present standing make interesting reading. Though not without minor flaws, the handsome bicentennial volume serves its purpose well and is recommendable to the general reader. (J.L.S.)

Urbahn de Jauregui, Heidi. "Denk ich an Heine." *SuF* 33 (1981): 1026-54.

With a rambling, somewhat pretentious essayistic style and a modest amount of information and insight, the author, said to be a literary scholar living in France, trims Heine to the orthodox Marxist outlook. He is used, among other things, as a stick with which to beat more complex modern poetry from Rimbaud to Celan. The piece is too long for its dilute content. (J.L.S.)

Vontin, Walther, ed. Heinrich Heine, *Schöne Wiege meiner Leiden: Hamburgische Miniaturen.* Hamburg: Hoffmann und Campe, 1981. Pp. 255. DM 19.80.

An allegedly revised reissue of a book originally published in 1956 orders Heine's observations on Hamburg in biographical sequence and connects them with a commentary compounded of more or less accurate fact and more or less reliable anecdote. It is of no scholarly value, but it contains a bibliographical chronology and identifications of all persons mentioned, along with some nice pictures. (J.L.S.)

Wehner, Walter. *Heinrich Heine: "Die schlesischen Weber" und andere Texte zum Weberelend.* (Text und Geschichte: Modell-analysen zur deutschen Literatur, ed. Gert Sautermeister and Jochen Vogt. Uni-Taschenbücher, 973.) Munich: Fink, 1980. Pp. 103. DM 9.80.

The volume, evidently intended for pedagogical purposes, contains information on the economic condition of Germany in the early nineteenth century and of the weaving industry; five exemplary poems on the weavers' rebellion, including Heine's, ranging from progressive to conservative; literary analysis; reception history; and documentary materials. The commentary is strictly Marxist, making large claims for Heine's debt to and affinity with Marx; the intention is to show that political partisanship is compatible with artistic excellence, insofar as it exhibits correct ideological in-sight, and to recommend the use of the text to oppose the bourgeoisie and capitalism. (J.L.S.)

Werner, Michael. "A propos des 'Mémoires' de Heine: la fin d'une légende et ses conséquences pour l'édition." Pp. 245-48 in Louis Hay and Winfried Woesler, eds., *Die Nachlassedi-tion--La Publication de manuscrits inédits: Akten des vom Centre National de la Recherche Scientifique und der Deutschen Forschungsgemeinschaft veranstalteten französisch-deutschen Editorenkolloquiums Paris 1977. (JIG, Series I, Vol. 4.)* Bern, Frankfurt am Main, and Las Vegas: Peter Lang, 1979. Pp. 248.

Rev. by Walter Huge in *HeineJ 1981*, pp. 193-96.
Editorial consequences of the work of Heinemann (see *ELN* 17, Supp., 202) indicating that Heine's memoirs were not mutilated by his family but that the lacuna was used for the *Geständnisse.* (J.L.S.)

Windfuhr, Manfred, ed. Heinrich Heine, *Historisch-kritische Gesamtausgabe der Werke.* Vol. VIII/2: *Zur Geschichte der*

*Religion und Philosophie in Deutschland. Die Romantische
Schule. Apparat*, ed. Manfred Windfuhr. Hamburg: Hoffmann
und Campe, 1981. Pp. 1,142 (continuously paged from Vol.
VIII/1, pp. 506-1,647.); 8 pls. Vol. XII/1: *Französische
Maler. Französische Zustände. Über die französische Bühne.
Text*, ed. Jean-René Derré and Christiane Giesen. Hamburg:
Hoffmann und Campe, 1980. Pp. 504. DM 48.00 each vol. (sub-
scription price).

The elaborate commentary volume to *Zur Geschichte der
Religion und Philosophie in Deutschland* and *Die Romantische
Schule* is a significant step forward for the Düsseldorf edition and establishes it not only as the major Heine edition
of all time but as one of the most impressive editing projects
in contemporary German scholarship. The philological work
on the texts, with their exceptionally complicated genesis
and publication history, is immense. Among the advances is
the decision to base the text of *Religion und Philosophie*
on the manuscript of 1834 rather than upon the second edition of *Salon II* (1852) as it appears, contaminated by editors with paralipomena, in almost all previous editions.
The annotation contains much new material. Of particular
interest to Americans is the information concerning the first
of Heine's works to be published in English in the United
States, the first version of *Die Romantische Schule*, translated by a New Hampshire banker in 1836 and extensively
reviewed at the time. A great deal has been accomplished
in tracing Heine's reading and sources, especially in
philosophy, although the breadth of his studies, much of it
in handbooks and secondary materials, may in places have
led the editor to overvalue Heine's philosophical competence,
as there is in general a tendency to apologetics in the
commentary from time to time. The extremely compendious and
detailed apparatus will not be very accessible to efficient
consultation by any but the most experienced students of
Heine; however, there is a useful index.

Vol. XII/1 contains Heine's reportage from Paris of the
1830s, along with their paralipomena and French versions.
The commentary is again postponed to a separate volume; one
looks forward to it with considerable expectation, as Heine's
views have never yet been set against an objective account
of French history of that time. (J.L.S.)

Zagari, Luciano, and Paolo Chiarini, eds. *Zu Heinrich Heine*.
(LGW-Interpretationen, ed. Theo Buck, Manfred Durzak, and
Dietrich Steinbach, in the series Literaturwissenschaft--
Gesellschaftswissenschaft, ed. Theo Buck and Dietrich Stein-
bach.) Stuttgart: Ernst Klett, 1981. Pp. 145. DM 19.00.

An interesting feature of this volume is that it arises out of Italian Heine scholarship, which has been quite sophisticated, though not completely well known to other scholars owing to the language barrier. The book is not, however, restricted to Italian contributors. Its purpose is to provide examples of a more modern Heine criticism, and, while the articles vary in their originality, all are of high quality and value. The introduction by the editors Zagari and Chiarini expresses the purpose of making Heine more accessible and acceptable to the modern intellectual temper, and along the way gives an instructive summary of the history of Heine criticism in Italy. Manfred Durzak argues that Heine's lyrical style reflects an awareness of a world without religious or metaphysical legitimation in which image and reality have separated; he rightly contends that Heine and Platen were not so different in this regard, and he concludes with Benjamin's concept of allegorical incongruity in preference to symbolic unity. Chiarini, in a carefully nuanced, though perhaps not wholly original analysis, sees Heine historically situated in a conflict between the private and the collective, the individual and the social, so that the hope of a genuinely emancipated autonomy exercises a resistance to the claimed revolutionary commitment. Alberto Destro points out the many points of contact between Heine's poetry and the common verse of the time; yet Heine failed to communicate his anti-conformist, emancipatory message. Some aspects of the argument are debatable. Ida Porena discusses Schumann's relation to Heine, observing that Schumann discovered his own self in all the poets and that he, like Heine, introduces disturbing elements into familiar forms. The Polish scholar Karol Sauerland provides a well-informed if brief effort to illuminate the genre of the *Reisebilder* comparatively, though in my opinion genre considerations do not go far toward understanding those texts. Lia Secci attempts a feminist interpretation of the dionysiac element in Heine, which seems a rather odd way of going about it, although she has some persuasive observations on Heine's "alienated" erotic constitution. This article suffers even more than most in the volume from inattention to English-language resources. In one of the best of the essays, Mazzino Montinari analyzes the subsumption of politics and philosophy under religion in the *Geständnisse*; there are some original and interesting philological observations on the genesis of the text. Wolfgang Preisendanz discusses Heine's images of India in the context of the modern idyll as a poetic, explicitly fictive counter-world to the real world of alienation and dissonance. Zagari, in a thoughtful and challenging essay, endeavors to show that in Heine's

late poetry the power of the word to reach the core of reality
has dissipated, the images and myths of the poetic imagination cannot be used but only shown in chaotic incoherence;
yet somehow the flow of words and images continues and the
imaginary poetic realm is the only worthwhile one.
The value of this volume cannot be captured in a brief
notice. Much in it is open to debate, but it exhibits an
effort to capture and define the quality of Heine's imagination more serious and nuanced than much of what we have had
recently. The essays should be carefully considered by Heine
scholars from now on. (J.L.S.)

Zinke, Jochen. "Heine und Hegel. Stationen der Forschung."
Hegel-Studien 14 (1979): 295-312.

A review of the modern scholarship on Hegel and Heine.
Much of Zinke's evaluation is motivated by the urge to ex-
aggerate Heine's connection to Hegel and his philosophical
competence in general. (J.L.S.)

See also Seiverth ("Hoffmann").

Reviews of books previously listed:

AKADEMIE der Wissenschaften der DDR, Zentralinstitut für
Literaturgeschichte, Centre National de la Recherche Scientifique, Centre d'Histoire et d'Analyse des Manuscrits
Modernes, eds., *Heinrich Heine und die Zeitgenossen* (see
RMB for 1980, pp. 295-96), rev. by Fritz Mende in *DLZ* 102
(1981): cols. 319-22; BRUMMACK, Jürgen, *Satirische Dichtung:
Studien zu Friedrich Schlegel, Tieck, Jean Paul und Heine*
(see *RMB* for 1980, p. 297), rev. by M[ichel] Espagne in *EG*
36 (1981): 89-90; CLASEN, Herbert, *Heinrich Heines Romantik-
kritik* (see *RMB* for 1980, pp. 297-98), rev. by Fritz Mende
in *HeineJ 1981*, pp. 189-91; HÖRLING, Hans, *Heinrich Heine
im Spiegel der politischen Presse Frankreichs 1831-1841*
(see *ELN* 17, Supp., 204), rev. by Michel Espagne in *Germanistik* 21 (1980): 354-55; HUEPPE, Frederick E., *Unity and
Synthesis in the Work of Heinrich Heine* (see *RMB* for 1980,
p. 302), rev. by Helge Hultberg in *Germanistik* 21 (1980):
710-11; JACOBI, Ruth L., *Heinrich Heines jüdisches Erbe*
(see *RMB* for 1979, p. 284), rev. by Karlheinz Fingerhut in
Germanistik 21 (1980): 711; JAHN, Maria-Eva, *Techniken der
fiktiven Bildkomposition in Heinrich Heines "Reisebildern"*
(see *RMB* for 1979, p. 285), rev. by Joseph A. Kruse in
HeineJ 1981, pp. 196-97; KÄFER, Karl-Heinz, *Versöhnt ohne
Opfer* (see *ELN* 17, Supp., 204), rev. by Hans-Georg Werner
in *DLZ* 101 (1980): cols. 930-31; KRÄMER, Helmut, *Heinrich*

Heines Auseinandersetzung mit zeitgenössischer Philosophie
(see *RMB* for 1980, p. 303), rev. by Fritz Mende in *Germanistik* 21 (1980): 711; LÜDI, Rolf, *Heinrich Heines Buch der
Lieder* (see *RMB* for 1980, pp. 303-04), rev. by Gerd Heinemann in *Germanistik* 21 (1980): 355-56; MEIER-LENZ, D.P.,
*Heinrich Heine--Wolf Biermann: Deutschland. ZWEI Winter-
märchen* (see *ELN* 17, Supp., 206), rev. by Volkmar Hansen
in *CG* 14 (1981): 86-88; NETTER, Lucienne, *Heine et la peinture
de la civilisation parisienne 1840-1848* (see *RMB* for 1980,
p. 306), rev. by Volkmar Hansen in *Germanistik* 22 (1981):
184-85; by Robert C. Holub in *GQ* 54 (1981): 351-52; by Alain
Montandon in *Romantisme* no. 32 (1981): 109-10; OEHLER, Dolf,
Pariser Bilder 1 (1830-1848) (see *RMB* for 1979, pp. 286-87),
rev. by Monika Noll in *Romantisme* no. 30 (1980): 121-22;
RADDATZ, Fritz J., *Heine: Ein deutsches Märchen* (see *ELN* 16,
Supp., 163), rev. by Béla G. Németh in *ALittASH* 21 (1979):
449-50; REESE, Walter, *Zur Geschichte der sozialistischen
Heine-Rezeption in Deutschland* (see *RMB* for 1980, p. 307),
rev. by Volkmar Hansen in *Germanistik* 21 (1980): 712;
SAMMONS, Jeffrey L., *Heinrich Heine: A Modern Biography* (see
RMB for 1979, p. 288), rev. by Rosemary Ashton in *New States-
man*, April 11, 1980, p. 557; by G. Richard Dimler, S.J., in
CollL 8 (1981): 110-11; by Richard C. Figge in *JEGP* 80 (1981):
388-90; by Henry Hatfield in *SiR* 19 (1980): 551-53; by Fritz
Mende in *DLZ* 102 (1981): cols. 35-38; by Ferdinand Mount in
S, April 5, 1980, pp. 17-18; by Nigel Reeves in *MLR* 76 (1981):
994-96; by Ludwig Rosenthal in *HeineJ 1981*, pp. 203-07; by
Hanna Spencer in *Seminar* 16 (1980): 259-61; SPENCER, Hanna,
Dichter, Denker, Journalist (see *ELN* 17, Supp., 208), rev.
by Manfred Windfuhr in *CG* 13 (1980): 275-77; ZEPF, Irmgard,
Heinrich Heines Gemäldebericht zum Salon 1831 (see *RMB* for
1980, p. 311), rev. by Fritz Mende in *DLZ* 102 (1981): cols.
597-99; by Fritz Mende in *EG* 35 (1980): 484; by Gerhard Weiss
in *HeineJ 1981*, pp. 211-13.

HEYSE

See Berno ("Italian 3. Leopardi").

HÖLDERLIN

Austerlitz, Robert. "Hölderlin's Asclepiad Strophe." Pp. 17-
28 in Erhard F. Schiefer, ed., *Explanations et Tractationes
Fenno-Ugricae in Honorem Hans Fromm*. Munich: Fink, 1979.
Pp. ix+453.

The article investigates Hölderlin's Asclepiad strophe
from the perspective of coherence in the strophe. Austerlitz
presents essential and characteristic cohering features
rather than a traditional metrical analysis. Original, if
tentative. Hölderlin research is included in rudimentary
form only. (W.G.K.)

Beck, Adolf. "Hölderlins Weg zu Deutschland: Fragmente und
Thesen. III. Teil: 'O guter Geist des Vaterlandes.'" *JFDH*
(1979): 278-348.

    Rev. by R. Ayrault in *EG* 35 (1980): 351-53.
    A thorough discussion, filled with an abundance of quota-
tions, of the complex image of Suebia and Germany in late
poems and fragments by Hölderlin, such as "Vom Abgrund nemlich ...," "Ihr sichergebaueten Alpen ...," "Die Wanderung,"
"Deutscher Gesang," "Sonst nemlich, Vater Zeus ...," and
"Germanien." (W.G.K.)

Beck, Adolf. "Hölderlins Weg zu Deutschland: Fragmente und
Thesen. IV. Teil: Hesperischer Orbis." *JFDH* (1980): 300-46.

    This article completes Beck's four-part series and includes
discussions of Hölderlin's poems and fragments "Am Quell der
Donau," "O Mutter Erde!," "Brod und Wein," and "Mnemosyne."
Also, Beck announces a book based on the series. (W.G.K.)

Böckmann, Paul. "Über eine Frage Hölderlins: 'Saget, wie bring'
ich den Dank?'" *JDSG* 24 (1980): 182-204.

    Employing a methodology along the lines of *Geistesgeschichte*,
Böckmann reflects on Hölderlin's language and his poetic
consciousness in relation to the possibilities of thinking.
In an appendix, Böckmann sharply criticizes Heidegger's
ahistorical 1934/35 approach to Hölderlin (see Murray,
Ziegler below). (W.G.K.)

Böschenstein, Bernhard. *Leuchttürme: Von Hölderlin zu Celan:
Wirkung und Vergleich. Studien*. Frankfurt: Insel Verlag,
1977. Pp. 331. DM 34.00.

    Rev. by Walter Naumann in *Germanistik* 21 (1980): 248-49.
Hölderlin, Jean Paul.

Constantine, David J. *The Significance of Locality in the
Poetry of Friedrich Hölderlin*. (MHRA Texts and Dissertations,
Vol. 12.) London: The Modern Humanities Research Association,
1979. Pp. vii+159. £9.00; $22.00.

Rev. by Beth Bjorklund in *Monatshefte* 73 (1981): 353-54; by Ralph W. Ewton, Jr., in *GSR* 4 (1981): 461-62; by P.H. Gaskill in *MLR* 75 (1980): 947; by Marjorie Gelus in *GQ* 54 (1981): 96-97; by G. Raynal-Mony in *EG* 35 (1980): 353.

The localities of Hölderlin's poetic world are presented and discussed in a thorough but frequently laborious manner, with particular emphasis on the two poles of Germany, especially Swabia, and an idealized Greece. Constantine points out the close relationship between Hölderlin's changing imagination and his various poetic landscapes. He shows some prejudice in his discussion of Hölderlin's works after the time in Bordeaux by passing negative value judgments derived from an outdated view of Hölderlin's madness and of the so-called disintegration of his creative abilities. Here, as well as in some other areas of the book, Hölderlin scholarship has been neglected. (W.G.K.)

Dallett, Joseph B. "Hölderlins Ätna: Zur Quellenfrage und Bildlichkeit der Empedokles-Dichtungen." Pp. 251-64 in Gerhart Hoffmeister, ed., *Goethezeit: Studien zur Erkenntnis und Rezeption Goethes und seiner Zeitgenossen: Festschrift für Stuart Atkins.* Bern and Munich: Francke, 1981. Pp. 392.

In this thorough comparison between Hölderlin's *Empedokles* and Patrick Brydone's travel book *A Tour through Sicily and Malta*, which appeared in German translation in 1744, Dallett emphasizes the differences between the two works. The question of Hölderlin's knowledge of Brydone's work is left open, and, to a large extent, it appears to be irrelevant for an understanding of *Empedokles*. Clarifying. (W.G.K.)

Fortugno, Franco. "Il primo programma di sistema dell'idealismo tedesco." *SGr* N.S. XVI (1978): 41-72 (part 1) and 291-336 (part 2).

Gaskill, P.H. "Hölderlin's 'Friedensfeier' and the 'Living Building.'" *NGS* 8 (1980): 169-88.

A thorough article which concentrates on the opening lines of Hölderlin's "Friedensfeier." In contradistinction to Beissner and in agreement with numerous other critics, Gaskill sees in these lines a metaphor for a wide-open, living landscape rather than an enclosed "Saal." In support of his argument, Gaskill refers to similar passages by Hölderlin and others, and also to the Bible. (W.G.K.)

Gaskill, P.H. "'Ich seh,' ich sehe, wie das enden muss ...': Observations on a Misunderstood Passage in Hölderlin's 'Hyperion.'" *MLR* 76 (1981): 612-18.

Arguing against a 1972 article by Lawrence O. Frye,
Gaskill convincingly contends that Hyperion, at the end of
the first volume, does not anticipate the main course of
the narrative in the second volume. (W.G.K.)

Hamburger, Michael, trans. *Friedrich Hölderlin: Poems and
Fragments*. Cambridge: Cambridge University Press, 1980.
Pp. xx+674. $16.50.

Rev. by [Peter] Howard Gaskill in *Lines Review* 75 (1980):
27-30.
In addition to the 1966 edition of Hamburger's Hölderlin
translations, this bi-lingual volume contains new translations of twelve poems and fragments, among them "The German's
Song," "Heidelberg" in an alcaic version, "The Traveller,"
"Stuttgart," and "Colombo." With success, Hamburger continues
to stay close to the original texts. (W.G.K.)

Horster, Detlef. *Die Subjekt-Objekt-Beziehung im Deutschen
Idealismus und in der Marxschen Philosophie*. (Campus For-
schung, Vol. 114.) Frankfurt am Main: Campus, 1979. Pp. 264.
DM 34.00.

In agreement with well-known research, Horster, in large
segments of this book, reemphasizes Hölderlin's seminal significance for Hegel's and Schelling's critique of knowledge.
Marx's philosophy is seen as a further and critically modified phase along lines originating with Hölderlin. Particular
stress is placed on the interrelationship of forms of knowledge and their underlying social conditions. Horster ignores
much relevant Hölderlin research, thus reaching oversimplified
conclusions with regard to the social significance of Hölderlin's thinking and suffering. (W.G.K.)

Liebrucks, Bruno. *Sprache und Bewusstsein*. Vol. 7, "Und."
*Die Sprache Hölderlins in der Spannweite von Mythos und
Logos, Realität und Wirklichkeit*. Bern: Lang, 1979. Pp. 847.

Rev. by Lawrence Ryan in *Germanistik* 22 (1981): 165-66.
Hölderlin is the focus of the nearly 600 pages comprising
the second part of this monumental volume. Within the context of his philosophical reflections on myth and logos,
Liebrucks discusses various levels of consciousness in Hölderlin's work. Particular attention is paid to the philosophical
status of Hölderlin's language. Throughout his book, Liebrucks warns against an overly objectivistic scholarship
and emphasizes the profoundly open nature of Hölderlin's
work. While Liebrucks offers searching and engaged reflections, various details of his argument as well as his sweep-

ing philosophical stance call for questions and criticism.
(W.G.K.)

McLean, William Scott. "Private Song and the Public Sphere:
Some Remarks on the Development of Hölderlin's Later Poetry."
Pp. 265-80 in Gerhart Hoffmeister, ed., *Goethezeit: Studien
zur Erkenntnis und Rezeption Goethes und seiner Zeitgenossen:
Festschrift für Stuart Atkins*. Bern and Munich: Francke,
1981. Pp. 392.

An overview of Hölderlin's shift away from a subjective
mode of writing toward a communal, reflective, universally
balanced kind of poetry. A good introduction, which includes
some references to the superficial literary life Hölderlin
was suffering from. (W.G.K.)

Methlagl, Walter. "'Die Zeit und die Stunde der Zeit': Rekon-
struktion des Hölderlin-Bildes im letzten 'Brenner.'" Pp.
153-78 in Johann Holzner, Michael Klein, and Wolfgang Wies-
müller, eds., *Studien zur Literatur des 19. und 20. Jahrhunderts in Österreich: Festschrift für Alfred Doppler zum
60. Geburtstag*. (Innsbrucker Beiträge zur Kulturwissen-
schaft: Germanistische Reihe, Vol. 12.) Innsbruck, 1981.
Pp. 295.

Focusing on the later years of Ludwig von Ficker's intellectual and editorial activities--the final issue of his
journal *Der Brenner* appeared in 1954--Methlagl mainly discusses Heidegger's friendly and Adorno's complex relationship to the journal's philosophy, particularly in the light
of different views of Hölderlin. Detailed, informative.
(W.G.K.)

Murray, Michael. "Heidegger's Hermeneutic Reading of Hölderlin: The Signs of Time." *The Eighteenth Century* 21 (1980):
41-66.

An informative and thoughtful overview of essential
aspects of Heidegger's reading of Hölderlin. Heidegger's
1934/35 lecture course appeared too late for inclusion in
this article. The lectures suggest a reexamination of Murray's
evaluation of Heidegger's attitudes toward the political
realities of that time (see Böckmann above, Ziegler below).
(W.G.K.)

Prévost, Claude. *Littératures du dépaysement*. Paris: Les
Editeurs Français Réunis, 1979. Pp. 314.

Includes well-written reflections on Hölderlin's situation
as an outsider (pp. 154-82), with some emphasis on his reception in France. (W.G.K.)

Sattler, D.E. *Friedrich Hölderlin: 144 fliegende Briefe.* 2 vols.
Darmstadt and Neuwied: Luchterhand, 1981. Pp. 320; 335.
DM 68.00.

Rev. by Peter Härtling in *Frankfurter Allgemeine Zeitung*,
Oct. 13, 1981; by Klaus Jeziorkowski in *Die Zeit*, Nov. 13,
1981; by Albert von Schirnding in *Süddeutsche Zeitung*, Oct.
14, 1981.
In subtly structured form, the two volumes contain numerous
texts by Hölderlin, edited and explicated by Sattler, as well
as various reflections, allusions, and quotations, directly
and indirectly related to Hölderlin—a multi-referential,
highly complex assemblage which shows Sattler's originality
and his dedication to his subject of many years: Hölderlin
and his works. At the same time, Sattler alerts the reader
to the present interruption of his—eminently useful—Frankfurt Hölderlin edition. (W.G.K.)

Sattler, D.E., ed. *Friedrich Hölderlin: Sämtliche Werke.* Vol.
14, *Entwürfe zur Poetik*, ed. Wolfram Groddeck and D.E. Sattler. (Frankfurter Ausgabe.) Frankfurt am Main: Roter Stern,
1979. Pp. 391.

Rev. by Henning Boetius in *Germanistik* 20 (1979): 818–19.
Another valuable volume of the Frankfurt edition. Hölderlin's poetological writings are presented with philological
precision and accompanied by numerous facsimiles of the
originals. (W.G.K.)

Schmidt, Jochen, ed. *Friedrich Hölderlin: Hyperion oder Der
Eremit in Griechenland.* Frankfurt am Main: Insel, 1979. Pp.
229.

A well-written, informative, and thoughtful postscript
(pp. 199-229) by Schmidt concludes this *Hyperion* edition.
A reference to the textual source of this volume is lacking.
(W.G.K.)

Söring, Jürgen. "'Die Apriorität des Individuellen über das
Ganze': Von der Schwierigkeit, ein Prinzip der Lyrik zu
finden." *JDSG* 24 (1980): 205-46.

A wide-ranging study which is not only concerned with
clarifying Hölderlin's formulation "Die *apriorität* des
Individuellen über das Ganze," but also with basic questions
of lyrical theory. At the end, Hölderlin's "latest" poetry
and other writings are discussed in the light of a dissolution of individuality, a phenomenon which could have been
elucidated further in connection with Hölderlin research.
(W.G.K.)

Verbeeck, Ludo. "Récit mythique ou appel transgressif? A propos du poème 'Der Winkel von Hardt' de Friedrich Hölderlin." Pp. 231-39 in Jacques Lerot and Rudolf Kern, eds., *Mélanges de linguistique et de littérature offerts au Professeur Henri Draye à l'occasion de son éméritat.* (Université de Louvain: Recueil de travaux d'histoire et de philologie, Ser. 6, Vol. 14.) Louvain: Bibliothèque de l'Université, Editions Nauwelaerts, 1978. Pp. xxv+258.

A "modern" reading of Hölderlin's late poem, emphasizing its fragmentary and disharmonious structure. (W.G.K.)

Ziegler, Susanne, ed. *Martin Heidegger: Hölderlins Hymnen "Germanien" und "Der Rhein."* (Gesamtausgabe, Vol. 39.) Frankfurt am Main: Klostermann, 1980. Pp. xi+296. DM 42.00.

Rev. by Paul Böckmann in *JDSG* 24 (1980): 201-04.
See Böckmann, Murray above.

An edition of Heidegger's 1934/35 lecture course on Hölderlin's hymns "Germanien" and "Der Rhein," this volume focuses on the two hymns in the context of Heidegger's thinking, with numerous references to Hölderlin's late poetry. In its vagueness, its arbitrary irrationalism, and its supportive allusions to the Third Reich, the volume is another document of Heidegger's blindness toward the Nazi regime. (W.G.K.)

See also Itô, Reed, Schmidt-Dengler ("German 2. General"); Kuhn ("Goethe").

Reviews of books previously listed:

BECK, Adolf, ed., *Hölderlins Diotima: Susette Gontard* (see *RMB* for 1980, p. 314), rev. by Willy Leygraf in *Schwäbische Heimat* 199 (1981): 68; by Johannes Mahr in *Germanistik* 21 (1980): 675-76; BERTAUX, Pierre, *Friedrich Hölderlin* (see *ELN* 17, Supp., 213), rev. by David Constantine in *MLR* 75 (1980): 944-46; by Alfred Ehrentreich in *NDH* 26 (1979): 616-19; by Helm Stierlin in *Psyche* 35 (1981): 747-49; HÄRTLING, Peter, *Hölderlin* (see *ELN* 15, Supp., 169), rev. by J.-L. Pinard-Legry in *QL* 340 (Jan. 16-31, 1981): 10-11; [French version] by Gilles Quinsat in *NRF* 339 (April 1, 1981): 121-22; HAUSCHILD, Hans-Ulrich, *Die idealistische Utopie: Untersuchungen zur Entwicklung des utopischen Denkens Friedrich Hölderlins* (see *ELN* 17, Supp., 212), rev. by Johannes Mahr in *Germanistik* 21 (1980): 675; KONDYLIS, Panajotis, *Die Entstehung der Dialektik: Eine Analyse der geistigen Entwicklung von Hölderlin, Schelling und Hegel bis 1802* (see *RMB* for 1980, p. 317), rev. by Wolfgang Schirmacher in *PL*

34 (1981): 297-98; MIETH, Günter, *Friedrich Hölderlin: Dichter der bürgerlich-demokratischen Revolution* (see *RMB* for 1980, p. 318), rev. by Claus Friedrich Köpp in *WB* 27 (1981): 182-85; by Tadeusz Namowicz in *Kwartalnik Neofilologiczny* 27 (1980): 481-82; NÄGELE, Rainer, *Literatur und Utopie: Versuche zu Hölderlin* (see *ELN* 17, Supp., 213), rev. by Marjorie Gelus in *Monatshefte* 73 (1981): 354-55; by R.B. Harrison in *MLR* 76 (1981): 747-48; by Wm. Scott McLean in *MLN* 96 (1981): 699-702; NALBANTIAN, Suzanne, *The Symbol of the Soul from Hölderlin to Yeats* (see *ELN* 16, Supp., 170), rev. by Maria M. Tatar in *Monatshefte* 71 (1979): 343-44; SCHMIDT, Jochen, *Hölderlins später Widerruf in den Oden "Chiron," "Blödigkeit" und "Ganymed"* (see *ELN* 17, Supp., 211), rev. by Beth Bjorklund in *Monatshefte* 73 (1981): 353-54; by Richard W. Hannah in *GSR* 4 (1981): 135-36.

HOFFMANN, E.T.A.

Behrmann, Alfred. "Zur Poetik des Kunstmärchens: Eine Strukturanalyse der 'Königsbraut' von E.T.A. Hoffmann." Pp. 107-34 in Wolfgang Haubrichs, ed., *Erzählforschung 3. Theorien, Modelle und Methoden der Narrativik*. (*LiLi*, Beiheft 8.) Göttingen: Vandenhoeck & Ruprecht, 1978.

An excellent, thorough, and highly illuminating model analysis of one of Hoffmann's greatest narrative achievements, hitherto largely unappreciated by Hoffmann scholars (laudable exceptions: Maassen and Negus). Behrmann draws on up-to-date narrative theory and folktale research on an international scale and succeeds in providing a soberly critical textual and structural interpretation. (S.P.S.)

Boie, Bernhild. "Die Sprache der Automaten: Zur Autonomie der Kunst." *GQ* 54 (1981): 284-97.

The unresolved mystery of the talking Turk in Hoffmann's *Die Automate* serves as the prime example for Boie's spirited and, in many interpretive details, novel excursus on the aesthetic, philosophical, and linguistic implications for literature of the eighteenth-century fascination with the theory and construction of automatons. *Kater Murr*, Novalis' *Monolog*, André Breton's *Manifeste du Surréalisme*, Arnim's *Gräfin Dolores*, and Villiers de l'Isle-Adam's *L'Eve future* are also briefly discussed. (S.P.S.)

Bourke, Thomas. *Stilbruch als Stilmittel: Studien zur Literatur der Spät- und Nachromantik. Mit besonderer Berücksichtigung von E.T.A. Hoffmann, Lord Byron und Heinrich Heine.* Frankfurt: Lang, 1980. Pp. 355.

See also Bourke ("Heine").
Consideration of Hoffmann (with an unremarkable chapter on *Kater Murr*) is curiously out of place in this Munich dissertation primarily concerned with lyric poetry. (S.P.S.)

Cheauré, Elisabeth. *E.T.A. Hoffmann: Inszenierungen seiner Werke auf russischen Bühnen. Ein Beitrag zur Rezeptionsgeschichte.* Heidelberg: Winter, 1979. Pp. 269. DM 94.00.

Cheauré's circumspect and absorbing study, a seminal contribution to Hoffmann research, offers a comprehensive historical and critical account of early twentieth-century stage adaptations of Hoffmann's works under influential theatermen of international stature such as Meyerhold and Tairov. After reviewing the history of nineteenth- and twentieth-century Russian Hoffmann-reception (based on previous work by Passage, Zitomirskaja, and Ingham), Cheauré discusses the fascinating theoretical, ideological, and technical aspects concerning dramaturgy and performance practices in the theatrical realization of four works in particular: *Nußknacker und Mausekönig, Die Brautwahl, Prinzessin Brambilla,* and *Signor Formica.* As a direct result of the innovative 1920 adaptation of *Prinzessin Brambilla,* treated in exhaustive analytical detail by Cheauré, Hoffmann has been regarded in Russia also as a pioneering theoretician of the theater. (S.P.S.)

Currie, Robert. "Wyndham Lewis, E.T.A. Hoffmann, and *Tarr.*" *RES* 30 (1979): 169-81.

Cited previously without review; see *RMB* for 1979, p. 295. Currie offers concise yet penetrating side-by-side interpretations of *Kater Murr* and Wyndham Lewis' *Tarr* (1918) and concludes that "though Lewis never publicly acknowledged the debt, *Tarr* was chiefly dependent, not on Dostoevsky, but on E.T.A. Hoffmann's *Murr*" (171-72). (S.P.S.)

Curzon, Henri de, trans. *E.T.A. Hoffmann: Fantaisies dans la manière de Callot.* Préf. de Jean-Paul Richter. Paris: Phébus, 1980. Pp. 426.

Rev. by G.-A. Goldschmidt in *QL* 318 (Feb. 1-15, 1980): 5-6.

Delabroy, Jean. "L'ombre de la théorie. (A propos de *L'Homme au sable* de Hoffmann)." *Romantisme* 24 (1979): 29-46.

Deterding, Klaus. "Der Zusammenhang der Dinge: Zum Phänomen
der Integration in Hoffmanns Werk." *MHG* 25 (1979): 46-50.

A sensible and necessary reconsideration of loose critical
usage of several concepts central to proper interpretation
of Hoffmann's works such as "die unsichtbare Kirche," "wun-
derlich," "wundersam," "Kunst," and "Moral." (S.P.S.)

Dyck, Joachim. "Heines Neujahrsglückwunsch für seine Kusine
Fanny in E.T.A. Hoffmanns 'Elixiere des Teufels.'" *HeineJ*
18 (1979): 202-05.

Elardo, Ronald J. "E.T.A. Hoffmann's Klein Zaches, the Trickster." *Seminar* 16 (1980): 151-69.

After defining the trickster as an archetypal figure in
world mythology and locating Zaches as Hoffmann's trickster
in this larger framework, Elardo offers an informed and illuminating analysis of the tale's principal characters,
perhaps all too firmly based on the relevant writings of
C.G. Jung and Erich Neumann (but also of G.H. Schubert and
Schelling). (S.P.S.)

Elardo, Ronald J. "E.T.A. Hoffmann's *Nussknacker und Mausekönig*: The Mouse-Queen in the Tragedy of the Hero." *GR* 55
(1980): 1-8.

This exaggeratedly one-sided psychological reading clearly
shows the dubious value of indiscriminate adoption of Jungian
(as well as E. Neumann's and J.G. Frazer's) premises for
meaningful literary interpretation. (S.P.S.)

Ellis, John M. "Clara, Nathanael and the Narrator: Interpreting Hoffmann's *Der Sandmann*." *GQ* 54 (1981): 1-18.

This circumspect essay offers the most thoroughly convincing and comprehensive reading to date of Hoffmann's
best-known masterpiece. With exemplary critical acuity,
Ellis identifies the numerous major and minor flaws in
earlier interpretive efforts (also in Freud's celebrated
essay on "Das Unheimliche") and proceeds to resolve the
"two major textual problems" which he regards as "so closely
linked that one provides the answer to the other": "the
meaning of the figure of Coppelius/Coppola" and "the function of the narrator's excursus" (1). Ellis' interpretation
abounds in so many well-documented insights (e.g., that
Clara proves to be a destructive force to Nathanael, pushing
"him into madness by actions which are *not* responses to him,
but instead entirely initiated by her," p. 11) and is so

closely argued that any attempt at summarizing it would do injustice to the validity of its analytical results. (S.P.S.)

Ettelt, Wilhelm. *E.T.A. Hoffmann--Der Künstler und Mensch.* Würzburg: Königshausen & Neumann, 1981. Pp. 143. DM 19.80.

Popularizing biography (pp. 7-54), critical monograph (pp. 55-88), and comprehensive Hoffmann handbook and reading companion (pp. 89-137), all in one slim volume? Too good to be believed! Yet this seems to be the aim of this ambitious undertaking. The result of this curious attempt to draw a composite and all-inclusive portrait of Hoffmann's life and works is deeply flawed and proves disappointing for both the expert and the uninitiated on all counts. To be sure, Ettelt displays thorough familiarity with his subject and offers occasional valuable interpretive insights. But his presentation is colored throughout by an overly subjective perspective and a disturbingly chatty tone which, together with a generally superficial level of discourse, produce more confusion than illumination. Even the potentially useful miniature synopses of 67 individual Hoffmann works (pp. 89-137) are often too vague, uneven, or inaccurate to constitute meaningful plot summaries. Ettelt's choice of consulted and cited secondary material is strangely arbitrary. The dilettantish overall impression of this book surprises all the more since Ettelt is also the author of the commendable publication reviewed below. (S.P.S.)

Ettelt, Wilhelm. "Philosophische Motive im dichterischen Werk E.T.A. Hoffmanns." *MHG* 25 (1979): 31-45.

This important article offers, for the first time, a penetrating and comprehensive assessment of Hoffmann's awareness, reception, and assimilation of contemporary philosophical ideas. After recording the few negligible traces of Kant and Hegel, Ettelt turns to a thorough consideration of Fichte's and particularly Schelling's (as well as G.H. Schubert's and J.M. Klein's) perceptible influence on Hoffmann's poetics as reflected in several works. Ettelt's insight concerning the inspirational presence of Schellingian thought ("Weltseele," "Weltgeist") in Hoffmann's formulation of his "Serapiontic principle" is especially illuminating and original. (S.P.S.)

Felzmann, Fritz. "Der böhmisch-mährische Raum bei E.T.A. Hoffmann." *MHG* 25 (1979): 24-30.

Felzmann, Fritz. "Michalina—Ein Frauenschicksal." *MHG* 26
(1980): 5-15.

A compassionate biographical portrait of Michalina Rorer
(1778-1859) whom Hoffmann married in 1802. (S.P.S.)

Freund, Winfried. "Verfallene Schlösser—Ein gesellschafts-
kritisches Motiv bei Kleist, E.T.A. Hoffmann, Uhland and
Chamisso." *Diskussion Deutsch* 11 (1980): 361-69.

Fühmann, Franz. *Fräulein Veronika Paulmann aus der Pirnaer
Vorstadt oder Etwas über das Schauerliche bei E.T.A. Hoffmann.*
Rostock: Hinstorff, 1979; Hamburg: Hoffmann und Campe, 1980.
Pp. 151; 165. M 6.20; DM 22.00.

Rev. by Eckart Kleßmann in *MHG* 25 (1979): 71-72.
A welcome volume of five recent essayistic contributions,
three of them previously published (see *RMB* for 1977, p.
172, and *RMB* for 1979, p. 216), by a prominent East German
author and Hoffmann connoisseur. Fühmann is here at his
Hoffmannesque best, skillfully blending fiction and creative
criticism. His positive reassessment abounds in fresh insights, particularly concerning the unduly neglected "Nacht-
stück" *Ignaz Denner* which he interprets in the light of
Hegel's *Phänomenologie des Geistes* and in comparison with
Kleist's *Michael Kohlhaas*. (S.P.S.)

Gantz, Jeffrey. "Mozart, E.T.A. Hoffmann, and Ingmar Bergman's
'Vargtimunen.'" *LFQ* 8 (1980): 104-15.

Gantz makes a spirited case for the more than merely inspirational omnipresence of Mozart's *Zauberflöte* and Hoffmann's *Der goldne Topf* and *Der Sandmann* as primary sources
in Bergman's 1966 film *Vargtimunen* (The Hour of the Wolf).
(S.P.S.)

Geißler, Rolf. "Kunst und Künstler in der bürgerlichen Gesell-
schaft: Eine Unterrichtsreihe über Goethes 'Torquato Tasso,'
Grillparzers 'Sappho,' E.T.A. Hoffmanns 'Kreisleriana,'
Buschs 'Balduin Bählamm,' Wedekinds 'Der Kammersänger' und
Th. Manns 'Tonio Kröger.'" *Literatur für Leser* 2 (1978):
130-64.

Includes a brief, didactically useful analysis (pp. 145-
51) of three prominent topics in *Kreisleriana*: "die bürger-
liche Gesellschaft," "die Musik," and "die Kulturkritik."
(S.P.S.)

Gersdorff, Dagmar von. *Thomas Mann und E.T.A. Hoffmann: Die Funktion des Künstlers in den Romanen "Doktor Faustus" und "Lebens-Ansichten des Katers Murr."* Frankfurt am Main: Lang, 1979. Pp. 321.

Rev. by Gunter Reiss in *MHG* 26 (1980): 126-27.

Gorski, Gisela. *E.T.A. Hoffmann: Das Fräulein von Scuderi.* Diss., Stuttgart: Akademischer Verlag Heinz, 1980. Pp. 229. DM 38.00.

This first dissertation devoted in its entirety to the interpretation of *Scuderi* contains few new insights: it is thorough and competent, if somewhat pedestrian. Gorski's bibliography, rich in wide-ranging background material, is particularly recommendable (pp. 219-29). (S.P.S.)

Gorski, Gisela. "Das Fräulein von Scuderi in Schauspiel, Oper, Film und Fernsehen." *MHG* 26 (1980): 76-87.

Gorski presents concise critical assessments of four memorable instances of *Scuderi*-reception: Otto Ludwig's play *Das Fräulein von Scuderi* (written 1846/47), Hindemith's opera *Cardillac* (1926), Eugen York's film *Das Fräulein von Scuderi* (1955), and Karl Wittlinger's television play *Das Fräulein von Scuderi* (1976). (S.P.S.)

Hartung, Günter. "Anatomie des Sandmanns." *WB* 23,9 (1977): 45-65.

Few interpretative insights emerge from this poorly focused presentation of standard quotations characterizing Hoffmann's poetics and straightforward plot summary of the well-known story. Hartung's lecture, written without access to the considerable body of provocative and controversial criticism on *Der Sandmann*, is no more than a disappointing compilation of subjective generalizations and stereotyped (often negative) critical reactions. (S.P.S.)

Hertz, Neil. "Freud and the Sandman." Pp. 296-321 in Josué V. Harari, ed., *Textual Strategies: Perspectives in Post-Structuralist Criticism.* Ithaca: Cornell University Press, 1979.

Yet another abortive attempt to demonstrate the critical validity of Freud's reading of *Sandmann*. Hertz's indiscriminate psychologizing inevitably results in undue disregard for the fictionality of Hoffmann's text (treated here in English translation only) and mistaking interpretive distortion for psychological insight. (S.P.S.)

Holbeche, Yvonne. "The Relationship of the Artist to Power:
E.T.A. Hoffmann's *Das Fräulein von Scuderi.*" *Seminar* 16
(1980): 1-11.

An illuminating discussion of "the beneficial influence
of art on the use of political power" (10) in *Scuderi*, with
reference to parallel treatment perceived in Brentano's
Geschichte vom braven Kasperl und dem schönen Annerl.
(S.P.S.)

Kesselmann, Heidemarie. "E.T.A. Hoffmanns 'Klein Zaches':
Das phantastische Märchen als Möglichkeit der Wiedergewinnung
einer geschichtlichen Erkenntnisdimension." *Literatur für
Leser: Zeitschrift für Interpretationspraxis und geschicht-
liche Texterkenntnis* 2 (1978): 114-29.

Köhler, Ingeborg. *Baudelaire et Hoffmann.* (AUU.SRU 27.)
Stockholm and Uppsala: Almquist & Wiksell, 1979. Pp. 275.

Rev. by Michèle Jeanvoine in *MHG* 26 (1980): 121-23.

Köhler, Ingeborg. "Ein Wegbereiter Hoffmanns in Frankreich:
Der Doktor Koreff." *MHG* 26 (1980): 69-72.

A spirited biographical sketch of Dr. David Ferdinand
Koreff (1783-1851), from 1814 Hoffmann's close friend in
Berlin and after 1822 champion of his works in France. (S.P.S.)

Kosim, J. "Ernst Theodor Amadeus Hoffmann in Warschau." *ZS*
24 (1979): 615-36.

Polish historian Kosim's exhaustively documented comprehensive account of Hoffmann's formative Polish associations
before, during, and after his stay in Warsaw should prove
invaluable for biographical research. (S.P.S.)

Kraft, Herbert. "E.T.A. Hoffmann: Geschichtlichkeit und
Illusion." Pp. 138-62 in Ernst Ribbat, ed., *Romantik: Ein
literaturwissenschaftliches Studienbuch.* (Athenäum Taschenbücher, 2149.) Königstein/Ts.: Athenäum, 1979. Pp. 236.
DM 19.80.

See also Ribbat ("German 2. General").
Apart from the disturbingly dense style of presentation,
this is a spirited plea against interpreting Hoffmann's
poetic development--here exemplified by *Ritter Gluck, Kreisleriana, Der Sandmann,* and *Des Vetters Eckfenster*--as leading gradually to narrative realism. (S.P.S.)

Krolop, Bernd. *Versuch einer Theorie des phantastischen Realismus: E.T.A. Hoffmann und Franz Kafka*. Frankfurt am Main and Bern: Lang, 1981. Pp. 165.

"Der phantastische Realismus ist eine spezifische Form heterogener Ganzheit, in der die Mechanismen des fiktional-phantastischen Symboltransfers dominieren, determiniert von realistischen Zeichenketten" (157). With this definition, deduced from an unfortunate overdose of turgid theorizing (vaguely based on Lukács, Althusser, Goldmann, and Sartre) which fills most of his pages, Krolop attempts to introduce a new category into literary theory that (he claims) could provide the "key to adequate interpretation" (158) of works such as Goethe's *Faust*, Brecht's *Der gute Mensch von Sezuan*, and Grass's *Die Blechtrommel*. If his all too superficial and unoriginal consideration (not comparison) of three texts each by Hoffmann (*Kater Murr*, *Das Majorat*, and *Klein Zaches*) and Kafka (*Der Prozeß*, *Das Urteil*, and *In der Strafkolonie*) as test cases for his theory are any indication, Krolop's tautological construct will not become a household word in criticism. It certainly adds little that is new to understanding Hoffmann. (S.P.S.)

Kuchenmeister, Rolf. "Einige Beispiele für Ortsnamenkodierung bei E.T.A. Hoffmann." *MHG* 26 (1980): 22–24.

Plausible decoding of two place names in *Kater Murr*: "Sieghartshof" as "Schloß Seehof" near Bamberg and "Kauzheim" as "Kloster Banz am Main." (S.P.S.)

Laval, Madeleine, trans. *E.T.A. Hoffmann: Les Elixirs du Diable*. Pref. par Jacques Haumont. Paris: Phébus, 1980. Pp. 357.

Rev. by G.-A. Goldschmidt in *QL* 318 (Feb. 1-15, 1980): 5-6.

Laval, Madeleine, and André Espiau de la Maestre, trans. *E.T.A. Hoffmann: Contes nocturnes*. Pref. par Albert Béguin. Paris: Phébus, 1980. Pp. 360.

Rev. by G.-A. Goldschmidt in *QL* 318 (Feb. 1-15, 1980): 5-6.

Lehmann, Hans-Thies. "Exkurs über E.T.A. Hoffmanns 'Sandmann': Eine texttheoretische Lektüre." Pp. 301-23 in Gisela Dischner and Richard Faber, eds., *Romantische Utopie--utopische Romantik*. Hildesheim: Gerstenberg, 1979.

Lehmann superimposes fashionable semiotic terminology à la Kristeva and Saussure on strained psychoanalyzing à la Freud, Lacan, and Deleuze. The result is an unintentional parody of textual interpretation, entertaining at best. (S.P.S.)

Lindken, Hans-Ulrich. *E.T.A. Hoffmann: Das Fräulein von
Scuderi. Erläuterungen und Dokumente.* (Universal-Bibliothek,
Nr. 8142.) Stuttgart: Reclam, 1978. Pp. 136.

Rev. by Klaus D. Post in *MHG* 25 (1979): 69-71.

Lindken, Hans-Ulrich, ed. *E.T.A. Hoffmann: Ein universaler
Künstler.* Stuttgart: Klett, 1980. Pp. 135.

Rev. by Friedhelm Auhuber in *MHG* 26 (1980): 120-21.
Intended as an introductory teaching aid, Lindken's somewhat arbitrary compilation of original texts and excerpts
as well as selected secondary materials does succeed in
providing a fairly representative composite portrait of Hoffmann the writer, musician, painter and caricaturist, and
lawyer. The reprinted texts include *Don Juan*, *Jaques Callot*,
Die Geschichte des Einsiedlers Serapion, *Der Sandmann*, *Die
Vision auf dem Schlachtfelde bei Dresden*, and the Knarrpanti
episode from *Meister Floh*. (S.P.S.)

McGlathery, James M. "Demon Love: E.T.A. Hoffmann's *Elixiere
des Teufels*." *CG* 12 (1979): 61-76.

Cited previously without review; see *RMB* for 1979, p.
296.
A searching, informed, and plausible interpretation of
"the sexual psychology operative in Medardus' story" (71).
(S.P.S.)

McIntyre, Allan J. "Romantic Transcendence and the Robot in
Heinrich von Kleist and E.T.A. Hoffmann." *GR* 54 (1979):
29-34.

Rev. previously for "Kleist" by Leonard Schulze; see *RMB*
for 1979, p. 304.
A sober and insightful comparative analysis, defining and
illustrating the image of the robot as distinctly different
in the two authors: for Kleist the robot is a symbol of
perfection, self-directed and godlike (e.g., Käthchen and
Penthesilea), while Hoffmann's robot is non-human and puppet-
like (Olimpia). (S.P.S.)

Magris, Claudio. *Die andere Vernunft: E.T.A. Hoffmann.* Königstein: Hain, 1980. Pp. 118. DM 28.00.

This collection of four essays by Magris, translated from
the Italian, shows the prominent Italian Germanist as a
knowledgeable and imaginative Hoffmann scholar. The contribution on *Elixiere* appeared here before the publication of
the Italian version. The essays were originally introductions

to various volumes of the latest Italian Hoffmann edition.
Three of them are devoted to the novels and stories, *Elixiere*,
and *Prinzessin Brambilla*, respectively. The fourth considers
briefly Hoffmann's possible authorship of *Schwester Monika*.
(S.P.S.)

Malandain, Gabrielle. "Récit, miroir, histoire: aspects de la
relation Nerval-Hoffmann." *Romantisme* 14 (1978): 79-93.

   An intertextual analysis of the problem of identity and
the dream-reality dichotomy in *Prinzessin Brambilla* and
Sylvia and *Die Abenteuer der Sylvesternacht* and *Pandora*,
respectively. (S.P.S.)

Mitteilungen der E.T.A. Hoffmann-Gesellschaft. Sitz in Bamberg.
25. Heft 1979; 26. Heft 1980. Bamberg: E.T.A. Hoffmann-
Gesellschaft e.V., 1979, 1980 [= *MHG*].

   In addition to the articles listed by author in this
section, the 1979 and 1980 volumes contain pictures, portraits, facsimiles, reports on commemorative celebrations,
announcements, and other miscellany of interest to Hoffmann
scholars. The separate review section, expertly edited by
Wulf Segebrecht, continues to bring extensive reviews of
recent Hoffmann editions, criticism, and selected dissertations. Beginning with the 1979 volume, an additional review
section offers concise commentary on selected recent bibliographical items not reviewed in detail. (S.P.S.)

Montandon, Alain. "Ecriture et folie chez E.T.A. Hoffmann."
Romantisme 24 (1979): 7-28.

Moore, Anneliese W. "E.T.A. Hoffmann's 'Haimatochare': Translation and Commentary." *Hawaiian Journal of History* 12
(1978): 1-27.

   Moore identifies *Haimatochare* (1819) as the first piece
of fiction using Hawaii as its setting. Her English version
is not the first ever, as claimed; Edward Spencer's translation appeared in Philadelphia in *Graham's Illustrated
Magazine*, 53, no. 5 (Nov. 1858): 418-23. Moore's informative
commentary "Hawaii in a Nutshell--E.T.A. Hoffmann's Haimatochare" (13-27) provides interesting source material and
a concise interpretation of the charming miniature. (S.P.S.)

Mühlher, Robert. "Das Bild der Wiener Klassik in den Werken
E.T.A. Hoffmanns." Pp. 427-43 in Herbert Zeman, ed., *Die
österreichische Literatur: Ihr Profil an der Wende vom 18.*

zum 19. Jahrhundert (1750-1830). Graz: Akademische Druck-
und Verlagsanstalt, 1979.

A well-documented discussion of Hoffmann's unique perception of Haydn, Mozart, and Beethoven as "Romantic" composers.
Mühlher concludes that for Hoffmann "Romantic" meant "Erkenntnis des Wesens der reinen Musik" (442): a value judgment
rather than a period designation. Mühlher also underscores
the important connection between Hoffmann's musical aesthetics
and his conception of humor and irony, as reflected in his
pioneering positive assessment of Mozart's *Così fan tutte*.
(S.P.S.)

Mühlher, Robert. "E.T.A. Hoffmanns Bamberger Jahre." *LJGG* 21
(1980): 75-88.

A succinct account of well-known biographical details
concerning Hoffmann's stay in Bamberg (1808-13), in appeal
and tone popularizing rather than scholarly. (S.P.S.)

Nagel, Bert. "Kafka and E.T.A. Hoffmann." *MAL* 14 (1978): 1-11.

In spite of the undeniable affinity between Hoffmann and
Kafka which Nagel concedes, he rightly cautions against
all too hasty comparisons of the two authors: "was die
beiden verbindet, trennt sie zugleich" (1). But since Nagel
fails to define his terms and continues to argue on much too
high a plane of generalization, potentially plausible insights such as the following affect us as amateurish and
tentative: "Der Hochschätzung des Hoffmann-Einflusses liegt
wohl eine Gleichsetzung bzw. Verwechslung des Kafkahaften
mit dem Kafkaesken zugrunde" (10). (S.P.S.)

Nahrebecky, Roman. *Wackenroder, Tieck, E.T.A. Hoffmann, Bettina
von Arnim: Ihre Beziehung zur Musik und zum musikalischen
Erlebnis*. Bonn: Bouvier, 1979.

Rev. by Charles V. Miller in *Monatshefte* 73 (1981): 469-
70.
Nahrebecky's voluminous Hoffmann-chapter (87-194) is sadly
inept and derivative in every respect; it should best remain
unconsulted. (S.P.S.)

Neubauer, John. "The Mines of Falun: Temporal Fortunes of a
Romantic Myth of Time." *SiR* 19 (1980): 475-95.

In the relevant theoretical framework of Romantic philosophy, aesthetics, and science, Neubauer surveys manifestations of the quest motif in fictional representations of
the Falun incident by G.H. Schubert, J.P. Hebel, Arnim,

Hoffmann, Wagner, and Hofmannsthal. "The metaphor of descent
is a journey into the self for all the Romantics, but descent yields self-knowledge and thereby knowledge of the
world for Fichte, Schelling, and Novalis; for Hoffmann the
journey ends with extinction of consciousness" (489). (S.P.S.)

Patzelt, Johanna. "Erfüllte und verfehlte Künstlerliebe: Ein
Versuch über das Menschenbild E.T.A. Hoffmanns in seinem
Phantasiestück 'Don Juan.'" *JWGV* 80 (1976): 118-48.

This important study of almost monographic proportions
delivers much more than its vague title promises: it is to
date the most comprehensive interpretation of Hoffmann's
Don Juan. Patzelt felicitously combines sensitive, sober,
and exhaustive textual analysis with informed consideration
of crucial themes and motifs which recur prominently in
Hoffmann's fiction. She also locates the elusive narrative
in the canon of literary works inspired by the infamous Don
and evaluates the lasting impact of Hoffmann's "fruchtbare
Umformung des Stoffes" (141) on subsequent critical perception of Mozart's *Don Giovanni*. (S.P.S.)

Petzel, Jörg. "E.T.A. Hoffmann und Arno Schmidt." *MHG* 26
(1980): 88-98.

Predictably, the affinity between Schmidt and Hoffmann
is considerable and complex. Petzel's penetrating critical
commentary of Schmidt's Hoffmann reception in general and
of traces and echoes of specific Hoffmann works in Schmidt's
oeuvre in particular shows thorough familiarity with both
authors. (S.P.S.)

Pitcher, Edward W. "From Hoffmann's *Das Majorat* to Poe's
'Usher' via 'The Robber's Tower': Poe's Borrowings Reconsidered." *ATQ* 39 (1978): 231-36.

Pitcher presents plausible textual evidence for his conclusion that E.A. Poe's borrowings from Hoffmann's *Das
Majorat* derive directly from John Hardman's adaptation of
Hoffmann in *The Robber's Tower* (1828) rather than from Poe's
familiarity with Walter Scott's summary of Hoffmann's tale
in the *Foreign Quarterly Review*. (S.P.S.)

Porter, Laurence M. "Hoffmannesque and Hamiltonian Sources
of Nodier's *Fée aux miettes*." *RomN* 19 (1979): 341-44.

Romero, Christiane Z. "M.G. Lewis' *The Monk* and E.T.A. Hoffmann's *Die Elixiere des Teufels*: Two Versions of the Gothic."
Neophil 63 (1979): 574-82.

A rather pedestrian, though occasionally insightful comparison of the two novels and their common sources. Romero's view that "*Die Elixiere* cannot be counted among Hoffmann's greatest achievements" (575) is startling. (S.P.S.)

Schemmel, Bernhard. "Die E.T.A. Hoffmann-Sammlung der Staatsbibliothek Bamberg: Zugleich ein Beitrag zur Geschichte der Rezeption E.T.A. Hoffmanns in Bamberg." *Bibliotheksforum Bayern* 6,3 (1978): 167-87.

   Rev. by Wulf Segebrecht in *MHG* 25 (1979): 90-91.
   A detailed description of the Hoffmann holdings of various museums, libraries, and other collections located in Bamberg.

Scher, Steven Paul, ed. *Zu E.T.A. Hoffmann*. Stuttgart: Klett, 1981. Pp. 207. DM 29.00.

   This collection of 14 essays published between 1960 and 1979 offers a representative sampling of modern Hoffmann research on an international scale. The authors: Wulf Segebrecht, Klaus G. Just, Wolfgang Preisendanz, Knud Willenberg, Hartmut Steinecke, Karl Riha, and Norbert Miller (West Germany); Hans-Georg Werner and Franz Fühmann (GDR); Siegbert Prawer (England); Bonaventura Tecchi (Italy); and Wolfgang Nehring, Christoph Schweitzer, and Steven Scher (U.S.A.). Except for one article devoted to Hoffmann and music, the contributions focus exclusively on Hoffmann's fiction. Among the individual works interpreted in detail: *Der goldne Topf*, *Der Sandmann*, *Ritter Gluck*, *Die Fermate*, *Rat Krespel*, *Klein Zaches*, *Prinzessin Brambilla*, *Kater Murr*, and *Des Vetters Eckfenster*. (S.P.S.)

Schnapp, Friedrich. "Das 'Anmuthige Beispiel' einer Luftfahrt 'Geschätzter Gräflicher Freunde.'" *MHG* 26 (1980): 16-21.

   Schnapp identifies Hoffmann's acquaintance Graf Pückler-Muskau as the unnamed "Baron" referred to in an obscure passage from the story *Die Irrungen*. (S.P.S.)

Schnapp, Friedrich. "Der Musiker E.T.A. Hoffmann." *MHG* 25 (1979): 1-23.

   A concise, informative, and meticulously executed chronological account of every relevant detail known about Hoffmann's musical associations, including his musical education, lifelong preoccupation with music, and professional activities as musician, composer, conductor, and music critic. Indispensable overview for biographical research. (S.P.S.)

Schnapp, Friedrich, ed. *E.T.A. Hoffmann: Nachlese. Dichtungen, Schriften, Aufzeichnungen und Fragmente.* Munich: Winkler, 1981. Pp. 536. DM 64.00.

In reprinting the authoritative five-volume Hoffmann edition (1960-65), Winkler Verlag decided to publish the *Nachlese* (hitherto contained in volume 5) separately as volume 6. The new volume is identical with the earlier publication (though not in pagination), except for three texts which are included here for the first time: "An das gesamte hochverehrte Publikum in und um Bamberg" (1812), the full text of the 1808 Singspiel *Liebe und Eifersucht* (available previously only as a facsimile reprint of Hoffmann's handwritten manuscript published by Winkler in 1970), and "Neudichtungen und Abänderungen in Sodens Melodram 'Sabinus'" from 1810, the full text of which Schnapp published in *MHG* 20 (1974): 1-41. (S.P.S.)

Schneider, Marcel. *Ernest Théodore Amadeus Hoffmann.* Paris: Julliard, 1979. Pp. 286.

Cited previously without review; see *RMB* for 1979, p. 296. Rev. by Gonthier-Louis Fink in *MHG* 26 (1980): 115-17.
Marcel Schneider, French novelist, essayist, and author of books on Schubert and Wagner, has been an eloquent advocate of German literature and culture in France for some time. His new biography of Hoffmann (the first biography since Ricci's *E.T.A. Hoffmann, l'homme et l'oeuvre*, 1947) is popularizing in the best sense of that word: eminently readable, based on thorough knowledge of the life and works and the contemporary historical and social background, free of erudite scholarly references and over-documentation, and mindful of most of the essential aspects and special features (i.e., music, painting, music criticism) which permit the average reader to form an adequate composite picture of Hoffmann's predicaments, aspirations, and artistic achievement. No positivist in approach, as biographer Schneider makes every effort to differentiate between life and oeuvre. Clearly, he writes for an exclusively French audience: all quotations from the correspondence, diaries, and works are in French. This orientation is also reflected in the short bibliography which, along with a few older German titles, lists only French secondary sources. While learning little that is new from this biography, specialists will benefit from Schneider's refreshingly sober general overview of Hoffmann's artistic stature and lasting impact. (S.P.S.)

Schneider, Peter. "Verbrechen, Künstlertum und Wahnsinn: Untersuchungen zur Figur des Cardillac in E.T.A. Hoffmanns *Das
Fräulein von Scuderi*." *MHG* 26 (1980): 34-50.

  A stimulating and for the most part convincing psycho-
  analytic study, selectively drawing on relevant insights by
  Freud and his more recent followers such as Sándor Ferenczi,
  Michael Balint, and Heinz Kohut. (S.P.S.)

Segebrecht, Wulf. "Die E.T.A. Hoffmann-Gesellschaft." *JIG* 12
(1980): 204-05.

  A concise statement characterizing the history, purpose,
  membership, holdings, publications, and organized activities
  of the Hoffmann Society in Bamberg.

Seiverth, Andreas, and Christiane Seiverth. "Kein Talent,
glücklich zu seyn: Alltag und Traum bei E.T.A. Hoffmann."
Pp. 163-215 in Hans-Christian Kirsch, ed., *Klassiker heute*.
Frankfurt am Main: Fischer Taschenbuch Verlag, 1980.

  Commensurate with the aim of the volume to make classic
  authors like Jean Paul, Brentano, Arnim, Kleist, Hoffmann,
  Eichendorff, Heine, and Büchner more accessible and relevant
  for the contemporary reader, this concise, reliable, and
  eminently readable survey serves as a superb first encounter
  with Hoffmann's life story and major works. A short excerpt
  from *Meister Floh* is included as a reading sample. (S.P.S.)

Sera, Manfred. "Peregrinus: Zur Bedeutung des Raumes bei E.T.A.
Hoffmann." *Aurora* 38 (1978): 75-84.

  Focusing on aspects of spatiality in *Der Sandmann* and *Der
  goldne Topf*, Sera arrives at refreshingly new interpretive
  conclusions. (S.P.S.)

Smith, Albert B. "Variations on a Mythical Theme: Hoffmann,
Gautier, Queneau and the Imagery of Mining." *Neophil* 63
(1979): 179-86.

  Consideration of Hoffmann's *Bergwerke zu Falun*, Gautier's
  Le Preneur de Rats de Hameln, and a text by Raymond Queneau
  (from *La Révolution Surréaliste*) as initiation narratives,
  exemplifying the motif of quest for a journey to hell.
  (S.P.S.)

Steinecke, Hartmut. "E.T.A. Hoffmanns 'Kater Murr': Zur
Modernität eines 'romantischen' Romans." *JWGV* 81/82/83
(1977/78/79): 275-89.

Steinecke's exemplary, comprehensive interpretation of the
novel successfully integrates the latest analytical results
of *Murr*-research and also includes an informed and suggestive
critical discussion of the history of *Murr*-reception in the
context of European literature. (S.P.S.)

Stiller, Günther. "Lithographien aus Aluminiumplatten? Zu
E.T.A. Hoffmanns *Der Sandmann.*" *Philobiblon* 22 (1978): 50-51.

Tatar, Maria M. "E.T.A. Hoffmann's 'Der Sandmann': Reflection
and Romantic Irony." *MLN* 95 (1980): 585-608.

Working with clearly defined distinctions between the
various types of irony and with key concepts for interpreting Hoffmann such as humor, the comic, the fantastic, the
uncanny, and the marvelous, Tatar systematically demonstrates
that "of all the German Romantics, E.T.A. Hoffmann perhaps
most successfully translated the theoretical pronouncements
of his colleagues [e.g., Friedrich Schlegel, Tieck, and
Novalis] into literary practice" (585). Her cogent analysis
of the famous authorial intrusion and incisive corrective
insights concerning Freud's celebrated but flawed reading
of *Der Sandmann* are particularly memorable. (S.P.S.)

Tietz, Manfred. "E.T.A. Hoffmann und Spanien." *MHG* 26 (1980):
51-68.

After a concise review of the few, but significant, traces
of Spain and "things Spanish" in Hoffmann (e.g., in *Berganza*,
Sanctus, *Datura Fastuosa*, and *Der Zusammenhang der Dinge*),
Tietz offers an informative critical survey of Spanish Hoffmann-reception: until recently a disappointing story of inadequate translations, severe misrepresentations, and a
general lack of affinity, due in part to a documentable
tradition of insensitivity toward literary manifestations
of the fantastic. (S.P.S.)

Trautwein, Wolfgang. *Erlesene Angst--Schauerliteratur im 18.
und 19. Jahrhundert: Systematischer Aufriß. Untersuchungen
zu Bürger, Maturin, Hoffmann, Poe und Maupassant.* München,
Wien: Hanser, 1980. Pp. 273.

Rev. by Gunter Grimm in *Germanistik* 21 (1980): 301-02.
Contains a chapter on Hoffmann's *Der unheimliche Gast*
(155-83), analyzed as a typical example of what Trautwein
terms the "Unheimliche Geschichte" (242). (S.P.S.)

Vietta, Silvio. "Das Automatenmotiv und die Technik der Motivschichtung im Erzählwerk E.T.A. Hoffmanns." *MHG* 26 (1980):
25-33.

Taking the story *Die Automate* as a paradigmatic example
for his highly suggestive narratological argument, Vietta
reconsiders the fundamental notion of ambiguity ("Vieldeutigkeit") that pervades Hoffmann's fiction in the light of critical concepts such as perspectivism, stratification of motifs
("Motivschichtung"), and self-projection of characters.
Vietta's concluding insights are seminal: "Hoffmann vereinigt
verschiedene Motivstränge zu *einem* Motivkomplex, dies aber
so, daß die Divergenz der Motivkomponenten eine eindeutige
Auflösung des Motivs gerade nicht mehr erlaubt" (27) and
"In bezug auf die Motivik zeigt sich die Kategorie der
'Vieldeutigkeit' als eine Form der Motivschichtung, erzähl-
technisch als gegenläufige Tendenz von Chiffrierung und
Auflösung" (32). (S.P.S.)

Vom Hofe, Gerhard. "E.T.A. Hoffmanns Zauberreich Atlantis: Zum
Thema des dichterischen Enthusiasmus im *Goldnen Topf*." *Text &
Kontext* 8 (1980): 107-26.

Central to this interpretation is a suggestive comparison
of Hoffmann's tale with Novalis' *Heinrich von Ofterdingen*
(similarities as well as divergencies). For vom Hofe *Der
goldne Topf* exemplifies "Hoffmanns skeptische Romantik"
(123). While the generous dose of satire and irony in the
tale does signal the advent of a poetic realism, "gerade in
den 'idyllisch' und 'elegisch' gestimmten Erzählphasen
dieses 'modernen' Märchens [ist] die fortwährende Romantik
unverkennbar" (112). (S.P.S.)

Von der Lippe, George B. "La vie de l'artiste fantastique:
The Metamorphosis of the Hoffmann-Poe Figure in France."
CRCL 6 (1979): 46-63.

Wellbery, David E. "E.T.A. Hoffmann and Romantic Hermeneutics:
An Interpretation of Hoffmann's 'Don Juan.'" *SiR* 19 (1980):
455-73.

This succinct article contains some striking interpretive
insights into Hoffmann's complex creative process, as reflected in and exemplified by basic narratological and
structural strategies of *Don Juan*. Wellbery's carefully
contemplated argument is so rich in suggestive theoretical
propositions signalling new directions of far-reaching significance for Hoffmann research that each of its steps merits
serious consideration. (S.P.S.)

Wirth, Irmgard, ed. *E.T.A. Hoffmann und seine Zeit. Gemälde--
Graphik--Dokumente--Bücher--Photographien*. Berlin: Walter
Bohm & Co., 1976. Pp. 76 (text); illus.

Expertly compiled and annotated and attractive in format,
this catalogue of the 1976 exhibit at the Berlin Museum to
commemorate Hoffmann's 200th birthday brings together a rich
assortment of Hoffmanniana, including many rare collector's
items loaned from private sources for the occasion. 119 of
the 274 exhibited items are reproduced here, some of them
in color. Of considerable information and illustration value,
the volume also contains brief essays by Hans Mayer, Friedrich
Schnapp, Herbert A. Frenzel, Hans Günther, Irmgard Wirth,
and Elke Riemer which consider Hoffmann's multiple talent
as writer, composer, and law official in the light of his
associations with contemporary Berlin. (S.P.S.)

Wittkowski, Wolfgang. "E.T.A. Hoffmanns musikalische Musiker-
dichtungen *Ritter Gluck, Don Juan, Rat Krespel.*" *Aurora* 38
(1978): 54-74.

Largely due to impressionistic use of musical vocabulary
and the absence of a sound musicological framework, these
lengthy speculations on the plausible presence of contra-
puntal strategies in Hoffmann's narratives remain incon-
clusive. (S.P.S.)

Wolff, J. "Romantic Variations of Pygmalion Motifs by Hoffmann,
Eichendorff, and Edgar Allan Poe." *GL&L* 33 (1979-80): 53-59.

Brief mention of the motif in *Elixiere, Die Fermate,* and
Meister Martin.

Wright, Elizabeth. *E.T.A. Hoffmann and the Rhetoric of Terror.
Aspects of Language Used for the Evocation of Fear.* Institute
of Germanic Studies, University of London, 1978. Pp. viii+
307.

Rev. by Richard Littlejohn in *JES*, Sept. 1981, pp. 225-
26; by James M. McGlathery in *GQ* 53 (1980): 387-88; by Maria
Tatar in *GR* 56 (1981): 78-79; by James Trainer in *MHG* 26
(1980): 124-26.

Yushu, Zhang. "In China wird E.T.A. Hoffmann entdeckt." *MHG*
26 (1980): 73-75.

A brief and fascinating account of Hoffmann-reception in
China; until 1976 essentially a story of non-reception.
Peking Germanists have recently initiated a rehabilitation
process. (S.P.S.)

See also Berger, Dessauer, Frank, Freund, Nemoianu, Pikulik, Trautwein, Völker ("German 2. General"); Hunter-Lougheed ("Bonaventura"); Dammann ("Grimm, Jacob and Wilhelm"); Gendolla ("Jean Paul").

Reviews of books previously listed:

BLOMEYER, Arwed, *E.T.A. Hoffmann als Jurist* (see *ELN* 17, Supp., 215), rev. by Philip Kunig in *MHG* 25 (1979): 72-73; EILERT, Heide, *Theater in der Erzählkunst: Eine Studie zum Werk E.T.A. Hoffmanns* (see *ELN* 17, Supp., 215), rev. by Horst S. Daemmrich in *MLN* 95 (1980): 720-22; by Gisela Vitt-Maucher in *Monatshefte* 72 (1980): 443-44; LAVAL, Madeleine, trans., *Les Elixirs du Diable* (see *RMB* for 1979, p. 296), rev. by G.-A. Goldschmidt in *QL* 318 (Feb. 1-15, 1980): 5-6; LLOYD, Rosemary, *Baudelaire et Hoffmann: Affinités et Influences* (see *RMB* for 1979, p. 296), rev. by Lilian R. Furst in *CL* 32 (1980): 302-04; by Francis S. Heck in *ECr* 21 (1981): 110; by James M. McGlathery in *GQ* 54 (1981): 354-55; by Elisabeth Teichmann in *MHG* 26 (1980): 123-24; SAHLIN, Johanna, ed. and trans., *Selected Letters of E.T.A. Hoffmann* (see *ELN* 17, Supp., 220), rev. by Michael T. Jones in *GQ* 52 (1979): 122-23; by James M. McGlathery in *GSR* 1 (1978): 231; SCHUMM, Siegfried, *Einsicht und Darstellung: Untersuchung zum Kunstverständnis E.T.A. Hoffmanns* (see *ELN* 15, Supp., 176), rev. by Gisela Vitt-Maucher in *Monatshefte* 69 (1977): 463; WAWRZYN, Lienhard, *Der Automaten-Mensch. E.T.A. Hoffmanns Erzählung von "Sandmann"* (see *ELN* 17, Supp., 221), rev. by Steven P. Scher in *Germanistik* 20 (1979): 178; WINTER, Ilse, *Untersuchungen zum serapiontischen Prinzip E.T.A. Hoffmanns* (see *ELN* 17, Supp., 222), rev. by Ernst F. Hoffmann in *Monatshefte* 71 (1979): 68-69.

HOFMANNSTHAL

See Neubauer ("Hoffmann"); Speier ("Jean Paul").

HUMBOLDT, A. VON

See Kuczynski ("German 2. General").

JEAN PAUL

Campe, Joachim. "Die moralische Revolution: Zu Jean Pauls
   Romanen." *STZ* 76 (1980): 287-311.

   Campe traces the development of Jean Paul's novels through
his major work *Titan* and critically analyzes Jean Paul's
variation of the "Bildungsroman." He emphasizes the difficult
maturation process of Jean Paul's heroes from a childhood
narcissism to a confrontation with the real world which almost never takes place. Jean Paul's "idealism" is viewed in
this context. (W.K.)

Campe, Joachim. *Der programmatische Roman: Von Wielands
   "Agathon" zu Jean Pauls "Hesperus."* (Abhandlungen zur Kunst-,
   Musik- und Literaturwissenschaft, Vol. 292.) Bonn: Bouvier,
   1979.

   Rev. by Christoph Braun in *JJPG* 15 (1980): 172-74.

Fink, Gonthier-Louis. "Der proteische Erzähler und die
   Leseorientierung in Jean Pauls *Leben des vergnügten Schulmeisterlein Maria Wuz.*" Pp. 271-87 in Günter Schnitzler,
   ed., *Bild und Gedanke: Festschrift für Gerhart Baumann.*
   Munich: Wilhelm Fink, 1980.

Gendolla, Peter. *Die lebenden Maschinen: Zur Geschichte der
   Maschinenmenschen bei Jean Paul, E.T.A. Hoffmann und Villiers
   de l'Isle Adam.* (Reihe Metro No. 10.) Marburg: Guttandin &
   Hoppe, 1980. Pp. 260.

   Rev. by Gunter Grimm in *Germanistik* 22 (1981): 94.

Hannah, Richard W. "The Tortures of the Idyll: Jean Paul's
   Wutz and the Loss of Presence." *GR* 56 (1981): 121-27.

Jahrbuch der Jean-Paul-Gesellschaft (= *JJPG*). Im Auftrag der
   Jean-Paul-Gesellschaft, Sitz Bayreuth, ed. Kurt Wölfel, 15.
   Jg. Munich: C.H. Beck, 1980. Pp. 179.

Jahrbuch der Jean-Paul-Gesellschaft (= *JJPG*). Im Auftrag der
   Jean-Paul-Gesellschaft, Sitz Bayreuth, ed. Kurt Wölfel, 16.
   Jg. Munich: C.H. Beck, 1981. Pp. 179.

   The second collection of contemporary reviews of Jean Paul's
works, the first being published as *JJPG* 13 (1978). This
collection includes reviews from eight different journals.
Most important are perhaps those of the *Gothaer gelehrte
Zeitungen*, *Oberdeutsche allgemeine Literaturzeitung*, and
especially the *Zeitung für die elegante Welt*. (W.K.)

Köpke, Wulf. "Eine Jean-Paul-Parodie im 'Taugenichts'? Bemer-
kungen zu Eichendorffs Jean-Paul-Rezeption." *Aurora* 41 (1981):
172-82.

Postulating that a passage at the end of the first chapter
of Eichendorff's *Taugenichts* contains a parody of Jean Paul's
style, the study traces the relationship of Jean Paul's and
Eichendorff's concept of art and the artist and compares
Eichendorff's hero with Jean Paul's poet Walt in *Flegeljahre*
whose trip "ins Blaue" is presumed to be one of the models
for Eichendorff's story.

Montandon, Alain. "Albertine Necker de Saussure et Jean Paul."
RLC 55 (1981): 76-89.

Although Jean Paul's treatise on education, *Levana*, had
little direct impact on France due to partial and ineffective
translations, it exerted some little-noticed influence through
Albertine Necker's *L'Education progressive*, published between
1828 and 1832, which is heavily indebted to Jean Paul. Alain
Montandon demonstrates this indebtedness with the help of
Madame Necker de Saussure's excerpts from Jean Paul's *Levana*.
Being the cousin of Madame de Staël, she was familiar with
German literature, and her rather successful book trans-
mitted many German ideas, especially those of Jean Paul, to
French educators, although with a specific Christian ten-
dency. (W.K.)

Naumann, Ursula. "Urania in Ketten: Jean Pauls 'Titaniden.'
Mit einem Anhang: Fünf Briefe der Charlotte von Kalb." *JJPG*
15 (1980): 82-130.

Compares Jean Paul's Linda in *Titan* with the historical
Charlotte von Kalb and provides new material on Charlotte
von Kalb and an analysis of her character and relations to
writers. (W.K.)

Oehlenschläger, Eckart. *Närrische Phantasie: Zum metaphorischen
Prozeß bei Jean Paul.* (Untersuchungen zur deutschen Literaturgeschichte, Vol. 29.) Tübingen: Max Niemeyer, 1980. Pp. 85.

After the period of Jean Paul research which centered on
sociological problems, Oehlenschläger wants to initiate a
discussion of the poetological foundations of Jean Paul's
work. Oehlenschläger concentrates on the nature of metaphors and metaphoricity and uses examples from Jean Paul's
shorter narrative texts which he tries to extricate from
the cliché of "idyls." Oehlenschläger analyzes Jean Paul's
dualism in his world view and the combination of metaphorical

and dicontinual mode of narration. In spite of some one-
sidedness due to shortcuts, this is a welcome new departure.
(W.K.)

Pauler, Klaus, ed. *Jean Paul: Die unsichtbare Loge*. Text der
Erstausgabe von 1793 mit den Varianten der Ausgabe von 1826.
Erläuterungen, Anmerkungen und Register. Munich: Edition
Text u. Kritik, 1981. Pp. xxxii+463.

The first reedition of the first version of Jean Paul's
Unsichtbare Loge, his first novel, together with text
variants, earlier drafts, sources, explanatory notes. A very
useful tool for the interpretation of Jean Paul's most
neglected novel. (W.K.)

Pietzcker, Carl. "Narziβistisches Glück und Todesphantasie in
Jean Pauls *Leben des vergnügten Schulmeisterlein Maria Wutz
in Auenthal*." Pp. 30-52 in Klaus Bohnen, ed., *Literatur und
Psychoanalyse: Kopenhagener Kolloquien zur deutschen Literatur*.
(Text & Kontext, Sonderreihe Vol. 10.) Munich: Wilhelm Fink,
1981.

Spaemann, Robert. "Fénélon und Jean Paul." *JJPG* 15 (1980):
55-81.

Reprint of an "appendix" to the book by Robert Spaemann
on Fénélon, *Reflexion und Spontaneität*, published 1963. The
comparison with Jean Paul focuses mainly on the use of
Fénélon in *Titan*, women, and the concept of love. (W.K.)

Speier, Hans-Michael. *Die Ästhetik Jean Pauls in der Dichtung
des deutschen Symbolismus*. Frankfurt am Main: Rita G. Fischer
Verlag, 1979. Pp. 2223.

A detailed description of Jean Paul's reception by Stefan
George and his circle, as well as by Hugo von Hofmannsthal;
on the basis of this deep-reaching influence the affinity
between a number of motifs, stylistic traits, and esthetic
structures of Jean Paul and those of the German symbolists
such as George and Hofmannsthal is demonstrated. Jean Paul's
Vorschule der Ästhetik appears as the key textbook for this
esthetic approach and as a basic text on poetic creation.
The study largely ignores any problematic aspects of German
symbolism, Stefan George in particular, and of his image of
Jean Paul. (W.K.)

Wölfel, Kurt. "Zwei Studien über Jean Paul: I. Über die
schwierige Geburt des Gesprächs aus dem Geist der Schrift;
II. Kosmopolitische Einsamkeit. Über den Spaziergang als
poetische Handlung." *JJPG* 15 (1980): 7-54.

See also Greiner, Nemoianu, Reed, Richter ("German 2. General"); Kuhn ("Goethe"); Böschenstein ("Hölderlin"); Seiverth ("Hoffmann").

Reviews of books previously listed:

KÖPKE, Wulf, *Erfolglosigkeit: Zum Frühwerk Jean Pauls* (see *ELN* 16, Supp., 174), rev. by Rainer Wuthenow in *CG* 14 (1981): 181-84; LINDNER, Burkhardt, *Jean Paul: Scheiternde Aufklärung und Autorrolle* (see *ELN* 16, Supp., 174-75), rev. by Christoph Braun in *JJPG* 15 (1980): 178-79; MÜLLER, Volker Ulrich, *Narrenfreiheit und Selbstbehauptung* (see *RMB* for 1980, p. 326), rev. by Christoph Braun in *JJPG* 15 (1980): 174-77; SPRENGEL, Peter, ed., *Jean Paul im Urteil seiner Kritiker* (see *RMB* for 1980, pp. 324-25), rev. by Wulf Koepke in *GQ* 54 (1981): 510-12; by Engelhard Weigl in *JJPG* 15 (1980): 154-71; WIETHÖLTER, Waltraud, *Witzige Illumination: Studien zur Ästhetik Jean Pauls* (see *RMB* for 1979, p. 299), rev. by Wulf Koepke in *GQ* 54 (1981): 512-13.

JUNG

See Elardo ("Hoffmann"; both items).

KAFKA

See Krolop, Nagel ("Hoffmann"); Barrack ("Kleist").

KANT

See Mann ("German 2. General"); Hunter-Lougheed ("Bonaventura"); Ettelt ("Hoffmann"); Corkhill ("Kleist"); Freier ("Schelling").

KLEIST

Barrack, Charles M. "Prince Friedrich: Hero or Victim?" *GR* 56 (1981): 13-19.

    Summarizes the prevailing interpretations of *Prinz Friedrich*, and offers a reading of the play as a dramatization of the theme of "tragic guilt." According to Barrack, previous views of the play may be characterized as (1) "The

Subordination and Education Theory," according to which the Prince learns to submit himself to public order, (2) "The Glorification of Individualist Bravado," under which it is the Kurfürst who learns that he cannot legitimately tyrannize the individual, and (3) "Peripheral Theories," which usually argue that some sort of genuine reconciliation occurs in the play. Barrack argues that the Elector is as much a victim as the Prince, "the tragic hero-victim [of] the forces of irrational destruction and the saving powers of creation ..." (18). Such a reading links the Elector with other figures in Kleist's works who are plagued by Kafkaesque guilt. (L.S.)

Belhalfaoui, Barbara. "'Der Zweikampf' von Heinrich von Kleist, oder die Dialektik von Absolutheit und ihrer Trübung." *EG* 36 (1981): 22-42.

A close reading of *Der Zweikampf*, in which Belhalfaoui argues that the metaphysical structures of the essay on the marionett-theater find their clearest expression in this "novella," which she claims has been unfairly neglected by Kleist criticism. While her analysis is thorough and, at times, illuminating, she is so captivated by what she takes to be "das metaphysisch gesellschaftliche Anliegen Kleists" (41) that she is blind to any irony in this story or elsewhere in Kleist. She takes the three-stage history of mankind propounded by "C" in "Über das Marionettentheater" to be the basic explicatory structure underlying Kleist's thought and "Der Zweikampf": initial innocence, loss and dissolution, resolution and atonement on an even higher plane. Because she has invested so much in this mythological structure, "wo Inneres and Äusseres sich [wieder] decken" (42), she sees no irresolution or irony in the apparent theodicy of the conclusion of the story. And, most strikingly, she wishes to privilege *Der Zweikampf* over *Prinz Friedrich* as more typically Kleistian; what it is, by her reading at least, is more typically Belhalfaouiesque. (L.S.)

Corkhill, Alan. "Kleists *Das Erdbeben in Chili* und Brechts *Der Augsburger Kreidekreis*: Ein Vergleich der Motivik und des Erzählstills." *WW* 31: 152-57.

Argues that the two stories share a critical concern with the establishment of true motherhood in a just social order. But for Kleist after the Kant crisis, it was impossible to believe in a programmatic historical improvement of society à la Brecht. The narrators of both tales adopt ironic stances, but in Kleist such irony serves to undercut all authority,

whereas in Brecht it serves to liberate judgment from prevailing bourgeois ideology, thus providing the opening for
a dialectical development toward the ideal social state.
(L.S.)

Exner, Richard. "Androgynie und preußischer Staat: Themen,
Probleme und das Beispiel Heinrich von Kleist." *Aurora* 39
(1979): 51-78.

Freund, Winfried. "Verfallene Schlösser--Ein gesellschafts-
kritisches Motiv bei Kleist, E.T.A. Hoffmann, Uhland and
Chamisso." *Diskussion Deutsch* 11 (1980): 361-69.

Gillespie, Gerald. "Kleist's Hypothesis of Affective Expression: Acting-out in Language." *Seminar* 17 (1981): 275-82.

A suggestive, if brief, argument that the somewhat neglected essay "Über die allmähliche Verfertigung der Gedanden
beim Reden" contains the kernel of Kleist's philosophy of
language. His rejection of the Horatian ideal of clearly
structured public rhetoric links Kleist to the general
Romantic turn toward subjectivity; language is no longer
an instrument of expression, but constitutes the very possibility of thought. This suggests that Kleist lies in the
mainstream of the Romantic revolt against socially sanctioned
reason. (L.S.)

Goldschmidt, Didier. "Une figure d'amoureuse: Catherine de
Heilbronn: un entretien avec Eric Rohmer." *LanM* 74 (1980):
393-98.

Report of a discussion held on 4 Oct. 1979 with the director of the film *La Marquise d'O*. Rohmer discusses the idio-
syncrasies of Kleist's language and the need he felt to
make entirely new translations of his own; he displays an
acute sensitivity for the implications of style: "Il y a
une traduction qui a été faite par Anouilh, il y a
quelques années, elle a été très critiquée, mais en fin
de compte elle est très exacte, je l'ai regardée de pres,
elle donne bien l'équivalent français de toutes les intentions de la phrase allemande: mais, peut-être même à cause
de cela, elle dénature complètement le style de Kleist, ne
serait-ce que parce qu'elle précise des choses que Kleist
parfois a laissées dans le flou" (395). (L.S.)

Heine, Roland. "'Ein Traum, was sonst?' Zum Verhältnis von
Traum und Wirklichkeit in Kleists 'Prinz Friedrich von
Homburg.'" Pp. 283-313 in Jürgen Brummack et al., eds.,
*Literaturwissenschaft und Geistesgeschichte: Festschrift für
Richard Brinkmann*. Tübingen: Niemeyer, 1981.

Hinderer, Walter, ed. *Kleists Dramen: Neue Interpretationen*.
Stuttgart: Reclam, 1981. Pp. 298. DM 32.80.

The strength of this volume lies in its broadness of scope
and thoroughness of coverage: all eight of Kleist's dramas
(including the "fragment" *Robert Guiskard*) are treated in
separate essays by major Germanists, including Lawrence Ryan
(on *Die Hermannsschlacht*), Hans Robert Jauss (on *Amphitryon*),
and Walter Müller-Seidel (on *Penthesilea*). Helmut Hermann
provides a useful chronology of the works, including posthumous events such as the premieres of five of the dramas
(e.g., *Guiskard* in April 1901, in Berlin). Most useful is
Hermann's 51-page bibliography, organized chronologically
and broken down into five sections: reference works and
editions, general studies of Kleist's life and work, studies
of the individual dramas, *Wirkungsgeschichte*, and miscellane-
ous. The list comprises 1096 entries, and concentrates on the
heretofore neglected period 1880-1914 (to include commemorative studies marking the centennial of Kleist's death); it
is the most comprehensive Kleist bibliography available
today. The individual essays on the dramas are solid, if
somewhat traditional readings; there seem to be no new para-
digms of interpretation offered. In fact, the editor's conception of the entire enterprise is still dominated by a
Rousseauistic reading of the marionett-theater essay. He has
specifically included a lead essay on "Über das Marionettentheater," in which Rolf-Peter Janz defends the astonishingly
outdated position that "der Marionetten-Aufsatz [stattet]
die Grazie als Ausdrick vollendeter Ich-Identität mit der
geschichtsphilosophischen Beglaubigung aus, sie sei die
Bestimmung des Menschen" (48). That Hinderer views such an
interpretation as the foundation of Kleist criticism is
confirmed not only by the inclusion of Janz's essay, but by
Hinderer's own claim in his introduction: "In seinen Dramen
und seinen Erzählungen zeigt er wieder und wieder, wie der
Mensch durch sein Bewusstsein getäuscht, ein Opfer des
Scheins wird und nur das Unbewusste, das spontane Gefühl,
die Anmut des *Marionettentheaters*, das wahre Sein trifft"
(21). To judge from this volume as a whole, German Kleist
criticism is still captivated by a view of Kleist as the
prophet of interiority: a figure safely within the *Geistesgeschichte* of Romanticism. Thus this book is useful not
only as a bibliographical source, but as a document revealing the continuing struggle of criticism to free itself
from received ideas. (L.S.)

Horn, Peter. *Heinrich von Kleists Erzählungen. Eine Einführung*.
Königstein/Ts.: Scriptor-Verlag, 1978. Pp. 215.

Rev. by Hans-Georg Werner in *DLZ* 102 (1981): 593-95.

After introductory essays on Kleist's style and his social position as a writer, Horn offers readings of each of the eight stories. He demonstrates a thorough acquaintance with the secondary literature, and each of the chapters is worth reading, particularly those on "Das Bettelweib von Locarno" and "Der Zweikampf." In some instances, the reader feels that Horn is rehashing old issues, with nothing new to contribute to them, especially in "Was geht uns eigentlich der Gerechtigkeitsbegriff in Kleists Erzählung 'Michael Kohlhaas' noch an?" and in "Anarchie und Mobherrschaft in Kleists 'Erdbeben in Chili.'" In general, one has the impression of a collection of discrete essays, some of them more insightful than others, but lacking a unity of perspective, or even of problematics. (L.S.)

Horn, Peter. *Kleist-Chronik*. Königstein/Ts.: Athenäum, 1980. Pp. 140. DM 18.00.

Rev. by R. Masson in *EG* 36 (1981): 341.

Hoverland, Lillian. *Heinrich von Kleist und das Prinzip der Gestaltung*. Königstein/Ts.: Scriptor-Verlag, 1978. Pp. 269.

Rev. by Hans-Georg Werner in *DLZ* 102 (1981): 593-95.

Kanzog, Klaus. *Edition und Engagement: 150 Jahre Editionsgeschichte der Werke und Briefe Heinrich von Kleists*. Band 1: *Darstellung*. Band 2: *Editorisches und dokumentarisches Material*. (Quellen und Forschungen zur Sprach- und Kulturgeschichte der germanischen Völker, Nrs. 74 and 75.) Berlin, New York: Walter de Gruyter, 1979. Pp. 342; 386.

Rev. of Vol. I by Marjorie Gelus in *GQ* 54 (1981): 350-51.

With these volumes, Kanzog continues presenting the fruits of his reconsideration of the publication history of Kleist's works, as well as the theoretical and practical issues which must be addressed by modern text-editing. Volume One contains a series of essays tracing editorial issues from Kleist's death up to Erich Schmidt's "Kämpfe um eine definitive Kleist-Ausgabe." There are fine chapters on Tieck's 1821 and 1826 editions, and on Eduard von Bülow's biography and edition of the letters. Volume Two contains a wealth of documentary material indicative of the principle of various editors of Kleist's letters and works. Anyone interested in the legitimacy and authority of specific editions, or in the hermeneutic and material dimensions of producing editions of canonized authors, will be grateful for the painstaking precision and thoroughness with which Kanzog has presented these materials. (L.S.)

Löb, Ladislaus. *From Lessing to Hauptmann: Studies in German Drama.* London: University Tutorial Press, 1974. Pp. 383. £3.50.

Rev. by Joachim Müller in *Germanistik* 19 (1978): 753. Kleist is among the six selected for discussion.

Reeve, W.C. "An Unsung Villain: The Role of Hohenzollern in Kleist's *Prinz Friedrich von Homburg.*" *GR* 56 (1981): 95-110.

A carefully developed, well-documented claim that Count Hohenzollern should be considered the *agent provocateur* in the struggle between the "objective, rational sphere of the sovereign and the subjective, irrational world of the Prince" (96). Although Hohenzollern casts himself as the friend of the Prince, he is quick to associate himself with the Elector when it is expedient to do so. He thus emerges as a Machiavellian sadist, gleeful in the gratuitous conflict he generates between the two orders. Since he is the only character whom Kleist created (the rest are derived from the Brandenburg genealogy), he could "act" with utter disregard for historical accuracy, and it is his arbitrariness that is the true initiator of all the major actions of the play. (L.S.)

Ruffet, Jean, trans. *Heinrich von Kleist: Anecdotes et petits écrits.* (Petite Bibliothèque Payot.) Paris: Payot, 1981.

Seidlin, Oskar. *Von erwachendem Bewußtsein und vom Sündenfall: Brentano, Schiller, Kleist, Goethe.* Stuttgart: Klett-Cotta, 1979. Pp. 171.

See also Seidlin ("Brentano").
Rev. by Egon Schwarz in *GQ* 54 (1981): 119-20.
All of the essays printed here have appeared elsewhere; thus the main attraction of this volume is that of convenience; those interested in Seidlin's recent work are spared the labor of collecting his writings. Most of the emphasis in this *Sammelband* falls on Brentano (four chapters of seven). The chapter on Schiller deals with *"Das Vorspiel zum Wilhelm Tell,"* the one on Goethe with irony in *Neue Melusine.* The essay on Kleist, "Was die Stunde schlägt in *Der zerbrochne Krug,*" originally appeared in English as "What the Bell Tolls in Kleist's *Der zerbrochne Krug*" in *DVLG* 51 (1977): 78-97 (see *ELN* 17, Supp., 232). (L.S.)

Sembdner, Helmut. *Das Detmolder "Käthchen von Heilbronn": Eine unbekannte Bühnenfassung Heinrich von Kleists.* (Beihefte

zum *Euphorion*, Nr. 17.) Heidelberg: Carl Winter Universitäts-
verlag, 1981. Pp. 198. DM 58.00.

Siebert, Eberhard. *Heinrich von Kleist: Leben und Werk im
Bild*. Frankfurt am Main: Insel, 1980. Pp. 252. DM 10.00.

Rev. by R. Masson in *EG* 36 (1981): 341.

Thum, Reinhard. "Kleist's Ambivalent Portrayal of Absolutism
in *Prinz Friedrich von Homburg*." *GR* 56 (1981): 1-12.

Agreeing with Walter Silz's 1936 article claiming that
most readings of the play neglect the complexity and ambiguity of its "resolution," Thum contends that Kleist criticism has not yet rectified its misreadings. Close readings
of scene after scene reveal, he argues, that Kleist's position cannot be firmly pinned down, but that it remains
ambivalent to the core. Kleist's simultaneous critique and
celebration of an absolutist society "indicate the moral
dilemma of a man who longed to preserve, to join and even
to honor and be honored by a society whose weaknesses and
failings he could not ignore" (3). Thus Kleist's claim to
have written "ein vaterländisches Schauspiel" must be seen
as "a description of national realities of which [he] was
painfully aware" (11). (L.S.)

Wegener, K.-H. *"Amphitryon" im Spiegel der Kleist-literatur*.
Bern: Lang, 1979. Pp. 305. Sw.Fr. 53.00.

Wegener's main achievement is a thorough review of the
major attempts to come to terms with Kleist's play, from
contemporary reactions to the most recent (post-1960)
secondary literature. As a *Stand-der-Forschung* report, this
book will be welcomed by all students of Kleist; it is en-
hanced by a chronologically arranged bibliography. Such a
cosmopolitan perspective, however, has apparently crippled
Wegener's ability to contribute anything significant of his
own to the issues of reading *Amphitryon*. "Part Two" of the
volume, "Exkurse zur Rezeptionsgeschichte und zur Interpretation des 'Amphitryon,'" is thoroughly dominated by the
perspectives and terminology of his predecessors. It is
curiously pallid and noncommittal on textual cruces, e.g.,
the significance of Alkmene's final "Ach!" Go to this book
for solid historical scholarship, not for new insights.
(L.S.)

Willeke, Androne B. "The Tightrope-Walker and the Marionette:
Images of Harmony in Wedekind and Kleist." Pp. 89-96 in
Eduardo Zayas-Bazan and M. Laurentino Saurez, eds., *Selected*

Proceedings of the Twenty-Seventh Annual Mountain Interstate Foreign Language Conference. Johnson City: East Tennessee State University Press, 1978.

See also Freund, Pongs, Reed ("German 2. General"); Fühmann, McIntyre, Seiverth ("Hoffmann").

Reviews of books previously listed:

DÜRST, Rolf, *Heinrich von Kleist: Dichter zwischen Ursprung und Endzeit* (see *ELN* 17, Supp., 226-27), rev. by Maria Tatar in *Monatshefte* 73 (1981): 461-65; ELLIS, John M., *Heinrich von Kleist: Studies in the Character and Meaning of His Writings* (see *RMB* for 1979, pp. 301-02), rev. by Erika Swales in *MLR* 75 (1980): 947-49; GERLACH, Kurt, *Heinrich von Kleist: Sein Leben und Schaffen in neuer Sicht* (see *ELN* 17, Supp., 227), rev. by Hilda Brown in *Seminar* 16 (1980): 58-62; by Maria Tatar in *Monatshefte* 73 (1981): 461-65; SCHMIDT, Herminio, *Heinrich von Kleist: Naturwissenschaft als Dichtungsprinzip* (see *ELN* 17, Supp., 232), rev. by Maria Tatar in *Monatshefte* 73 (1981): 461-65; WITTKOWSKI, Wolfgang, *Heinrich von Kleists "Amphitryon"* (see *RMB* for 1979, p. 305), rev. by Ludwig W. Kahn in *GR* 55 (1980): 164-65; by R. Masson in *EG* 36 (1981): 90-91.

LENAU

Kostič, Strahinjak. "Lenaus Zeitgenossen unter den serbischen Dichtern aus Südungarn." *LenauF* 11 (1979): 49-56.

Nivelle, Armand. "Notes sur l'imagerie de Lenau." Pp. 89-103 in Richard Thieberger, ed., *Etudes allemandes et autrichiennes*. (Annales de la Faculté des Lettres et Sciences Humaines de Nice, No. 33.) Paris: Les Belles Lettres, 1978. Pp. 145.

Weiss, Walter. "Nikolaus Lenau: Poesie und Politik." Pp. 289-309 in Gerlinde Weiss and Gerd-Dieter Stein, eds., *Festschrift für Adalbert Schmidt zum 70. Geburtstag*. (Stuttgarter Arbeiten zur Germanistik, Nr. 4.) Stuttgart: Heinz, 1976. Pp. 563. DM 78.00.

LESSING

See Hunter-Lougheed ("Bonaventura").

MAHLER

See Rölleke ("Brentano").

MANN, TH.

See Heinrich-Heine-Institut, Düsseldorf, ed. ("Heine"); Gersdorff ("Hoffmann").

MARX

See Kaufmann, Nabrotzky, Wehner ("Heine"); Horster ("Hölderlin").

MENDELSSOHN

See Prawer ("Heine").

MÖRIKE

Belmore, H.W. "Two Romantic Poems of Solitude: Leopardi and
Mörike." GL&L 31 (1977-78): 313-18.

Turner, D. "Romantic Motifs in Mörike's 'Früh im Wagen.'"
NGS (1976): Special Issue, 41-54.

See also Dessauer ("German 2. General").

MOZART

See Miller ("German 2. General"); Gantz, Mühlher, Patzelt
("Hoffmann").

MÜLLER, A.

Richter, Karin. "Der 'böse Dämon' in der deutschen Romantik:
Betrachtungen zum Werk und Wirken Adam Heinrich Müllers
(1779-1829)." WB 25 (1979): 82-105.

NIETZSCHE

Behler, Ernst. "Nietzsche und die frühromantische Schule" [incl. discussion]. *Nietzsche-Studien: Internationales Jahrbuch für die Nietzsche Forschung* 7 (1978): 59-87, 88-96.

Heller, Peter. "Nietzsche Kampf mit dem romantischen Pessimismus" [incl. discussion]. *Nietzsche-Studien: Internationales Jahrbuch für die Nietzsche Forschung* 7 (1978): 27-50, 51-58.

See also Wuthenow ("German 2. General"); Behler ("Schlegel, Fr.").

NOVALIS

Heller, Erich. "Novalis: Die Christenheit oder Europa." *Merkur* 400 (1981): 1034-44.

Kreuzer, Ingrid. "Novalis 'Die Lehrlinge zu Sais': Fragen zur Struktur, Gattung und immanenten Ästhetik." *JDSG* 23 (1979): 276-308.

Leroy, Robert, and Eckart Pastor. "Die Initiation des romantischen Dichters: Der Anfang von Novalis' *Heinrich von Ofterdingen*." Pp. 38-57 in Ernst Ribbat, ed., *Romantik: Ein literaturwissenschaftliches Studienbuch*. (Athenäum Taschenbücher, 2149.) Königstein/Ts.: Athenäum, 1979. Pp. 236. DM 19.80.

See also Ribbat ("German 2. General").

Nakai, Ayako. "Die 'Natur' bei Novalis" [Japanese with German summary]. *DB* 60 (1978): 64-74.

Niscov, Viorica. "Orientul în opera de fictiune a lui Novalis." *Revista de istorie şi teorie literară* 25 (1976): 369-80.

Scrase, David A. "The Movable Feast: The Role and Relevance of the *Fest* Motif in Novalis' *Heinrich von Ofterdingen*." *NGS* 7 (1979): 23-40.

See also Dessauer, Firchow, Greiner, Itô, Mann, Metzner, Timm ("German 2. General"); Boie, Neubauer, Tatar, Vom Hofe ("Hoffmann"); Samuel ("Schlegel, Fr.").

RAABE

See Rölleke ("Brentano").

RUNGE

Feilchenfeldt, Konrad. "Gedanken zu einer textkritischen
   Ausgabe der 'Schriften' von Philipp Otto Runge." *Philobiblon*
   22 (1978): 286-97.

Toyoda, Jun-ichi. "Philipp Otto Runge und Goethe" [Japanese
   with German summary]. Pp. 109-26 in *Gête Nenkan* [*Goethe-
   Jahrbuch*, Japan] 18 (1976): 109-26.

SAVIGNY

*Savigny y la ciencia jurídica del Siglo XIX. Anales de la
   catedra Francisco Suárez* (University of Granada) 18-19
   (1978-79). Pp. 393.

   Rev. by André Reix in *RMM* 86 (1981): 134.

SCHELLING

Freier, Hans. *Die Rückkehr der Götter: Von der ästhetischen
   Überschreitung der Wissensgrenze zur Mythologie der Moderne.
   Eine Untersuchung zur systematischen Rolle der Kunst in der
   Philosophie Kants und Schellings.* Stuttgart: Metzler, 1976.
   Pp. 297. DM 54.00.

Lehmann, Jürgen. "Schelling (1775-1854)." Pp. 151-66, 330-35
   in Horst Turk, ed., *Klassiker der Literaturtheorie: Von
   Boileau bis Barthes.* (Becksche schwarze Reihe, Bd. 192.)
   München: Beck, 1979. Pp. 374. DM 24.00.

   Rev. by Jürgen Söring in *Germanistik* 20 (1979): 377.

Schaffer, Elinor. "Schelling and Romantic Science: The Frontier
   between Disciplines." Pp. 191-93 in Robert D. Eagleson, ed.,
   *Language and Literature in the Formation of National and
   Cultural Communities.* Proceedings of the XIIIth Congress of
   the Fédération Internationale des Langues et Littératures
   Modernes and the XVIIth Congress of the Australian Universi-
   ties Language and Literature Association held at Sydney University, 25 to 29 August 1975. Sydney: Australian University
   Language and Literature Association, 1976. Pp. xiv+274.

See also Mann ("German 2. General"); Horster ("Hölderlin");
Elardo, Ettelt, Neubauer ("Hoffmann").

SCHILLER

Donnenberg, Josef. "Die Jungfrau von Orleans--und Brecht: Die
heilige Johanna der Schlachthöfe. Zur Interpretation und
Rezeption." Pp. 257-87 in Gerlinde Weiss and Gerd-Dieter
Stein, eds., Festschrift für Adalbert Schmidt zum 70. Geburtstag. (Stuttgarter Arbeiten zur Germanistik, Nr. 4.) Stuttgart: Heinz, 1976. Pp. 563. DM 78.00.

Sellner, Timothy F. "The Lionel-Scene in Schiller's Jungfrau
von Orleans: A Psychological Interpretation." GQ 50 (1977):
264-82.

Wieden, Fritz. "S.T. Coleridge's Assimilation of Ideas from
Schiller's Early Writings." Pp. 170-81 in A. Arnold, ed.,
Analecta Helvetica et Germanica: Eine Festschrift zu Ehren
von Hermann Bueschenstein. (Studien zur Germanistik, Anglistik und Komparatistik, Bd. 85.) Bonn: Bouvier, 1979. Pp.
392. DM 52.00.

See also Conger ("English 4. Shelley, Mary"); Freund ("German
2. General"); Seidlin ("Brentano"); Seidlin ("Kleist").

SCHLEGEL, A.W.

Guthke, Karl S. "Benares am Rhein--Rom am Ganges: Die Begeg-
nung von Orient und Okzident im Denken A.W. Schlegels."
JFDH (1978): 396-419.

Nakai, Chiyuki. "Literaturgeschichte als Bildungsgeschichte
der Menschheit: Über die 'Berliner Vorlesungen' (1801-
1804) von August Wilhelm Schlegel" [Japanese with German
summary]. DB 56 (1976): 1-10.

See also Firchow, Lefevere ("German 2. General").

SCHLEGEL, FR.

Behler, Ernst. "Friedrich Schlegels 'Rede über die Mythologie'
im Hinblick auf Nietzsche." Nietzsche-Studien: Internationales Jahrbuch für die Nietzsche-Forschung 8 (1979): 182-209.

Gockel, Heinz. "Friedrich Schlegels Theorie des Fragments."
    Pp. 23-37 in Ernst Ribbat, ed., Romantik: Ein literatur-
    wissenschaftliches Studienbuch. (Athenäum Taschenbücher,
    2149.) Königstein/Ts.: Athenäum, 1979. Pp. 236. DM 19.80.

    See also Ribbat ("German 2. General").

Hacks, Peter. "Der Meineiddichter." NDL 25 (1977/75): 8-19.

Huyssen, Andreas. Friedrich Schlegel: Kritische und theore-
    tische Schriften. (Universal-Bibliothek, Nr. 9880.) Stutt-
    gart: Reclam, 1978. Pp. 243. DM 4.80.

Sakata, Ken'ichi. "Die Idee der Literaturgeschichte als
    Wissenschaft bei F. Schlegel." DB 56 (1976): 11-20.

Samuel, Richard. "Friedrich Schlegel's and Friedrich von
    Hardenberg's Love Affairs in Leipzig: A Contribution to
    Their Biographies." Pp. 47-56 in Anthony Stephens, ed.,
    Festschrift for Ralph Farrell. (Australisch-neuseeländische
    Studien zur deutschen Sprache und Literatur, Bd. 7.) Bern,
    Frankfurt, and Las Vegas: Lang, 1977. Pp. 233. Sw.Fr.
    38.00.

Timpanaro, Sebastiano, ed. with intro., prepared by E.F.K.
    Koerner. Friedrich Schlegel: Über die Sprache und die
    Weisheit der Indier. Ein Beitrag zur Begründung der Alter-
    tumskunde. (Amsterdam Studies in the Theory and History
    of Linguistic Science, Serial 1, Vol. 1.) Amsterdam: Ben-
    jamins, 1977. Pp. 70.

See also Firchow, Lefevere, Mann, Timm ("German 2. General");
    Tatar ("Hoffmann").

SCHLEGEL-SCHELLING, CAROLINE

Stern, Carola. "Zierlich, klein, mit Silberblick: Nicht nur
    eine Erinnerung an Caroline Schlegel-Schelling." Merkur
    398 (1981): 703-09.

SCHLEIERMACHER

Birus, Hendrik. "Hermeneutische Wende? Anmerkungen zur
    Schleiermacher-Interpretation." Euphorion 74 (1980):
    213-22.

See also Timm ("German 2. General").

SCHMIDT, ARNO

See Petzel ("Hoffmann").

SCHUBERT, FRANZ

See Knepler ("Goethe"); Brauner ("Heine").

SCHUBERT, G.H.

See Frank ("German 2. General"); Elardo, Ettelt, Neubauer
("Hoffmann").

SCHUMANN, ROBERT

See Brauner, Motte-Haber, Zagari ("Heine").

TIECK

Ribbat, Ernst. "Poesie und Polemik: Zur Entstehungsgeschichte
der romantischen Schule und zur Literatursatire Ludwig
Tiecks." Pp. 58–79 in Ribbat, ed., *Romantik: Ein literaturwissenschaftliches Studienbuch.* (Athenäum Taschenbücher,
2149.) Königstein/Ts.: Athenäum, 1979. Pp. 236. DM 19.80.

  Listed without a review in *RMB* for 1979, p. 317.
  See also Ribbat ("German 2. General").

See also Dessauer, Frank, Pikulik ("German 2. General");
Nahrebecky, Tatar ("Hoffmann"); Kanzog ("Kleist").

Reviews of books previously listed:

CORKHILL, Alan, *The Motif of "Fate" in the Works of Ludwig
Tieck* (see *RMB* for 1979, p. 314), rev. by Ernst M. Oppen-
heimer in *Germanistik* 20 (1979): 494; RIBBAT, Ernst, *Ludwig
Tieck* (see *ELN* 17, Supp., 240–41), rev. by Uwe Schweikert
in *Germanistik* 20 (1979): 495; SEGEBRECHT, Wulf, ed.,
Ludwig Tieck (see *ELN* 16, Supp., 188), rev. by Ernst Fedor
in *LMFA* 12 (1979): 60–62.

UHLAND

Freund, Winfried. "Verfallene Schlösser—Ein gesellschafts-
kritisches Motiv bei Kleist, E.T.A. Hoffmann, Uhland and
Chamisso." *Diskussion Deutsch* 11 (1980): 361-69.

Lenerz, Jürgen. "Dichterische Freiheit, linguistisch betrach-
tet: Zur Syntax des poetischen Dialekts von Ludwig Uhland."
Pp. 80-95 in Klaus Grubmüller, ed., *Befund und Deutung:
Zum Verhältnis von Empirie und Interpretation in Sprach-
und Literaturwissenschaft.* Tübingen: Niemeyer, 1979. Pp.
viii+545. Dm 120.00.

VARNHAGEN VON ENSE, KARL AUGUST

Bähtz, Dieter. "Der 'rothe' Varnhagen: Tagebucher als poli-
tische Zeitchronik." *WZUH* 27,2 (1978): 79-84.

See also Kuczynski ("German 2. General").

WACKENRODER

See Greiner ("German 2. General"); Nahrebecky ("Hoffmann").

WAGNER

See Frank ("German 2. General"); Neubauer ("Hoffmann").

ITALIAN

(Compiled by Augustus Pallotta, Syracuse University; Daniela Bini, University of Texas, Austin)

1. GENERAL

Bellina, Anna Laura, and Gilberto Pizzamiglio. "Balli scaligeri e polemiche romantiche." *LI* 33 (1981): 350-84.

The ballets staged at La Scala during the Romantic period not only represented important cultural events in themselves, but public and critical reaction to them had a precise correspondence to the battle waged by the Romantics and Neoclassicists. A novel perspective on the cultural ramifications of Italian Romanticism; hence a welcome contribution. (A.P.)

Berengo, Marino. *Intellettuali e librai nella Milano della Restaurazione*. Torino: Einaudi, 1980. Pp. 426.

Rev. in *ON* 5 (1981): 329-30.

De Caprio, Vincenzo. "*L'Attaccabrighe*: ideologia conservatrice e classicismo senza classici." *Paragone* 31 (1980): 139-56.

Giornetti-Incarbone, Rossella. "*Lo Spettatore* e la cultura italiana nella prima Restaurazione." *CrL* 9 (1981): 19-61.

Rich in factual documentation, this study brings to light the role played by *Lo Spettatore* in the *querelle* between Romantics and Neoclassicists and in Italian culture in general. Less influential than *La Biblioteca Italiana*, with which it shared a conservative outlook, *Lo Spettatore*, lacking an ideological program, sought to avoid social and political issues "per concentrarsi nel campo innocuo della letteratura e dell'erudizione" (21). But the periodical proved a positive force nonetheless: it circulated widely and it exposed readers to European literature. (A.P.)

Tissoni, Roberto. "La *Biblioteca Italiana* e la cultura della
Restaurazione nel Lombardo-Veneto." *Studi storici* 2 (1980):
421-36.

2. STUDIES OF AUTHORS

DE SANCTIS

Bellucci-Celli, Novella, and Nicola Longo. *Francesco De
Sanctis tra coinvolgimento e ideologia*. Roma: Bulzoni,
1979. Pp. 224.

  Rev. by Filippo Bettini in *RLI* 84 (1980): 368-70; in *ON*
5 (Jan.-Feb. 1981): 332-33.

De Sanctis, Francesco. *Un viaggio elettorale. Racconto*. Introduzione di Gilberto Finzi. Milano: Garzanti, 1977. Pp. 121.

  Rev. by Anthony Verna in *FI* 14 (1980): 115-16.

See also Dell'Aquila ("Foscolo").

FOSCOLO

Barbarisi, Gennaro. "Il fine della poesia e la responsabilità
del letterato nel pensiero di Ugo Foscolo." *Il Risorgimento*
31 (1979): 117-43.

Betti, Franco. "Primitivismo e morte nell'*Ortis* e nei *Sepolcri*.
Nota junghiana." *Italianistica* 9 (1980): 491-95.

Bosisio, Paolo. "La rappresentazione dell'*Ajace* e la tecnica
teatrale foscoliana." *Belfagor* 35 (1980): 139-56.

Cambon, Glauco. *Ugo Foscolo, Poet of Exile*. Princeton University Press, 1980. Pp. 356. £11.80.

  Rev. by Mary Ambrose in *DUJ* 43 (1981): 144-46.

Cardini, Roberto. "A proposito del commento foscoliano alla
Chioma di Berenice." *LI* 33 (1981): 329-49.

Dell'Aquila, Michele. "Foscolo nel progetto pedagogico del
De Sanctis." *Italianistica* 9 (1980): 283-96.

Conclusion of a two-part study (Part I is reviewed in *RMB* for 1980, p. 344). The author continues to illustrate De Sanctis' lukewarm interest in Foscolo influenced in part by a negative assessment of *Jacopo Ortis* ("gli appariva come il sintomo di una malattia, non solo foscoliana, ma di una intera generazione nazionale," 285). A more balanced criticism of Foscolo is found in De Sanctis' *Saggi*, written after the poet's death, at the time, in fact, that his remains were brought to Italy. This segment of the essay lacks the interest and the critical breadth so evident in the first part. (A.P.)

De Luca, Raffaele. "La tomba nel Foscolo come immagine ossessiva e mito personale." *Italica* 58 (1981): 16-27.

Fasano, Pino. "La vita e il testo: introduzione a una biografia foscoliana 1978." *RLI* 84 (1980): 161-78.

As he reviews Foscolo's biographies through the years, the author singles out three historical periods reflecting as many approaches to Foscolo: (a) the Risorgimento period, marked by a coherent vision of the writer and his life; (b) the 1871-1927 period, which, partly under Croce's influence, stressed a net distinction between "personalità biografica" and "personalità estetica"; (c) the "atteggiamento anti-biografico" of recent criticism. Laying the groundwork for a different biography of Foscolo, Fasano points out that Foscolo's life (an important aspect of which are his letters) represents "metodologicamente il sostrato organico" of his work, a "doloroso preambolo al testo letterario, segnale del tormentato rapporto che Foscolo ha con la sua opera" (176). And to prove his point the critic cites Foscolo's revealing words: "Friggo, rifriggo, macero, tormento in mille modi ogni verso fra me." (A.P.)

Flint, R.W. "Ugo Foscolo: Exiles Return." *Canto* 4 (1981): 136-47.

Foscolo, Ugo. *Lettera apologetica*. A cura di Giuseppe Nicoletti. Torino: Einaudi, 1978. Pp. LII+143.

Rev. by Mario Chiesa in *GSLI* 158 (1981): 301-06.

Girardi, Enzo Noè. *Saggio sul Foscolo*. Milano: SPES, 1978. Pp. 106.

Rev. by Alberto Brambilla in *Italianistica* 9 (1980): 341-43; by Alfredo Cottignoli in *SPCT* 23 (1981): 253.

Goffis, Cesare Federico. "Il romanzo anglo-elvetico del
    Foscolo." *Italianistica* 9 (1980): 251-77.

    A lengthy discussion of *The Italian Bride*, a novel barely
    sketched by Foscolo. Goffis dwells on biographical elements,
    especially Foscolo's relationship with Carolina Russell, and
    he does so to advance some educated guesses on what might
    have been the content of the work. (A.P.)

Nicoletti, Giuseppe. *Il "metodo" dell'"Ortis" e altri studi
    foscoliani*. Firenze: La Nuova Italia, 1978. Pp. 216.

    Rev. by Mario Chiesa in *GSLI* 158 (1981): 301-06.

Rosada, Bruno. "Rassegna foscoliana: 1976-1979." *LI* 32 (1980):
    364-99.

    A rich, if incomplete, survey of recent Foscolo scholar-
    ship. Rosada discusses the papers given at various *convegni*,
    but he virtually ignores Foscolo studies published outside
    Italy--the norm rather than the exception in studies of this
    sort. One such omission: vol. 12 (Winter 1978) of *Forum
    Italicum* devoted to Foscolo. (A.P.)

Santoro, Marco, ed. *Foscolo e la cultura meridionale. Atti
    del Convegno Foscoliano* (Napoli, 29-30 marzo 1979). Napoli:
    Società Editrice Napoletana, 1980. Pp. xvi+332.

    Rev. by Gustavo Costa in *FI* 15 (1981): 227-29; by Wanda
    De Nunzio Schilardi in *Italianistica* 10 (1981): 271-74.

Scarcia, Riccardo. "Mediazioni scolastiche neoclassiche di Ugo
    Foscolo e di alcuni altri." Pp. 21-64 of Scarcia, *Due studi
    di filologia*. Roma: Palombi, 1979.

Schilardi-De Nunzio, Wanda. "In nota al rifiuto del Foscolo
    all'edizione dell'*Ortis* del '99." *ON* 5 (1981): 219-29.

    Deals with Foscolo's reaction to the apocryphal edition
    of his novel, the *Vera storia di due amanti infelici ossia
    Ultime lettere di Jacopo Ortis*, published in Bologna in
    1799. Foscolo's protest is perceived as an intellectual
    statement on literature: "Era rifiuto della ideologia che
    era dietro il romanzesco, era rifiuto della ipocrisia, della
    retorica, della contraffazione della realtà" (221).
    Schilardi's cogent references to Foscolo's critical works
    substantiate his aversion to the "follie romanzesche" and
    point to Foscolo's concept of the novel as a didactic medium
    of moral enlightenment. (A.P.)

Toschi, Luca. "*To Callirhoe* ed altri inediti foscoliani." *RLI* 84 (1980): 520–37.

Offers a detailed account of several versions and editions of the poem *To Callirhoe*, including three unpublished copies of the work Toschi found in the Osborn Collection at Yale University. The other *inediti* are five letters relating to Foscolo's arrival in England, the publication of his *Essays* on Petrarch, and a series of lectures he gave in 1823. (A.P.)

Tripodi, Vincenzo. *Studi su Laurence Sterne ed Ugo Foscolo.* Madrid: Ediciones José Porrúa Turanzas, 1978. Pp. 207.

Rev. by Sante Matteo in *FI* 14 (1980): 253–55.

See also Amoretti ("Leopardi").

Reviews of books previously listed:

FOSCOLO, Ugo, *Scritti di critica storica e letteraria, 1817–27* (see *RMB* for 1980, p. 345), rev. by Gennaro Barbisi in *GSLI* 158 (1981): 125–45; by Gustavo Costa in *FI* 15 (1981): 92–94; by D.M. White in *IS* 36 (1981): 110–12; FOSCOLO, Ugo, *Studi su Dante* (see *RMB* for 1980, p. 345), rev. by Mario Chiesa in *GSLI* 158 (1981): 254–61.

GROSSI

Cerri, Angelo. "I manzonismi nel *Marco Visconti* di Tommaso Grossi." *GSLI* 158 (1980): 557–91.

A minute analysis of Grossi's extensive lexical borrowings from Manzoni's novel. Heavy reliance on *I promessi sposi* not only affected adversely the formal structure of *Marco Visconti* but "finisce per squilibrare ulteriormente uno stile già compromesso dalla mancanza di un tono costante e personale" (558). Cerri offers substantial evidence to support this position, but goes too far in tracing to Manzoni words, idioms, and lexical constructs which Grossi could have drawn from other literary sources as well as everyday usage. (A.P.)

LEOPARDI

Amoretti, Giovanni G. *Poesia e psicanalisi: Foscolo e Leopardi.* Milano: Garzanti, 1979. Pp. 200.

The book contains two essays. The first deals with Foscolo.
The second, "'L'ultimo orizzonte.' Lettura psicanalitica
dell''Infinito' di Giacomo Leopardi" (pp. 79-200), is published here for the first time. The aim of the essay is to
explore the expressive contents of the "Infinito" with the
tools of psychoanalysis without applying to them preconceived
ideas about Leopardi's neurosis. Through the psychoanalytical
approach, the poem appears as a regression to the pre-oedipal phase, where the goal is identification with nature and
annulment in it (mother-symbol). In Amoretti's view, Leopardi
was never able to flee ahead, challenging his father, for
he could not take the risk of life. His flight was, therefore, backwards: to become again a son rather than a man.
Leopardi's loves are also interpreted by Amoretti as repe-
titions of love for the mother; thus their failure. The author
uses the "Discorso" to show how the refusal of the new poetry,
the romantic, was the symptom of Leopardi's fear of growing
up. His negation of progress had its roots in the trauma of
separation from his mother. Hence Leopardi's narcissism and
praise of the prerational phase of man (ancients, children).
Beside the fact that Leopardi did not "refuse" Romantic
poetry--pages and pages of the *Zibaldone* can prove this--it
is somewhat simplistic to reduce Leopardi's serious attack
on progress to this psychological motive. The author himself,
in fact, after recognizing the value of using some of the
more recent critical contributions to Leopardi, admits that
a psychoanalytical reading does not pretend to be exhaustive.
He adds, however, that it can be a valid contribution to
other types of criticism. Yet he is convinced that the fundamental component of inspiration, not only in the "Infinito,"
but in all *Canti*, is the poet's ambivalent feeling of desire
and fear of pre-oedipal regression. (D.B.)

Berno, Giuseppe. "Leopardi in Germania: due traduzioni dell'
    Infinito." *CeS* 77 (Jan.-March 1981): 7-18.

    In addition to a close analysis of two German translations
of the poem (by P. Heyse and Rilke), the author offers some
incisive remarks on the craft of translation and its ultimate
objectives. (A.P.)

Binni, Walter. "La poesia di Leopardi negli anni napoletani."
    RLI 84 (1980): 427-57.

Binni, Walter. "Il saggio di Luporini e la svolta leopardiana
    del '47." *RLI* 84 (1980): 538-45.

Cesare Luporini's essay *Leopardi progressivo*, published first in 1947, marked a turning point in Leopardi studies (for a review of the 1980 reprint, see *RMB* for 1980, p. 357). In this article, Binni recalls the cultural atmosphere of the time, defends the attribute "progressivo" applied to Leopardi, and points out the relevance of Leopardi's thought to our time. (A.P.)

Bonadeo, Alfredo. "Leopardi e il vero." *Italica* 58 (1981): 28–42.

Bonadeo follows Leopardi's thought from his refusal to accept the harsh realities of life (around 1819 when the poet becomes seriously ill) to his acceptance of life, indeed his "exaltation" of human existence (the expression seems rather strong) that culminates in "La Ginestra." Bonadeo analyzes different connotations of Leopardi's "disperazione" present in his letters, poetry, and the *Zibaldone*. The poet's total despair becomes gradually the pleasure of despair. His constant dwelling on evil and pain gives despair a masochistic connotation. Yet this experience is overcome when Leopardi realizes its inherent weakness and learns to accept the "orrido vero" shared by all beings. The acceptance of truth and suffering separates the noble man from the "volgo." Leopardi is now proud to be a "souffrant." In the conclusion to this well-written essay, Bonadeo fails to see, however, that the pleasure of suffering persists to the end, originating now from Leopardi's sense of inferiority toward the common man who refused to accept the hard truth. What differentiates this from the previous phase of masochism is the final awareness that suffering makes man nobler. The pleasure of suffering, therefore, has in the end an even stronger foundation. (D.B.)

Bosco, Umberto. *Titanismo e pietà in Giacomo Leopardi e altri studi leopardiani*. Roma: Bonacci, 1980. Pp. 103.

Rev. by Emilio Bigi in *GSLI* 158 (1981): 461–65.

Brioschi, Franco. *La poesia senza nome. Saggio su Giacomo Leopardi*. Milano: Il Saggiatore, 1980. Pp. 303.

Rev. by Novella Bellucci-Celli in *RLI* 85 (1981): 346–48.

Carrannante, Antonio. "Il pensiero linguistico di Giacomo Leopardi." *RLI* 84 (1980): 179–98.

Caserta, Ernesto G. *L'ultimo Leopardi. Pensiero e poesia*. Roma: Bonacci, 1980. Pp. 289.

Cecchetti, Giovanni. *Sulle "Operette morali": tre studi con
  proscritto sull'elaborazione dei "Canti."* Roma: Bulzoni,
  1978. Pp. 126.

  Rev. by Clavio Ascari in *Forum Italicum* 15 (1981): 226-27.
  Contains four studies published first in 1962-64. Cecchetti
examines the leitmotives and keywords that recur in the
Operette, focusing on the poetic rather than philosophical
qualities of the work. In the Preface, Scrivano comments
on Cecchetti's subtle analysis of the linguistic and stylistic
aspects of the *Operette*. (D.B.)

Circeo, Ermanno. *La poesia satirico-politica del Leopardi.*
  Roma: Edizioni dell' Ateneo and Bizzarri, 1978. Pp. 121.

  Rev. by Ernesto G. Caserta in *IQ* 22 (1981): 115-17.
  The analysis is limited to Leopardi's ideological-political
satire, which Circeo wants to reevaluate and which he sees
as a fundamental part of Leopardi's literary work. The author
examines first the relationship between Leopardi and French
sensationalism and materialism as philosophical sources of
Leopardi's work. He then concentrates on his satirical
works ("Palinodia," "I nuovi credenti," and "I Paralipomeni").
The picture that emerges is of a Leopardi in polemics with
his times and politics *tout-court*, an isolated intellectual
who, while reaffirming his faith in the principles of the
Enlightenment, passes over his times to reach out into our
century. His materialism is "neither progressive nor apologetic" and it presents neither a political project nor a
utopic view of the future, as Prete well saw (Introduction
to *Operette morali*, Milan, 1976). Circeo, however, believes
that though pessimistic, Leopardi's philosophy maintains an
adamant faith in history and in man.
  The book has as an Appendix the essay "Metafora e satira
in Leopardi e Montale" where the affinity of the two poets
is found in their constant and painful search for truth and
in their consequent negativism. The difference between them,
according to Circeo, who examines comparatively the satirical works of the two poets, is that, whereas Montale's
irony is the sign of admitted defeat and a renunciation of
fighting, Leopardi's is, to the end, the combative voice of
a man who will not withdraw from the battle for he still
has faith in reason, and thus in man's power. (D.B.)

Cook, Albert. "Leopardi: The Mastery of Diffusing Sorrow."
  CJIS IV,1-2 (1980-81): 68-81.

  The essay dwells on Leopardi's technique of diffusing
sorrow; that is, of poetically conveying the idea of vague-

ness and indefiniteness. Cook ties together Leopardi's
thoughts on poetics expressed in the *Zibaldone* ("il linguaggio
poetico ... consiste ... in un modo di parlare indefinito")
with Leopardi's philosophical belief: the yearning for the
infinite never fulfilled. He briefly examines "A Silvia,"
"L'infinito," "Le ricordanze," and "La ginestra" in order
to point out the connection between formal and thematic
aspects. The movement between precision and vagueness, disappointment and joy, discovery of truth and rejection, reveals
Leopardi's unshaken belief "that man fulfills himself by
being unfulfilled" and that poetry is the only language
capable of expressing this insight. (D.B.)

Di Carlo, Franco. "Ungaretti tra *La Ronda* e Leopardi." *ON* 4
(1980): 249-55.

Ungaretti's psychological need for order and stability
after World War I corresponded, poetically, to the rescue
of Italian literary tradition. Leopardi appeared to him as
a hermetic poet *ante litteram* for the metaphysical value he
gave to memory, lasting time, and innocence. Furthermore,
Leopardi's greatest formal lesson was, according to Ungaretti,
his hendecasyllable which had to be rescued and used as a
model. (D.B.)

Fontanella, Luigi. "L'*Aspasia* leopardiana: una rilettura."
CL 9 (1981): 253-65.

Frattini, Alberto. *Letteratura e scienza in Leopardi e altri
studi leopardiani*. Milano: Marzorati, 1978. Pp. 237.

Contains the following studies published previously:
"Leopardi e gli ideologi francesi del Settecento" (1966),
"Leopardi e Dante" (1965), "Leopardi e il neoclassicismo"
(1970), "Leopardi e l'immaginazione creatrice" (1969-70),
"Leopardi e il Novecento" (1972-73), "La critica leopardiana
negli anni Settanta" (1975), "Leopardi e Petrarca. I" (1975),
and "Letteratura e scienza in Leopardi" (1976). The only
essay published for the first time is "Leopardi e Petrarca.
II." Here Frattini examines previous comparative studies
on the relationship Leopardi-Petrarch (Ungaretti, Noferi)
and tries a new approach. He seeks to find the reason for
Leopardi's rejection of Petrarch after his Commentary on
the *Rime* and finds it in Leopardi's new poetics, where
style is no longer the substance of poetry as it was for
Petrarch, Virgil, and Horace. Modern times, Leopardi believes,
require a poetry "di cose, d'invenzione, d'immaginazione."
A second point Frattini wants to clarify is the persistent

presence after that date (the date of the Commentary) of
Petrarchian echoes. He examines "A Silvia," "Le ricordanze,"
and "Il canto notturno" and finds that the Petrarchian
stylistic elements present there are used in a context and
with a rhythm which completely transform their quality (he
uses the word "transustanziare"). The reminiscences are simply
lexical, whereas the philosophical situation has totally
changed. Leopardi's assimilation of and confrontation with
the greatest lyric poet, Frattini concludes, was the *conditio
sine qua non* for supplanting him. (D.B.)

Gabrieli Iselin, Maria. "Giacomo Leopardi in Scandinavia."
ON V,3-4 (1981): 249-61.

Compared to that of contemporary writers, especially
Montale, Moravia, and Pavese, Leopardi's popularity in
Scandinavian countries is said to be negligible.

Giordano, Emilio. "Rassegna di studi critici su Giacomo Leopardi (1976-1978)." *MC* 9-10 (1979-80): 169-72.

This exhaustive survey comments on the major critical
studies on Leopardi and on the reprints and the editions
of his works, done between 1976 and 1978. It is an extremely
valuable tool for Leopardi scholars. Giordano analyzes
Leopardi scholarship chronologically without omitting, to
my knowledge, anything--the titles of the essays he does not
comment on appear in a long footnote at the end of the
article--and he even succeeds in outlining critical debates,
e.g., the still open polemics between the supporters of a
Leopardi "progressivo" (Timpanao) and those of a Leopardi who
"rifiuta la politica in quanto tale" (Carpi). By far the most
complete and intelligent bibliographical tool available. (D.B.)

Jodi Macchioni, Rodolfo. "Leopardi e l'anonimo del *Sublime*."
Belfagor 36 (1981): 145-57.

Studies the effects of Longinus' treatise on Leopardi's
work, a subject treated by, among others, N. Perella's
Night and the Sublime in G. Leopardi (1970), duly acknowledged by Jodi. To Leopardi, "il *Del Sublime* fu un libro
utile e importante, ma sarebbe troppo attribuirgli il ruolo
di *livre de chevet*" (157). Even so, Leopardi's interest
in the work attests that he was not extraneous to "le sug-
gestioni della cultura europea più recente." Adds little
to the existing scholarship on the subject. (A.P.)

Leopardi, Giacomo. *Canti.* Introduzione e note a cura di Franco
Brioschi. Milano: Rizzoli, 1979. Pp. 210.

Rev. by Novella Bellucci-Celli in *RLI* 85 (1981): 346.

Leopardi, Giacomo. "Dialogue Between Torquato Tasso and his
Familiar Spirit"; "In Praise of Birds." A new Translation
by Giovanni Cecchetti. *IQ* 22 (Summer 1981): 105-16.

Marti, Mario. *Dante, Boccaccio, Leopardi*. Napoli: Liguori,
1980. Pp. 414.

  Rev. by Roberto Ballerini in *SPCT* 23 (1981): 169-73.

Mattesini, Francesco. "Tra storia e antologia: *Leopardi nella
poesia italiana*." *Italianistica* 9 (1980): 197-201.

  A review of Renzo Negri's book on Leopardi, initially
published in 1970 and reexamined here as a tribute to the
author.

Matteucci, Sapo. "I guardiani del minotauro." *NARG* 65-66 (1980):
260-66.

  Article inspired by Antonio Ranieri's *Sette anni di soda-
lizio con Giacomo Leopardi* (see *RMB* for 1980, p. 359).
Matteucci offers a psychoanalytical reading of the work,
dwelling on Ranieri's ambivalent disposition toward the
poet: admiration of an ideal image of Leopardi, "il grande
poeta, l'estrema sensibilità, la cultura profondissima";
tolerance for a physically deteriorating being whose
presence is accepted "come farebbe con un fratello mongo-
loide." (A.P.)

Melani, Viviana. *Leopardi e la poesia del Cinquecento*. Con
un'appendice su G.B. Belli. Messina: D'Anna, 1978. Pp. 219.

  Rev. in *GSLI* 158 (1980): 630-31.

Musti, Mario. "La sintassi sonora: analisi delle fonie leo-
pardiane in 'A Silvia' (V. 1-6)." *MC* 9-10 (1979-80): 56-73.

  Twenty-three pages go to analyze the phonetic signs of
six lines in order to prove that Leopardi's choice of words
was not only determined by meanings but by sounds as well.
The author thinks it necessary to have a new science or
discipline for this type of analysis: "Sintassi sonora"
he calls it, a study of the system behind the organization
and disposition of sounds. He examines the vocalic and
consonantic "fonie" (phonetic signs) in the first six lines
of "A Silvia" discovering a *"fonia"* made by two opposing
sounds. The sound structure of Leopardi's verse is built
on very few phonic groups which constantly reappear. Beside
these, Musti distinguishes the "fronde," thematic variations
which, as in music, enrich the "primary groups." The essay

is a painstaking exercise that, as the author himself admits,
serves to prove the existence of something the ear already
knew was there. (D.B.)

Peruzzi, Emilio. *Studi leopardiani*. *"La sera del dì di festa."*
Firenze: Olschki, 1979. Pp. 196.

This long and detailed essay aims at bringing to light the
unity of the poem through a thorough stylistic analysis of
phonetics, semantics, and syntax. Peruzzi uses for this
analysis Leopardi's two manuscripts, Paolina's copy, and the
four editions of the poem (1825, 1826, 1831, 1835) where he
examines the use and the recurrence of key words, sounds as
well as punctuation marks. This he does, finding clarification and support in Leopardi's *Lettere* and *Zibaldone*. The
result is the discovery of a theme which develops in three
different phases: the silent sorrow, the furor, and the
final, spiritual prostration. The whole poem shows a strong
coherence between feelings expressed and means of expression,
thus confuting, in Peruzzi's view, the common criticism of
its lack of unity.
     The last chapter of the book, "Grecità di Leopardi," deals
with the interpretation of Leopardi's expression "le immagini
antiche" (in a letter to Giordani) which Peruzzi attributes
to the inspiration of "La sera." Homer, Callimacus, and
Simonides are the literary sources, but to Peruzzi "le
immagini antiche non sono superficiali somiglianze tematiche,
ma coincidenze di sensibilità" (183). (D.B.)

Prete, Antonio. *Il pensiero poetante. Saggio su Leopardi*.
Milano: Fetrinelli, 1980. Pp. 177.

Rev. by Ugo Dotti in *Belfagor* 36 (1981): 368-71.
     The book focuses on the analysis of the *Zibaldone* which
appears to Prete as a corrosive critique of modern thought,
of optimism and progressivism. To retrace the moments of
such criticism is to do justice to Leopardi's complex but
coherent thought. It has too often been dismembered in pointless antitheses (reason-imagination, philosophy-poetry),
which cannot be appropriated either by conservative or
progressive thinkers. The systematic and fragmentary quality
of the *Zibaldone* is seen here as a statement by Leopardi
on the impossibility of the *"opus,"* on the absence of cer-
tainties, absolute truths, objective systems. The fragmentary style of this essay, as Prete admits, tries to keep
up with the movement of the *Zibaldone*. In spite of this,
he reveals a profound understanding of Leopardi's obsession
with the impossibility of reaching a fixed end. Prete, how-

ever, finds the unbroken thread, that is, the unifying motive,
of the *Zibaldone* in Leopardi's investigation of pleasure,
identified with the poetic experience. The book begins, like
the *Zibaldone*, with an analysis of Leopardi's doctrine of
pleasure; thus it starts from the experiencing subject (desire, remembrance, infinite, are all examined). It then
follows Leopardi's inquiry on nature, society, history, and
the discovery of their false pretension to bridge contrasts,
and it ends where it had started, like the *Zibaldone*: over
the experiencing subject still concerned with pleasure. Yet
the subject is now totally aware that the only possible happiness is poetic creation which alone can bridge the gap
between reason and imagination. The best part of the essay,
in fact, is Prete's analysis of an apparent contradiction
between Leopardi's statements about the incompatibility of
imagination and reason, and his belief in a philosophical
poetry. Through the passages of the *Zibaldone*, Prete can
show that for Leopardi poetry can only be the product of
both reason and imagination. Having understood this, Prete
concludes, the close affinity between the *Zibaldone* and
Leopardi's poetry becomes obvious, that is, between the
place where Leopardi examines the relation imagination-
theory with the place where the unity between symbols and
theoretical language is actually performed. (D.B.)

Ruggeri, Sidonia. "Carducci e Leopardi." *ON* 4 (1980): 307-20.

Except for brief references in his *Epistolario*, Carducci
wrote only two essays on Leopardi, both in 1898: "Degli
spiriti e delle forme nella poesia di Giacomo Leopardi"
and "Le tre canzoni patriottiche di Giacomo Leopardi." Carducci, writes Ruggeri, lacked an understanding of Leopardi's
artistic personality and praised only the eloquent and
patriotic spirit of his first *Canzoni*--those closest to his
own. Yet Carducci pointed out Leopardi's high literary technique and the social value of "La ginestra." In his speech
to the Senate in 1897, Carducci called attention to the
Zibaldone, neglected until that date. (D.B.)

Singh, G. "Melville and Leopardi." *RLMC* 33,1 (1980): 23-37.

Singh finds Leopardi's name mentioned twice in Melville's
"Clarel," a philosophical poem, an indication that Melville
was probably interested in Leopardi's thought and philosophy
rather than his poetry. Both Leopardi and Melville were "in-
trepid truth-seekers," believers only in their own experience
and observation.
    After mentioning a few of Melville's poems in which some
Leopardian themes appear, Singh focuses his attention on

The Confidence-Man, which he regards as a Melvillian version
of Leopardi's *Pensieri* and *Operette*. The skepticism and
belief in the destructive nature of truth, the divergence
between principles and practice they discover in life, the
intolerance of ignorance and hypocrisy, are elements common
to both. Besides the similarity of content, Singh points
out a formal similarity as well. Both Melville's novel and
Leopardi's *Operette* present characters who are not important
in themselves, but who function "as mouthpieces of contradictory points of view" (33). Furthermore, the complex form
of irony they both use in "ridiculing what is affirmed" and
in "vindicating the truth of what is implicitly denied by
the affirmation" becomes a fundamental part of their dialectical reasoning. Singh's comparative analysis is interesting, although his negation of Leopardi's misanthropy is not
fully supported. It does not help his case that some passages
in Italian are not correctly quoted. (D.B.)

Tartaro, Achille. *Leopardi*. Bari: Laterza, 1978. Pp. 203.

An exhaustive and rich monograph on Leopardi's life and
thought with an intelligent selection from all his works.
Tartaro develops lines of interpretation opened by Sapegno
and Binni. He takes into consideration the major works of
Timpanaro, Luporini, and their followers, and, indeed,
demonstrates a deep familiarity with the texts, a complete
knowledge of Leopardi's critical bibliography. (The bibliographical appendix, at the end, is a valuable tool for any
Leopardi scholar.) Like Prete (in his edition of the *Operette
morali*), he recognizes the poet's negative philosophy from
beginning to end, materialistic, atheistic, and antisocial.
The open gesture toward humanity of "La ginestra," Tartaro
concludes, is not a sign of "un progetto di rinnovamento
politico-sociale," but a moral hypothesis, or rather another
and final challenge performed by reason against the mystifying presumption of political science. (D.B.)

V.A. *Leopardi e la letteratura italiana dal Duecento al
Seicento: Atti del IV Convengo internazionale di studi
leopardiani*. Firenze: Olschki, 1978. Pp. 852.

The proceedings of the fourth international congress of
Leopardi studies (Recanati, Sept. 13-16, 1976) includes an
introduction by Umberto Bosco, eight "relazioni" which follow
a chronological order, and twenty-seven "communicazioni."
This volume greatly surpasses in size and range the *Atti*
of earlier conferences. The structure and methodology, however, are similar to those employed in the previous volumes.

The major topics covered are the relations Leopardi-Dante
(D. Consoli, G. Di Pino, C.F. Goffis), Leopardi-Petrarch
(E. Bonora, B. Biral, N. Bonifazi, M. Feo, E. Bigi, A. Frat-
tini, R.M. Ruggieri), Leopardi-Ariosto (E. Bigi), Leopardi-
Tasso (R. Scrivano, A. Tortoreto), Leopardi-Vico (V. Pacella),
Leopardi-Arcadia (C. Di Biase, N. Borsellino, N. Feo),
Leopardi-Machiavelli (J. Figurito, G. Singh).

Other essays cover the relation Leopardi and sixteenth-
century prose (M. Martelli), Leopardi and the seventeenth
century (M. Scotti, V.U. Capone, M. Cataudella, M. Dell'
Aquila, R. Macchioni Jodi, E.M. Maiani, P. Mazzamuto). As
Bosco points out in his Introduction, the aim of the present
conference was to complete the cycle of Leopardi's position
vis-à-vis the major moments and authors of Italian literature.
In this congress the focus was exclusively on the influences
and impact that Italian literature between 1200 and 1600
had on Leopardi's own work and his view and interpretation
of it. (D.B.)

See also Belmore ("German 3. Mörike").

MANZONI

Bàrberi-Squarotti, Giorgio. *Il Romanzo contro la storia. Studi
sui "Promessi Sposi."* Milano: Vita e Pensiero, 1980. Pp. 293.

Bezzola, Guido. "Un'ipotesi sulle teorie linguistiche del
Manzoni." *ON* V,1 (1981): 185-99.

In advocating the use of Florentine as the national language,
Manzoni was moved, according to Bezzola, by practical and
political considerations, not by elitist motives as Ascoli
and other dissenters seemed to think. Manzoni regarded
Florentine as a "basic language," a medium of communication
for all Italians which, in time, would foster the objectives
of national unification. Bezzola also touches on Manzoni's
increasing disinterest in literature after 1845 but on this
subject he offers nothing really new. (A.P.)

Borlenghi, Aldo. *Il successo contrastato dei "Promessi Sposi"
e altri studi sull'Ottocento italiano.* Napoli: Ricciardi,
1980. Pp. 337.

Rev. by Fiorella Gobbini in *EL* VI,2 (1981): 135.

Branca Del Corno, Daniela. "Strutture narrative e scansione
in capitoli tra *Fermo e Lucia* e *Promessi Sposi*." *LI* 32 (1980):
314-50.

Reflecting a structuralist approach to the organization
of fictional material, the study analyzes the principles of
modification and transformation marking the transition from
the first draft to the final edition of Manzoni's novel. The
analysis includes narrative techniques, plot elements, various forms of cesura, and the organization of narrative material into chapters. Interesting analogies emerge between
Manzoni's fiction and that of Cervantes, Fielding, and
Scott. In many respects, this is an impressive study, reflecting a rigorous methodology and exhaustive documentation of literary and critical sources. Yet Branca's technical,
nearly mechanical approach to the text discounts the author's
intellectual and artistic discernment. Specifically, she
underestimates the fact that such matters as language, style,
and characterization are carefully weighed and reelaborated
in the transitional process from the provisional text of
Fermo e Lucia to the definitive edition of the novel. (A.P.)

Chandler, Bernard S. "Individual Ages in Manzoni's Conception
of History." *Quaderni d'italianistica* 1 (1980): 64-79.

Chandler traces the differing perception of historical
ages in Vico, Hume, Herder, Montesquieu, among others, in
order to establish a firm foundation for Manzoni's thought
on the subject, which develops from a conception of history
representative of all ages in *Adelchi* and *Carmagnola* to
the "acceptance of an individual epoch with its own characteristics" in the *Discorso* on the Lombards. From a somewhat
vague representation of the special features of seventeenth-
century history in Lombardy (partly "a failure to understand the age in itself") reflected in *Fermo e Lucia*, Manzoni comes to the conclusion in *I promessi sposi* that "each
man belongs to his age, must live his life and make decisions in *that* age and in those conditions" (76). Well researched and intellectually stimulating. (A.P.)

Chandler, Bernard S. "Rassegna sul 'lieto fine' ne *I Promessi
Sposi*." *CrL* 8 (1980): 581-97.

The seemingly idyllic ending of Manzoni's novel, climaxing
with the reunion and marriage of Renzo and Lucia, is seen
by most critics as a rejection of idyllic life, rejection
punctuated by the protagonists' departure from their native
town. Chandler does not accept the devaluation of the "lieto
fine" in these terms. He approaches the subject from a formal viewpoint, linking the structure of *I promessi sposi*
to the comic mode as well as the quest-romance treated by
Northrop Frye in his *Anatomy of Criticism*. But Chandler

also points to the element of tragedy present in Manzoni's
work in the form of individual choice to accept or reject
spiritual salvation. At the surface level, the structure of
I promessi sposi offers some analogies, according to Chandler, with the comic fictional mode in the sense that the
happy ending epitomizes the cyclical nature of the Renzo-
Lucia story and, metaphorically, the cyclical character of
human life. More consequential is the analysis of Renzo
from the standpoint of the quest-romance. Through this optic,
Renzo is seen as the quest-embodying hero substantiating
Frye's definition of the genre as "the search of the libido
or desiring self for a fulfillment that will deliver it from
the anxieties of reality but will still contain that reality."
   In departing from the interpretation of the "lieto fine"
offered by such critics as Bàrberi-Squarotti, De Michelis,
and Varese, Chandler introduces a critical perspective which
enables us to see certain formal aspects of Manzoni's narrative in a different light. Yet the necessity to point as
well to "variazioni e deviazioni formali" (such as the dimension of tragedy) attests to the difficulty and the risks
of applying generic categories to *I promessi sposi*. More
than Frye's fictional modes, what defines the structural
movement of Manzoni's novel (and the actions of the characters connected to that movement) is, I believe, the elusive
interaction between history and Providence--two everpresent
forces controlling human events (but not individual actions)
in different ways and at different existential planes. (A.P.)

Chandler, Bernard S. "Spazio e tempo nella conversione dell'
innominato." *EL* VI,2 (1981): 32-34.

   An intuitive note on the interaction between time and
space in the conversion scene of the Innominato. In the
element of spatialized time Chandler sees a potentially
ironical intent, for "il selvaggio signore [che] dominava
all'interno tutto lo spazio dove piede d'uomo potesse posarsi"
(Ch. XX) acquires a different perception of time in the
course of his spiritual crisis: "L'elemento del tempo
acquista un'importanza decisiva quando l'innominato giunge
alla verità fondamentale che [il tempo], e non lo spazio,
domina la vita umana" (32). (A.P.)

Cottignoli, Alfredo. "Inquietudine e consolazione nelle lettere
familiari del Manzoni." *Italianistica* 9 (1980): 145-52.

   Expressions of suffering and religious comfort, reflected
in Manzoni's letters, are examined with full appreciation
of Manzoni's inner life. No speculative psychology, only
sensitivity and mature judgment. (A.P.)

Di Benedetto, Arnaldo. "Un Manzoni inattuale: il *Discorso* sui Longobardi." *GSLI* 157 (1980): 210-29.

The qualifier "inattuale" present in the title refers to Manzoni's time, to the misconceived effort of his contemporaries to view the *Discorso* as an indirect attack against Austrian rule in Italy. Di Benedetto argues that the genesis of the work is found in Manzoni's intent to refute Machiavelli, who maintained, in his *Historie fiorentine*, that, after 232 years in Italy, the Lombards "non ritenevano di forestieri altro che il nome," and that "tutte le guerre che ... furono dai barbari fatte in Italia furon in maggior parte dai pontefici causate." Manzoni sought to show that Lombards and Italians remained distinct ethnic entities for as long as the former dominated the latter and that the Popes consistently protected the interests of the Latin people. Having clarified this important point (which has been treated by other scholars as well), Di Benedetto focuses on what is the main interest of the essay: the ultimate merit of Manzoni's *Discorso* rests on its treatment of history as a source of moral reflection, on the perception of history as tangible proof that political power leads inevitably to moral corruption. (A.P.)

Di Rienzo, G. *L'avventura della parola nei "Promessi Sposi."* Roma: Bonacci, 1980. Pp. 160.

Ficara, Giorgio. "Le parole e la peste in Manzoni." *LI* 33 (1981): 3-37.

Sheds new light on the meaning of the plague in *I promessi sposi*, including the various connotative functions the term assumes in the course of the narrative. The essay's exceptional merit rests on its treatment of the plague as a metaphor of evil and death in society. The binomium plague-evil is thus perceived, in conjunction with Manzoni's metaphysical view of the world, as a constituent and inextricable force in human history. Excellent textual analysis. (A.P.)

Fido, Franco. "Due inediti del Manzoni." *Italica* 57 (1980): 93-95.

Publishes two documents not included in Cesare Ariete's comprehensive edition of Manzoni's correspondence. The first concerns James Robert Hope, a British writer acquainted with Manzoni; the second is a letter to Louis Claude Baudry, the well-known French publisher of Manzoni's works. Both *inediti* are followed by very useful comments. (A.P.)

Marri, Fabio. "Manzoniani e no tra i prosatori lombardi."
Italianistica 9 (1980): 409-44.

Examines the effects of Manzoni's linguistic writings on
the work of five Lombard authors: Arrighi, Dossi, De Marchi,
Lucini, and Linati. We come to learn that in a region deservedly called "fucina di sperimentalismo linguistico" (and
the allusion to Gadda is most fitting), Manzoni's ideas on
a unified language found widespread, but less than full,
acceptance. (A.P.)

Nevola, Maria Luisa. "Su un recente intervento manzoniano."
EL V,3 (1980): 104-08.

Expands on Karl Witte's visit to Manzoni discussed in Mario
Puppo's *Poesia e verità*. *Interpretazioni manzoniane* (see
RMB for 1980, p. 364).

Nigro, Salvatore. "Il sorpasso di Lucia." *Italianistica* 9
(1980): 141-44.

In one of his sermons, Bourdaloue describes divine Providence as "la puissance et sagesse supérieure à celle des
hommes, qui se joue de leurs desseins." To Nigro, this
thought represents the controlling force of the epilogue
of *I promessi sposi* and explains why Renzo's optimism is
tempered by Lucia's belief in the inscrutable designs of
Providence. (A.P.)

Pallotta, Augustus. "Characterization through Understatement:
A Study of Manzoni's Don Rodrigo." *Italica* 58 (1981): 43-55.

Pallotta, Augustus. "Manzoni's Relationship with Spain."
Italica 57 (1980): 107-13.

Examines two works that throw new light on Manzoni's
connection with Spain: *La Guerra e la Peste nella Milano
dei "Promessi Sposi." Documenti inediti tratti dagli archivi
spagnoli* (see *ELN* 17, Supp., 252) and Oreste Macrí's *Varia
fortuna del Manzoni in terre iberiche* (Ravenna: Longo,
1976).

Portier, Lucienne. "I silenzi del Manzoni." *Italianistica* 9
(1980): 153-58.

Discusses three important events on which Manzoni did not
pronounce himself: the Vatican Council of 1869-70; the
proclamation of papal infallibility by Pius IX; the occupa-
tion of Rome by Italian troops which completed Italy's unification and marked an end to the temporal power of the

Vatican. Portier speculates that Manzoni had little admiration for Pius IX and that he may have been opposed to the dogma of papal infallibility. (A.P.)

Puppo, Mario. "Due note manzoniane." *Italianistica* 9 (1980): 123-29.

To corroborate the fact that Goethe's study "Klassiker und Romantiker in Italien sich heftig bekämpfend" was based largely on Gaetano Cattaneo's account of Italian letters in the early Ottocento sent to the duke of Weimar, Puppo publishes both texts in question. The second note discusses Manzoni's pessimism regarding the ability of traditional literary forms to survive in the modern world. In the essay *Del romanzo storico*, writes Puppo, "è contenuta la profezia della morte del romanzo storico, anzi di ogni genere letterario, destinato ad essere assorbito nella storia" (128). (A.P.)

Rati, Giancarlo. "Alessandro Manzoni e la critica: 1973-1980." *CeS* 77 (Jan.-March 1981): 27-41.

A careful assessment of recent Manzoni criticism. The studies examined by Rati deal chiefly with biographical and cultural matters, literary criticism, and socio-political questions reflected in Manzoni's works. Useful bibliography. (A.P.)

Salsano, Roberto. *Ritrattistica e mimica nei "Promessi Sposi."* Roma: Palombi, 1979. Pp. 152.

Rev. by Filippo Bettini in *RLI* 84 (1980): 375-76; by Lucia Miele in *EL* V,1 (1980): 138-39.

Saro, G. "Le sens politique des *Promessi Sposi*." Pp. 9-60 in V.A., *Idéologies et politique. Contributions à l'histoire des intellectuels italiens du Risorgimento au fascisme.* Abbeville: Paillart, 1978.

Rev. by Gian Carlo Menichelli in *EL* V,3 (1980): 139-40.

Tonucci-Mazza, Antonia. "Gli studi manzoniani di Renzo Negri." *Italianistica* 9 (1980): 191-96.

A homage to the critic Renzo Negri to whom this issue of the journal is dedicated. In surveying Negri's contribution to Manzoni studies, the author draws attention to his analysis of *La colonna infame* as "romanzo-inchiesta"--a felicitous assessment which enables us to see Manzoni's neglected novel in the same light as the works of Gide, Sciascia, and Solzhenitsyn. (A.P.)

Trombatore, Gaetano. "I *Sermoni* e la crisi del giacobinismo manzoniano." *Belfagor* 36 (1981): 501-12.

Although they were written, for the most part, in a different cultural environment (Venice), the *Sermoni* are said to betray the same socio-political and moral concerns reflected in *Il trionfo della libertà*. The *sermone* to Pagani is seen as "il più compiutamente significativo" offering "elementi costitutivi di un autoritratto, di una autoraffigurazione dell' autore come poeta civile" (506). And the verse "Or ti dirò perché piuttosto io scelga/ Notar la plebe con sermon pedestre" is viewed as Manzoni's criticism of his own poetic style. Trombatore comments: "Ci troviamo di fronte a una tensione stilistica, in cui praticamente si scaricava la tensione polemica" (510). Sound scholarship. (A.P.)

See also Cahiers mennaisiens 13 ("French 2. Lamennais"); Cerri ("Grossi").

Reviews of books previously listed:

CASERTA, Ernesto G., *Manzoni's Christian Realism* (see *RMB* for 1980, p. 362), rev. by Lucienne Portier in *REI* 4 (1979): 353-56; GIRARDI, Enzo Noè, and Gabriella Spada, *Manzoni e il Seicento lombardo* (see *ELN* 17, Supp., 254), rev. by Augustus Pallotta in *Forum Italicum* 14 (1980): 124-26; PUPPO, Mario, *Poesia e verità. Interpretazioni manzoniane* (see *RMB* for 1980, p. 364), rev. by Angiola Ferraris in *GSLI* 157 (1980): 151-55; SIMONINI, Augusto, *L'ideologia di Alessandro Manzoni* (see *ELN* 17, Supp., 256), rev. by Augustus Pallotta in *CMLR* 38 (1981): 121-22.

MAZZINI

Sipala, Paolo. "Mazzini e il romanzo storico." *Italianistica* 9 (1980): 159-67.

PORTA

V.A. *La poesia di Carlo Porta e la tradizione milanese.* Milano: Feltrinelli, 1976. Pp. 223.

Rev. by Filippo Bettini in *RLI* 84 (1980): 360.

TENCA

Tenca, Carlo. *Poesie edite e inedite*. A cura di Alfredo Cottignoli. Bologna: Patron, 1979. Pp. 200.

  Rev. in *GSLI* 158 (1980): 631.

TOMMASEO

Puppo, Mario. *Poetica e poesia di Niccolò Tommaseo*. Roma:
Bonacci, 1980. Pp. 153.

VISCONTI

Visconti, Ermes. *Saggi sul bello, sulla poesia e sullo stile*.
A cura di Anco Marzio Mutterle. Bari: Laterza, 1979.

  Rev. by Pino Fasano in *RLI* 85 (1981): 344-45.

SPANISH

(Compiled by Brian J. Dendle, University of Kentucky)

1. BIBLIOGRAPHY

Aguilar Piñal, Francisco. "La Academia de Letras Humanas (1793-1801). Manuscritos conservados." *CB* 38 (1979): 159-80.

Manuscripts listed include those by Arjona, Blanco, Mora, Lista, Reinoso.

Aguilar Piñal, Francisco. "La prensa española en el siglo XVIII." *CB* 35 (1978): v-xxi, 3-134.

Periodical works listed by place of publication and year. Some early nineteenth-century works included. Index.

Alberich, José. *Bibliografía Anglo-hispánica 1801-1850*. Oxford: Dolphin Book Co., 1978. Pp. xl+197.

Alberich notes British interest in the Peninsular War (British professional soldiers had scant regard for Spanish military prowess) and Spanish America, Tory support for the Carlists, and the prevalence of Spanish themes in Gothic literature. Alberich lists by subject 1600 works published in the British Isles and Gibraltar dealing with Spain, Gibraltar, Spanish America, and the Philippines. Indices of authors, translators, titles, topics, places. Most useful.

Chatham, James R., and Carmen C. McClendon. *Dissertations in Hispanic Languages and Literatures*. Vol. II. University Press of Kentucky, 1981. Pp. xi+162.

Lists dissertations completed in USA and Canada, 1967-77.

Ferreras, Juan Ignacio. *Catálogo de novelas y novelistas españoles del siglo XIX*. Madrid: Ediciones Cátedra, 1979. Pp. 454.

2158 references to novels in Castillian. The listings are
by author, by title (when author is unknown), and by series,
are annotated, and include occasional sparse references to
criticism. List of pseudonyms. Essential work of reference.

Gómez Rea, Javier. "Las revistas teatrales madrileñas (1790-
1930)." *CB* 31 (1974): 65-140.

Pérez-Rioja, José Antonio. *Bibliografía soriana*. Madrid:
Patronato "José María Quadrado," C.S.I.C., 1975. Pp. 199.

Works grouped by topic ("Literatura," pp. 141-54). Listing of periodical publications. Onomastic and geographical
indices.

Romero Tobar, Leonardo. "Textos inéditos de escritores
españoles del siglo XIX relacionados con la censura guber-
nativa." *CB* 32 (1975): 89-108.

Texts relating to censorship by Aribau, Escosura, Madrazo,
Ochoa, Navarro Villoslada, Reinoso, Gallego, Lista, Quadrado,
Rivas, Rodríguez Rubí, Tapia, et al.

Rudder, Robert S., ed. *The Literature of Spain in English
Translation*. New York: Frederick Ungar, 1975. Pp. 637.

Translations of nineteenth-century works are listed,
pp. 270-335. Indices of authors, anonymous works.

Ruiz Lasala, Inocencio. *Bibliografía zaragozana del siglo
XIX*. Zaragoza: Institución "Fernando el Católico," Excma.
Diputación Provincial, 1977. Pp. xv+394; illus.

Brief descriptive notes on Zaragozan printers. 2676
bibliographical entries by year. Index.

Simón Palmer, María del Carmen. "Manuscritos dramáticos de
los siglos XVIII-XX de la Biblioteca del Instituto del
Teatro de Barcelona." *CB* 39 (1979): 1-248.

Indexed by title, first line, and author.

Simón Palmer, María del Carmen. "La mujer en el siglo XIX:
notas bibliográficas." *CB* 31 (1974): 141-98; 32 (1975):
109-50; 37 (1978): 163-206; 38 (1979): 181-211.

Simón Palmer, María del Carmen. "Revistas destinadas a la
familia en el siglo XIX." *CB* 40 (1980): 161-70.

Villa-amil y Castro, José. *Ensayo de un catálogo sistemático y crítico de libros, folletos y papeles que tratan de Galicia*. Barcelona: Ediciones El Albir, 1975. Pp. 309.

Facsimile edition of work of 1875.

2. GENERAL

Artola, Miguel. *Partidos y programas políticos 1808-1936*. 2 vols. Madrid: Aguilar, 1974-75.

Bozal, Valeriano. *La ilustración gráfica del siglo XIX en España*. Madrid: Comunicación, 1979. Pp. 234; illus. Ptas. 2,600 (cloth); ptas. 2,000 (paper).

A lavishly-produced volume, valuable above all for its profusion of illustrations. Bozal discusses the development of the press in the Romantic period, and treats the satirical and *costumbrista* illustrations in such journals as *El Semanario Pintoresco Español*, Modesto Lafuente's *Fray Gerundio*, *El Matamoscas* (1836-37), and Ayguals' journals of the 1840s. Indices of names, publications, and illustrations.

Brines i Blasco, Joan. "Reforma agraria y desamortización en la España del siglo XIX." *Estudis* 7 (1980): 125-54.

The *desamortización* of the *trienio* prepared the way for that of Mendizábal. The disentailments formed part of the process of dissolution of the *Antiguo Régimen*.

Callahan, William J. "The Origins of the Conservative Church in Spain, 1793-1823." *ESR* 10 (1980): 199-223.

Cánovas Sánchez, Francisco. "La nobleza senatorial en la época de Isabel II." *Hispania* (Madrid) 39 (1979): 51-99.

Castells, José Manuel. *Las asociaciones religiosas en la España contemporánea (1767-1965)*. Madrid: Taurus, 1973. Pp. 502.

Cervera Pery, José. *Marina y política en la España del siglo XIX*. Madrid: Editorial San Martín, 1979. Pp. 327; illus.

Chaho, J. Augustin. *Viaje a Navarra durante la insurrección de los vascos (1830-1835)*. San Sebastián: Editorial Auñamendi Argitaldaria, 1976. Pp. 183.

Re-edition of the translation of a work first published
in Paris, 1836.

Gassier, Pierre. "Goya and the Hugo Family in Madrid, 1811-
12." *Apollo* 114 (1981): 248-51.

Gil Novales, Alberto. *Textos exaltados del Trienio Liberal.*
Madrid: Ediciones Júcar, 1978. Pp. 202.

Useful collection of pamphlets and manifestoes. Index.

Glendinning, Nigel. "Goya's Patrons." *Apollo* 114 (1981):
236-47.

Grases, Pedro. *Britain and Hispanic Liberalism (1800-1830).*
(Diamante, XXV.) London: Hispanic and Luso Brazilian
Council, 1975. Pp. 23.

Spanish and Spanish American intellectuals sought refuge
in London in the first two decades of the nineteenth century. There they learned the science of government and
acquired broader perspectives (which included the concept
of the city, as well as Romanticism).

Juretschke, Hans. "Du rôle médiateur de la France dans la
propagation des doctrines littéraires, des méthodes historiques et de l'image de l'Allemagne en Espagne au cours
du XIXe siècle." Pp. 9-34 in *Romantisme, Réalisme,
Naturalisme en Espagne et en Amérique Latine.* (Publications
de l'Université de Lille III.) Lille: Centre d'Etudes
Ibériques et Ibéro-Américaines du XIXe Siècle, 1978.

French culture had a preponderant role in Spain at least
until 1860. German literature and scholarship entered
Spain from France. The most influential works were those
of Mme. de Staël and Friedrich Schlegel's *L'Histoire de
la littérature ancienne et moderne* (1829 translation).
Other important influences were Heine (known from 1835
on in the plagiarisms of Fontcuberta), Hegel (on Pi y
Margall), and articles in the *Revue des Deux Mondes.*

López-Rey, José. "Goya's *The Taking of Christ*: Challenge
and Achievement." *Apollo* 114 (1981): 252-54.

*Manifiesto que la m. n. l. y h. ciudad de Zaragoza ofrece
al público.* Zaragoza: Libros Pórtuo, 1980. Pp. 232; illus.

Facsimile edition of work celebrating Fernando's visit
to Zaragoza in 1828; contains laudatory verse.

Marrast, Robert. "Le drame en Espagne à l'époque romantique de 1834 à 1844: contribution à son approche sociologique." Pp. 35-55 in *Romantisme, Réalisme, Naturalisme en Espagne et en Amérique Latine*. (Publications de l'Université de Lille III.) Lille: Centre d'Etudes Ibériques et Ibéro-Américaines du XIXe Siècle, 1978.

For Marrast, the true spirit of Romanticism is "progressive." The spectators of Spanish Romantic drama were from the middle class; "Romantic Spain" is a bourgeois myth; the Spanish Romantic theater is superficial and rhetorical. Marrast notes that there were no Spanish Romantic dramas dealing with contemporary political themes. The revolution does not triumph in *La conjuración de Venecia*; love defies social convention in *Macías*; domestic virtues are proclaimed in *Los amantes de Teruel*; Zorrilla was the spokesman for historical nationalism.

Navas-Ruiz, Ricardo. *Imágenes liberales. Rivas--Larra--Galdós*. Salamanca: Ediciones Alnar, 1979. Pp. 197.

Revised versions of previously published articles: "Ticknor en España" (contains text of letter from Rivas to Ticknor) (pp. 29-38); "Trayectoria política de Larra" (pp. 41-126); "*Don Alvaro* y el teatro del Duque de Rivas" (pp. 137-75); "*Don Alvaro* y Don Juan. Contribución a una mitología romántica española" (pp. 176-88).

Pageard, Robert. "Le romantisme vu par la critique espagnole autour de 1860, notamment dans *La América*." Pp. 75-115 in *Romantisme, Réalisme, Naturalisme en Espagne et en Amérique Latine*. (Publications de l'Université de Lille III). Lille: Centre d'Etudes Ibériques et Ibéro-Américaines du XIXe Siècle, 1978.

Romanticism was hazily defined by Spanish critics *ca*. 1860. Bécquer ignored or derided Romanticism in his publications. Valera (1854) considered Romanticism obsolete. Pi y Margall (1857) guardedly accepted Romantic freedom of expression and demanded a social or moral content in literature. Menéndez Rayón (1859) associated Romanticism with Spanish tradition and believed it weakened by societal change. José Leopoldo Feu (1861-62) similarly associated Romanticism and tradition and regretted French influence. Giner de los Ríos (1862) attacked the French cult of the medieval and exaggerated sentimentality and sensationalism. Alcalá Galiano (1862) defended "good taste" and attacked thesis literature.

Palacio Atard, Vicente. *La España del siglo XIX, 1808-1898*.
Madrid: Espasa-Calpe, 1978. Pp. 668; illus.

Panoramic political history; no mention of literature.

Picoche, Jean-Louis. "Existe-t-il un drama romantique espagnol?"
Pp. 47-63 in *Romantisme, Réalisme, Naturalisme en Espagne
et en Amérique Latine*. (Publications de l'Université de
Lille III.) Lille: Centre d'Etudes Ibériques et Ibéro-
Américaines du XIXe Siècle, 1978.

Picoche notes that Spanish Romantic dramatists (Roca de
Togores, Gil y Zárate, Larra, Zorrilla, Hartzenbusch,
García Gutiérrez, Príncipe, García de Villalta, Asquerino)
transcended their French model by varying the number of
acts, mixing prose and verse, and by constructing dramas
which were lyrical or operatic, realistic (*Don Juan Tenorio*
is the exception; *Macbeth* was rejected by Spanish spectators), or optimistic and nationalistic. Rivas, with his
pessimism, is an exception; *Don Alvaro*, with its deliberate
absurdities, is "le drame d'un incroyant, d'un athée, même
d'un désabusé."

Saurín de la Iglesia, María Rosa. *Apuntes y documentos para
una historia de Galicia en el siglo XIX*. La Coruña: Diputación Provincial, 1977. Pp. 379.

Fascinating, well-documented survey of rural life, emi-
gration, poverty, military service (unpopular), and administration in nineteenth-century Galicia. The Romantic myth
of a martyred Galicia is touched on (pp. 27-32).

Simbor Roig, Vicent. *Els orígens de la Renaixença valenciana*.
Valencia: [n.p.], 1980. Pp. 218.

Refuting received opinion, Simbor Roig amply documents
the literary use of the Valencian vernacular from the
beginning of the nineteenth century. He documents the
origins of the *Renaixença* in the writings of neoclassical
and pre-Romantic authors, 1790-1830; he also lists popular
and scholarly works of this period. In the chapter devoted
to the beginning of the *Renaixença* (1830-59), Simbor Roig
quotes at length from such poets as Pérez y Rodríguez,
Arolas, Boix, Bonilla, and Llorente. He also lists satirical
journals and religious and dramatic works in *valenciano*.
A useful corrective to those who would claim the Valencian
Renaixença to be a tardy offshoot of Catalan Romanticism.
Bibliography; index.

"Solo Goya." *Apollo* 114 (1981): 212-19.

Soria, Andrés. "Notas sobre Hugo Blair y la retórica española en el siglo XIX." Pp. 363-88 in *Estudios sobre literatura y arte dedicados al profesor Emilio Orozco Díaz*. Vol. III. Universidad de Granada, 1979.

Villasante, Luis. *Historia de la literatura vasca*. Burgos (?): Editorial Aranzazu, 1979. Pp. 487; illus.

Revised edition of work first published in 1961. Pp. 157-297 discuss individual nineteenth-century authors. Indexed.

3. STUDIES OF AUTHORS

ALCALA GALIANO

See Pageard ("Spanish 2. General"); Carnero ("Böhl von Faber").

AMADOR DE LOS RIOS

Amador de los Ríos, José. *Historia de la villa y corte de Madrid*. 4 vols. Madrid: Abaco, 1978. Illus.

Lavishly illustrated facsimile edition.

ARIBAU

See Romero Tobar ("Spanish 1. Bibliography").

ARJONA

See Aguilar Piñal ("Spanish 1. Bibliography").

AROLAS

See Simbor Roig ("Spanish 2. General"); Dowling ("Rivas").

ASQUERINO

See Picoche ("Spanish 2. General").

AVELLANEDA

Harter, Hugh A. *Gertrudis Gómez de Avellaneda*. (Twayne's World Authors Series, 599.) Boston: Twayne Publishers, 1981. Pp. 182.

A competent discussion of Avellaneda's life, poetry, dramas, novels, and brief fiction. In her life, Avellaneda epitomized Romanticism, "oscillating between the extremes of passionate love and religious devotion, the fevers of the flesh and the fervors of prayer, intense participation in life and temporary withdrawals into melancholy disenchantment...." A constant theme of her works is the Romantic consecration of love; noble souls suffer at the contact of reality. One minor correction needs to be made: the heresy in *Recaredo* is Arianism, not "Aryanism." Selected, annotated bibliography. Index.

AYGUALS DE IZCO

See Bozal ("Spanish 2. General").

BECQUER

Herzberger, David K. "The Contrasting Poetic Theories of Poe and Bécquer." *RomN* 21 (1981): 323-28.

Jofre, Alvaro Salvador. "Gustavo Adolfo Bécquer: una poética melodramática." Pp. 267-84 in *Estudios sobre literatura y arte dedicados al profesor Emilio Orozco Díaz*. Vol. III. Universidad de Granada, 1979.

For Jofre, Bécquer is a "modern" in his personal anguish and confusion and for the conflict within him between inspiration and reason. The melodramatic structure of his poems conceals a void, created by the clash of the values of the ruling class and reality. A useful exploration of Bécquer's political and ideological context.

Letemendía, Emily. "Galdos and Bécquer." *RomN* 21 (1980): 178-83.

By uncritically accepting Galdós' article "Las obras de Bécquer" at face value, Letemendía suggests an affinity between Bécquer and Galdós. She also indicates parallels between the *episodios nacionales* and *Tres fechas*.

See also Pageard ("Spanish 2. General").

BLANCO WHITE

See Aguilar Piñal ("Spanish 1. Bibliography").

BÖHL VON FABER

Carnero, Guillermo. *Los orígenes del romanticismo reaccionario español: el matrimonio Böhl de Faber*. Universidad de Valencia, 1978. Pp. 331; illus.

Carnero examines in detail the financial and marital vicissitudes of Frasquita de Larrea and Juan Nicolás Böhl von Faber: Frasquita was far from the submissive wife Böhl desired; Böhl, Carnero suspects, as agent for the Rothschilds bribed the deputies of Cadiz to secure the release of Fernando. Frasquita reveals a Romantic sensibility in her descriptions of Nature; her patriotic exaltation, monarchical enthusiasm, deep religious feeling, execration of liberalism, idealized vision of the people, and exclamatory style suggest (although Carnero fails to develop this topic) her strong influence on her daughter, Fernán Caballero. Carnero details Böhl's readings and establishes his relations with Blanco and Durán. The bulk of his commentary is devoted to the Calderonian polemic; the contributions of Vargas Ponce, Cavaleri (the text of Cavaleri's *folleto* on *A secreto agravio secreta venganza* is printed in full), Mora, and Alcalá Galiano are described. Böhl's ideology, Carnero concludes, is ultraconservative: for Böhl, Calderón represents ancient Spanish virtues; the Spanish people is essentially religious, patriotic, and monarchical; enlightened thought becomes, in the conservative worldview, a dangerous toxin; hence, neoclassicism is associated with revolution and treason. Carnero's work is meticulously researched and based on documents not accessible to earlier critics, whose errors Carnero frequently corrects. Bibliography.

Gies, David Thatcher. "The Plurality of Spanish Romanticism (Review Article)." *HR* 49 (1981): 427–42.

Gies urbanely discusses Guillermo Carnero, *Los orígenes del romanticismo en España: el matrimonio Böhl de Faber* (see above), and Antonio Orozco Acuaviva, *La gaditana Frasquita Larrea, primera romántica española* (Jerez de la Frontera: Sexta, 1977).

See also González del Castillo ("González del Castillo").

BOIX

See Simbor Roig ("Spanish 2. General").

BONILLA

See Simbor Roig ("Spanish 2. General").

CASTRO

Castro, Rosalía de. *Obras completas*. Recopilación e introducción por Victoriano García Martí. Nueva edición aumentada por Arturo del Hoyo. 2 vols. Madrid: Aguilar, 1977.

ESCOSURA

See Romero Tobar ("Spanish 1. Bibliography").

ESPRONCEDA

Vasari, Stephen. "Aspectos religioso-políticos de la ideología de Espronceda: *El Estudiante de Salamanca*." *BH* 82 (1980): 94–149.

For Vasari, *El estudiante de Salamanca* is "un poema alegórico y simbólico," in which Espronceda portrays the struggle between the intolerant Past and the proud, tolerant, liberated Present. Don Félix de Montemar symbolizes progressive Humanity, liberal Spain, Espronceda himself, and Lamennais (the rebel against Rome, whose apocalyptic vision resembles Espronceda's). Doña Elvira represents the Church, the past; the *blanca dama* is the Pope or "dead" Church. Don Diego is the monarchy which supports the traditional role of the Church. Setting also is allegorical: Salamanca is the Church, tradition, the old social order; the dead city is Rome. Because Espronceda was disheartened by the failure of the liberal progressive regimes of the 1830s, he portrays the new, progressive Spain (Don Félix) as succumbing to the power of the past and of the Church; his spirit alone refuses to surrender.

The source of Espronceda's poem, apart from Lamennais and Larra (the vision of Spain as a cemetery), is above all Balzac's tale *L'Eglise* (1831); works with a similar theme are Gautier's *Albertus* (1831), Hugo's *Notre Dame de Paris* (1831), and poems by Vigny and Dondey.

Vasari's novel interpretation is too far-fetched to convince. (The only "hard" evidence he presents is an ambiguous statement by Quinet in *Mes vacances en Espagne* in 1857.) It is, however, vividly presented, cogently argued (if one accepts Vasari's initial premise that the poem is allegorical), and stimulates the reader to reexamine previous approaches to this work.

FERNAN CABALLERO

See Carnero (Böhl von Faber").

FLORES

Rubio Cremades, Enrique. *Costumbrismo y folletín. Vida y obra de Antonio Flores*. Vol. III. Alicante: Instituto de Estudios Alicantinos, 1979. Pp. 147.

(For Volume I, see *ELN* 17, Supp., 263; for Volume II, see *RMB* for 1979, p. 329.) Annotated list of Flores' journalistic publications. Brief conclusions to all three volumes assimilate Flores to Larra and Mesonero Romanos. Listing of printing laws. Reproduction of documents concerning Flores. List of editions of Flores' works. Bibliography. Index to all three volumes.

FONTCUBERTA

See Juretschke ("Spanish 2. General").

GALLEGO

See Romero Tobar ("Spanish 1. Bibliography").

GARCIA DE VILLALTA

See Picoche ("Spanish 2. General").

GARCIA GUTIERREZ

See Picoche ("Spanish 2. General").

GIL Y ZARATE

See Picoche ("Spanish 2. General").

GONZÁLEZ DEL CASTILLO

González del Castillo, Juan Ignacio. *El café de Cádiz y otros sainetes.* Edición, introducción y notas de Carmen Bravo-Villasante. Madrid: Editorial Magisterio Español, 1977. Pp. 285.

González del Castillo (1763-1800), the teacher of Böhl von Faber, was the author of forty-four *sainetes.* Carmen Bravo-Villasante, in the brief introduction, claims that the comedy *Una pasión imprudente ocasiona muchos daños* contains pre-Romantic traits (unspecified). Bibliography. Annotated text of twelve *sainetes.*

GONZALEZ ELIPE

See Dowling ("Rivas").

HARTZENBUSCH

Fournier, Anne. "Les ressorts dramatiques dans le théâtre de J.E. Hartzenbusch: étude du drame *Alfonso el Casto.*" Pp. 57-63 in *Romantisme, Réalisme, Naturalisme en Espagne et en Amérique Latine*. (Publications de l'Université de Lille III.) Lille: Centre d'Etudes Ibériques et Ibéro-Américaines du XIXe Siècle, 1978.

Brief exposition of the intrigue of *Alfonso el Casto*; the dénouement is conformist and bourgeois.

Hartzenbusch, Juan Eugenio. *Los amantes de Teruel*. Edición, estudio y notas de Jean-Louis Picoche. Madrid: Editorial Alhambra, 1980. Pp. 353.

Study of sources, structure, variants, critical reception. Bibliography. Annotated text, with variants.

Iranzo, Carmen. *Juan Eugenio Hartzenbusch*. (Twayne's World Authors Series, 501.) Boston: Twayne Publishers, 1978. Pp. 151.

An ill-arranged study, in which Iranzo discusses at excessive length the sources of *Sancho Ortiz de las Roelas*, indicates "absurdities" and historical errors in Hartzenbusch's dramas, dismisses Hartzenbusch as "basically an unoriginal mind," and--at her most nit-picking--lists faults in Hartzenbusch's edition of Cervantes. Selected bibliography.

See also Marrast, Picoche ("Spanish 2. General").

LAFUENTE

See Bozal ("Spanish 2. General").

LARRA

Benítez, Rubén, ed. *Mariano José de Larra*. Madrid: Taurus, 1979. Pp. 315.

Useful anthology of articles concerning Larra, written over the last century and a half. Bibliography.

Lorenzo-Rivero, Luis. "La corrida en *Pan y Toros*, Goya y Larra." *CA* 235,ii (March-April 1981): 182-91.

For Arroyal, Goya, and Larra, bullfights express the barbarity of absolutist regimes.

Marún, Gioconda. "Apuntaciones sobre la influencia de Addison y Steele en Larra." *Hisp* 64 (1981): 382-87.

  "Larra como Addison y Steele esgrime el costumbrismo ético-social para reformar la conducta humana, para lograr el desarrollo completo del ser y su sociedad."

Monleón, José. *Larra, escritos sobre teatro.* Madrid: Edicusa, 1976. Pp. 386.

  Monleón stresses the progressive nature of Larra. Text of Larra's articles concerning the theater.

Varela, José Luis. "Larra, diputado por Avila." Pp. 515-45 in *Estudios sobre literatura y arte dedicados al profesor Emilio Orozco Díaz.* Vol. III. Universidad de Granada, 1979.

  Letters to Larra, concerning his electoral campaign, Feb. to Aug. 1836.

See also Marrast, Navas-Ruiz, Pioche ("Spanish 2. General"); Vasari ("Espronceda"); Rubio Cremades ("Flores").

LARREA

See Carnero, Gies ("Böhl von Faber").

LISTA

See Aguilar Piñal, Romero Tobar ("Spanish 1. Bibliography").

LLORENTE

See Simbor Roig ("Spanish 2. General").

LOPEZ SOLER

Picoche, Jean-Louis. "Ramón López Soler, Plagiaire et Précurseur." *BH* 82 (1980): 81-93.

  In *Los bandos de Castilla*, López Soler massively plagiarized Scott and, to a lesser degree, Byron.

MADRAZO

See Romero Tobar ("Spanish 1. Bibliography").

MARTINEZ DE LA ROSA

See Marrast ("Spanish 2. General").

MESONERO ROMANOS

Mesonero Romanos, Ramón de. *Escenas costumbristas.* Prólogo de Agustín del Saz. Barcelona: Editorial Juventud, 1978. Pp. 256.

Varela Hervías, Eulogio. *Don Ramón de Mesonero Romanos y su círculo.* Madrid: Caja de Ahorros y Monte de Piedad, 1975. Pp. xvi+436.

  Letters from authors (A to M) to Mesonero. Comprehensively indexed.

See also Rubio Cremades ("Flores").

MONTOTO

See Dowling ("Rivas").

MORA

See Aguilar Piñal ("Spanish 1. Bibliography"); Carnero ("Böhl von Faber").

NAVARRO VILLOSLADA

See Romero Tobar ("Spanish 1. Bibliography").

OCHOA

See Romero Tobar ("Spanish 1. Bibliography").

PEREZ Y RODRIGUEZ

See Simbor Roig ("Spanish 2. General").

PI Y MARGALL

See Juretschke, Pageard ("Spanish 2. General").

PRINCIPE

See Picoche ("Spanish 2. General").

QUADRADO

Quadrado, José María. *Salamanca, Avila y Segovia*. Barcelona: Ediciones El Albir, 1979. Pp. 733; illus.

Facsimile edition.

See also Romero Tobar ("Spanish 1. Bibliography").

QUINTANA

Dérozier, Albert. *Manuel José Quintana y el nacimiento del liberalismo en España*. Madrid: Ediciones Turner, 1978. Pp. 818.

Translation of *Manuel Josef Quintana et la naissance du libéralisme en Espagne*.

REINOSO

See Aguilar Piñal, Romero Tobar ("Spanish 1. Bibliography").

RIVAS

Dowling, John. "The King with the Clicking Knees: The Duque de Rivas' *Una antigualla de Sevilla*." *SAB* 46,i (Jan. 1981): 1-15.

Professor Dowling offers medical evidence of the nature of King Pedro's infirmity, and suggests numerous sources for Rivas' poem. Other Romantics interested in the tale were Trueba y Cosío, Arolas, Mérimée, Montoto, Romero Larrañaga, and González Elipe.

Pinto, Paul A.M. "Rivas' Operatic Characters: The Personages of Giuseppe Verdi's *La forza del destino*." *RomN* 21 (1980): 184-92.

Rivas, Duque de. *Don Alvaro o La fuerza del sino. El desengaño en un sueño*. Prólogo de Carlos Ruiz Silva. Madrid: Espasa Calpe, 1980. Pp. 275; illus.

Solanas, Juan V. "Estructuras de superposición temporal en los *Romances históricos* del duque de Rivas." Pp. 65-73 in *Romantisme, Réalisme, Naturalisme en Espagne et en Amérique Latine*. (Publications de l'Université de Lille III.) Lille: Centre d'Etudes Ibériques et Ibéro-Américaines du XIXe Siècle, 1978.

Temporal superpositions assist in establishing the authenticity of the narrative and involve the reader.

See also Romero Tobar ("Spanish 1. Bibliography"); Navas-Ruiz, Picoche ("Spanish 2. General").

ROCA DE TOGORES

See Picoche ("Spanish 2. General").

RODRIGUEZ RUBI

See Romero Tobar ("Spanish 1. Bibliography").

ROMERO LARRAÑAGA

See Dowling ("Rivas").

TAMAYO Y BAUS

Tamayo y Baus, Manuel. *Un drama nuevo*. Edición de Alberto
Sánchez. Madrid: Ediciones Cátedra, 1979. Pp. 144.

TAPIA

See Romero Tobar ("Spanish 1. Bibliography").

TRUEBA Y COSIO

See Dowling ("Rivas").

VENTURA DE LA VEGA

Dowling, John. "El anti-Don Juan de Ventura de la Vega."
Pp. 215-18 in *Actas del Sexto Congreso Internacional de
Hispanistas*. University of Toronto, 1980.

   Julián Romea, the rival of Carlos Latorre (who played the
role of Don Juan in Zorrilla's drama), performed in *El
hombre de mundo* (1845), which enjoyed greater immediate success than *Don Juan Tenorio*.

VICETTO

López de Serrantes, Josefina. *Benito Vicetto iñorado*. Lugo:
Editorial Alvarellos, 1978. Pp. 205.

   Novelized biography of the moody and sensitive historical
novelist Benito Vicetto (1824-1878). Although short on facts
and sentimentalized, López de Serrantes' work is nevertheless written *con amor*. List of editions of Vicetto's works.
Bibliography.

ZORRILLA

Feal, Carlos. "Conflicting Names, Conflicting Laws: Zorrilla's
Don Juan Tenorio." *PMLA* 96 (1981): 375-87.

   The outstanding feature of Don Juan is his exaggerated
theatricality. Don Juan defies the paternal figure (i.e.,

God); he desires to embrace a life of order, to abandon his donjuanism, at the very moment when Inés (affected by that same donjuanism) frees herself from the convent and her father. Inés, like the Virgin Mary, intercedes between man and God. Although Zorrilla (Don Juan) apparently desexualizes Inés, her nature is passionate. Finally, love challenges, but does not overthrow, the patriarchal order. "Law (marriage or death) finally entraps those who endeavor to be exempt from it.... On the one hand, Don Juan is a perpetual threat, but on the other he is an indispensable component that a man has to assimilate if he wishes to win a woman's heart."

Zorrilla, José. *Don Juan Tenorio*. Edición de Aniano Peña. Madrid: Ediciones Cátedra, 1979. Pp. 226.

A brief discussion of Zorrilla's life, the Romantic nature of *Don Juan Tenorio*, its sources, the theological basis for Don Juan's salvation, selected bibliography. Annotated text of the drama.

See also Marrast, Navas-Ruiz, Picoche ("Spanish 2. General"); Dowling ("Ventura de la Vega").